A BETTER LIFE

IN

A BETTER WORLD

Can Mindfulness Save Us From Ourselves?

PIERO FALCI

ALSO BY PIERO FALCI

Pay Attention! Be Alert! Discovering Your Route to Happiness

Silent Peace Walk: From Inner Peace to World Peace

Peaceful Ways: The Power of Making Your Wishes Come True

....

The author of this book does not dispense medical advice or prescribe the use of any technique as a form of treatment for medical problems. You should always seek the advice of physicians who will evaluate your physical, mental, and emotional condition, and suggest the appropriate treatment. The intent of the author is only to offer information of general nature to help you in your quest for living a better life and enhancing your well-being. What is presented in this book is not meant to replace medical care. Consult with physicians and mental health professionals about the practices contained in this book. In the event you use any information in this book for yourself, the author and publisher assume no responsibility for your actions and the outcomes of such actions.

DEAR WILL,
 I AM VERY HAPPY THAT
MATEUS AND YOU ARE TOGETHER,
MAKING GOOD MUSIC THAT
WILL HELP BRING ABOUT A
BETTER WORLD,
 KEEP IT UP!

This book is dedicated to those who endeavor to consciously unlearn the falsehoods they have unconsciously learned.

CONTENTS

ACKNOWLEDGMENTS

I would like to express my sincere gratitude to Dr. Sharon Theroux, the founder of the South Florida Center for Mindfulness, for patiently mentoring me on this journey. Without her generous support I would not be teaching mindfulness today.

A deep bow of gratitude to Cindy Ricardo, from the West Broward Insight Meditation Community, Sandra Tillett, from Shiwa Yoga, Karen Darrow, from Yoga Source, and Sheila Griffin, from the Calcagnini Center for Mindfulness at the Jupiter Medical Center, for their trust in me, for inviting me to teach, and for all they do to bring the gift of mindfulness to others.

I owe a lot to Saki Santorelli, Florence Meleo-Meyer, Judson Brewer, Beth Mulligan, Carolyn West, Lynn Koerbel, Anne Twohig, and Bob Stahl, my Mindfulness-Based Stress Reduction teachers; Patricia Isis, my Mindful Self-Compassion teacher; Ted DesMaisons and Charisse Spencer Minerva, my Mindfulness in Schools Project teachers; and Joseph Goldstein, Jack Kornfield, Sharon Salzberg, Jon Kabat-Zinn, Dan Harris, and many other wise teachers who instruct me all the time through their books and recordings.

I am thankful to Bhante Gunaratana, Bhante Saddhajeewa, Bhante Seelananda, Bhante Dhammaratana, Bhante Jayasara, Gilles Goulet, Alain Lepine, Akincano, Chris Cullen, Jaya Karen Rudgard, and Bruce Stewart, my silent retreat guides, for creating environments where I deepened my practice, enhanced my understanding, and saw clearer.

I am grateful to Valerie York-Zimmerman, Gus Castellanos, Shelly Sitton Tygielski, Knellee Bisram, Suzanne Jewell, Delia Calixtro, Paula Winkler, Nicole Davis, Mary Beth Stern, Debbie Steinberg, and Linda Gradess, who, among many others, passionately work to spread the seeds of mindfulness in South Florida.

My expressions of love to my friends Leslie Lott, Jack Bloomfield, John Linn, Kevin McGee, Paul Veliyathil, Wally Dale, Sabrina Romero, Reina Gomez Medina, Florencia Clement de Grandprey, Penelope Arango, Rivera Sun, and Jameson Henkle. My sincere gratitude to Kristen Prater for her unreserved willingness to help me. And finally, an immense expression of thankfulness to my family, my friends, and all my students. You are my teachers. I learn from you. Thank you.

i

INTRODUCTION

This book is a compilation of two hundred and seventy articles that I wrote between January 2014 and December 2019, a time when mindfulness became central in my life. Consider it a notebook with insights and musings of an explorer.

During this period, I looked for answers to many questions that visited me, such as, "What is mindfulness? Why should I practice it? What are its individual and collective benefits, if any? How should I meditate? How do I overcome the inherent difficulties of the practice? How can I live more mindfully?"

I practiced, studied, pondered, and came to a point when I felt that sharing my discoveries could be of value to others. That's why I assembled this book.

Since we have many roles in life and everything is inter-related, this book collects not only my reflections as a mindfulness practitioner, but also as a spiritual seeker and as a social justice and environmental activist. Therefore the writings on death, the sporadic poetry attempting to express what I was unable to fully articulate through prose, and the call to action, with an encouragement for us to roll up our sleeves and get involved in the work of saving our planet and bringing about a more humane and less violent society. In this book you will find an invitation to give free reins to your imagination, and contemplate the possibility that Heaven is here, if we want it to be.

Mindfulness is much more about exploration than explanation. I am aware that many times my writing, with all the advice giving, sounds preachy, professorial, and perhaps even condescending. I apologize for that. But I hope this doesn't turn you away. As the Buddha repeatedly said, "Come and see for yourself." You don't have to believe anything I say. Use your intelligence and sustained inquiry. Investigate and make up your own mind. And among all suggestions presented here, pick those that make sense to you at this stage of your life.

Since these pieces were written as standalone essays, you may notice the repetition of themes, references, and quotes now and again. I hope this will not discourage you from giving consideration to the ideas expressed herein.

Finally, feel free to read the articles in this book in any order that feels right for you.

Wishing you many mindful moments, today and every day.

Piero Falci

Deerfield Beach, December 2019

MINDFULNESS MEDITATION AND MINDFUL LIVING

THE CHILD

I love those moments when night becomes day. Watching the sun coming up on the horizon and coloring our world — the sky, the clouds, the water — is, for me, an unmatchable spectacle. I simply adore this quiet time of observation, introspection, and reflection.

I was again at the beach this morning-- meditating and watching the sunrise. Birds were gliding effortlessly above the water. Fish were jumping. I felt the cool morning air filling my lungs, the breeze caressing my skin, and as the sun came up, I felt it warming my face. Everything was perfect and serene, and I was grateful.

As I was standing at the shoreline, suddenly, out of nowhere, this little child, about two years old, came running in my direction with open arms and a big smile on his face. He was so close and running with such a clear confidence in me, that I didn't have time to think twice; I instinctively squatted down and took him in my arms.

As I stood and lifted him up, he held my cheeks with both hands, looked me in the eyes, and gave me the most beautiful smile. I was astounded. I turned around to see where his parents were, but didn't see anyone else. Awkwardly, it was just the two of us.

His head was now moving in all directions. He was clearly in awe with the beauty around, looking at everything with the wonder of one who is seeing for the first time. He softly rested one arm on my shoulders, around my neck, and with the other hand he pointed at the sun, the clouds, the birds, as if inviting me to look at them too. I accepted his invitation, and immediately we found ourselves together in a place of beauty where distances shortened and time slowed down.

I looked at him again and noticed that he seemed oddly familiar, and suddenly I realized that the one I was holding in my arms was me. I was that beautiful, innocent child. The Universe had brought me back, as a little one, to meet me now, at this point in time when I am completing several decades of journeying on this planet. I was instantly filled with immense love for this little boy, a love that inundated me in such an overwhelming way that I began to cry. I was in a state of supreme exhilaration and uncontrollable tears of joy ran down my face. There I was, experiencing this colossal love for this child, while holding him in my arms.

"What should I tell him?" I thought. "He has his whole life ahead of him. I cannot let this opportunity go by without telling him everything that I have learned. There's so much I know now. I must tell him not to waste time. I must tell him to pursue his dreams and follow his bliss…" While I was in the middle of my thoughts, the child held my cheeks again, looked me in the eyes, and smiled. With that, I was immediately transported to a dimension of calm and peace where, without uttering a word, I heard him say, "Everything is OK. Everything will always be OK. Don't worry about anything. Just be grateful, and give away the gifts that you were brought here to give. Don't hold them back. And know that you are loved. I love you."

In that moment, in the middle of all my sobbing, I felt the weight of the world being lifted from my shoulders, and I knew that I was healed. In that very moment, I realized who the real teacher was. I smiled, brought his body closer to mine, hugged him with all tenderness of the Universe, and gave thanks.

········

MINDFULNESS MEDITATION

"Meditation is the only intentional, systematic human activity which is about not trying to improve yourself or get anywhere else, but simply to realize where you already are." ~ Jon Kabat-Zinn

········

Mindfulness is a word used to describe both a practice and a way of living. When introducing mindfulness, I like to make a distinction between mindful living and mindfulness meditation.

Mindful living is a special way of being in which we live paying more attention to life in the present moment, and mindfulness meditation is the training that, by developing our ability to focus attention, prepares us for this more attentive existence.

Mindfulness meditation can be understood as a fitness program for the brain, a series of mental exercises that strengthen 'the brain muscle' and develop concentrated attention, calmness, stability, and equanimity. When I meet new students for the first time, I jokily say, "Welcome to the brain fitness gym. I'm Piero, your personal brain fitness trainer."

The most basic form of meditation is very simple: we are instructed to focus our attention on something, such as the breath, which is the most traditional object of attention in mindfulness meditation. As we begin paying attention, and feeling the physical sensations associated with the act of breathing, what inevitably happens is that our minds stray, carried away by thoughts. And this happens simply because this is what the mind does. The mind is an independent and unstoppable thought-producing machine.

So, during the meditation, when we notice that the mind has wandered and we are no longer paying attention to the physical sensations of the breath, we gently let go of the distraction and bring our attention back to feeling the breath. No matter if the mind wanders five times or five hundred times during meditation, we should simply start over, gently redirecting our attention back to the breath. Each time we catch ourselves distracted, we should celebrate and congratulate ourselves because this is a moment of success, a moment similar to flexing a muscle in a physical fitness program. And each time we flex our brain muscles, we strengthen our capacity to pay attention and be alert.

……...

"Thoughts are like birds flying about in the air. You can calmly watch them fly by without becoming involved with them and letting them nest in your hair." ~ Saint Francis of Assisi

……...

So, to begin with, meditation is a way of developing concentrated attention, the ability to let go of distractions and notice whatever may be going on in the present moment, around us and within us. It is a practice that develops the ability to become aware of thoughts, emotions, body sensations, and life in general.

Mindfulness meditation is not an exercise aimed at producing relaxation. We don't engage on this practice in order to clear the mind, stop thoughts – which, by the way, is impossible -- or create a state of tranquility, although this may happen. What the practice does is to train practitioners to be at peace with what is, whatever it may be, while developing the ability to notice the impermanence of everything.

With practice we will be less reactive and choose better responses to the challenges in our lives. We will grow in resilience and bounce back from adversity faster. We will reduce the physical, mental, and emotional wear-and-tear caused by stress, and enhance our overall well-being.

. . . .

Pausing and practicing:

Find a comfortable position for your body, close your eyes, and observe your breathing. For the next few moments, every time you become aware of your thoughts, acknowledge them, and gently let them go by bringing your attention back to the sensations of your body breathing. Observe the activity of the thinking mind from a removed place of silence and stillness.

. . . .

WHAT IS MINDFULNESS?

"In the beginner's mind there are many possibilities. In the expert's mind there are few." ~ Shunryu Suzuki Roshi

. . . .

Mindfulness is a training that leads to a way of living with more instances of present-moment awareness. It is the practice of focusing attention and observing what is going on in the present moment, by observing our own bodies, emotions, thoughts, experiences, and life in general. Not only observing, but observing without interfering, without the presumption that we already know, without adding commentary and judgment, and without hurriedly rushing to conclusions; observing with the openness and curiosity of a child, or, as we say, with the mind of a beginner, not the mind of an expert.

This manner of observing is one that allows us to discover the new in the old, the unusual in the usual, and the extraordinary in the ordinary.

Learning to focus and observe is just the beginning of the mindfulness practice. What follows focusing and observing is inquiring and reflecting as a diligent Greek philosopher from times past would. This exercise of questioning and surmising has the potential of liberating us from wrong perceptions. It brings us to that state of lucidity marked by clearly seeing, clearly understanding, and clearly knowing. We become better able to see beyond the veil of ignorance and delusion, and see things as they really are. We see the impermanent and ever-changing nature of everything, and realize that everything that arises also passes away.

……..

"Mindfulness is a way of training yourself to become aware of things as they really are." ~ Bhante Henepola Gunaratana

……..

Mindfulness refers to two things: the practice that develops our awareness, and the way of life in which we live with this more developed awareness. Mindfulness is both the practice that enhances the ability to observe and notice, and the clearer knowing that arises from observing and noticing.

Mindfulness practice develops the ability to know what's going on inside our heads right now, without getting carried away by it. It allows us to notice those times when we are being tossed around by unhealthy thoughts and emotions, when the mind is lost in desire, aversion, regret, and anguish, ruminating the past and worrying about the future. It equips us to redirect our attention to the here-now and from unwholesome thoughts to wholesome ones.

Mindfulness acts like a discerning guardian at the gates of the realm of the mind, selecting who should be allowed in and who should not. So, what follows the practice of diligent observation and reasoning is discerning wisdom, is seeing what is beneficial and what is not; seeing cause and effect at play, and learning what the consequences of our actions are.

From realizing that thoughts are insubstantial and ephemeral; from learning that we are not our thoughts; from discerning which thoughts bring about affliction and suffering and which bring about tranquility and joy; from seeing what is really important, and distinguishing what we can from what we cannot change, we can begin to be more selective, and choose which thoughts we should give our attention to and which ones we should dismiss.

The practice of mindfulness develops a better understanding of ourselves, and as we begin to get more familiar with our habitual patterns of reaction, we begin to see, with more clarity, the possibility to choose healthier responses.

Equanimity, that calmness and composure under tension, that expanded levelheadedness, imperturbability, and stability, begins to show up more often in our lives, perhaps to our own surprise. We become better able to recognize the disturbances when they emerge, and rather them resisting and pushing them away, we do the opposite: we accept their presence, allow them to be, and with interest and curiosity we lean toward them, trying to know them better. This investigation may be very revealing. We may notice our urges, our habitual patterns of reaction, and by pausing and asking, "What do I get from this?" we can begin to choose healthier responses. And as we learn to respond mindfully instead of reacting mindlessly -- as we learn to take time to ponder before choosing what to say and do -- we become better able to create more peaceful and joyful lives.

Doing whatever it is that we may be doing with awareness, observing, noticing, and knowing what is happening, is of tremendous value.

Living mindfully is a fresh way of living in which we engage with life fully awake, aware, and appreciative. By living in such a way, the suffering that exists in the world becomes more evident, and we feel called to engage in the work of promoting justice and enhancing the quality of life for all sentient beings.

Practicing to be still, to retreat, to gather ourselves, to befriend and pay loving attention to our minds is not a selfish activity. Throughout this process we experience, in a very natural and organic way, the growth in us of qualities such as tolerance, acceptance, solidarity, compassion, kindness, hospitality, and generosity. We become less selfish and more selfless. We become more inclined to cooperate than to compete with others. It becomes evident that when we take care of ourselves we are taking care of others, because when we work to know ourselves, we get to know others as well, and in the process we make the entire world a better place for all.

In a nutshell, the practice of wise assessment, wise discernment, and wise choices leads to liberation, awakening, and enlightenment. Living with more gratitude, ease, joy, lightness, and aliveness encapsulates what mindful living is.

....

Pausing and practicing:

Sit comfortably, close your eyes, and bring your awareness to your body. Soon you will notice that you become more aware of your body breathing. Choose a spot in your body to observe your breathing more closely, such as your nostrils, your chest, or your abdominal area. As your attention gravitates away from your breathing -- as you notice that you are thinking about something that is not in this very moment – congratulate yourself for noticing, acknowledge the thought, gently release it, and bring your awareness back to the physical sensations of your breathing. Keep doing this for the entire duration of the meditation. As you go about your day, practice observing your thoughts and emotions, and bringing your awareness back to the here-now. Be mindful of what you are thinking, feeling, saying, and doing. Observe yourself. Whenever you feel agitated -- or at any other time of your day, even for no reason at all -- gently bring your awareness to your breathing; this will help you redirect your awareness to the present moment. Such diligent daily discipline will reward you with enhanced well-being.

....

WHAT IS EQUANIMITY?

"Between stimulus and response there is a space. In that space is our power to choose our responses. In our responses lie our growth and our freedom." ~ Viktor Frankl

....

Equanimity is that attribute of impartiality, equilibrium, and ease of mind that allows us to see the totality of the situations clearly, and understand them dispassionately. It's an open space between stimulus and response that holds everything without excluding anything. In the turbulent region of our likes and dislikes, equanimity is that calm space of stability and non-reactivity, where we don't immediately submit to our cravings and aversions. We stay in the middle, serene and relaxed, exercising active assessment and discernment, while refraining from acting abruptly and impulsively. For such qualities it can be said that equanimity is applied wisdom, or wisdom in action.

Being equanimous doesn't imply that we become non-reactive to a point where our lives lose their allure. It simply means that we don't get carried away by our thoughts and emotions too easily and hastily. By practicing this non-reactive equanimity, we stay longer periods of time in the serene middle, and very seldom visit the turbulent extremes.

....

Pausing and practicing:

During meditation, choose to not push anything away. Observe the mental and emotional activity, and calmly and patiently be with all disturbances as a good host would. Go to that place of stillness and silence where you will have a clearer vision of who you really are, and also of who you are not. Close your eyes and observe your breathing. Now, observe your thoughts, emotions, and the feelings in your body. With each exhalation, relax and calm down a little more. Be gentle with yourself. Treat yourself with love, patience, and kindness. Give yourself the gift of rest. Acknowledge what is bothering you, but do not give those disturbing thoughts and emotions any further power. Do not engage in the process of imagining. The moment you realize that you have been captured by your thoughts and emotions, gently set yourself free, and softly release them; let them go. Do not fight your undesirable thoughts. Do not be angry at them. Do not try to chase them away. Do not get angry at yourself for having such thoughts either. This doesn't work; it only empowers them further.

Be here, now. Come back to the present moment by focusing on your breathing. By doing so, over and over again, you will be spending more and more time in this place of immense serenity. Meditation will train you to be a better observer of your thoughts and moods when you are not meditating, and this will enhance the quality of your life immensely.

A FULFILLING EXISTENCE

The practice of mindfulness meditation prepares us to live more mindfully in the present moment. It is a training that sharpens our ability to pay attention and notice what is going on, both around us and within us.

This practice allows us to live more attentively and be more aware during those other moments of our lives when we are not formally meditating. This expanded awareness, and the more mindful choices that it brings about, enhances our well-being and the overall quality of our lives. As we practice, we begin to pay more attention to our own selves and to the world around us, and begin to notice beauty that we didn't see before, or that we once saw, but don't see any more. We discover magic, mystery, and miracles even in the simplest things, and begin to live in a state of amazement with the wonders that surround us. We experience a sense of gratitude for all that has been freely given to us, and feel richly blessed, realizing how fortunate we already are.

This more mindful way of living – a life in which the pace is slower and the attention greater – allows us to savor and enjoy a lot more. It is as if, with the slower pace and greater attention, high doses of elegance and refinement are introduced in our days. With our sharpened ability to sense, every unremarkable item suddenly becomes a masterpiece for our sensory enjoyment; every meal, no matter how simple, becomes a banquet; every occurrence, no matter how ordinary, is sensed as extraordinary. Noticing nature, the vegetation, the leaves moving with the wind, and feeling the cool breeze caressing the skin, awakens in us awe and wonder. We begin to feel extremely rich, but in a different way: we feel owners of a kind of wealth that has nothing to do with one's financial situation, or with the accumulation of possessions that money can buy, but a wealth that is already present, available, and immensely more satisfying.

This more mindful way of living leads us to a joyful acceptance of what we have, what we do, and who we are. We begin to experience a sense of contentment that tames our relentless urge to have more, do more, and be more. And when we find ourselves engulfed in this restful cloud of peace, we suddenly realize that we are happier already, right here, right now.

Mindful living is a love affair with our own lives.

Pausing and practicing:

Pause, close your eyes and direct your attention to your breathing. Observe what happens when you breathe. Don't do anything else; just observe. That's all. As you are doing this, observe also how your attention shifts away from your breathing to your thoughts. We are, by nature, thought-producing machines who give rise to tens of thousands of thoughts a day. We operate in this world with a constant background noise generated by thoughts that have nothing to do with the present moment. Well, during meditation, our job is to become aware of our thoughts. When this happens, we choose not to engage with them; we don't start a mental conversation. After congratulating ourselves for noticing, we simply acknowledge them, and gently invite them to leave. We release them and bring our attention back to our breathing. We do this, over and over again. This is a very basic and easy form of meditation that is recommendable to be done for twenty minutes, twice a day, every day. Why? Because this gives us some control over our minds, and, in the final analysis, control over our lives. How? As you practice, you will develop the ability to observe yourself, your thoughts, and your moods. You will develop a present moment awareness that will help you stay with what is important while releasing what is not. This moment-to-moment present moment awareness is what will enhance your inner peace.

....

MINDFUL LIVING

I always come back to the saying, "It's not difficult to be mindful. Difficult is to remember to be mindful."

To live mindfully is to live a life with plenty of mindful moments, moments when we remember to purposely pay attention and observe whatever may be happening in the present moment with calm, interest, openness, and curiosity.

Although observing the here-now is fundamental for mindful living, it is not enough. Living mindfully invites inquiry, investigation, and reflection on what is being observed. It is an engagement with the present moment through the philosophical method of questioning, learning, and knowing. For me, it is a vibrant and exciting way of living that fulfills my aspiration to explore and inspire.

In order to live more mindfully, we should increase the amount of mindful moments in our days. It is difficult, if not impossible, to be mindful all the time, but it is possible, through training and practice, to increase the number of times we remember to be mindful. Mindful moments are those when we remember to embody the qualities of six words that begin with the letter A: awake, alert, attentive, aware, appreciative, and alive.

It all begins with being awake, meaning that we are not sleepwalking through life. Things are not happening totally on their own without our conscious participation. We are not on automatic pilot mode, going through our days without being on the pilot seat. We are not going through life mindlessly repeating negative patterns of behavior that may be degrading the quality of our lives. We are engaged with the present moment, purposely focusing our attention on the here-now, and deliberately slowing down to observe with openness and curiosity what is going on in this present moment, without rushing to add commentaries, opinions, or judgments.

Living mindfully produces such an empowering feeling!

It should be clear to everyone how our choices affect our lives. Living mindfully involves being a good observer, seeing clearly, making wise assessments, using wise discernment, and making wise decisions. That's why focusing on the present moment is so important. Because it is in this moment that we choose, and these choices are the ones that ultimately affect the quality of our lives.

....

"Everything can be taken from me, but one thing: the way I choose to respond to what you do to me. The last of one's freedoms is to choose one's attitude in any given circumstance." ~ Viktor Frankl

....

Pausing and practicing:

Sit down, close your eyes, and focus on your breathing. Observe what happens when you inhale and exhale. As you do this for some time, inevitably the mind will get distracted with thoughts. Your job is to catch yourself when you get distracted. Congratulate yourself for noticing that you were distracted. Become aware of what you are thinking, but don't continue to give your thoughts further power. Simply invite them to leave, and do this gently. Think of yourself as someone who is sitting by the side of the road watching cars go by; each car carries a thought. See each car passing by, going away, and disappearing in the distance. Don't go to the middle of the road and try to direct the traffic. Don't jump into any car either. Do not judge the thought, the practice, or yourself. Just bring your attention back to your breathing. Do this over and over again. Soon the activity in the mind will slow down and you will spend less time with the thoughts and more time in the space between thoughts. The traffic on that road will dwindle substantially. This simple practice will develop in you the ability to be aware of your thoughts and emotions during the other hours of your day, and allow you to be more selective of what you should give your attention to, and this way of living more mindfully will enhance the quality of your life.

....

LIVING MORE MINDFULLY

Why should we practice mindfulness?

Well, perhaps because the practice of mindfulness leads us to live more mindfully, and a more mindful way of living enhances the quality of our lives: the unpleasant occurrences do not wound us as deeply or last as longer, and the pleasant ones are noticed sooner and enjoyed fuller.

The practice of mindfulness develops skills that allow us to see beyond what we normally see, and to see again those things that, with the passing of time, became invisible to us.

To live mindfully is to live noticing what is real; being aware of life as it is, without wasting time and energy fruitlessly protesting because it is not as we would like it to be. Living mindfully is to see who we really are, and also who we are not. It is living with the ability to notice the pleasant and the unpleasant, calmly resting in the knowing that both are inevitable and transitory. It is to peacefully live in the knowing that everything is impermanent, that nothing lasts forever, and that transformation is the only constant in life. It is living with the power to be at peace with what is, accepting and dealing with both the good and the bad that life gives us. It is living with the skill to pause, breathe, and ask, "What is called for now, in this moment?" It is living with the capacity to augment the space between stimulus and response, and choose health-enhancing responses rather than health-damaging reactions.

The consistent practice of mindfulness meditation -- the cultivation of moment-to-moment, non-judgmental awareness -- helps develop a skill set that allows us to live more mindfully. With the regular practice of paying attention to the present moment, on purpose, and non-judgmentally, new qualities of mind arise, which reduce the physical, mental, and emotional wear-and-tear and enhance our overall well-being.

We practice mindfulness meditation in order to live more mindfully, and, in doing so, we not only live better lives, but also make the world a better place. With our peaceful presence, we become bringers of peace, and a blessing to every person we meet.

. . . .

Pausing and practicing:

Sit down, close your eyes, and observe your breathing. Focus. Whenever you realize that you are thinking about things of the past, or imagining the future, catch yourself doing it. Do it gently. Don't get mad, criticize, or chastise yourself for getting distracted. Don't judge the quality of your meditation practice. Don't tell yourself that you are not doing it right. Having thoughts is absolutely normal, and, in fact, the more you catch yourself and your wandering thoughts, the better the exercise for the brain is. Catch the thought. Congratulate yourself. Take a good look at it. Decide to release it, no matter how important and interesting the thought may be. Release it, gently, and return to the here-now, bringing your attention back to your object of attention, your breathing.

I call it the CCARR method of meditation: Catch - Congratulate - Acknowledge - Release - Return.

This simple acronym serves as a mnemonic aid to help us remember what to do, not only during our meditation sessions, but also throughout our days, in order to live more mindful lives. Catch the thought, congratulate yourself for catching it, acknowledge it, release it, and return to the activity of paying attention to the physical sensations of your breathing.

. . . .

ETERNAL SILENCE

Immersed in the eternal silence
Surrounded by the sounds of the ocean
The sun slowly moves up on the horizon and I feel its warmth upon my face.
"Feel the breeze" I remind myself, "and the freshness of the water, and the
softness of the sand"
The smooth pebble smiles and wakes me up from my dreams
"Smoothness comes with time," I say to myself
I breathe deeply and mindfully
I smile
I am here
You are here
We are here
Now

········

EARLY APRIL MORNINGS IN ATHLONE

Cold air and long shadows
Trees waking up after a long retreat
Fresh bulbs and little leaves decorating branches tired of fighting the winter
winds
Pigeons and crows protecting their nests
A coming back to life
And an infinite number of diamonds floating down the river Shannon,
shining jewels that can only be seen in this present moment, but cannot be kept
for later enjoyment, just like every single moment of our lives

········

FOR THE FIRST TIME

See as if you were seeing for the first time. Listen as if you were listening for the first time. Taste as if you were tasting for the first time. Smell as if you were smelling for the first time. Touch as if you were touching for the first time. Move as if you were moving for the first time. There's a lot to observe, discover, and be amazed and grateful for.

········

In the late 1980s I spent some time in Japan. Looking back at that experience now, I see that I was a completely different person then. I was an unrefined individual, almost a western barbarian if you will, and the worst of it all is that I was completely unaware of it. Only later in my life I became aware of my lack of awareness. Back then I had no idea of what mindfulness was or of the many rituals people in the East practice in order to develop it.

There were two events on that trip that contributed to raise my awareness. First, I was invited to attend a tea ceremony. Although I approached the entire service with reverence, I had no idea that it had little to do with the tea itself. Only later in my life I came to understand that it had to do with the attention we give to every single detail of what is going on: from the shape of the tea pot to the designs made by the steam rising up to the sky; from the color and smell of the infusion to the feelings generated by the warm ceramic cup in our hands. I now understand that it has little to do with the tea itself, and, at the same time, as paradoxical as it may sound, it has everything to do with it. The tea ceremony is, in reality, a practice of mindfulness, of being attentive to what is going on in the here-now. It is an exercise that teaches us to see and appreciate beauty. It is a way of developing skills that expand the moments of alertness during our lives.

A similar eye-opening experience happened to me when I was invited to stay in a ryokan, a traditional Japanese inn, and participate in a communal bath. Japan is famous for its hot springs, those bodies of subterranean water which are made warm by the underground volcanic activity, and for its shared baths where guests bathe together with the water that comes to the surface naturally hot. It was only later in life that I came to understand that what was taking place in that communal bath had little to do with the bath itself, and a lot to do with paying attention to the present moment.

I was taken aback by the extended length of time it took those in there to bathe themselves. It amazed me how slowly they moved from one part of the body to another, and how conscientiously they washed each area while paying attention to the all details, such as the texture of the skin, the aroma of the soap, and the temperature of the water. It also struck me how they did all this in absolute silence. It dawned on me, later in life, that what they were doing there had little to do with the bath itself, and, at the same time, everything to do with it.

I now understand that it is by paying attention to the present moment that we become able to recognize what is going on in the center of our beings. The reflection on tea ceremony and the communal bath experiences taught me about mindfulness, about meditation in motion, about the ability to see beyond what we see. They initiated me in the art of living a contemplative life, the life that allows us to connect, communicate and commune with the magic, mystery, and miracles.

……..

DOING SOMETHING AND DOING NOTHING

"I like to describe mindfulness as threefold attentional skill set: concentration power, sensory clarity, and equanimity working together." ~ Shinzen Young

……..

Mindfulness meditation is not a practice we engage in order to create a desirable state, such as peace or bliss, but one we practice to develop the ability to be more aware and less reactive. It is a training that enhances our ability to pay attention to the present moment with kindness and curiosity, noticing what is going on, curbing our most-of-the-time hasty and thoughtless reactions, while taking time to choose the wisest responses.

The idea that we can meditate to stop the arising of thoughts and clear the mind is a myth. In meditation, our aspiration is not to stop thinking but rather to observe the thinking, and realize that the mind has a mind of its own. We don't meditate with the intention to have a completely blank mind, devoid of thoughts, but rather to be aware of thoughts when they arise, getting to know them better. We become more conscious of the constant activity of our minds and realize the non-stop pursuit of sorting out what we like from what we dislike, what we approve from what we disapprove. We notice our relentless tendency to compare, contrast, categorize, classify, compete, complain, criticize, and condemn.

Besides awareness of our thoughts, the practice of mindfulness meditation allows us to be more aware of our emotions and body sensations. By resting in awareness -- by staying put and doing nothing, except observing – we become more aware of our periods of restlessness, drowsiness, and doubt. We realize the impermanence of everything, become less judgmental and self-centered, and grow in appreciation, contentment, gratitude, kindness, generosity, patience, and compassion.

And, in the middle of this whole process, we may experience greater calm and serenity.

It is said that the most important moment in the meditation practice is the one when we transition from being lost in thoughts to becoming aware of where our minds had been. The moment we realize that we haven't been mindful is itself a mindful moment of mindfulness, a magic moment when we are awake and aware. By bringing energetic curiosity to our lives, we are able to clearly see the difference between the moments when we are not aware and those moments when we are. It is when we become aware of a thought, that we are able to realize the difference between being an observer of thoughts and being lost in the middle of a story.

Paying greater attention to these moments of transition, noticing them over and over again, is what develops our mindfulness and enhances the quality of our lives. By having the intention and exercising the commitment to be awake, alert, attentive, aware, and appreciative, we feel fully alive.

. . . .

I am paying attention, noticing what is going on, aware of what is happening. I am able to see events, thoughts, feelings, emotions, and sensations in my body with clarity. I have insights. I investigate, ponder, and understand. I see all the beauty of this world, and appreciate the magic, mystery, and miracles that surround me. I experience energy, vigor, and vitality. I am able to discern and make wise decisions that improve the quality of my life. I am awake, alert, attentive, aware, and appreciative of life. I am fully alive.

. . . .

THE EIGHT C'S

We all have some habitual thought patterns. What I mean is that we develop habits to process information in certain ways that become well established habits. In general, given our negativity bias -- the one that states that "the brain works like velcro for the negative and teflon for the positive" -- we tend to focus on the negative more often. We habitually criticize, judge, and condemn.

The mind engages in the Eight C's process a lot, if not all the time.

Comparing and contrasting, categorizing and classifying, competing and complaining, criticizing and condemning, are all habitual behaviors. Let's ponder for a while. Aren't we unceasingly comparing and contrasting how things and people are with our ideas of how they should be? "She should do this. He should be like that. I don't approve her behavior. I don't like the way he is." We are also constantly categorizing and classifying, in other words, creating categories, labeling, putting things and people in this or that specific category. "I like this. I don't like that. This goes over here, together with the things that I like. This goes in that shelf, together with those I dislike."

Unfortunately, once we have made up our minds of what goes where -- for example, which group, in our minds, certain individuals belong to -- we begin to live with our beliefs about them, not with the reality of whom they are in the present moment. We don't see them; what we process in our minds are our ideas of them.

And then comes criticism, judgment, and condemnation. "She should not act like this. He should not talk like that. This car in front of me is moving too slow; it should go faster. This car that just passed me is moving too fast; it should go slower." When we criticize others -- which happens most of the time -- we unconsciously engage in a mind-created competition in which we compare ourselves with others and invariably, although unconsciously, declare ourselves to be the winners. "He is not as good as I am. I am much better." And untrained minds produce those unrelenting complainers for whom nothing is ever good enough, those nit-pickers for whom there's always something wrong to grumble about.

……..

"Small people, big problems. Big people, no problem."

……..

Finally, we become those presumptuous and self-righteous judges, and we proclaim our verdicts, condemning others. It is a very seductive process, very easy to get in, and difficult to get out. It is an unconscious and therefore not easily perceptible way of processing information. Fortunately, mindfulness practice allows us to see how often we are lost in the eight C's and how easily we put ourselves on pedestals, high above others, from where we judge and condemn everyone and everything.

So, let us be more mindful and notice when we are comparing, contrasting, categorizing, classifying, competing, complaining, criticizing, and condemning. By doing so, we can begin to tame those negative tendencies. As my teacher says, "You cannot fix what you cannot see. You cannot heal what you cannot feel. You cannot tame what you cannot name." Let's be mindful, and remember that the mind is trainable. Let's practice ways of developing more positive thinking habits, noticing and reducing the time we spend with the eight C's.

Let's give ourselves more time to intentionally take in the good that is all around us, allowing the time to notice, appreciate, linger, savor, and absorb it.

………

THE HABITUAL VISITORS

The unrestrained and unruly thoughts are habitual visitors. We are called to treat our thoughts the same way good hosts treat all their guests: kindly and skillfully. Diligent practice will prepare us to be better hosts, so, later on, when visiting thoughts knock on our doors, we will be ready to welcome and entertain both the lower and the higher quality ones. We will also know how to gently ask the rowdy visitors to leave, and be successful in doing so.

………

"Hi! There you are again, my recurring thoughts, my little, agitated monkey-like friends! I didn't notice you were there. I just saw you. Before we go any further, give me a moment so I can congratulate myself for having noticed you. This makes me very happy! Please, sit down. I would like to know you better. May I ask you how long have you been here? OK, I see. OK, I hear you. I understand your suggestion, but it doesn't sound like a good idea right now. Thanks, but 'No, thanks.' Well, unfortunately I can't give you any further attention right now. We will have to get together some other time. I am sorry but I have to ask you to leave. I need to get back to my breath. Anyway, it was good seeing you again. Thank you for stopping by. Bye!"

………

Pausing and practicing:

We begin this awareness of the breath meditation acknowledging

21

place and time. The place is here and the time is now. We are here, now, and no-where else, and no-when else. We are right here, right now. And actually we are always here, now. If someone asks, "Where are you?" the answer, "Here" is always right. And if someone asks, "What time is it?" the answer, "Now" is also always right. We are always here, now. But although the body is here, perhaps the mind is not. Perhaps the mind is else-where and else-when, lost in space and time, visiting the past or the future. So the invitation is to bring the mind to where the body is, right here, right now. James Joyce, the famous Irish author, introducing a character in one of his short stories wrote, "Mr. Duffy lived a short distance from his body," and we, too, many times, are living short distances from our bodies. So the invitation is to bring the mind to inhabit the body, right here, right now. And we do this by paying attention to the physical sensations in our body, noticing how the body feels right here, right now. And as we become more aware of the physical sensations, and of the body as a whole, we also begin to become more aware of the body breathing, noticing the air coming in and going out, paying detailed attention to the entire cycle of breathing: the in-breath, the lungs full, the out-breath, and the lungs empty. And when the mind wanders, we simply bring it back, starting over, beginning again, paying attention to this breath, this one; not the previous one, not the next one, but this one, this breath, right here, right now.

·········

MINDFUL EATING

Take a few deep breaths and center yourself before you begin eating. Set the intention to eat deliberately, to give eating your full attention, and to get the most possible enjoyment out of this meal. Check your belly and ask yourself, "How hungry am I?" Be curious and assess your food. Look attentively. Use your senses and re-discover the colors, the textures, the aromas. Appreciate it. Smell it. Now, taste it. Feel its temperature. Move slowly, bite by bite. Put your fork down between bites, close your eyes if you so wish, and be conscious of all the different sensations you are experiencing. Even if you have eaten something similar in the past, treat this food as if you were savoring it for the first time in your life. Taste and eat it as if you've never tasted or eaten it before, because, actually, you've never eaten this one before.

Be mindful of mental images and memories while eating. Since mind-wandering is inevitable, bring it back to the present moment and the enjoyment of this meal. If the mind wanders, you may use this opportunity to express gratitude to the seeds, the soil, the sun, the rain, and the people involved in producing, distributing, and preparing the food you are now eating. But come back, as much as possible, to the here-now, paying attention to this moment and mindfully eating this food, this one, right here, right now. Slowing down is extra important in this process. Stay with this bite, this one. Not the previous one. Not the next one. This one. This bite. Chew it thoroughly, and savor it, like a refined gourmet would. Staying with this bite is staying in the present moment, practicing mindfulness, living mindfully. Detect any expectation. If we keep thinking about other things, such as what we will be eating next, we are not fully connected with the food that we are eating now. Also, since it takes time for the brain to register that we have already eaten enough, if we eat too fast, we either eat too much, or we finish the meal too quickly and still feel hungry. Since overeating is not good for anyone's health, slow down and savor this one bite. The more you savor, the you we eat.

……..

THE MIRACLE IN YOUR MIND

Our friend Kevin reminded us of the power of our thoughts, and the beauty and wisdom of populating our minds with good thoughts, with images of health, happiness, prosperity, wealth, and peace. He reminded us to stop wallowing in our self-pity, and to stop telling those stories of our suffering, distress, or misfortune, the ones we tell to evoke sympathy. He encouraged us to let go of those poor me stories and replace them with stories of success and victory. He reminded us to look at those who have it worse than we do, and to express gratitude for all that was given to us, always. He talked about giving thanks for the good that we already have and also all the good that is coming our way. He encouraged us to engage, or reengage, in a daily discipline of meditation, imagination, and visualization of the life and world we want.

I thanked him for re-igniting in me the desire to do what is important: to give thanks. I am now motivated to reengage in a more diligent practice of expressing gratitude for life in this present moment, and imagining the great outcomes I want for my life.

……..

"The miracle is in your mind. But just the same, so is every negative outcome. Think you can't and you won't. It is time to shift your awareness. It is time to expect miracles. It is time to have gratitude for what you have. Without gratitude, we live in a state of want. We need to wake up to the fact that what we THANK about, we bring about. Do you desire to be happy, healthy and prosperous? Is that what you wish for yourself? It is time for change. It is time for renewal. It is time to realize that the miracle of your life, the miracle of your destiny, the miracle of your dreams lies in the miracle of your mind. Ask for it. Seek it. Knock on the door. And be prepared to receive the many gifts and blessings that are waiting for you. It is time for action! It is time to believe in the miracle in your mind."~ Reverend Kevin McGee

……..

I love the part when he said, "what we THANK about, we bring about." There is great wisdom in these words. Kevin encouraged us to practice imagining that we already are in the future, already living our ideal lives, and already giving thanks for every good thing that happened to us. In other words, he encouraged us to mentally project ourselves into our ideal futures, and, then, feel how good it feels, and give thanks, because "what we THANK about, we bring about."

……..

"And now, dear brothers and sisters, one final thing: Fix your thoughts on what is true, and honorable, and right, and pure, and lovely, and admirable. Think about things that are excellent and worthy of praise."~ Paul, the apostle

……..

Pause and think for a moment about it. Isn't this a very, very clear instruction? Be conscious of what you are thinking. Let go of the negative and embrace the positive. Change your thoughts, change your mind, change your choices, and change your life!

……..

WALKING WITH PEACE AND PRESENCE

Carefully. Slowly. Lifting one foot from the ground. Standing and balancing on just one leg, with all the weight of my body sustained by this one limb. Moving the foot that is in the air forward, lowering it. Heel touching the ground, and then my instep, the ball of my foot, and my toes. My entire foot, from heel to toes, is touching the ground. Both feet are now resting on the ground. Pausing for a moment. The heel of the back foot is now leaving the ground, and for a moment only its toes are in contact with the floor. The weight of my body is shifting from the foot in the back to the one in the front.

………

Lifting. Moving. Placing.
Heel of the back foot leaving the floor.
Pausing.
Weight shifting to the front leg.
Starting again.

………

Moving slowly, lifting the foot in the back, trying to keep my balance, controlling all sorts of muscles, compensating here and there in order not to fall. Correcting. Tightening. Releasing. Adjusting and readjusting. Maintaining the balance. Moving the foot forward and placing it on the ground: heel, instep, arch, ball, toes. Resting. Starting the movement all over again.

………

Up. Forward. Down.
Lifting. Moving. Placing.
Resting.

………

"Am I here? Am I really here? Can I feel my feet? Can I feel the soles of my feet? Can I feel the weight shifting from heel to toes? Can I feel that? Can I come back to paying attention to my walking and the sensations in my body when I catch myself distracted with other things? Am I thinking or am I feeling the sensations?"

"Too much thinking! Less thinking and more sensing!"

………

Redirecting the attention back to the sensations in my body as I walk. Walking slowly and mindfully. Lifting, moving, placing, and resting. Walking as if I had never walked before. Paying attention to the entire body, and the breathing. Staying alert to the sensations. Discovering how to walk again.

"How did I learn such a complex movement? How can I, in my day-to-day living, perform it without even consciously thinking about it? How is this possible?"

……..

Lifting. Up.
Moving. Forward.
Placing. Down.
Resting.

……..

Observing. Noticing. Witnessing. Investigating. Exploring. Extracting great joy from walking mindfully. Not only marveling at the intricate and complex movement that I was able to master, but also at what I am able to mindfully capture with my senses, what I am able to see, hear, smell, touch, and perhaps even taste now that I am moving slowly and mindfully. Paying greater attention to the world that surrounds me. Seeing things that I wasn't able to see before. Stopping. Looking at the big things and the little ones, looking at what is near and what is far away from me. Seeing all the magic, mystery, and miracles that surround me. Letting the beauty penetrate me. Noticing it. Appreciating it. Savoring it. Absorbing it. Seeing what arises and what passes way. Noticing birth and death, the pleasant and the unpleasant, and the impermanence of all. Letting it all in.

……..

I feel the coolness of the breeze! I feel the warmth of the sun!
I breathe and walk; I walk and breathe... slowly, mindfully!
I am here, now, whole, perfect, and complete.

……..

"Walk as if you your feet are kissing the Earth… The kingdom of God is available to you in the here and the now. But the question is whether you are available to the kingdom. Our practice is to make ourselves ready for the kingdom so that it can manifest in the here and the now. You don't need to die in order to enter the kingdom of heaven. In fact, you have to be truly alive in order to do so." ~ Thich Nhat Hanh

……..

"When was the last time you really, really looked around you, and took the time to wonder and appreciate even the smallest of things in their awesome perfection? Today, right now, take five minutes out of your phone and look at something with new eyes; observe its shape, the variation in color, the texture, how the light bounces off it, how it feels, or even how it smells... Ever wonder how it got to be that way? What it went through and what it must still endure? Stop, observe, and be aware of your surroundings and all its magic! Don't sleepwalk through life! If my dog, Chico, can stop to smell the flowers, so can we!" ~ Florencia Clement De Grandprey

....

FOR TOO LONG

For too long now I have confined myself. I haven't touched the pebble, or laid my hands on the tree, or admired the colors of the feathers of the duck.

For too long now I haven't seen you in the clouds, or in the reflections on the pond. I have not felt you in the morning breeze, or sensed you in the empty spaces.

For too long now I haven't allowed the squirrels to look me in the eyes, or listened to what the birds had to tell me. I haven't heard you in the whispers beyond the noises.

For too long now I have not felt you gently kissing my feet as I walk. I have not noticed the leaves dancing with the wind. I have not seen you in what is dying and what is being born. I have not reflected on the impermanence of all.

For too long now I have not seen you shining in the drops of water on the blades of grass.

I have not been paying attention.

I haven't felt that you and I are one.

But today I am out again,

I am here, now

In ecstasy

With you

With me

....

DOING WITHOUT DOING

"Nature does not hurry, yet everything is accomplished." ~ Laozi

……..

Wu Wei is Chinese for non-doing or non-action.

It refers to creating without striving, without trying desperately to control the outcomes.

Wei Wu Wei is action without action, the aptitude of achieving results without excessive effort.

It brings to my mind images of allowing Life to flow naturally while trusting the Universal Wisdom, offering ourselves to be used by the Universe to create through us, aware of the commands whispered by our Inner Voices.

……..

FLOWING IN THE ZONE

"The Sage is occupied with the unspoken and acts without effort. Teaching without verbosity, producing without possessing, creating without regard to result, claiming nothing, the Sage has nothing to lose." ~ Laozi

…….

Do you remember those times in your life when you were fully focused and energized, thoroughly enjoying what you were doing, feeling that you weren't really doing anything and that things were being done through you? Do you remember being in that state of complete immersion in the present moment while performing a task, with a calm confidence that everything you wanted to achieve was possible? Do you remember your amazement with the extraordinary results you were getting spontaneously and effortlessly, without thinking or striving too much? Do you remember losing track of time, feeling that everything slowed down like in a slow motion movie, and hours went by like minutes?

Many athletes and artists have hyper-focused experiences when they feel as if they are in a special zone where everything flows naturally, easily, without obstructions. The practice of mindfulness expands one's ability to enter "the zone" and stay in this state of "flow."

NO MIND

The Last Samurai is a 2003 movie that tells the story of the changes that took place in Japan in the late 19th century, and in the life of a man who learns mindfulness. In the movie, an American mercenary is captured in battle and taken to live among those he was fighting against. After some time, although still a prisoner, he is allowed to live as any other member of the community. He begins to participate in many of the village activities, such as samurai sword-fighting training (kata and iaido). In the beginning, his performance is pitiful. After many defeats in the practice fights, he is told that he has too many minds, and is advised to have no mind. He is told to let go of the many thoughts that are crowding his head, thoughts that do not allow him to focus on the here-now. Once he learns to reduce the over thinking and increase his present-moment-mindfulness, he begins to reach that flow state that brings about noticeable improvements in his performance. With time, he learns the Bushido tradition -- the code of the samurai -- and becomes more grounded, centered, and present. Experiencing greater peace of mind, he grows in respect for the samurai way of life.

Mushin is a Japanese word that means no mind. Mushin no shin is a Zen expression that can be translated as the mind without mind, a mental state where there is a greater immersion in the present moment without discursive thought and judgment. Jon Kabat-Zinn defined mindfulness as "the awareness that arises from paying attention, on purpose, in the present moment, non-judgmentally." Mindfulness practice is the way we cultivate this no mind state, where we are in the present moment, knowing what is going on, without adding a lot of commentaries, opinions, and judgments. It is that state of bare knowing and continuous mindfulness, mentioned by the Buddha in the Satipatthana Sutta, his discourse on the four foundations of mindfulness:

"In this way, in regard to the body one abides contemplating the body internally, or one abides contemplating the body externally, or one abides contemplating the body both internally and externally. One abides contemplating the nature of arising in the body... the nature of passing away in the body... or the nature of both arising and passing away in the body. Mindfulness that "there is a body" is established in one to the extent necessary for bare knowledge and continuous mindfulness. And one abides independent, not clinging to anything in the world. That is how in regard to the body one abides contemplating the body." ~ the Buddha

....

We practice in order to establish enough mindfulness to apprehend and understand what is unfolding in the here-now, noticing when mental commentary -- likes and dislikes, approvals and disapprovals, criticism and condemnation -- arises. We practice in order to let go of those mental commentaries, and simply be with what is. By doing this constantly, moment after moment, we develop bare knowledge and continuous mindfulness.

....

"The mind must always be in the state of 'flowing,' for when it stops anywhere that means the flow is interrupted and it is this interruption that is injurious to the well-being of the mind. In the case of the swordsman, it means death. When the swordsman stands against his opponent, he is not to think of the opponent, or of himself, or of his enemy's sword movements. He just stands there with his sword which, forgetful of all technique, is ready only to follow the dictates of the subconscious. The man has effaced himself as the wielder of the sword. When he strikes, it is not the man but the sword in the hand of the man's subconscious that strikes" ~ Takuan Sōhō, Zen master

....

Seeing clearly is the meaning of the Pali word vipassana, usually translated as insight meditation. Seeing clearly implies objectively observing and directly knowing what is without making up stories and getting lost in thoughts and emotions, reactions and associations. That's the bare knowledge mindfulness practitioners cultivate. Mindfulness practices are used to refine the mind and equip those who practice it with that level of complete present-moment awareness which enhance the overall well-being and quality of life.

....

BEING IN THE ZONE

To be in the zone is to be in that desirable state in which you are fully immersed and completely absorbed by the activity at hand, feeling energized and focused. When you are in the zone, you are flowing with the flow, achieving great things effortlessly, enjoying the process, and feeling happy. To be in the zone is to be totally in the here-now, without entertaining any thoughts that do not pertain to the present moment. When we are in the zone, we are completely immersed in what we are doing, and we don't think about anything else. In fact, we feel that we are not actually doing anything; we feel that the doing is being done through us. Our perception of time and space is altered, and we feel that time slows down, that everything is unfolding in slow motion, and that we are mere observers of ourselves while we do extraordinary things. We become one with our environment, and our sense of being a separated self vanishes; we merge with the Universe and experience oneness. This state of expanded awareness allows us to do amazing feats.

To be in the zone is a profound experience of deep connection and communion with everyone and everything which can bring about a new understanding of life.

We should strive to be in the zone as often as possible. The paradox is that although we cannot get in the zone through our striving, we have to first put in effort in order to break through a threshold and reach that state in which effort is no longer needed. In other words, we have to do some things in order to reach that level in which we don't do anything, and great things are done through us. Then, this refined instrument that we have become effortlessly brings what needs to be brought to the world.

Apply yourself to do, and reach that point when you don't do, but simply allow it to be done through you. Experience the wondrous shift from human-doing to human-being, a human who is in the zone, flowing with the flow.

Apply yourself to learn, but live in that state where you don't struggle to learn because you have realized that the wisdom you seek is already in you. You already know what needs to be known.

……...

The desire to be better is praiseworthy, and the commitment to do what is necessary to improve ourselves is honorable, but let us not be oblivious to the fact that the motivation behind self-improvement is, most of the time, a selfish one. Even on the journey to let go of the self, the self wants to feel that it is better than someone else. It is constantly comparing itself with others in order to produce emotional rewards through feelings of superiority. Let us pay attention and be aware of what the ego is engendering, being cognizant of its arrogance. Let us grow in selflessness, and make of the effort and dedicated work we are putting into our personal development our sacrificial gift for the betterment of all.

....

FLOWING

The Flow is experienced in those moments when we feel that we have been transported to another dimension -- another sphere of existence -- where we experience an intensification of senses, feelings, and emotions so powerful as to produce a kind of trance that leads to a dissociation from everything but the experience itself. Those are moments of total immersion in the here-now, when we feel as if we are out of ourselves, observing ourselves doing great things, and feeling that we are not doing them, but they are being done through us. In sports, we say of athletes who are operating at this flow state as being in the zone. The Flow is those moments of heightened perception, unrestricted self-confidence, and masterful performance. The Flow is accompanied by a host of intense feelings and overpowering emotions such as rapture, joy, ecstasy, delight, euphoria, bliss, elation, exaltation. It carries us to a place of peaceful contentment, supreme happiness, and poetic inspiration.

....

HOW DO WE GET IN THE FLOW?

- Meditate and befriend the six S's: Silence, Stillness, Solitude, Seclusion, Simplicity, and Service, knowing that the first five prepare us to properly perform the sixth one.

- Immerse yourself in nature, striving to see the magic, mystery, and miracles all around you, being amazed, grateful, and happy. Never underestimate the power of nature to bring you to a flow state.

- Develop mastery in the art of mindful living, practicing moment-to-moment awareness, always paying attention and being alert to what is.

- Apply yourself to figure out who you are, and what you were brought here to do. Also realize who you are not, liberating yourself from imposed conditionings.

- Dedicate yourself to do what you love. Give expression to your creativity. Refine your craft and become the best you can be. Immerse yourself totally in whatever you may be doing, losing yourself in that dimension where time and space are altered.

- Don't get distracted by thoughts that don't pertain to the present moment. Catch your distracting thoughts, congratulate yourself for catching them, acknowledge them, gently release them, and return to the appreciation of this present moment.

- Be here, now, not spending much time in the past, replaying old mental tracks. Leave behind memories that bring up regret, resentment, and remorse, letting go of lives that have played themselves out and do not serve you anymore. Don't obsess with what lies ahead either, but if you do, be hopeful, optimistic, and imagine positive outcomes.

- Simplify. Unclutter your life, and get rid of distractions. Focus on what is important now, at the current stage of your life.

- 'Clean your vessel and become like a hollow bone,' allowing the energy to flow through freely. Remove inner obstacles such as envy, anger, and hatred, allowing compassion and forgiveness to flow freely through you. Send love, all the time, to everyone, and to your own self too, regardless of time. Send love to your younger and to your older self.

- Be present to others, giving your undivided attention to whoever may be with you at any given time. Practice kindness, patience, and generosity, becoming an individual who exudes love.

- Operate with a beginner's mind, not letting our preconceived ideas taint the here-now. Approach every moment as a new moment, every situation as a new situation, discovering them with the freshness and curiosity of a little child.

- Finally, believe that Heaven is here, if we want it to be. Believe that Earth is our garden and our playground, and our joyous fate is to enjoy the beauty of this stunning garden, and have fun in this amazing playground. Believe that we can make the garden more beautiful, and the playground more enjoyable. Believe in sharing your toys, because the joy of your fellow playmates will increase your own.

....

EXPLORING WHATEVER ARISES

Mindfulness meditation is quite simple, but it's not easy. In the beginning of this journey of mindfulness practice, the goal is to develop the ability to concentrate attention and notice the details of what is being observed. This practice of focusing the mind is done by choosing an object of attention -- the breath, for instance -- and setting the intention to pay attention to it. A great aid to keep the focus on this object of attention is to be interested in it, investigating it with curiosity -- with a so-called 'beginner's mind' -- exploring the physical sensations of the process of breathing, and discovering them anew.

Now, while one is focusing, or trying to focus on the object of attention, the mind wanders. This is common and inevitable, something to be expected. Nothing wrong there. So, when the practitioner notices that she is lost in thoughts, she is called to congratulate herself for noticing, acknowledge what the distraction was, gently release it, and bring her attention back to the chosen object of attention. Quite simple, but not necessarily easy.

This practice sharpens our noticing skills, and develops one-pointed focused attention. It brings awareness to the non-stop internal chatter -- the proliferation of distracting, always self-referential, and mostly non-constructive thoughts -- and reveals how transient and impermanent thoughts are.

Once the practitioners get a good understanding of this practice and develop the ability to retain focus on the object for some time without distractions, they are introduced to an expanded and more encompassing meditation. Rather than choosing beforehand one object to pay attention to, they are instructed to investigate with curiosity whatever arises and calls for attention during the meditation. This is known as choiceless awareness meditation. It is also called open awareness or open monitoring. Again, it is quite simple but not necessarily easy. In this meditation, practitioners are initially instructed to ground themselves, noticing sensations, and becoming aware of the body, and the body breathing in the here-now.

....

Sit, and know you are sitting. Breathe, and know you are breathing. Breathing in, know you're breathing in. Breathing out, know you're breathing out.

34

Once they settle down and settle in; once, as we say, they bring their minds to inhabit their bodies; once mind and body are together in the present moment, they are invited to investigate with greater curiosity whatever catches their attention, such as thoughts, emotions, sounds, or body sensations. Whatever arises becomes the object to be investigated and known.

……..

This Open Monitoring practice can be divided in the following four phases:

1 - Settle,
2 - Open up
3 - Explore
4 - Return.

Settle: Rest in the awareness of your body and your body breathing. Settle down and settle in. This will be your 'anchor,' a safe place to return to whenever you get distracted, agitated, or lost.

Open up: Once you have settled, give yourself permission to observe other experiences. Open up and remain open to whatever arises. Notice whatever becomes predominant in your field of awareness.

Explore: Investigate with curiosity what is calling you; what is requesting your attention. Remember that there is a difference between observing thoughts and emotions, and being lost in them. Stay as the observer.

Return: If at any moment you get confused, agitated, or lost, return with gentleness and compassion to the anchor. Reconnect with the body and the body breathing in this moment, and once you feel settled, return to your practice, opening up and exploring again.

……..

It is important to have it clear when you are observing thoughts and emotions and when you are caught, carried away, and lost in them. It is important to develop the ability to stand in the role of the observer, the one who is watching the movie that is unfolding. The following reminders may be helpful:"Observe that you are observing. Notice that you are noticing. Be mindful that you are being mindful."

……..

LOST

"Midway along the journey of our life I woke to find myself in a dark wood, for I had wandered off from the straight path."~ Dante Alighieri

……..

There's a story, told by David Wagoner in poetry, of a young Indian who asks an older member of the tribe "What do I do when I am lost in the forest?" In the answer, the elder instructs the young Indian to stand still and observe the woods with the utmost attention, seeing all the details, and even listening to the forest breathing. If we are able to get out of our heads, and let go of our worries of impending tragedies, and focus on the here-now, we will find ourselves. We will not be lost. The place where we find ourselves has to be deeply known, because no place is like any other: each place is unique. The final words of the recommendation of the elder are of great beauty. "Stand still. The forest knows where you are. You must let it find you.'"

……..

"Stand still. The trees ahead and bushes beside you
Are not lost. Wherever you are is called Here,
And you must treat it as a powerful stranger,
Must ask permission to know it and be known.
The forest breathes. Listen. It answers,
I have made this place around you.
If you leave it, you may come back again, saying Here.
No two trees are the same to Raven.
No two branches are the same to Wren.
If what a tree or a bush does is lost on you,
You are surely lost. Stand still. The forest knows
Where you are. You must let it find you."
~ David Wagoner

……..

MEDITATION IS NOT WHAT YOU THINK

"I have not found anything else anywhere near as powerful, as nurturing, and as illuminating as cultivating the capacity for embodied presence in my own life." ~ Jon Kabat-Zinn

……..

We don't meditate to create any particular state or unusual experience, such as a state of calmness, or an experience of transcendence. Whenever we expect the meditation practice to produce a desirable state, we are setting ourselves up to frustration. Our intention during meditation should be to remain gently open and observe whatever arises, without striving for anything special to happen, knowing that sometimes what arises can be quite unsettling.

Sometimes the meditation will be easy and blissful, other times it will be difficult and tormenting, but we should be careful with our tendency to classify our meditations as good or bad. Not all pleasant meditations are good, and not all unpleasant ones are bad. A good meditation is one that gives the brain a good workout, develops focus, sharpens the ability to notice, and augments the appetite to investigate, discover, and learn. Despite all the ups and downs we face during this journey of exploration through meditation, as long as we keep practicing, we will be moving forward, making progress, and developing our ability to live more mindfully, which is what will, in the end, improve the quality of our lives. And it's quite easy to understand that the more 'mindful moments' we have, the more of those moments we will have. It's like saying that mindfulness brings about more mindfulness: it is by noticing what is unfolding that we activate and strengthen neural pathways that allow us to more frequently, and clearly, notice what is unfolding. So, during meditation, don't expect anything enjoyable or extraordinary to happen. If it happens, great! Enjoy it! The problem is not with the experience itself, but with the desire, the expectation, and the strong impulse to control the process in order to produce certain results. The advice is, "Do not strive to produce any specific outcome. Let go and let it be. Expectation will lead to frustration. Just meditate without expectations, and trust that a regular and committed practice will bring about improvements in your life."

Jon Kabat-Zinn recommended the cultivation of these nine mindfulness-enhancing attitudes in our daily lives:

- Beginner's Mind,
- Non-Judging,
- Acceptance,
- Letting Go, Letting It Be,
- Trust,
- Patience,

- Non-Striving,
- Gratitude, and
- Generosity.

By incorporating these attitudes, and practicing regularly, we will develop this invaluable ability to more skillfully process the ups and downs in our lives -- the good and the bad occurrences, the easy and the difficult situations, the pleasant and unpleasant experiences -- with greater equanimity, balance, serenity, and ease. We will learn to reduce unnecessary reactivity and useless struggle, accept life as it presents itself, and use wise assessment and discernment to choose the best responses, all of them skills that are truly priceless.

....

NEITHER GOOD, NOR BAD MEDITATIONS

It is not uncommon, even for experienced meditators, to fall in the trap of classifying their meditations as good or bad. When asked, "How was your sit?" the answers, "Oh, I had a good meditation. I was poised and centered," or, "I had a terrible meditation. I was agitated and restless. My mind was all over the place," are usual responses.

We should refrain from judging our meditations because the effectiveness of a meditation is not measured by how good we feel, but by how it moves us forward to become more awake, alert, attentive, aware, and alive.

We don't meditate to become better meditators. We meditate to become better human beings. We practice in order to be who we really are, live better lives, bless the world with our presence, and make the world a better place.

We meditate in order to learn to accept what is without pointless resistance, and to deal with what reality presents to us in the wisest possible ways.

....

IMPROVING WITHOUT STRIVING

We all want to be better. This is natural. That's why we study and practice. But we should let go of forceful striving, and approach the endeavor with joy, ease, and lightness. We should accept that there's no linear progression in mindfulness meditation and mindful living: some days we will move forward, while other days we will move backward. But we should rest in the knowing that, in the end, after all the ups and downs, there will be a noticeable improvement in the quality of our lives.

Yes, there is improvement with consistent practice; this is not debatable. But although practicing regularly is desirable and necessary, we also have to accept that life gets in the way, and we will falter; that's a given. So, when we find ourselves not practicing, we should be gentle with ourselves, letting go of the self-criticism that we are not doing enough, or that we are not good enough. We should remember that the only thing we need to do is to simply start over, because the only moment that counts is the present one.

Our training brings about a mind that is more focused and better able to sustain attention. The interesting thing is that if we try too hard, we are unable to attain this state of mind. On the other hand, if we don't try hard enough, the same will happen. It's counterintuitive. We have to go through this process patiently, with perseverance, and without giving up. Stoic willpower, forcing, and striving will not do it. Our continued, gentle practice is what will allow it happen. So, the challenge seems to be to find balance between trying too hard, and not trying hard enough.

Practicing mindfulness to achieve some special condition, such as a state of permanent peace, can be misguided because nothing is permanent. So this enterprise demands a difficult balance: we must have goals, and put ourselves in motion to accomplish them, while, at the same time, not being too rigid about achieving them. We should cultivate the ability to accept whatever may come with openness and flexibility, even if what comes is not what we originally set ourselves in motion to achieve. It's a difficult dance: it's OK to want, but not too much; it's OK to strive, but not too much.

Bottom line, we should take a good look at our lives and at the world, and put ourselves in motion to make our lives and the world better, while, at the same time, not striving too forcefully, and accepting the present situation and whatever else may come with gratitude and contentment.

Yes, we have to work to hone our skills, but we should remember that the flow is a state of non-doing. Yes, we should practice diligently, so when the moment comes we may be able to do what we have practiced without thinking. Although the practice demands willpower, a flow performance doesn't. We don't get in the flow through our wanting, our striving, and our efforting. Going after a state of flow does not work: the more we chase it, the more it moves away. We experience the flow spontaneously through our continuous and diligent practice, through our acceptance of what is, and through our total immersion in the here-now.

....

MINDFULNESS IS SIMPLE, BUT NOT EASY

After four weeks of mindfulness practice, one of my students wrote, "I'm learning that mindfulness is not easy. All the many distractions and obligations in life make it hard to stay mindful. The practice is demanding: it takes time, effort, persistence, dedication, and motivation." True. There's a popular saying in the mindfulness world: "Mindfulness is simple, but not easy." It is not uncommon for meditators to feel frustrated, discouraged, and unmotivated during the early stages of mindfulness training. Novice practitioners soon realize how tiresome it can be to focus and sustain concentration, and how much less tolling it is to continue acting mindlessly and automatically. They notice how challenging it is to sit still to investigate the feelings that arise, and how much easier it is to distract and numb themselves. They get to know firsthand how difficult it is to try to be mindful throughout the day.

The truth is that old habits die hard, and that although all of us are capable of having some moments of great awareness, only diligent training can elevate us to that state when living mindfully most of the time – when we are awake, alert, attentive, aware, and appreciative -- becomes second nature. It also takes practice to get in touch with that inner wisdom that helps us discern what we should and what we shouldn't be demanding from ourselves, and reminds us to be gentle with ourselves. Not striving forcefully to generate anticipated outcomes, but remaining open to accept what life brings to us, perhaps doesn't make the mindfulness practice easier, but, at least, makes is lighter.

The saying that I keep reminding my students is, "It's not difficult to be mindful. Difficult is to remember to be mindful." Mindfulness practice allows us to have more moments of mindfulness, and the more of such moments we have, the more we will have. If in the beginning it may be difficult to maintain mindfulness, with gentle effort, commitment, and diligent practice it becomes easier. What was inconsistent, hard, and burdensome, with practice becomes fluid, light, and effortless.

Easy does it! Easy does it!

So, if you are at the beginning of this mindfulness journey, don't chastise yourself because right now you cannot be mindful most of the time. On the contrary: congratulate yourself when you catch yourself being mindful, even if such moments are infrequent. Experience shows that moments of mindfulness for those with still untrained and untamed minds are few and far between. Setting reminders throughout the day to pause, breathe, and observe works well for a lot of practitioners. So you may want to give it a try!

And continue practicing because the liberation from suffering can only be found in our daily lives.

....

A GOOD NIGHT OF SLEEP

Many students come to me because they have a hard time falling and staying asleep. They go to bed at night and the old mental recordings, full of doubts and predictions, begin: "How is it going to be tonight? Am I going to be able to sleep? If I have another sleepiness night I'll have another miserable day tomorrow. What's happening? There's something wrong with me."

I encourage them to explore their own individual situations, by telling them, "Come to the realization that these are just thoughts, and that thoughts think themselves. Recognize the old recording when it starts running. Bring to mind that this is a new moment which you haven't lived yet. This moment doesn't have to be similar to moments you've lived before. It is a new one and it can be completely different. Worries will not help you fall asleep. Relax and consider that there's nothing wrong with you in this moment." I suggest that they put aside the old script and write a new one, full of positivity: "I will sleep well for whatever amount of time by body needs. I will wake up rested and energized."

I also recommend that they try different things while keeping a journal to see what works and what doesn't work for them. I ask them to record the activities they did and at what time they did them. I ask them to register things such as the food and drinks they ingested, if they exercised, if they took a bath before going to bed, if they watched TV, if they stayed on the computer, if they listened to a guided visualization or to music conducive to sleep before bedtime, if they did a body scan in bed, etc.

I also tell them not to worry about the prevailing standards, about what is considered normal regarding sleep, at least not at this stage. "Don't tell yourself that there's something wrong with you for not being able to sleep as much as others do. You may say, 'I am not normal,' and I will reply, "Correct. You are not normal. You are unique. You are not like anyone else, so accept your current sleep pattern." Acceptance, not resistance, is the field where change starts. Acceptance will create the conditions for your body, with its self-regulatory system, to bring you to sleep well.

Are you awake? OK. Accept that. Start the process that will bring you to have good nights of sleep without self-condemnation. At this stage, comparing yourself with others -- with what is considered normal -- is not helpful. What is helpful is to concentrate on yourself, not others, and explore what is going on with curiosity. Ask yourself, "What is right for me?" Liberate yourself from the cultural conditioning, from what is culturally accepted, from the mandate of the collective, and live out your individuality and uniqueness. And recite these words often, "These are just thoughts. This is a brand new moment. I'm fine. There's nothing wrong with me."

Here are some ideas from experts in the field, ideas that may help you:

Learn and practice mindfulness meditation. This is an ample field with many resources that can help you sleep better. Exercise, but not too close to bedtime. Consult with a doctor before starting an exercise program, especially if you have been sedentary. Start slowly. Reserve four hours before bedtime for relaxation and preparation for sleep. Reduce the intensity of the light in the rooms you find yourself in. Have a bedtime ritual, one that helps you wind down and relax before going to bed, and repeat it every night, consistently. Take a warm shower. Reserve your bedroom for 'rest and romance' only. Make sure your bed, mattress, pillows, and linens are of the best quality you can afford, and make you feel as comfortable as possible. If possible do not use your bedroom as an office. Remove all clutter, and everything that may bring to mind your 'to-do list.' Keep the bedroom quiet, cool, and dark. If you can control the temperature, bring it down to a point you feel it's cold. Have curtains in the windows to block light from the outside. If possible, remove all computers, phones, and TV sets from the bedroom, and if you have an alarm clock, turn it around, so its illuminated display is facing away from you. Listen to guided meditations, nature sounds, or relaxing music before sleeping, and see if they are helpful. If using a smartphone for that, keep the display dark. Avoid turning bright lights on in the middle of the night. If you have to get up to go to the bathroom, for instance, choose a flashlight that produces a soft light. Try to get out of the bed at the same time every day. Expose yourself to bright light every morning. This will help sync your circadian rhythm.

Above all, explore each day with curiosity. No one knows you better than you.

Sleeping well is important. Believe that with training you will be able to sleep the recommended eight hours without any, or perhaps with very few interruptions.

....

LOVING-KINDNESS MEDITATION

Loving-kindness is a specific kind of love characterized by acts of kindness. Loving-kindness meditation (also known as metta) is an exercise that combines the techniques of meditation, creative visualization, and positive affirmations. It is used to develop inner peace and well-being through the very simple practice of mentally directing well-wishes and expressions of love towards others and your own self. In simple terms, it consists in empathizing, feeling compassion, sending love, and wishing all beings to be well and happy.

Although very simple, metta meditation is very powerful. It really enhances the quality of life of those who practice it regularly because the simple act of wishing well makes one feel well. It is not difficult to understand that if we are using our time to think good things, then we will have less time for ruminating over the bad things. The practice of wishing well during meditation cultivates a type of attitude that makes us more likely to respond with compassion, kindness, love, generosity, and patience during the other moments of our lives when we are not formally meditating, all of which makes of us a more loving and lovable person.

Here's how to do a combined Loving-Kindness and Compassion meditation:

Begin by bringing to your mind's eye a person that you love; a person that is easy for you to love; a person that when you think about him or her, brings a smile to your face. Imagine both of you in a beautiful location where you can give each other undivided attention. With great love for this person, mentally recite with honest intention sentences such as, "May you be safe. May you be happy. May you be healthy. May you live with ease." And notice how it feels to express these well-wishes. Imagine this person receiving these well-wishes with an open heart, feeling deeply loved and appreciated. And feeling the love you have for this person, try to feel how he or she feels. Feel that he or she, just like you, has aspirations and faces challenges. Now imagine that your compassionate understanding encourages this individual to open up his or her heart and unload all the pain and suffering that is there, while feeling supported and loved by you.

And now imagine this person returning these well-wishes to you. Feel the great love this person has for you. And while feeling truly and deeply loved receive the well wishes directed to you: "May you be safe. May you be happy. May you be healthy. May you live with ease. May you receive lots of love." Open up your heart to receive. Notice how it feels to be the recipient of love and compassion. Experience the transformative power of these wishes. See yourself smiling and joyful.

Bring to mind a benefactor, any person who has generously helped and supported you -- a relative, a friend, a mentor, a teacher, a supervisor or a co-worker – and go through the same steps of extending well-wishes as you did with the person you love. Express your gratitude for everything he or she has done or continues to do for you.

Now, shower yourself with love. While remaining open to receive, mentally send yourself well-wishes by reciting phrases such as, "May I be safe. May I be happy. May I be healthy. May I live with ease. May I receive lots of love." Feel all emotions. Feel love flowing to you. Feel deeply understood and loved.

After that, bring to mind a person you feel neutral about, someone you neither like nor dislike, someone you see often but know nothing about. Do the same as you did before: feel love and direct your loving energy to her, and mentally exercise compassion, allow her to pour out her suffering.

Then, do the same with a difficult person, someone you dislike, someone who upsets you, or whom you have a hard time with.

Now, think about an individual, or a group of individuals that you know are suffering. You may or may not know them. Take some time to feel as they feel. Develop heartfelt compassion. And then, as you did before, mentally recite the well-wishes.

Finally, bring to mind again all the people that were in your thoughts (someone you dislike, someone neutral, someone who is suffering, someone you like, and yourself) and once again send well-wishes and love to all of them, and to all beings by mentally saying, "May all beings everywhere be safe. May all beings everywhere be happy. May all beings everywhere be healthy. May all beings everywhere live with ease. May all beings everywhere receive lots of love."

Do this meditation cultivating, compassion, loving kindness, affection, amity, good will, benevolence, and active interest in all beings -- including yourself, loved ones, neutral ones, and difficult ones -- and experience a great improvement in the quality of your life. Feel free to modify these phrases and create well-wishes that may be more meaningful to you.

. . . .

"May all beings everywhere be well, be safe, be happy, be peaceful, be healthy, be free from troubles, be free from inner and outer harm, be free from suffering. May all beings everywhere live with ease and joy, and be abundantly loved."

. . . .

PLEASANT, UNPLEASANT, NEUTRAL

It is not difficult to develop the ability to realize when we are noticing what we like and what we dislike. "This is pleasant. I like this. I want more of it... This is unpleasant. I don't like this. I want none of it." What also comes about from this practice is the realization that the majority of the time we are mindlessly sleepwalking through life, in an auto-pilot state of living, not registering anything consciously. We realize how much of the time we are absent, not present to the present, but with our minds elsewhere and else-when. We become conscious of the amount of time we spend daydreaming, as if we were immersed in a fog, lost in a state of ignorance or false impressions of reality, unable to clearly see what is actually unfolding in the here-now. Mindfulness practice makes us better able to recognize pleasant and unpleasant feelings, notice how pleasant events generate attachment, and how unpleasant ones bring about aversion. It also helps us to realize how much goes by unnoticed, and how much of our lives we are in a state of oblivion.

. . . .

THE BENEFITS OF COPING WITH DISCOMFORT

"Mindfulness is simply being aware of what is happening right now without wishing it were different; enjoying the pleasant without holding on when it changes (which it will); being with the unpleasant without fearing it will always be this way (which it won't)." ~ James Baraz

. . . .

Learning to cope with the discomfort we experience during formal meditation practice -- especially when we are invited to be still and not move for extended periods of time -- is a great training to enhance the quality of our lives because it may lead to the reduction of mindless reactivity. It develops our noticing skills, especially of what is disturbing us, enhances patience and endurance, and augments the time between receiving a stimulus and choosing a response.

Many unpleasant sensations may come up during formal meditation practices, especially during those of longer duration. We instruct our students how to work with physical and non-physical discomfort when it shows up. We ask them to notice the pain and the urge to immediately do something about it, and we advise them to hold on and do nothing for a while -- if this option is available to them -- and just observe what is going on. We ask them to investigate the physical sensations, thoughts and emotions that may be arising, with a beginner's mind, without pushing them away, without hiding from, or running away from them, but getting closer and staying with them a little longer without rushing to react. We tell them to think of themselves as good hosts, and of the unpleasant sensations as unwanted guests who they should welcome and treat honorably (see Rumi's poem, "The Guest House"). Many times, the mere introduction of this element of curiosity reduces the discomfort, or dissipates it.

If that does not work, we instruct our students to remove the focus from the pain and refocus on some other object of awareness, such as the breath. Many times this profound and detailed observation of the breathing process has a calming effect which prevents a thoughtless reaction. It demonstrates that moving the focus of attention to something else other than the discomfort, and observing it with curiosity is another effective way of handling it.

Finally, if after trying these two suggestions meditators still feel that they have to do something, such as readjust their postures, we ask them to do so in a very mindful and well thought-out way. Our instructions emphasize the need to take time, not rush, and be very mindful of the entire process. With many possible variations, the instructions may sound like the following: "Once you have decided that you really want to move, imagine how you will do it, and mentally rehearse the steps you will take to readjust your posture. Visualize the entire process. Play a mental movie, if you will, of how you will move before actually moving. Once this step has been completed, then go ahead and move, but make sure you do it mindfully. This should not be a reaction, but a thoughtful response to the pain and discomfort. Move mindfully. Observe the way you move, observe the physical sensations, emotions, and thoughts, and mentally compare the actual movement with the one you imagined. Once the moving is over, check again to see how you feel. Compare the sensations now with those of moments ago."

This training is invaluable because it makes us better able to stay put in the middle of uncomfortable situations. The practice weakens those conditioned, automatic, fast, habitual, mindless reactions and strengthens the mindfulness-mediated responses. It gives us better tools to deal with the stressors in our lives, responding more thoughtfully to the triggers that activate stress.

We ask our students to become mindful of their automatic, habitual reactions and to make an assessment to determine if those reactions are producing outcomes that enhance the quality of their lives. If that's the case, there's no need to change, but if they are not satisfied with the outcomes, we encourage them to consider using mindfulness skills to explore alternatives, contemplate new options, and try something new, something that may be capable of making their lives better. We remind them that madness is doing the same things expecting different results, and we encourage them to ask themselves, "What could I do differently to improve the quality of my life? Am I willing to give it a fair try?"

The training of staying with the unpleasant sensations and refraining from reacting instinctively is of great use in daily life. It allows us to stay comfortable in the middle of uncomfortable situations, augmenting the time between stimulus and response. More time allows looking again at the situation with removed curiosity, seeing the new in the old, making a better assessment, seeing new options, and using wise discernment to decide on the best course of action.

Imagine the following internal dialogue in a difficult situation: "Oh, I have been challenged. I have been wounded. I feel the urge to react. I am going to strike back. Wait a second, I have done this many times before and what was the outcome? Not a good one. Perhaps I should do what they taught me in the mindfulness classes. S.T.O.P. Stop. Take a breath. Observe. Proceed. OK, let me do this before I do anything. Let me investigate my physical sensations, my emotions, and my thoughts. Yes, I feel a tightening in my throat, a contraction in my chest, a pain in the stomach. My hands are sweaty. My heart is racing. My breath is shallow and fast. I feel anger and rage. I feel aversion to this person and his behavior. OK. Noticing my dislike. Noticing my aversion. Noticing my desire to strike back. Oh, wait a minute. I see: this is my ego at work. Oh, the ego is bruised. Let me be curious. Let me understand the other person too. Why is this person acting this way? Oh, I see. Let me go back to my breath. Let me breathe consciously. OK. I am here now. I am here. I'm safe. I know who I am and I know the ground where I stand. This is home. Everything is OK. Let me make a wise assessment of the situation, use wise discernment, and choose the best possible course of action. I feel that urge to react subsiding. Interesting! OK, I don't need to go down the same path I have always traveled with my automatic, habitual, mindless reactions. I can choose a mindfulness-mediated response. OK. What am I going to do? How am I going to respond? Let me think this over before I move. And let me move mindfully. OK. I know who I am and I know the ground where I stand. I feel calmer. And it is from this calmness that I will act. I have the alternative of not engaging. I don't have to win this argument. I can let it go."

Formal meditation practice develops patience and endurance to stay comfortable in the middle of the uncomfortable. And why would we want to do all this? Because mindful choices will improve the quality of our lives, and enhance our physical, mental and emotional well-being by reducing the wear-and-tear caused by chronic stress.

Mindfulness allows us to get good at noticing the activators of stress. And this is fundamental because we cannot heal what we cannot feel; we cannot fix what we cannot see; we cannot tame what we cannot name. Mindfulness makes us better able to recognize stress when it is present by sharpening our ability to notice our body sensations, thoughts, and emotions.

Hopefully, with a better understanding of the Fight, Flight, Freeze reaction, and with the enhancement of noticing skills that diligent mindfulness meditation practice brings about, we will be able to step outside of the swirling circle of chronic stress, and let go of old patterns of behavior, those fast, automatic, habitual, mindless reactions that do not serve us anymore.

We have to remember to ask ourselves, "What can I do differently to improve the quality of my life?"

Since it is very difficult to be mindful all the time, our goal should be to increase the number of mindful moments during our days. Knowing that "It's not difficult to be mindful; difficult it is to remember to be mindful," mindfulness practitioners regularly bring to mind the following phrases:

- "Short moments, many times, "or
- "Brief moments, many times," or
- "Mindful moments, however brief, many times."

……..

The Buddhist monk, peace activist and promoter of mindfulness, Thich Nhat Hanh, was once asked, "Do you meditate every single day?" He answered, "Not only every day, but every moment. While drinking, while talking, while writing, while watering our garden, I am meditating. It is always possible to practice living in the here and the now. That's what we call meditation."

Mindful moments, however brief, many times. These six words instruct us how to practice the art of living mindfully. We are called to have as many moments of mindfulness as possible during our days, however brief they may be, knowing that we enhance the quality of our lives by bringing the same attentiveness and awareness we cultivate and develop during formal meditation to the other moments of our lives when we are not meditating.

·······

DESIRING OTHERS TO CHANGE

Mindfulness practice makes it easier for us to focus on the present moment and not worry as much about the past and the future. It brings us to a place where we are more centered, and where we begin to notice that focusing on the present moment is very liberating. We perceive that we are calmer and happier, and this realization produces even more calm and happiness.

When we start practicing mindfulness, it is not uncommon to experience a boost in the quality of our lives. We feel so excited with the progress we are making that a desire emerges in us: we want the people with whom we share our lives to do what we are doing and experience what we are experiencing: we want them to practice mindfulness too. And if this does not happen, we feel frustrated, because we think that we are changing for the better and they are not.

As we practice, we develop a feeling that we are developing, getting better, moving forward, all of which is very exciting! But although we may be changing by practicing mindfulness, this doesn't mean that those around us are also going through a similar process, or moving in the same direction, or even transforming themselves at the same pace as we are. Sooner or later, as we progress to a place of greater freedom, we catch ourselves desiring for the people in our lives to experience what we are experiencing; we want them to evolve as we sense we are, not only for their benefit, but also for our own because we suspect that their growth will make our journey easier.

Many times we feel that by not being on the same path as we are, they hinder our evolution, and pull us back to old ways that we have concluded are not beneficial for us, ways that we want to abandon. So a desire emerges in us: we want the people with whom we share our lives to change as we are changing. We want them to be different.

When this desire emerges, we need to be cautious and investigate it carefully. The first thing we should remember is that stress is created by not accepting reality, or, in other words, by desiring the present situation to be what it isn't, what actually is impossible. We have to always remember that the present situation is what it is. Period.

If we are mindful, we will catch ourselves and notice that we are not accepting others as they are. We will also notice that our lack of acceptance of 'what is' -- our desire for people to be different than who they are -- is generating a disturbance in us. In this particular case, we can immediate notice the Eight C's in action: comparing and contrasting, classifying and categorizing, competing and complaining, criticizing and condemning.

If we look deeply, we will notice that our assessment that others are not changing -- that they are stuck in their old ways, unwilling to change -- is inaccurate. Mindful observation makes it very clear that all of us are changing all the time, and that no one stays the same forever. It is very clear for mindfulness practitioners that change is perpetual, unstoppable, and inexorable.

A deeper examination may reveal that we are the ones who are stuck in our old ways of seeing. Perhaps we are not approaching the people in our lives with a 'beginner's mind,' with the necessary curiosity to discover who they really are now, in this moment. We have classified and categorized them in the past, and we continue to rely on these old assessments and labels that we have given them. We are oblivious to the fact that as we have changed, they have changed too, and that we need to look at them with fresh eyes in this present moment to see who they really are now.

The diligent practice of mindfulness makes the impermanence and interconnectedness of everything very evident. By paying attention, we realize that our growth and evolution are already affecting the people in our lives in positive ways. We will notice that as we are changing, they are changing too. The awareness of our interconnectedness produces an inner knowing that understanding and acceptance of others are not only good for them, but also for us.

All these aspects should be calmly considered when we feel the desire for people to be who they are not, but who we want them to be. Whenever we catch ourselves desiring the people in our lives to be different than whom they are, we should, at the outset, congratulate ourselves for noticing that. The mere fact that we are able to notice our judgment of others, and the upsetting emotions associated with our lack of acceptance is, in itself, a great step towards liberation from suffering.

Whenever these desires come up, may we be able to slow down, pause, take a deep breath, observe, and gleefully welcome these moments as great opportunities to mindfully cultivate curiosity, equanimity, acceptance, patience, and trust in the process of change. May we be able to notice our desires and welcome the opportunity to practice taking time to consider options and choosing the wisest and most constructive course of action.

Challenges like this one -- the desire for people to be different -- allow us to notice our own rigidity and prejudices. They remind us that there is a time for everything, and that the wisest thing we can do some times is to let things be as they are and unfold as they will, while focusing on living mindfully and enjoying the present moment. If the situation we wish is to come about, we trust that it will at the time it is meant to, without the need on our part to strive forcefully.

Finally, trying to bring the people in our lives to practice mindfulness may be difficult, if not impossible. In general, attempts to change others are usually destined to fail miserably. It's not up to us to change others; it's up to them to change themselves. It's their work, not ours. The best thing we can do is to be inspiring examples that may instill in them the desire to do something, perhaps the same we are doing, in order to make their lives better.

We can invite them, gently and skillfully, but we should never insist. People will experiment mindfulness when they see us changing for the better, become curious about it, get informed about its benefits, or are in such a degree of suffering that they are desperate to try.

Remember that despite your good intentions, unsolicited advice is often misinterpreted as criticism. Telling someone, "You should meditate. Meditation would be good for you," is usually not well taken. What the other person hears is, "You are flawed. Meditation will fix you." We didn't say that, but that's what, the majority of the time, they will hear; and no one wants to hear that there's something wrong with them. Whenever feeling compelled to talk about the benefits of mindfulness to people close to us, let us remember the saying, "No one is a prophet in his own land," and not get disappointed if what we have to say falls in deaf ears. So let's be very cautious and gentle when suggesting meditation, or inviting others to practice it.

Also, whenever we catch ourselves considering that others are stuck in their old ways, stubbornly ignoring our advice to do what we believe could improve the quality of their lives, we should pause and ponder. Let us realize that believing that we know what is best for others reveals arrogance, which may be an impediment for a leveled relationship. Let us mindfully investigate our drive to dispense advice and see the possible presence of a sense of superiority in us. If so, let's exercise humility. Everything considered, the best thing we can do is to avoid any proselytizing and just practice it ourselves. One of the rules I have adopted is, "Don't talk about mindfulness meditation, unless asked." But I am not completely strict. Sometimes -- very seldom I must say -- I take the initiative to talk to other people about the benefits of mindfulness, but I do so only in those instances when I feel that the person is under too much suffering.

May we be able to look at the people in our lives with lover's eyes again, seeing the new in the old, and the extraordinary in the ordinary. May we be the ones who bring understanding, compassion, and healing. May we be the ones who promote reconciliation, rekindle strained relationships, and end all conflicts with renewed love.

....

WAYSHOWERS AND THE PATHS TO AWAKENING

Whenever we find something beautiful we want to show it to others. This desire to share our findings is natural. But I have realized that no matter how much we may want to share, only those who have the right eyes will be able to see what we have found. If the time is not right for them, they will not see what we have to show, or understand what we have to say. Each individual is on a different path of purification, liberation, and enlightenment, and the timing of the findings for each person is different. Many individuals are sitting right on top of treasures without being able to see them. Although way showers are important, the paths must be opened and the findings must be made by each person on her own.

Nevertheless, do not hesitate to talk about your findings, and share your treasures with those who want to listen. But be sure that your sharing is made out of the love you have for others -- out of your desire to help them on their path of awakening -- and not to satisfy the need of your ego to boast itself. Be cognizant that if the time is not right for them, they will not be able to hear what you have to say, they will not be able to see what you have to show, and they will not understand you. But no matter what, with compassion in your heart, love them, even more than before.

． ． ． ． ． ． ． ．

EVERYTHING IN ITS TIME

"To everything there is a season, and a time to every purpose under the heaven: A time to be born, a time to die. A time to weep, and a time to laugh. A time to mourn, and a time to dance. A time to get, and a time to lose. A time to keep, and a time to cast away. A time to keep silence, and a time to speak." ~ Ecclesiastes 3:1-8

We cannot be vigorous and productive all the time. Laozi states that "There is a time for being ahead, a time for being behind; a time for being in motion, a time for being at rest..." Like the changing weather and seasons, we must recognize different times in our lives.

． ． ． ． ． ． ． ．

ADVICE TO MY FELLOW EXPLORERS

When we practice, wisdom grows. When we don't practice, wisdom wanes. ~ the Buddha

． ． ． ． ． ． ． ．

Dear fellow explorers, I would like to encourage you to continue practicing mindfulness. I begin by asking you not to wait for perfect conditions to meditate. We all want secluded and silent environments to practice, but the majority of the time these peaceful surroundings will not be available. Most likely, conditions will never be as perfect as you would like them to be. But don't allow this to prevent you from meditating regularly. Remember: "If you can't do it perfectly, do it imperfectly. Just do it anyway." Can't find a place inside your home? What about outside? Don't have time to meditate for twenty minutes straight? What about meditating for just one minute twenty times? Change the way you approach your desire for perfection and develop the ability to say to yourself, "This is a new moment. This is a new me. Everything is perfect, just the way it is. It is always perfect. Time to be mindful, right here, right now. One minute counts!" No excuses! Just do it!

Meditate regularly and continue developing your ability to focus your attention, noticing and investigating what is going on in the present moment with curiosity. The more you practice formal mindfulness meditation exercises, the better equipped you will be to live mindfully.

Remember that we don't meditate to become better meditators, but to become better human beings. We practice not only to enhance the quality of our lives, but also the quality of the lives of those we come in contact with.

Be mindful of your body, your mind, your feelings, and of your life in general. Be aware of your body when you are sitting, lying down, walking, and standing, noticing physical sensations and mindfully observing your body breathing. Be mindful of your mind, contemplating your mind states: your thoughts and emotions. Be mindful of wanting, aversion, restlessness, sleepiness, and doubt. Notice the workings of your judgmental mind and of the times when you are comparing and contrasting, categorizing and classifying, competing and complaining, criticizing and condemning.

Develop the ability to see thoughts and emotions for what they are: thoughts are just thoughts; emotions are just emotions. And recognize that your brain is an independent and unstoppable thought-producing and emotion-producing machine. Therefore, realize that you are not your thoughts and emotions. Thoughts and emotions are just visitors. They come and go. You don't need to be schlepped around or owned by them. You don't need to act impulsively on the bad suggestions that may arise. You are independent and free.

Be mindful of your daily activities, noticing the times when you are labeling your experiences as pleasant or unpleasant. Be aware of the instances when you are engaged in the process of liking or disliking, approving or disapproving. Examine your beliefs and explore new ideas. Be ready to consciously unlearn what you have unconsciously learned, and let go of what does not serve you anymore. Investigate and explore life with curiosity as a way of growing in understanding and wisdom. Practice seeing the new in the old, the unusual in the usual, and the extraordinary in the ordinary.

Realize the impermanence and constant change of everyone and everything, witnessing the unstoppable cycle of birth, growth, decay, death, and transformation. Develop the understanding that everything is a result of conditions coming together, including you: you exist because certain conditions came together and brought you into existence, and when such conditions cease to exist, so do you. Understand that life is manifesting through you, but that you don't own this life, this body, this lived experience. Notice how clinging brings about suffering, and remember that nothing whatsoever should be clung to as I, me, or mine. Let it go and let it be.

Realize that experiencing suffering and dissatisfaction in life is a given. Notice that the lack of awareness of the craving for sensual delight, craving to be someone, and the craving to feel nothing are all causes of suffering. Notice that greater awareness of the existence of these cravings lessens suffering. Work diligently to identify, understand, and tame desires.

Practice to pause and augment the time between stimulus and response, developing the ability to be comfortable in the middle of uncomfortable situations, accepting with serenity the things you cannot change. By doing so you will diminish the number of mindless reactions and increase the number of mindful responses, which all in all will have a positive impact in your life.

Cultivate the skills of concentration, observation, and investigation in order to grow your wisdom, 'the sword that cuts through delusion.' Be awake, alert, attentive, appreciative, and aware, in order to be fully alive. Know that the diligent practice will make your life better by, on one hand, taming desire, greed, aversion, hatred, delusion, ignorance, prejudice, and violence, and on the other hand, by increasing in you the reservoir of kindness, gentleness, peace, compassion, generosity, patience, love, and forgiveness.

Remember that the mind is trainable and choose to be happy! And because happy is somewhat an intangible and elusive state, at least choose to be happier now than you were before. For instance, to be happier today than you were yesterday is a definable and attainable goal. Strive to be happier!

Take inventory of all the things you say you have to do, and notice how many of them are self-imposed demands. Notice how much you demand of yourself and how hard you are on yourself. Develop some self-compassion, let go of the need to be perfect, and give yourself the gift of rest. It's your birthright. Savor your daily accomplishments, no matter how faulty, and rest. You deserve it.

Develop happiness, by practicing to notice, appreciate, savor, and absorb all the good things in life. If you do so, you will grow in gratitude which is the key that unlocks the gates to the kingdom of happiness.

Cultivate wisdom: wise effort, wise mindfulness, wise concentration, wise assessment, wise discernment, wise understanding, wise intention, wise action, wise speech, and wise livelihood. All this practice will allow you to gain the wisdom that cuts through delusion and ignorance and allows you to see reality and the truth of life clearly.

Surround yourself with good friends, people who like you are on this path of awakening.

And continue exploring and inspiring!

So remember that our practice is not selfish. We don't practice for ourselves alone. Our practice makes the entire world a better place. Whatever makes us better makes the world better because we are part of the world. I bow to you in gratitude. Thank you for your practice.

Wishing you many mindful moments, today and every day.

……..

"Show up and choose to be present.
Pay attention to what has heart and meaning.
Tell the truth without blame or judgment.
Be open to outcome, not attached to outcome."

~ Angeles Arrien, The Four-Fold Way

…….

PERSISTENT PRACTICE

Sometimes we feel like superheroes, ready to face life's greatest challenges. Other times we feel like timid cowards, wanting to flee and hide. Have you ever asked yourself, "Why?" Sometimes we feel courageous, optimistic, determined and confident, while other times we experience fear, pessimism, hesitation and doubt. Why? One day we wake up full of positive energy, but many are the days when we feel so depleted that even getting out of bed is difficult. Why? Why do we go through these mood fluctuations? What is it that hurls us to the highest peaks one day, and pulls us down to the lowest valleys the next? And is there a way to avoid the descent into the doldrums?

James Allen, the author of As A Man Thinketh, clearly made the point: "We are what we think!" Since the quality of our lives is determined by the quality of our thoughts, we better make sure we know how to select our thoughts wisely. The key that opens the door to the kingdom of happiness and serenity is the understanding that our thoughts influence our moods, and if we want to live a happy, productive life we must learn to observe, sort out, and select our thoughts. The prescription may sound simple, but implementing it is not always easy. But if we practice mindfulness with diligence, eventually we will be better able to screen and pick our thoughts, and this will help us tame melancholy and gloom.

So, here's my recommendation:

1 - Meditate every day. Separate yourself from your thoughts. You are not your thoughts. You are the one who observes them.

2 - Practice mindfulness. Be the one who observes your moods. Be aware of your feelings. Ask yourself, "What am I feeling? Why am I fearful? Why am I enraged? Why am I sad? Why am I feeling this way?" Be the one who identifies the thoughts behind the moods. Screen your thoughts many times during the day. "What am I thinking? How are my thoughts affecting my mood?" Remember that you are not your moods either; you are the one who observes them and is capable of welcoming them all, without resistance, and after a while choosing which ones should stay and which ones should go.

3 - Spot the ego at work, ready to get a hold of you and bring you down. Be the one who observes the ego. When the situation arises, be ready to say, "There you are, hiding in the bushes. I see you. I'm not going to stay here and play your game. I am moving on to a better place. Good-bye."

4 - Put a positive spin on your thinking. Learn techniques that allow you to shift from negative to positive self-talk. Practice the techniques of creative visualization and positive affirmations. The moment you identify a negative thought in your mind, remember to say to yourself, "This is just a thought. Thoughts are not real. I'm not my thoughts." Gently let it go, and replace it with the best positive image of yourself. It

doesn't hurt to say affirmations such as, "I am growing in health, love, wealth and wisdom everyday. I am advancing and moving forward everyday. I am prospering everyday. All that is good is coming my way."

5 - Finally, surround yourself with positive, supportive, happy people. Smile a lot and laugh more. Adopt a healthy lifestyle, a healthy diet, and learn techniques to manage stress. The practice of mindfulness meditation and mindful living helps immensely with these aforementioned points. When we meditate, we learn to observe our thoughts: we acknowledge the thoughts, and gently release them, without initiating an inner narrative or dialogue. The greatest benefit of meditation is equipping us to screen our moods, our thoughts, and our egos at work during the other hours of the day when we are not meditating. It is through the practice of meditation that we realize that we are not our moods, our thoughts and our egos; we are separated from them. We are the ones who observe them. Through practice, we learn to not engage with negative thoughts; we learn to simply let them pass by. The practice of creative visualization and positive affirmations helps us reduce the negative self-talk. Soon, we will find ourselves criticizing less, looking for the good in every situation, and expressing gratitude more often. It may take some time, but this practice produces optimists. Remember: "As a man thinks in his heart, so is he." Do these things and not only you will be blessed, but you will be a blessing to the world.

……..

DEVELOPING MINDFULNESS: PRACTICAL ADVICE

There is an immense amount of excellent material out there on mindfulness. Do not let the desire to read, watch, and listen to everything be another source of anxiety. Remember that nothing is more important than the daily practice of mindfulness meditation and moment-to-moment mindful living.

- Develop the habit of pausing and having mindful moments throughout your days: "Short moments, however brief, many times."
- Continue your daily individual mindfulness meditation practice (in solitude, or not)
- Meditate regularly with a group, at least once a week if possible.
- Create your own Silent Days.

- Enroll in multi-day Silent Retreats.
- Establish a relationship and seek advice from a teacher.

……...

Daily Formal Practice - The most important thing you can do now, in my opinion, is to practice every day. Create the habit and a routine of practicing mindfulness meditation daily. What works for me is to wake up early and practice. I choose from the menu of practices: a combination of sitting meditation, body scan, mindful walking, mindful stretches, etc. My motto is "R.P.M. – Rise. Pee. Meditate." Remember that if you cannot do it perfectly, do it imperfectly. Just do it anyway. Remember that one single minute counts. And if you haven't meditated for any period of time, short or long, it's no big deal. It doesn't matter. Don't condemn yourself. Don't give up. Just start over; begin again, because what matters is the present moment. If you are unable to meditate daily, remember that still a 'daily-ish' practice is better than not meditating at all.

Daily Informal Practice – Well, mindfulness meditation is the training; mindful living is the game. And that's where the rubber meets the road. You've heard the saying, "It is not difficult to be mindful. Difficult is to remember to be mindful." How are you going to remember to be mindful? How are you going to live mindfully? What works for me is to practice formal meditation every day, and then pause many times during the day (whenever I remember!) to check-in: I connect with my breath and my body, with my thoughts and emotions. My motto is, "Mindful moments, however brief, many times." I try to practice what I teach. I try to remember things I have learned, such as:

- to slow down,
- to remember to be mindful in order to have many mindful moments, however brief, many times,
- to use meditation as a tool for investigation, examination, exploration, and discovery,
- to cultivate the attitudes of non-judging, patience, curiosity, trust, acceptance, non-striving, letting go and letting it be, gratitude, and generosity,
- to approach every moment with a Beginner's Mind,
- to be less critical and judgmental,
- to accept what I can't change,
- to let go of outcomes trusting in the organizing intelligence of the

Universe,
- to listen and speak mindfully,
- to be less passive or aggressive, but be gently assertive in my communications,
- to be more patient and generous,
- to be kinder and gentler,
- to give more and serve more,
- to be proactive in establishing and maintaining relationships,
- to make healthy choices,
- to sort out what is really important,
- to stay away from toxicity (toxic people and toxic environments),
- to notice how similar and interconnected we all are,
- to be a bringer of peace,
- to expand the time between receiving a stimulus and choosing a response,
- to 'catch myself,' hopefully prior to reacting, but if not, at least in the middle of a reaction, or after a reaction,
- to be gentle with myself,
- to treat myself kindly, taking good care of myself, reducing the self-criticism and self-judgment, monitoring the self-imposed demands to make sure I am not demanding too much of myself,
- to be humble,
- to remember who we are and who we aren't, and not give my "self" too much importance,
- to be honest, authentic, and true to myself,
- to practice "S.T.O.P. Stop. Take a breath. Observe. Proceed or Park,"
- to notice all the magic, mystery, and miracles that surrounds us and be grateful.

Meditation Recordings – These are great helpers to maintain a daily practice. There are many sources of recorded guided meditations. My daily companions, at this time of my life, are the 10% Happier and the Insight Timer smartphone apps. Finally, I listen to audio books and mindfulness podcasts, such as the 10% Happier and those on the Be Here Now Network, especially when I am driving.

Weekly Group Practice – Surrounding yourself with spiritual friends, and meditating together regularly will not only keep your mindfulness practice going, but give it a boost. Look for meditation drop-ins in your area.

Silent Retreats – These are gorgeous times for me! I really love the silence and the growth it brings about. I encourage you to consider enrolling in a silent retreat if you haven't had this experience yet. And if you have already, you know how good they are. So, find a silent retreat, and give yourself this beautiful gift. Extended periods of mindfulness practice really have a positive impact on the plasticity of our brains. (See the book "Altered Traits" by Davidson and Goleman) I recommend teacher-led mindfulness retreats.

Silent Days – Create your own days of silent practice, as if you were in noble silence in a silent retreat. Do everything as mindfully as possible, from the time you wake up in the morning until the time you go to bed at night. Do the meditations, read some poetry and inspiring passages, walk mindfully (in nature if possible), eat mindfully, etc. Stay awake, alert, attentive, aware, and appreciative all the time. If you live alone, naturally this will be easier. If you don't, perhaps you can find time during the week to be alone for a few hours here and there to intentionally practice mindfulness in silence. Take good care of yourself. Pamper yourself. Give yourself those little moments as if you were in a spa. Or act as if you were on vacation today and notice how this affects your mood and modifies your perception. Manage what you need to do in order to free up time to do more of what you want to do. Enjoy silence and calmness.

……..

Show up. Be present. Pay attention. Tell the truth. Be open.

……..

META AWARENESS

I've heard Dan Harris -- the author of Ten Percent Happier, a book that I constantly recommend to my students -- explain what Mindfulness Meditation is many times in his podcast. He usually begins his explanation by saying that mindfulness meditation is the practice of cultivating meta-awareness, that knowing that we know, the knowing that we are thinking. I like his explanation a lot.

Our species is called homo sapiens sapiens, which refers not only to our capacity to think, but also to our capacity to know that we are thinking. Pretty awesome, right? Now, if we observe our thoughts we will realize that we have this independent and unstoppable thought producing machine that is constantly generating these random, self-referential, and mostly negative thoughts. Observing and understanding this activity of the mind, through practices such as mindfulness meditation and mindful living, allows us to separate ourselves from our thoughts and not be owned by them.

This is extremely liberating. The problem is that most humans have not been trained to observe and become aware of their thoughts and emotions. They are pushed and pulled in all directions by this unruly thought process. A thought comes into our minds and without pausing to make an assessment and choosing the best course of action, we just do what we were commanded to do, even when such action is detrimental to us; there are no shock absorbers between the stimuli and our reactions.

Our practice helps us augment the time between stimulus and response which makes us less likely to be do unwise and harmful things suggested by the disorderly thoughts.

....

IT'S JUST A THOUGHT

Where do thoughts come from? Who generates them? What is this non-stop narration that we hear in our heads? Who does the talking? And who does the listening?

....

After a great performance of his band, my son was joyfully and justifiably relishing in the praise. He was celebrating, feeling really good, and having a great time. His band opened for another, and it was a great concert! Then, something happened that caused an interruption in those good feelings and spoiled that moment for him: he was accused of something he didn't do… stealing beer from one of the venue's many bars! Evidence was brought to light, and soon things were clarified, proving that he hadn't done anything wrong. The beer had been given to his band before the concert, and was in their rehearsal room. That's where he took it from after playing the opening act and coming to the floor to watch the rest of the concert. Those who accused him quickly apologized with great sincerity, and even gave him a gift as a compensation for their hurried misjudgment: more free beer! Now, rather than returning to the enjoyment of the present moment, and taking in the joy of a great performance, my son kept ruminating the accusation, totally ignoring all the good he had recently experienced, and could be experiencing still. He had a difficult time letting go of the accusations and redirecting his attention to the good that came out of it -- a sincere apology and a gift -- proving, one more time, that "the brain is like Velcro for negative experiences, and like Teflon for positive ones." He kept repeating to himself, "How could they think this of me? Who do they think I am? I would never do that! I am hurt." But, in reality, who or what was hurt? His image? His reputation? His ego? His 'self?' And what are those things if not mental constructs, if not abstractions, if not thoughts, just thoughts in other people's minds? And who is this 'I' that was hurt? The 'self,' the 'ego:' what is that if not a mental construct, a narrative of a life that we keep retelling ourselves?

....

Time to think: "Why does blame stick for such a long time and praise wash away so fast? Why do we retell negative stories and not so much the positive ones?"

....

Do not get stuck in the quicksand of what is negative. You can get out. Actually, with some practice, getting out of this quicksand becomes quite easy. There's no need to retell painful stories. There's no need to relive upsetting emotions. You can choose! You can remain their prisoner, or you can liberate yourself by simply saying, "It's just a thought. And I'm not my thoughts." Give them a shoulder shrug, and move on, of move back to the present! Enjoy what is good in your life, right here, right now, without magnifying what is bad. Remember that everything comes and goes. One moment gain, the next moment loss. One moment pleasure, the next, pain. One moment praise, the next, blame. Everything is impermanent, and nothing stays the same. Conditions are changing all the time. Remember that the past is gone. And what is the past if not a thought in the present moment, right? Let it go. It's just a thought! And I'm not my thoughts! You can choose. If you are going to get stuck, get stuck in the territory of the good events and good feelings. If you are going to retell stories, choose to retell the pleasant ones. This is a training for you. Practice to notice what is good, pleasant, and positive in your life. Notice them. Appreciate them. Savor them. Absorb them. Practice to retell the good moments of your life and be grateful. This is going to activate new neural pathways in your brain that will predispose you to notice more often all that is good, which in turn will enhance your positive outlook, optimism, and the quality of your life. So, whenever you are accused of doing something wrong, either repent and apologize if you have actually done it, or, if not, say to yourself, "I know who I am. I know the ground where I stand. I know what I did and what I didn't do. I will listen to those who accuse me first, and then I will speak my truth quietly and clearly, hoping to clarify the situation and be understood. But if I'm not, there's little I can do. If I'm unjustly condemned, so be it. I have no control over other people's judgments. If people choose to think bad of me and spread falsehoods about me, so be it. I have no control on what other people think, say, or do. Whatever others think of me is none of my business. I know who I am. I know the ground where I stand. I know what I did and what I didn't do. The people who know me and care about me, my true friends, know who I am. And those who doubt my integrity and character, don't really know me, and are not truly my friends. If they depart, there's no loss for me; only for them." Say it, and move on in peace. So, there you have it: a suggestion on how to mindfully respond when people falsely accuse you, misjudge you, or spread falsehoods about you. Remember Dr. Seuss's quote: "Be who you are and say what you feel, because those who mind don't matter, and those who matter don't mind." In the middle of those uncontrollable situations, may you be able to give a shoulder shrug, accept, let go, and move on in peace. "It's just a thought. Thoughts are not real. Thoughts are just thoughts. Thoughts think themselves. The thought of a thing is not that thing. The mind has a mind of its own. I am not my thoughts."

....

INJURED INNOCENCE

When an innocent is wrongly accused of something he hasn't done, the sense of righteous indignation and hurt that is experienced reveals the concept of 'self' in very vivid ways: "How could they think this of 'me?' Don't they know who 'I' am? 'I' would never do that." Recalling such experiences when we feel that we were treated with lack of respect creates great opportunities to expose 'self' as a mental construct. The reactivity that comes up when we are attacked and wounded shows our attachment to images and notions of who we believe we are: 'self' becomes very evident.

The practice of insight meditation makes it very evident that everything is constantly changing and ephemeral. Meditating on our injured innocence -- exploring physical sensations, thoughts, and emotions -- takes us to territories where we can intuitively understand selflessness. The exploration to find the 'self' will reveal that there's nothing concrete and unchanging there. There's nothing fixed to hold on to. There's nothing to be found. And the not finding is the finding.

………..

"In order to understand the notion of emptiness, egolessness, selflessness you first have to find the self as it actually appears to you in your own real experience." ~ Mark Espstein

……..

THE PLACE IS HERE, THE TIME IS NOW

What is the past? Is it not just a thought in the present moment? And what about the future? Is it not, also, just a thought in the present moment? How do we experience the past and the future if not as thoughts in the present moment?

Pause for a moment, take a deep breath, and observe yourself: "What am I thinking? Am I, in this moment, regretting the past or worrying about the future?" Whenever you catch yourself ruminating or anticipating, remember to say to yourself, "It's just a thought. And I'm not my thoughts." Take some gentle steps to reduce this time traveling of the mind, and to be grounded in the here-now, the only real moment of choice-making and life-creation. Connect mindfully with this present moment, refocusing your attention on your breath, your body, on whatever you may be doing, paying detailed attention to the simplest things. The place is here, and the time is now, so be here, now, and no-where else and no-when else. Right here. Right now. And by doing so you will be alleviating suffering, reducing anxiety, taking better care of yourself, and bringing more happiness and peace to the world.

……..

What is the past or the future if not a thought in the present?

……..

It's just a thought, and life, in this moment, is not this thought. Thoughts are not real. Thoughts are just thoughts. Thoughts think themselves. The thought of a thing is not that thing. The mind has a mind of its own. I am not my thoughts.

....

OBSERVING THOUGHTS

I've heard people say that an untrained mind is like a drunken monkey stung by a bee. That's an interesting image of an agitated, restless, inebriated, and ineffective being due to his foggy mind. It reminds me of the story of a man who comes to a revered master and implores, "Please, help me. I am suffering immensely. I am restless. Please, pacify my mind." The wise man replies, "Show me your mind and I will pacify it." Unable to fulfill the request, the man leaves. After some time he returns with the same plea, "Master, please, help me. I am suffering. I am afflicted. Please, pacify my mind." Once again the wise man commands, "Show me your mind and I will pacify it." The man responds, "Master, I looked for my mind everywhere, but I could not find it." "There!" says the teacher, "It's already pacified."

....

There are those times when we are thinking without realizing that we are thinking. Thoughts are running amok, but we are unable to notice that we have been carried away by them and that we are lost in them. We hop on a train of thought and travel on it for a long distance and time. Then we make an immediate connection, hop on another train of thought, and do the same. And we keep going, jumping from train to train, from wagon to wagon, without ever disembarking. We go through life as if we were anesthetized and numb, lost in thoughts. We are not awake; we are sleepwalking through life.

Then comes a magic moment of awakening and awareness, when we catch ourselves thinking, and we engage in an exploration: "Oh, I have been thinking. What have I been thinking? Where did this thought come from?" We begin to notice that the appearance of thoughts have no logic, that they appear and go away randomly, only to be replaced by other thoughts that pop up in a chaotic, unorganized fashion.

This realization is very liberating. When we realize that we are carrying an independent and unstoppable thought-producing machine that keeps creating thoughts on its own, we are free to separate ourselves from our thoughts. We can calmly remind ourselves, "I can see that this is just a though created by the independent thought-producing machine, and I am not this thought." Then we reflect on the moment of mindfulness:"Wow! I'm able to observe thoughts without being carried away by them. This is pretty cool! What happened when I became aware of the thought: did it get stronger, weaker, or did it fade away?" As we get more curious, we may ask ourselves: "And what is a thought anyway? What is this thing we call 'thought?' What can I say about a thought? Actually, not much: a thought is pretty much nothing. It's ephemeral and lacks substance. Thoughts are just thoughts."

And as the inquiry continues, other questions arise, such as, "Who is having these thoughts? Who is doing the thinking? Who is the thinker?" and to add even another level of complexity to the exploration, another question emerges:"And who is asking all these questions?"

As we continue with this mindfulness practice, we soon begin to free ourselves from thoughts, these little dictators of the mind, and we become able to ponder, "Why do I spend so much time and energy with thoughts? Thoughts are not real. Thoughts are just thoughts. They are here one moment, and they soon vanish." And whenever we notice that we are enthralled in the drama, we can remember to say to ourselves, "It's just a thought!"

The truth is that no matter how thoroughly we may look for the one who is doing the thinking and the one who is asking the questions, we will not be able to find anyone. There's no one to be found. The mystery is that we know that we are knowing, but we don't know who is knowing. The one who is knowing cannot be found. It is a quandary, and realizing that we cannot find the mind, that we cannot find who is doing the thinking, and that we cannot find who is asking the questions, is the finding. Not finding the mind is the finding. Not finding who is doing the thinking is the finding. Not finding who is asking the questions is the finding. Not finding is the finding. Yes, sometimes the saying, "Life is a mystery to be lived, not an enigma to be solved" makes perfect sense.

....

It's just a thought. Thoughts are not real. Thoughts are just thoughts. Thoughts think themselves. I am not my thoughts.

....

WE ARE NOT OUR THOUGHTS

Pause for a moment and analyze: isn't it true that when we are suffering we are actually lost in unsettling thoughts? Obsessive thinking and identification with thoughts is the primary cause of suffering.

The practice of mindfulness meditation and mindful living allows us, first of all, to notice that we are thinking all the time. By creating a detachment that enhances our aptitude to objectively observe the activity of the mind, this practice gives us the ability to realize the omnipresence of thoughts. It makes us better able to notice that the brain is an unstoppable and independent thought-producing machine, thus the saying, "The mind has a mind of its own."

Mindfulness practice gives us opportunities to analyze the nature of thoughts, and realize that they are completely random and ephemeral mental formations. With practice we begin to notice that thoughts appear spontaneously, and that we don't know and cannot know what our next thoughts will be. We begin to notice how surprising they can be. We notice their impermanence -- how they arise and pass away -- and come to the conclusion that we have no idea about their origin or destination: we don't know where thoughts come from, and where they go when they are no longer present.

All these realizations are very liberating and lead us to see that thoughts are not real and that we are not our thoughts.

Mindfulness practice teaches us to recognize thoughts simply as transient appearances in our consciousness, which ultimately gives us a great resource for a better life: the ability to understand that we have some selective control. We realize that we can choose not to allow ourselves to be carried away by unsettling thoughts, and that we can choose which thoughts deserve our attention and which ones we should simply let go.

Mindfulness also gives us, during those moments of suffering, when we notice that we are lost in upsetting thoughts, the ability to simply say to ourselves, "It's just a thought, and I don't need to believe it!" In other words, it gives us freedom. It liberates us from being dominated by unwholesome thoughts.

This ability of noticing thoughts, letting some of them go, and redirecting the attention to the present moment is liberating, stress-reducing, and life-enhancing. Humans, unlike other animals, spend a lot of time thinking about what happened in the past, or might happen in the future. Matthew A. Killingsworth and Daniel T. Gilbert of Harvard University conducted a study and concluded that "The ability to think about what is not happening is a cognitive achievement that comes at an emotional cost. A human mind is a wandering mind, and a wandering mind is an unhappy mind."

Yes, the untrained and untamed human mind spends an immense amount of time ruminating and anticipating, but the good news is that we can train our minds. The practice of mindfulness meditation and mindful living can reduce mind-wandering, bring us back to the here-now, and enhance happiness.

Recognize the benefit of saying to yourself the following phrases and say them often:"It's just a thought, and I don't need to believe it. Thoughts are not real. Thoughts are just thoughts. Thoughts think themselves. The thought of a thing is not that thing. The mind has a mind of its own. I am not my thoughts."

....

To live mindfully is to deliver on the commitment to live with the intention to pay attention to the present moment, every moment, moment after moment, reducing the urge and rush to judge, criticize, express likes and dislikes, or act on our desires and aversions, but just calmly observing with curiosity and accepting whatever is given to us.

To live mindfully is to live fully awake, alert, attentive, aware, and appreciative of what is going on in the here-now, in order to be fully alive.

Unfortunately, we have the tendency to give too much attention to our thoughts, especially frightening ones. By allowing our minds to run out of control, the sense of despair that arises from the illusion that we are powerless to control our lives, many times takes hold of us. In such moments it is important to ask ourselves, "What exactly am I feeling? What sensations do I feel in my body? Why am I feeling this way? What thoughts are creating these sensations and feelings in me?" and remember that the dramatic plots with tragic consequences that we have imagined in the past rarely became reality.

....

"I am an old man and have known a great many troubles, but most of them never happened." ~ Mark Twain

……..

In a letter to John Adams dated April 8, 1816, Thomas Jefferson wrote, "I think with you that it is a good world on the whole, that it has been framed on a principle of benevolence, and more pleasure than pain dealt out to us. There are indeed gloomy & hypochondriac minds, inhabitants of diseased bodies, disgusted with the present, & despairing of the future; always counting that the worst will happen, because it may happen. To these I say, How much pain have cost us the evils which have never happened!"

The practice of Mindfulness Meditation develops in us the ability to better observe our thoughts and emotions. By becoming more aware of what we are thinking and feeling, we become better able to control our mood, which, ultimately, alleviates suffering and enhances the quality of our lives.

Have you noticed that you may be thinking one thing, one moment, and in the next you may be thinking another that is its total opposite? We have to realize that we have the ability to imagine the most absurd things, and that what we may be thinking is not always correct, and that what we may be afraid of is not certain to happen. And since our minds are like blank canvases upon which we can paint anything, we can choose not to get too involved with thoughts that produce fear, anxiety, and stress, but, instead, embrace the present moment with spaciousness, lightness, and freshness, and populate our minds with gratitude while noticing the good that surrounds us.

And let us be vigilant and not fall in the trap of criticizing ourselves for feeling a certain way, one that we think we should not be feeling. Let us be gentle with ourselves, honoring and accepting what is, all the time. As we get better at observing our thoughts, we conclude that we are not our thoughts, and that we should not give them too much credit. We realize that thoughts are mysterious entities with a life of their own: they spontaneously appear and vanish, and no one really knows where they come from and where they go after they leave. We also realize that thoughts are not always accurate, and that our minds can entertain contradictory thoughts.

…….

PERCEPTIONS AND REALITY

Research is showing that our memories are not only the sum of all those things that we have actually done and gone through. Our memories are not precise because they are also the sum of what we have thought, what we have imagined, what we have been told, and what we believe.

．．．．．．．．

The Woman on the Beach in Guaymas, a short story by Sylvia Boorstein featured in her book, It's Easier Than You Think, tells the story of two women in the middle of a storm, and how while one is full of fear, the other is relishing in the beauty and power of nature's spectacle. It shows how different people perceive and process what happens differently, and how our upbringing and past experiences influence our perceptions and the ways we interpret events.

It seems that reality -- everything we assume as indisputably real -- is merely a construct of our minds. What we call reality is what our minds create from the way we perceive and interpret what happens. That is why it is said that if we change the way we perceive and interpret events -- if we change the meanings we attach to occurrences -- we will inevitably change our realities.

．．．．．．．．

"When we change the way we look at things, the things we look at change." ~ Wayne Dyer

．．．．．．．．

Since the perceptions, interpretations, and meanings that we derive from the experiences are very personal and particular, and given that our memories and stories are unreliable because they keep changing as time goes by, we should come to terms that one, single, undisputable reality is something that does not exist.

．．．．．．．．

LIBERATING OURSELVES FROM OUR STORIES

Since we are constantly trying to extract meaning from what happens and putting together all sorts of stories, it would be wise to scrutinize the stories we tell.

Sometimes, when we are craving for sympathy and affection, we tell stories of our victimization, stories that highlight our wounds. Other times, when our egos are craving admiration and adulation, we tell stories that highlight our heroic courage in overcoming difficult times. These are the times when our flimsy egos reveal their craving for attention and love, and also their resistance to accept the impermanence of everything, and their yearning to outlive physical existence and be remembered and revered for eternity. We should be aware of how this longing of the insubstantial self to prove its existence influences our stories.

We should notice the differences between what happened and the many stories we tell about what happened. We should also be cognizant that we are constantly rewriting our stories and adapting them for different audiences. We pick and choose our memories, and arrange them in new narratives, unaware that our memories are changing all the time. We would be doing ourselves a favor if we started to doubt the veracity of the stories we tell, and came to conclude that stories are not an accurate account of the truth.

One practical advice for the improvement of life that comes out of all this could be to pay more attention to the stories we tell and practice to be skeptical of our own stories. Let's also be doubtful of the stories we hear. Let's be more careful of how we choose to make meaning of what happens. Let's also realize that we have the power to choose the stories we tell, and that we can tell stories that either empower or disempower us. Let's practice to let go of stories that do not serve us anymore. And since the power to interpret events and create stories resides in us, let us give ourselves the freedom to interpret what has happened differently if necessary, in order to create new, health-enhancing stories that improve the quality of our lives.

So, following this logic, picking and choosing and rearranging our narratives is not a bad thing. Seeing new possibilities and creating uplifting stories is actually a good move.

But what if we didn't do any of those things? What if we came to the conclusion that the main reason for creating stories is to strengthen the sense of self? Wouldn't our lives improve immensely if we realized that the attachment to our self-referential stories, and to the illusion of a separate self, is perhaps the major impediment to our liberation and transcendence?

Perhaps we would benefit a lot from becoming conscious that we can curb the habit of attaching meaning to our experiences. Perhaps we can let go of the characters we have created, treating every moment as new moment, and telling ourselves, "Who I was does not have to determine who I am, or who I will be. Who I was is not who I am. This is a new moment, and in this moment I am a new me." Perhaps we can come to a point where we may be able to refrain from creating stories altogether.

It is fair to state that we spend too much time trying to extract meaning from the occurrences. Possibly the best thing we can do is to slow down and observe life, and from this observation perhaps we may come to realize that life is nothing more than a series of random occurrences, and that we are the ones attaching either positive or negative meanings to them.

Wouldn't it be better if we paused, analyzed, and perhaps saw with more clarity the unpredictability of life? Wouldn't it be beneficial if we saw that trying to find logic explanations to what is random by nature prevents us from living more freely? Wouldn't it be good, in order to regain our sanity, to accept the uncertainty and randomness of life, while practicing to be vigilant in order not to be too carried away by the thoughts in our heads and the stories we create? A good advice would be, "Get out of your head!"

Another wise advice would be to focus on what really matters. And how do we know what really matters? Well, ask Death, the wisest adviser. When faced with impending physical death, 99% of the things we deemed important lose importance. This is when we will be ready to let go of a series of attachments, desires, and needs, such as the need to find meaning, the need to be recognized and remembered, and even the need to leave a legacy.

....

ACCEPTING WHAT IS WITH EQUANIMITY

We also have to be mindful of how much time we spend criticizing, judging, and condemning. We have to realize that we go through life like slaves under the domination of our cravings and aversions, unstoppably stating, "I like this. I don't like that. I want more of this. I want none of that." Pretty much, human lives could be summarized as the relentless movement between resisting what is and wanting something else.

We are the ones who trapped our own selves in this never-ending quest for pleasure and avoidance of pain, constantly wanting to maximize what is pleasant and minimize what is unpleasant. But what would happen if we decided to stop classifying things, people, and events? What would happen to us, and the quality of our lives, if we curbed this impulse to state what is pleasant and what is unpleasant for us? What if we exercised equanimity, and simply accepted people, things and events as they are, without having to tell ourselves, or anyone else, our verdicts about them, if we consider them good or bad?

I believe that as we move to empty ourselves of the unnecessary and self-imposed load of over thinking, meaning-attaching, and story-creating, we begin to open space in our lives to receive the blessings of the Universe. It is only when we become able to accept what is, that we become open to receive and appreciate the gifts.

My good friend Jack, again and again, reminds me to stay in the present. He made a copy of the following passage from Eckhart Tolle's book, The Power of Now, and gave it to me: "I have learned to offer no resistance to what is; I have learned to allow the present moment to be and to accept the impermanent nature of all things and conditions. Thus have I found peace." ~ Eckhart Tolle

………

FILTERING INFORMATION

We have to realize that although a vast amount of information is coming our way all the time, we are only able to process a small part of it. Our conscious mind can only absorb a fraction of reality, mainly what matches our understanding of what life is. It seems that our brains accept what is in accordance with our knowledge and reject what does not harmonize with our memories and expectations. It is as if we had filters that allow the entrance of that information that matches our stored experience, and keeps out what does not make sense to us. What is new and unexpected has little chance of breaking through and making its way to our conscience.

This explains why different individuals looking at the same event have different perceptions, or see different things altogether. Have you heard the saying, "People hear what they want to hear?" I am convinced that people hear what they are predisposed to hear. When listening to someone, we all look for those pieces of information that sustain our beliefs, and we reject the majority of those that go against them. Our filters are allowing some bits of information to pass through while keeping others out. We don't absorb everything that is being said because our brains are selectively looking for what confirms our understanding of the world. On the other hand, if we have a predisposition to oppose and find err in others, we listen to detect what does not match our beliefs, so we can solidify our position and increase our sense of self by opposing views we don't accept. We are not really open to listen to what others have to say. What we do is to pick and choose, and reinterpret what was said so it matches our preconceived ideas. It is very difficult to hear with an open mind, a beginner's mind, with curiosity, attention, and freshness, without judgment, because our beliefs, past experiences, accumulated knowledge, and memories look for those pieces of information that are in alignment with what we already know.

Again, we hear only what we are predisposed to hear. We have to understand that we don't hear with our ears; we hear with our brains. We don't see with our eyes; we see with our brains. Our perceptions are shaped by the things we accept as real and true, by the stories we tell ourselves. We all have our own views of the world, and because we crave security and comfort, we compare our beliefs with each other, we surround ourselves with people who think and understand the world as we do, and we come to agreements of what reality is. We, then, embrace this collective perception, the paradigm of our tribe, as reality. This explains why it is so difficult, especially for those of us with untrained minds -- those of us unfamiliar with intellectual exploration -- to change deep-seated opinions; the moment our understanding of the world is challenged, we feel threatened; fear kicks in, and we close ourselves up.

....

I always liked the words of F. Scott Fitzgerald: "The test of a first rate intelligence is the ability to hold two opposed ideas in the mind at the same time, and still retain the ability to function."

………..

The persistent questions are: "Why don't we allow ourselves to explore and examine what is new? Why do we resist considering other worldviews? Is it due to fear of the unknown? Or is it because we don't want to dissent with our group, and be perceived as disloyal? How do we get out of the habitual mind, the one that keeps replaying and running the same old programs and coming up with the same old [and mostly bad] solutions, and begin to take new looks at reality from different angles? Furthermore, since we have been trained to accept what comes through our five senses as real, and to pay little or no attention to our feelings, how do we train ourselves to pay more attention to our intuition? How do we hone our ability to listen to our inner voice, and reach a point where is not so much about making right decisions, as it is about making decisions that 'feel right?' Why don't we pay more attention and take action on our inspirations?"

And the great question, then, seems to be: "Knowing that individual and collective perceptions keep us stuck, and do not invite us to consider new ideas, new visions of life and the universe, new ways of relating to one another and organizing ourselves to live in community, how can we open our minds and begin to absorb new information that challenges our paradigms, and can lead us to embrace new ones?"

………..

BECOMING AWARE OF FILTERS

I don't claim to have an answer, but I believe that in order for us to open our minds we must first come to feel, as Socrates did, that an unexamined life is not worth living, and pledge that we will put our fears aside and boldly launch ourselves on a journey of exploration. We have to accept responsibility for our realities, believing that they were created by us through our chosen thoughts and perceptions, through our own, or our tribe's interpretation of the occurrences, through the meanings we attached to the events, through the stories we created. We must commit to deliberately remain open to listen and analyze other points of view with curiosity. We must decide that we will engage in a practice of questioning ourselves that will lead us to consciously unlearn the prejudices and self-defeating beliefs we have unconsciously learned. Curiosity, doubt, and skepticism should be our companions.

A good place to begin may be to ponder on the impermanence of all things, and on the unending cycle of birth and death. We should also consider the vastness of the universe and Einstein's views of unified time, because such reflection has a humbling effect that tames our egos and sets the stage for some radical transformations.

I believe that the process that leads to those life-changing experiences -- the epiphany of oneness -- demands the practice of some sort of inner work, which, based on my experience, involves Silence, Stillness, Solitude, Seclusion, Simplicity, and Service, a reverence for nature, and, among other practices, those of mindfulness and gratefulness; a commitment to stay in the present moment, appreciating the simple things in life, while opening ourselves up to receive and to give love.

Our goal should be to practice and get good at observing and controlling our thoughts, at refraining from comparing, hastily judging, and quickly reacting. It would be advisable to practice and get good at becoming the masters of the space between stimuli and responses, developing the ability to make time (yes, "make"), ponder, and choose the best responses to the challenges of life. Our goal should be to develop ourselves so we can live mindfully, responding thoughtfully instead of reacting mindlessly to what happens to us.

On this journey of seeking wisdom that can lead to the liberation from suffering, I have not found anything better than the practice of mindfulness meditation and mindful living. That's why I promote these practices of paying extreme attention to the here-now, to this present moment, in order to enhance our perceptions, see beyond what we see, and see magic, mystery, and miracles everywhere, all the time. By doing so, we shall experience that awakening that allows us to realize that we are, at the same time, body and soul, solid matter and vibrational energy, mortal and immortal, human and spiritual, earthly and divine, separated and united, independent and interdependent, many and one. We will gain a better understanding of this physical life, of the impermanence of all things, of the cycle of birth and death, and will be blessed with the revelation that life is more, immensely more than what we were ever able to imagine. And once we experience this enhancement of understanding -- this awakening, this enlightenment -- our perceptions, ideas, and beliefs will change, and all fear will subside. We will look at the world and see it differently. Those things we once thought were desirable will seem meaningless. We will look at all the struggle for power, fame, and privileges in the world, and will consider all of it senseless. We will look at all conflicts and squabbles and see them as absurdities. We will realize that when we change the way we look at things, the things we look at change.

When we seriously give consideration that what we accept as reality may not be real, and that, in fact, we may be living in a construct of our own minds -- an illusion, if you will -- our ability to perceive begins to enhance. And each individual shift in perception will add to the critical mass that will eventually tip the scale, and bring about a great planetary shift in the collective consciousness, when a whole new world -- new perceptions and realities -- will arise. Then, we will discover Heaven right here on Earth.

……..

C.C.A.R.R.

Mindfulness meditation is a great practice that can really enhance the quality of anyone's life. Let us meditate with regularity and be mindful of our thoughts and what is happening in the present moment.

During meditation, we will be invited to pay attention to a particular object. Traditionally, this object of attention is the breath. We will be instructed to focus our attention on the physical sensations associated with the act of breathing. The objective of this practice is to develop the ability to focus and maintain focused attention. While observing the breath, the mind will wander; it's normal and inevitable. We will be distracted by passing thoughts, and our minds will carry us to other places and times, away from the here-now. But sooner or later we will notice that we have not been paying attention to the breath. In that moment, it's important to congratulate ourselves for catching ourselves distracted because this is the high point of the meditation practice: the moment of mindfulness. And then, all we have to do is to return to the activity of paying attention to the breath. We simply have to start over, begin again, which is probably the most frequently repeated instruction in the world of mindfulness meditation. Start Over. Begin Again.

During meditation the mind will wander many times. It doesn't matter if it wanders five times, fifty times, or five hundred times. When we notice that we have been distracted, we should congratulate ourselves for noticing, and simply start over, bringing our attention back to the breath.

. . . .

CCARR

- Catch yourself distracted.
- Congratulate yourself for catching.
-Acknowledge the distraction, taking a good look at it.
- Release it, and
- Return your attention to the object of attention in this present moment.

. . . .

LIFE IS NOT THIS THOUGHT

"Leave your front door and your back door open. Allow your thoughts to come and go. Just don't serve them tea." ~ Shunryu Suzuki Roshi

. . . .

In order to preserve our sanity, many times it's useful to remember to say to ourselves, "It's just a thought, and I don't need to believe it."

Let's pause for a moment and ponder: What are these things we call thoughts? What are their characteristics, features, qualities? It doesn't take a lot of observation to realize that thoughts are just ephemeral mental formations. They come and go. They arise, are present for a moment, and soon vanish. Thoughts are not only ephemeral; they are also insubstantial. They are not real. They are temporary and empty mental formations. Thoughts are also independent. It is as if we are carrying around an independent thought-producing machine. When we become able to observe our thoughts and notice their independent nature, then we can liberate ourselves from their grip by realizing that we are not our thoughts. And whenever thoughts bring about disturbing emotions, it's also useful to remember to say to ourselves, "It is OK to feel like this. It's just a short-lived emotion that will soon go away." Because just like thoughts, emotions are also ephemeral and insubstantial. Observing thoughts and emotions is very liberating. The ability to observe thoughts and emotions without being carried away by them, without being owned by them, without allowing them to get a hold of us, is very empowering. So, whenever they arise, try not to push them away. Observe them with removed and dispassionate interest. Observe the desire to push them away but get closer to your disturbing thoughts and emotions instead. And if necessary, remember to say to yourself, "What I am thinking is not actually happening right now. It's just a fleeting thought, and thoughts are not real. I am not my thoughts. The thought of this occurrence is not the actual occurrence. The thought of this person is not the actual person. The thought of this thing is not the actual thing. It's just a thought. And it is OK to feel what I am feeling right now. It's OK to feel like this. These are just transient mind states that will soon pass away."

....

It's just a thought, and life, in this moment, is not this thought. It's just a thought, and I don't have to believe it. Thoughts are not real. Thoughts are just thoughts. Thoughts think themselves. The thought of a thing is not that thing. The mind has a mind of its own. I am not my thoughts.

....

SELF-FULFILLING PROPHECIES

"As a man thinks in his heart, so is he." ~ Book of Proverbs

....

What we imagine impacts our lives, therefore we need to be watchful of what we think and believe, always keeping in mind that we have the power to choose.

When we start to observe and be more aware of our thoughts, we begin to understand the thought process: how thoughts appear from nowhere, vanish, and reappear, and how one thought generates many others. Then we begin to realize that we have the power to be selective, and choose what thoughts we give our attention to. Once we realize that we can decide to give attention to thoughts, ideas, and beliefs that are beneficial to us, and disregard those that are not, our lives become immensely better.

It should be said that we don't push any thoughts away. The practice is one of recognizing all thoughts, even the disturbing ones, allowing them to be present, accepting them, and making an effort to get to know them better, investigating them with sincere curiosity, without identifying ourselves with them.

……..

"I am enough of an artist to draw freely upon my imagination. Imagination is more important than knowledge. For knowledge is limited, whereas imagination encircles the world." ~ Albert Einstein

……..

What possibilities do you imagine for yourself? What do you expect from your life? How do you see yourself in the future? Life is full of possibilities. You can be your own greatest motivator or your own greatest inhibitor; it is up to you.

Whether you think you can, or you think you can't, you are right.

……..

"If you think you are beaten, you are; If you think you dare not, you don't. If you'd like to win, but you think you can't, It is almost a cinch that you won't.

If you think you'll lose, you're lost; For out of the world we find Success begins with a fellow's will It's all in the state of mind.

If you think you're outclassed, you are; You've got to think high to rise. You've got to be sure of yourself before You can ever win the prize.

Life's battles don't always go To the stronger or faster man; But sooner or later the man who wins Is the one who thinks he can!"

~ Walter D. Wintle

……..

MINDFULNESS AND THE ILLUSION OF A SEPARATE SELF

NO SELF, NO PROBLEM

I was reflecting about the transformation I am going through, and this reflection led me to think about death. Not my physical death, but the death of my old lives, the ones that had played themselves out and did not serve me anymore. I reflected on how the clinging to my old stories had held me back, and how this death, the death of my old identities, was the factor that led to the beginning of my meaningful transformation.

As the deconstruction and reconstruction of Piero Falci – as I like to call my transformational journey – continues, I keep being taken aback by the insights that keep popping up. For instance, for a long time I thought that if I replaced 'the old me' with a newer and improved version of me, I would be happy. I kept thinking that if I left behind my less authentic self and showed up in the world as someone who knows what his purpose is, as someone who does what he likes and likes what he does, then I would have a fulfilling existence. Although I still believe that discovering your purpose and following your bliss is the right and noble thing to do, it struck me that, perhaps, this was not the final solution for the end of anguish. I began to entertain the idea that perhaps the problem was not 'the old me,' and that the solution was not 'the new me,' but that the problem resided in the concept of 'me,' and that, therefore, the ultimate solution was to be found in the dissolution of such a concept.

I like the idea that we were given this opportunity to live so we can learn the lessons we need to learn, and that, perhaps, by learning them well, we will graduate and not need to come back to 'school' again. For me, one of the most important lessons to be learned -- and one that is able to propel any individual on the journey of personal discovery and transformation -- is how to move from self-centeredness to other-centeredness; how to become a less selfish and a more selfless person. I have experienced how selfishness is a source of suffering, and how practicing generosity leads to the liberation from suffering.

………

Who am I? I can answer this question by saying that I am Piero, a human being, a man, a son, a husband, and a father. I can describe my body features, and state my age. I can list my education and professional achievements, and the titles and possessions I have accumulated. I can tell the stories of my successes, craving admiration, and I can also tell the stories of my defeats and show my wounds, begging for sympathy. But although, in one hand, I am all this huge structure of words, images, and feelings that I have built throughout my life to present my 'self,' on the other hand I am none of it. The 'self' is a concept, and like all concepts, it is useful, but we must remember that it is a concept nonetheless.

What gives rise to this sense of 'self?' As experiences arise we have the habit of identifying ourselves with the experiences as being 'my experiences,' and this mental process of indentifying ourselves with the experiences is what gives rise to the felt sense of 'self.' We feel an unpleasant sensation in the body and refer to it as 'pain in my body.' We feel emotions and say, 'I am sad,' or 'I am angry.' We talk all the time about 'my body, my emotions, and my thoughts.' This practice of claiming possession of impermanent states; of identifying ourselves with the experiences; of frequently using the words 'I, me, my, mine, myself' contributes to create and reinforce the concept of 'self.' My mindfulness teachers instructed me to be careful to not identify myself with my emotions. They taught me to refrain from saying "I am angry" or "I am afraid," but rather say, "Anger is visiting me," or "Fear is passing by."

The right attitude is the one of not taking our emotions personally. Observation puts in evidence the independent nature of emotions: they emerge when conditions are present, but the moment such conditions cease to exist, the emotions vanish. They have a life of their own. When we stop claiming emotions as our own, we feel less isolated and more connected, and we experience more freedom. We are not owned by the emotions: we notice them and calmly allow them to simply come and go.

Yes, I am my name, my body, my personality, my mental creations, my memories, my stories, my emotions, but I am more than that, and none of that. The more I am identified with this construct, the more I feel isolated from others. The more I believe that I am this made up 'self,' the bigger is my suffering. Therefore I can see that not grasping at or clinging to anything as being 'self,' or as belonging to 'self,' leads to the weakening of this identification with 'self' and diminishes the suffering.

The essential practice is not wanting, not craving, not grasping, not clinging.

We are continuously craving for the experience in the next moment, hoping that it will be the one that will bring us solace. But it never does because everything is impermanent. Since whatever has the nature to arise will also pass away, then there's nothing to want.

That's what the practice of mindfulness is about: noticing the impermanence of every-thing and wanting no-thing. And when there's nothing to want, achieved is the end of craving, a state of contentment and gratitude where freedom resides.

……..

"Nothing whatsoever should be clung to as 'I' or 'mine.'" ~ the Buddha

……..

The word selfless brings to my mind the joyful possibility of an existence without clinging to the concept of 'I' as a separate entity, and I ponder: "Could the 'self' be nothing more than an illusion created by the unending barrage of self-referential thoughts that populate my mind? Is the 'I' a notion conditioned and reinforced by the ceaseless narration inside my head of countless stories in which I always am the protagonist?"

……..

Alan Watts taught powerful lessons about the tricks the ego play. He asked, "Who is this self, behind the self, who is watching the self? Who is The Watcher, The Observer, The Witness? Isn't The Watching Self, The Observing Self, The Witnessing Self behind our thoughts and feelings a thought itself?"And isn't the act of identifying ourselves with the

Watcher, the Observer, the Witness, another attempt of the 'I' to find a new identity, a new hideout? When the ego is about to be unmasked it immediately identifies itself with a higher self. What drives us to do the work to be more spiritual and selfless people? Many times, the spiritual quest -- the quest for self-improvement -- is no different from the quest for material success; the drive is the same, it is ego-driven. In essence, we still see ourselves as separated from others, and in competition with others, and we engage in developing ourselves because our egos want to experience the rewards of feeling somewhat superior.

....

So this possibility that the 'I' is just a made up illusion – an illusion that brings about suffering due to the expressions of desires, cravings, and attachments -- transports me to think that we were given this opportunity to live this life so we can learn the ultimate lesson: how to practice non-identification, how to let go of the notion of 'self,' or, in other words, how to die before we die. Perhaps we will be able to internalize the concept of non-self, liberate ourselves from the grip of the 'self,' and experience greater freedom. This is my wish.

....

"One of the most radical, far-reaching, and challenging statements of the Buddha is his statement that as long as there is attachment to the pleasant and aversion to the unpleasant, liberation is impossible." ~ Joseph Goldstein

....

There is no self. We suffer because we live with the strong impression that there is a separate self. This is a delusion. We don't even notice it because we are so immersed in it, like fish that are unaware of the water they are in. To have a sense of self is, also, to have a sense that there are others. Babies aren't born with this duality; this is something that we learn through socialization. And this is problematic because the self is a mental construction, an abstraction. As we live we reinforce the sense of a separate self, but there isn't such a thing as a self to begin with. The separate self does not exist. There is nothing there. Therefore, this separate self is inherently insecure, and this condition brings about suffering.

There is the suffering that stems from our vain attempts to make the self, which is a mere mental construct, real. In other words, there is suffering that stems from the impossibility of giving substance to an illusory self that is, by nature, insubstantial. Trying to fill that internal void that we all experience -- that sense that something is not quite right -- we mistakenly sacrifice the enjoyment of the present moments, throwing ourselves in the frantic pursuit of positions, possessions, power, and privilege, believing that those things will be the ones that will placate our sense of lack, only to discover, perhaps later in life, that no matter how many of those things we may be able to accumulate, they will never be enough to pacify the feeling that something is missing. And then the suffering is made greater by the inevitable loss of the people and places that we became attached to, and the loss of our own physical existences.

......

KNOWING OURSELVES AND OUR NON-SELVES

"Knowing others, one is intelligent. Knowing oneself, one is enlightened" ~ Laozi

......

The disturbed individual slaps the master in the face. The disciples ask, "Why didn't you react?" The master responds, "He didn't slap me. He slapped his idea of me."

......

If we really know who we are, and also who we are not, and if we are comfortably and securely grounded on that knowing, what other people think, say, or do to us is of little relevance. If we develop a serene knowing of our non-selves, nothing will affect us, because the non-self never feels diminished. The non-self never feels the need to outsmart others, or prove that it is better. The non-self cannot be offended. The non-self will never feel threatened. The non-self will never feel the need to react because, in a way, the non-self is real, but the self is not.

......

"Nothing real can be threatened. Nothing unreal exists. Herein lies the peace of God." ~ A Course in Miracles

......

We'd better not listen to the ego. We'd better not take anything personally. We'd better not cling to anything as I, me, or mine, because we are more than these mortal physical beings that the ego makes us believe we are. We are manifestations of an energy that is ever present and immortal. Take a moment to reflect on this passage:

"There is a Light that lights every man and woman that comes into the world. That Light is Eternal, All-Powerful and Imperishable. Only that which is subject to birth is subject to death. The Light is the extension of God into man. It is not born nor can it die." ~ Douglas K. DeVorss

……..

Under the rule of our egos, we grew unaware of this Imperishable Light that lives in all of us. We have forgotten our original nature and pure essence. We have forgotten that every child comes into the world with this light, full of love, gentleness, and kindness. We have forgotten who we are and why we are here.

Under the rule of our egos, we have made of this planet a place of widespread insanity. Why do we feel this compulsion to compete and defeat others all the time? Why do we oppress, exploit, enslave, take advantage of, torture, and kill other beings? Why are we so violent? Why?

Let us remember who we are and why we are here. We are here to learn, and the most important lesson we all need to learn is to tame our egos. We are here to learn to diminish our selfishness and expand our selflessness. We are here to develop our modesty and contain our arrogance. We are here to learn to grow in compassion and service to others.

Now, let us pause and see what is really happening. Even though things may look bleak the truth is that for every selfish and harmful act there are millions of selfless acts of kindness. There's a lot more good than bad in the world, and we are perfectly equipped and capable of diminishing what is bad. How? By doing even more good. So let us love, care, and share. Let us focus on the abundant good that exists in our world. Let us realize that Heaven is here, if we want it to be.

……..

"Certainly there are a distinct "me" and a distinct "you" operating in our everyday relationships with the world. Each of us comes as a unique package of qualities and conditions shaped by myriad factors. We call this "my self." Yet, when we look closely into our lives, we see that we are made up of thousands of what the Vietnamese Zen master Thich Nhat Hanh calls "non-self" elements, such things as earth, water, fire, air, space, carbon, oxygen, parents, genes from the entire planet pool. The same constituents that make up the sun, the stars in the night sky, and the salty seas are part of our common, embodied heritage... it is easy to forget all this." ~ Saki Santorelli

....

When the Buddha was asked, "In brief, how is a monk liberated from the destruction of craving?" he replied, "He who has realized that nothing is worth clinging to as I, me, or mine, directly knows all things."

....

'The Buddha once said that the core message of all his teachings could be summed up in one sentence. ... That sentence is: 'Nothing is to be clung to as I, me, or mine.' In other words, no attachments—especially to fixed ideas of yourself and who you are.' ~ Jon Kabat-Zinn

....

PEACE COMES FROM ACCEPTING IMPERMANENCE

"I am of the nature to grow old. There is no way to escape growing old. I am of the nature to have ill health. There is no way to escape having ill health. I am of the nature to die. There is no way to escape death. All that is dear to me and everyone I love are of the nature to change. There is no way to escape being separated from them. My actions are my only true belongings. I cannot escape the consequences of my actions. My actions are the ground on which I stand." ~ the Buddha

....

I invite you to think if these are sources of joy for you.

The joy that comes from peacefully accepting the impermanence of all.

The joy of accepting and resting in this present moment as it is, with all it brings, without wanting it to be different, without rushing to judge it as good or bad, and without anxiously rushing to the next moment.

The joy of being in this ephemeral moment and realizing the impermanence of everything.

The joy of realizing that this moment is vanishing and will vanish as all other moments that came before this one, and that all future moments that we idealize, that we expect to be better than this one, will also vanish when they come to be.

The joy of realizing that this is it, that this moment is real, and is all that exists.

The joy of being totally absorbed and losing the sense of time while playing an instrument, or creating outstanding music that will never be repeated or recorded, and that no one else will ever hear, and being at complete peace with that.

The joy of cooking and creating a beautiful meal that will soon be consumed and disappear, and be fully content with that.

The joy of waking up very early and drinking a hot beverage while all around is silent and dark, and not feeling the urge to accomplish anything.

The joy of discovering that we actually don't need to do all the things we told ourselves that we need to do.

The joy that comes from freeing ourselves from all self-imposed and unnecessary obligations.

The joy of not having to do anything.

The joy of realizing that there is no need to rush to get anywhere.

The joy of giving ourselves the gifts of rest and gentleness.

The joy of mindfully being in this life while we are here.

The joy of enhancing the quality of life by being mindful, amazed, and grateful, by not having to do more, have more, or be more, but by being totally happy, content, and satisfied with this moment and with what it brings, whatever it may be.

The joy of realizing the self-imposed violence of getting it right and being perfect, and freeing ourselves of it.

The joy that we experience from liberating ourselves from the subtle violence of self-improvement.

The joy of giving ourselves permission to rest and enjoy life instead of feeling guilty for not working hard enough, or as hard as we think we should.

The joy of non-striving.

The joy of being curious, of discovering, and of learning to live a rich life in the process.

The joy of letting go of the desired outcomes and be open for amazement with the unexpected. The joy of accepting whatever may come.

The joy of realizing and accepting that we are not this important.

The joy of realizing and accepting that no matter what we do, in the great scheme of things, it doesn't really matter.

The joy of being at peace with the fact that although we may want to touch many lives, we will only touch a few, or maybe one, or none at all, except our own, realizing that whatever it may be, it is enough.

Impermanence is ever-present. Impermanence is eternity.

....

FAITHFUL COMPANIONS

Joni Mitchell's ability to carefully choose words to convey emotions is admirable. Two of her songs — "Down to You" and "Shadows and Light" — have been my faithful companions since my youth. I guess we are still together after all these years because as I change, I keep discovering something new in them. These are poignant chants that remind me of the impermanence of all things, that change is the only constant in life, that the pleasant does not exist without the unpleasant, and that good and bad, right and wrong, reside in all of us. Great wisdom through inspired, sublime poetry!

....

Excerpts from the lyrics of "Down to You" by Joni Mitchell, a reflection on impermanence:

"Everything comes and goes
Marked by lovers and styles of clothes
Things that you held high

And told yourself were true
Lost or changing as the days come down to you
Down to you
Constant stranger
You're a kind person
You're a cold person too
It's down to you"

"Everything comes and goes
Pleasure moves on too early
And trouble leaves too slow
Just when you're thinking
You've finally got it made
Bad news comes knocking
At your garden gate
Knocking for you
Constant stranger
You're a brute, you're an angel
You can crawl, you can fly too
It's down to you
It all comes down to you"

....
Excerpts from the lyrics of "Shadows and Light"

"Every picture has its shadows
And it has some source of light
Blindness, blindness and sight
The perils of benefactors
The blessings of parasites
Blindness, blindness and sight"

"Suntans in reservation dining rooms
Pale miners in their lantern rays
Night, night and day
Hostage smiles on presidents
Freedom scribbled in the subway
It's like night, night and day"

"Critics of all expression
Judges in black and white
Saying it's wrong, saying it's right
Compelled by prescribed standards
Or some ideals we fight
For wrong, wrong and right"

……...

ALL PROBLEMS, ONE PROBLEM

"Virtue is the foundation, the forerunner, and origin of all that is good. A strong foundation of morality helps us develop the discipline and serenity necessary for the practice of meditation." ~ Bhavana Vandana

……...

Who am I? What is the purpose of living? What am I doing here? Why is it so difficult to be content and stay happy? The mere contemplation of fundamental questions such as these -- even if we are unable to get conclusive answers -- takes us to an understanding that all problems derive from one problem: the lack of inner peace.

Inner peace can be cultivated by the practice of mindfulness meditation and mindful living which in order to be fruitful should be based on a strong foundation of morality. Without adherence to a code of moral and ethical conduct, we create disturbances that show up during the meditation and do not allow us to reap the benefits of the practice. They hinder our evolution. Following the general precept of doing no harm prepares the ground for the cultivation of a way of living that reduces life conflicts and takes us to experience greater peace.

Here are some precepts to live by: Abstaining from killing, stealing, and sexual misconduct. Abstaining from ingesting intoxicants that cause heedlessness. Abstaining from engaging in wrong livelihood, which means staying away from occupations with weapons, intoxicants, and those that harm animals. Abstaining from false, malicious, harsh, and useless speech.

Our job during our lifetime should be to go beyond our self-centeredness in order to reach the understanding that we are, at the same time, many and one. Once we get to this realization, we will move through the world more mindfully, caring for others and doing our best to do no harm.

. . . .

"The animals of the world exist for their own reasons. They were not made for humans any more than black people were made for white, or women created for men." ~ Alice Walker

. . . .

Everything we think, say, and do has consequences. Some are good, some are bad. Some are positive, some negative. Some bring peace, others bring unrest. That is why it is so important to take time between stimuli and responses, between impulse and action. It's important to pause and think before saying or doing anything. It is important to analyze our thoughts and moods, and evaluate if we are reacting without measuring possible consequences, or if we are responding after a thorough consideration of the possible outcomes. It is important to figure out what motivates our speaking and acting. Is it coming from the ego? Is the ego feeling threatened? Does the ego want to use this opportunity to aggrandize itself? Some of the great rules to remember are:

- Before speaking, ask yourself, "Is t true? Is it necessary? Is it kind?" If the answer is no, refrain from speaking.

- Before doing anything, remember that the most important thing is to do no harm. Ask yourself, "Will my chosen words and actions harm someone?" If so, choose another course of action.

The practice of mindfulness helps us because it makes of us inhabit the space and time between stimulus and response. It enhances that space and time. It trains us to be less reactive, and more capable of choosing the best responses.

What we sow is what we reap. What goes around, comes around. Every choice has consequences, so let's choose wisely.

. . . .

"At any moment, you have a choice that either leads you closer to your spirit or further away from it." ~ Thich Nhat Hanh

. . . .

MINDFUL COMMUNICATION

"If speech has five marks, O monks, it is well spoken, not badly spoken, blameless and above reproach by the wise. What are these five marks? It is speech that is timely, true, gentle, purposeful and spoken with a mind of loving-kindness." ~ the Buddha

……..

Should I participate or hold back? Should I give advice, or refrain from doing so? Should I offer ideas, or remain silent? Should I interrupt now, or patiently wait for my turn to speak? Should I say something? Why this urge to speak is so intense? Could it be that it is because I want to make sure that the things I'm thinking are not left out? Is it because I want everything to be perfect? But is the outcome really this important? Why this urge to take charge is so intense? Could it be that it is because I feel that I can do better? Shouldn't I let the process unfold without taking charge? Do I need to speak?

I know how excited I get when I make discoveries and establish connections, and how much I want to share my insights. I believe that my intentions are pure, and I see sharing ideas as acts of generosity.

OK. I'd better pause and remember the tenets of right speech: "Is it true? Is it useful? Is it beneficial? Is it timely? Is it necessary? Is it skillful? Is it gentle? Will my words be infused with care and kindness? Do they promote unity or division? Can I say what I want to say and still do no harm? The intentions that move me to speak, are they pure? What moves me: selfishness or selflessness? Am I going to speak in order to get something for my personal benefit, or in order to give something that will benefit others?"

I feel the need to be heard. I feel the desire to be approved, admired, and loved. Oh, I can see the ego at play! Perhaps the right move is to let go of the compulsion to intervene, while remaining aware of the difference between letting go and withdrawing. I can let go of the need to control the outcomes, and still stay engaged, actively participating and contributing, or I can decide to retreat and no longer take part because things are not unfolding in accordance to my wants. Withdrawing can be a very immature reaction. Time for wise assessment and wise discernment. Time for choosing the wisest course of action.

……..

Before speaking, T-H-I-N-K.
Is it:
T—True? Timely?
H—Honest? Helpful?
I—Insightful? Inspiring?
N—Necessary?
K—Kind?

………

Stephen R. Covey taught us in The 7 Habits of Highly Effective People, "Seek first to understand, then to be understood."

Here is communication's golden rule: First of all, listen attentively, empathize, and don't say anything; just listen and seek to understand. Then, utter the magic words, "Let me see if I understand," and then repeat in your own words what the people you are interacting with have said, finishing with the following magic words, "Is that so? Did I get it right?" This gives a chance for people to clarify what they have said, and gives you another opportunity to understand. Usually, they will answer, "Yes, but…" adding more details, or correcting misunderstandings.

Again, after listening attentively, you are called to repeat the magic words, "Let me see if I understand," repeat what they have said, and finish with, "Is that so? Did I get it right?" Repeat this process as many times as necessary until they feel that you feel what they feel, and that you have understood them completely. And, then, only then, say what you have to say, because only now they are ready to listen to you. If you try to say what you came prepared to say without mindfully listening to them first you drastically diminish the chances of producing the best possible outcomes from the interaction.

It is as if they approached the conversation ready for a fight, wearing a full armor, and now that they have witnessed your efforts to listen and understand them, they feel safe enough to let the shield and sword down, relax, and listen to you. Trying to say your side of the story before first listening to them, demands more effort and yields poorer results.

And now, when is your turn to speak, talk about you, not about them. Describe the situation from your perspective, expressing your feelings, your needs, your desires, avoiding, as much as possible, finding fault and criticizing them. Use the I-message. Start your phrases with I, not with You. This way of communicating mindfully and nonviolently usually yield the best results.

Seek first to understand, then to be understood.

……..

I've once heard that after the terrorist attacks that happened on September 11, 2001, in US soil, Thich Nhat Hanh was asked, "If you had the chance, what you would say to Osama Bin Laden?" His answer was something along these lines: "At first, I wouldn't say anything. I would remain silent and listen to what he had to say. I would seek to understand him."

……..

Here are some guidelines to consider before speaking:

- Is it true? Is my speech based on facts, or not?
- Is it necessary? Is it helpful? Should I say something, or not? Will my words add anything of value, or will my silence be more helpful? Will my words make situations and relationships better, or not?
- Is it kind? Do I speak gently or harshly? Will I speak with a mind of loving-kindness? Do I speak with a kind heart, or with malice? Will my words hurt someone? Will my words make someone uncomfortable? Will my words arise the impulse in others to defend and attack? Will my words damage relationships? Will my words be kind, affectionate, and endearing?
- Is it well-spoken, or poorly spoken? Is it skillful? Am I explaining myself properly? Am I making myself understood?
- Is it timely? Is this the right time to speak, or not?
- Is it inspiring? Is it peace-producing? Do my words carry criticism or praise, pessimism or optimism? Do I speak expressing love, understanding, and good will, or do I let my ego speak, wanting to be right and win? Are my words conducive to the visualization of a just solution, a win-win agreement, a future of harmony?

Sometimes it makes more sense to surrender and let go of the need to prove that you are right. Sometimes the best response is a shoulder shrug accompanied by "Whatever!"

……..

LOVE WASTEFULLY

Some years ago, while practicing mindfulness with a group of fellow meditators, the facilitator began to guide us on a compassion and loving-kindness meditation, a beautiful practice of mentally directing well-wishes and expressions of love towards your own self and others. Well, during the meditation the instructor directed us to look back at our lives and remember occasions when we felt abundantly loved. She instructed, "Go back in time. Remember how loved you were when you were a child."

To my amazement, I couldn't easily remember occasions when I received lots of love. I looked back at my life and I could not clearly remember being immersed in a sea of affection, being hugged, caressed, kissed, praised, and loved. Actually, I couldn't remember my parents showering me with an outpouring of affection. I am sure those moments existed. I am sure not only my parents, but also my relatives and friends bestowed affection in great quantities, but although I am sure those moments existed, honestly, I couldn't clearly remember them.

I also can't remember being copiously and munificently loved by any of the women in my life. Actually, I can't remember anyone being wastefully generous in giving me love, or doing things that made me feel unconditionally loved, with maybe one exception: I have a vague memory of my maternal grandmother holding me in her arms when I was a little child, dancing around, smiling, kissing me, and letting me know how much she loved me, and how happy she was to have me in her life.

Well, all those insights were surprising and shocking, and I began to ask myself: "Why can't I remember receiving love? Have I blocked those memories? If so, why?" But I also have learned that for many people, showing love is not an easy thing. I, then, asked myself, "Why so many people refrain from showing affection? Could it be because they have not learned how to do it, or have not experienced it themselves? Could this be the case with my parents? Or could it be that they don't show affection because they were taught that showing it is a sign of weakness?"

Immediately, other questions came to my mind: "Why do people measure and ration the love they give? Why do some people think that a person who receives love will become dependent and demanding and therefore, in order to avoid such a situation, love should be given parsimoniously? Why don't people love wastefully?"

I began to raise doubts about the existence of unconditional love: "Does unconditional love really exist? Or is all love conditional?"

And it became more personal when I started to investigate my own motivation, "Do I crave to be loved? Do I crave to be the recipient of affection?" Finally, bigger and more important questions emerged: "Am I able to be satisfied with all the love I have received throughout my life, and the love I still receive, without wanting more? Can I calmly accept my past and present life situation without longing for it to be different?"

Well, one of the requirements of the mindfulness journey I am in is to be aware of my cravings and aversions and practice equanimity. Yesterday's metta meditation brought to the surface some buried feelings. I felt deprived. I felt a craving for a kind of love and affection that I don't remember receiving. I saw myself as a needy being, a type of person that I don't want to be because I believe that such an unbalanced individual is not a magnet for love. On the contrary, I believe that those who are more easily loved are the ones who feel whole and complete. Those who are loved are the ones who are able to freely give lots of love, not the ones who desperately desire to receive it.

After a more calm, lengthy, and thorough reflection I realized that things have changed and are different these days. I sincerely feel generously loved these days by my wife, my father, my sister, my aunt, by all my relatives, especially by my sons, who, by the way, are the ones who receive, more than any other people in my life, my expressions of love. I constantly remind them of how much they mean to me and how much I love them. I realized that I have changed. With the passing of time, I became a less self-centered individual, and, therefore, better able to give love and affection.

What comes to my mind is a line in the Prayer of Saint Francis that reads, "It is in giving that we receive." So, from now on, I will make sure that I become more generous in my love-giving. I will give love and affection freely, abundantly, profusely, wastefully. And I will also make sure that I will remain wide open to receive. From now on, I will give myself the love I don't remember receiving, and I will remind myself that I am loved. From now on, I will let everybody know that they are loved.

………

NO NEED TO BE PERFECT

We don't have to be perfect, or fear criticism. A big obstacle for doing good things is the obsession with doing perfect things. Perfectionism prevents the materialization of many things that could be of great benefit to others. We don't need to be perfect. It is OK to be imperfect, fail, make mistakes, and be criticized.

……...

"Perfectionism is a slow death. If everything were to turn out just like I would want it to, just like I would plan for it to, then I would never experience anything new; my life would be an endless repetition of stale successes. when I make a mistake I experience something unexpected.... when I have listened to my mistakes I have grown."~ Hugh Prather

……...

The obsession with perfection -- and the fear of criticism and rejection -- is such a source of anxiety and stress, and the sad aspect is that it prevents us from offering many contributions to the world. We must practice to say, "Yes, it can be better, but right now it's good enough. Time to let go, savor the accomplishment, and give myself the gift of rest."

……...

"See simplicity in the complicated. Achieve greatness in little things. In the universe the difficult things are done as if they are easy. In the universe great acts are made up of small deeds. The sage does not attempt anything very big, and thus achieves greatness." ~ Laozi

……...

Leonard Cohen, the great Canadian songwriter instructed us to forget our obsession with perfection, and recognize that nothing is perfect because there is a crack in everything. But that's not a bad thing because it is through those cracks that we receive the blessings. He sang, "Forget your perfect offering. There is a crack in everything. That's how the light gets in."

……...

DEVELOP YOUR STRENGTHS

Yes, I can do a lot, but I cannot do everything I would like to do. I have my limitations. For instance -- and I know this may sound childish -- I would like to have a more flexible body, with a greater range of motion, so I could be able to do those yoga postures restfully, without striving. Mindfulness reminds me, "Here you are, again, with your desires, with wanting this and not wanting that. Stop. Practice equanimity. Simply accept what is."

Everyone is different. Each one of us is a different bundle of aggregated talents, attributes, skills, potentials, and limitations. I learned a great lesson from Tom Rath in his book Strengths Finder 2.0. He referred to it as a misguided maxim. He said that one of the most damaging things we can tell our children is, "You can be anything you want to be, if you just try hard enough."

The reality is that not everyone can be a Michael Jordan, or a Muhammad Ali, or a Pele, or a Michael Phelps, or an Einstein. A much more honest and less damaging advice is, "You cannot be anything you want to be -- but you can be a lot more of who you already are. You can develop your innate talents, and excel in what you already are good at."

We help our children succeed when our main focus is not on developing their weaknesses, but on maximizing their strengths. Our fault is that we keep trying to develop weaknesses. We invest a lot of time in developing what we are not good at, and not so much in what we enjoy doing and already are good at. We hear a lot people saying things such as, "You're failing in algebra. You need some extra classes." We rarely, if ever, hear someone saying, "You write so well, express yourself so precisely, and have such a rich vocabulary. I will hire a tutor to further enhance your writing and speaking proficiency."

It is evident that we need to give attention to both weaknesses and strengths, but wouldn't it make more sense to invest more time, resources, and energy to develop further what we already are good at? Wouldn't it make more sense to develop our strengths?

The things we should do are at the intersection of things we enjoy doing and things we are good at. That's what brings about excellence.

·······

NINE L'S

"In the end, just three things matter: How well we have lived. How well we have loved. How well we have learned to let go."~ Jack Kornfield

……...

Look. Listen. Learn. Lead. Laugh. Love. Live. Let go. Leave.

……...

Look deeply.
Listen attentively.
Learn unceasingly.
Lead compassionately.
Laugh profusely.
Love wastefully.
Live fully.
Let go of everything.
Leave an honorable legacy.

……...

FINDING YOUR OWN VOICE

We are, by nature, students and teachers. I am convinced that learning and teaching has no end and that we will be learning and teaching until the last moment of our physical existences, and, who knows, even beyond. I see evolution of consciousness as a never-ending journey.

In my attempts to learn and teach how to live a more joyful and fulfilling life, I have been blessed by the knowledge and wisdom of many amazing teachers who came before me; I read their books, listened to their recordings, watched their videos, attended their workshops, and experimented with the different practices they suggested. I recognize how tremendously important they were -- and continue to be -- in bringing me to where I am in my life, and I look forward to the amazing places they will be taking me in the future. They made and continue to make me better, and I am grateful to all of them. Not only those who have written books that I have read, or facilitated classes that I have attended, were my teachers. My friends, especially those with whom I have deep conversations, have taught and continue to teach me a whole lot. Conversations about our explorations and our findings are very inspiring. I remind myself that reading a book is another type of conversation; in a way, when I am reading, I am having a conversation with the author.

It is now very clear to me that we are all teachers to each other, and that everyone we meet can be a teacher to us, as long as we approach all situations with reverence and a sincere desire to learn. The source from where lessons come is inexhaustible, and the flow of lessons is unstoppable, simply because abundance is the very nature of our world. With the constant progress in technology, more and more information is produced and made available to us. Teachers keep showing up all the time: some of the lessons they bring are already known to us, some are improved versions of old lessons, and some are entirely new ones. I consider that we are fortunate for having such easy access to all this wisdom, and I am grateful for that. But the exposure to all this information, without clarity on how to process it, can become a source of bewilderment and anxiety. We must realize that the amount of available information is already immense and will continue to grow without end. No one will ever be able to process all the information contained in all the good books, audio recordings, videos, and courses that exist already, plus the ones that are coming out every day. They are all good for our growth, but we must realize that too much of a good thing can be bad. Imagine, for instance, a reckless glutton who overindulges in eating. We shall not allow our insatiable hunger for knowledge -- our desire to know it all -- to drive us crazy.

A sane approach to processing information demands a few guidelines. Here are seven that serve me, and that I submit to your consideration, hoping they can serve you as well:

1 - Choose wisely. Since there is more information available than you will ever be able to process, be selective. Consider that a lot of the life lessons are pretty much the same. Many times, what you think is new is just the same old lesson presented in a different way by the same teacher, or a new one. What you have to do is to ask yourself if what you are learning resonates with you. Does it excite you? Do you feel compelled to share it? Does it produce new insights? Does it produce a spark of creativity? Does it help you move forward in your life? Does it make you better? If so, stick with it. These are all signs that you are receiving what you need at the stage of life you are currently in.

2 - Be aware of change, and release what doesn't serve you anymore. We are constantly evolving. Maybe some beliefs and practices that made a lot of sense in the past, don't resonate with you anymore. That's OK. Let them go.

3 - Don't be judgmental. Don't condemn others. Consider that wherever they are on their journeys it's where they ought to be, and that, eventually, if it is to be so, they will see what you see, as you see it, although this is not really important. Look back and, if it is the case, say to yourself, "I too have been there and done that. I too have, in the past, believed what they believe now. It was good for me then, but it doesn't serve me anymore. I am at a different place now. What I know now, I didn't know then." Accept others wherever they may be, and gently help them to move on to better grounds, if they so desire.

4 - Don't be worried about what you don't know, or you think you don't know. Don't consume yourself trying to know it all. Consider that you know more than enough already, and that what you need to do now is to ponder what you already know and put the advice you have received to good use. Consider that whatever else you need to know will spontaneously come to you.

5 - Be aware of the difference between collecting information and exuding true knowledge. Consider dedicating less time to the frantic collection of information and more time to calmly processing what you already have acquired. Don't satisfy yourself in remaining on the surface and being a mere 'regurgitator' of someone else's ideas. Take time to go deeper. Study, analyze, reflect, internalize the concepts learned, and make that knowledge your own. The widespread availability of good information is a good thing, but information alone, no matter how much of it is available, or how easy it may be to access, will not change our world. Only the diligent daily practice, by each one of us, of what is being taught by the masters will change minds, and this is what will change the world. The world changes when we change. Remember that only actions bring about results. Information alone will not bring about change. Change comes from action, so practice what you have learned.

6 - Follow whoever you want to follow, but be ready to not follow anyone. The true master will tell you, "Don't follow me. Stay with me for as long as you want, but know that the day will come when you will have to leave me, and I will have to leave you. That will be the day when you realize that the guide you have been waiting for has always been

with you since the beginning. The sage is within you. The guru is you. Turn inward and get directions from the master who lives in you, and is you."

7 - Move your focus from the outside to the inside. Stop looking for answers outside and begin finding them inside. Recognize that there is a place of quiet, silence, stillness, and peace that is found beyond the incessant flow of thoughts. Meditate. Go to that place of knowing, to that inexhaustible source of intelligence and creativity that resides beyond the thinking mind. Pay attention. Be alert. Know yourself. Find your own voice and speak your own authentic truth. From all the knowledge and wisdom that already resides within you, allow something new and beautiful to be born. Don't look back. Look forward. Envision the great days that are going to come. Bring out your unique messages to the world. Be of service to others and give your contribution to bring about a better world.

My spiritual teachers have taught me to seek the silence, go within, and ask myself, over and over again, "Who am I?" and "Who am I not?" They guided me to become the silent observer, the witness of the conversations taking place inside my head. They taught me how to slow down my hyperactive mind, and calmly stay in the here-now. Their command is clear: "Know yourself, only to know that there is no self."

I can't deny that the works of great masters have taken me to higher levels of consciousness. Learning from them has been a great blessing, but I have realized that this journey is less about accumulation of information and knowledge, and more about my own intuitive and direct experience of who I am. More important than accumulating information is to continuously and sincerely investigate e explore with a beginner's mind. I have access to unlimited amounts of excellent information that keeps coming my way all the time, without interruption. But over and over again I was taught that the treasure I am seeking is not elsewhere; it is inside my own dwelling all the time. So, at this stage of my life, I am trying to limit my exposure to external stimuli. The external stimulus that I am receptive to is the one that guides me to silently observe the internal chatter inside my hyperactive mind, the one that calms me down, and brings me to rest in the present moment in the peaceful center of my being. I am turning inward and dedicating more of my time to hear, so I may speak with my own voice. If it is the right time for you, then turn inward and find your own voice.

TRY A LITTLE KINDNESS

These texts have been circulating through the Internet for a while. They are so beautiful! They express attitudes and simple actions that if performed often would really change things for the better.

……..

"As the world fights to figure this all out, I'll be holding doors for strangers, letting people cut in front of me in traffic, saying good morning, keeping babies entertained in grocery lines, stopping to talk to someone who is lonely, tipping generously, calling you by the name on your tag, waving at police, sharing food, giving children a thumbs-up, being patient with sales clerks and smiling at passersby as often as I am provided the opportunity, buying a total stranger a cup of coffee. Because? I will not stand idly by and live in a world where unconditional love is invisible. Join me in showing love, judging less. Find your own way to swing the pendulum in the direction of love. Be kind to a stranger today and every day. It just may be a friend you have never met. Pay it forward for any kindness shown to you in the past. Be the change! Be the light! Start today!"

……..

"Our door is always open. Our home is safe. Coffee could be on in minutes, and the kitchen table is a place of peace and non-judgment. Anyone who needs to chat is welcome anytime. It's no good suffering in silence. We have food in the fridge, coffee and tea in the cupboard, and listening ears, or shoulders to cry on. We will always be here. You are always welcome."

……..

I could not find the authors of these two passages above. Naturally, they were written by someone, but my research did not bring about any credible authorship. I would love to know who wrote them, so I can give them the credit they deserve.

……..

A LOVING AND PEACEFUL PRESENCE

"The most precious gift we can offer others in our presence. The most precious gift we can offer anyone is our attention. When mindfulness embraces those we love, they will bloom like flowers." ~ Thich Nhat Hanh

To live lives that uphold the well-being of others is one of the noblest things we can do, and to do it properly we must constantly work on our own selves. Let us cultivate peace and love in the inner garden of our hearts. Let us, intentionally, be presences of love and bringers of peace to all the people we meet and all the places we go. Let us radiate peace, and shower all people with love, knowing, as Meher Baba said, that "love cannot be forced upon anybody, yet it can be awakened in one through love itself." Let us be fully present and give all people our undivided attention. Then we will be the healers that the world needs. Then we will be real blessings to others, and people will naturally gravitate toward us, to grow in love, and to become spreaders of love themselves.

Love brings about love spontaneously. In any environment, the mere presence of a loving person expands the number of individuals who respond with love.

……..

"Love and coercion can never go together. Love has to spring spontaneously from within. It is in no way amenable to any form of inner or outer force and it cannot be forced upon anybody, yet it can be awakened in one through love itself." ~ Meher Baba

……..

BE THE PEACE YOU WANT TO SEE IN THE WORLD

"Fear is the path to the dark side. Fear leads to anger. Anger leads to hate. Hate leads to suffering. Remember, a Jedi's strength flows from the Force. But beware of the dark side. Anger, fear, aggression; the dark side of the Force are they. Once you start down the dark path, forever will it dominate your destiny, consume you it will." ~ Yoda

……..

It is during dark times that dark thoughts and feelings creep up. Beware! Hatred is not overcome by hatred; through love alone is hatred overcome. Do not feed the dark side with more hostility and rage. This only makes it stronger. Beware, because, in the end, it may engulf and consume you completely. Pause, and ask yourself, "What am I thinking? What am I feeling?" And if the thoughts and feelings may strengthen the dark side, don't let them get a hold of you. Try something different. Ask yourself, "How can I dispel these dark thoughts and emotions with love? How can I be a bringer of optimism and peace?" Remember S. T. O. P. -- Stop, take a breath, observe, and only then proceed. Choose wisely, and respond with love. Be the peace you want to see in the world.

....

MY INTENTIONS ARE PURE

"Ill treatment by opponents is a catalyst for your meditation. Insulting reproaches you don't deserve spur your practice onward. Those who do you insult are teachers challenging your attachment and aversion. How could you ever repay their kindness?" ~ Shantideva

....

At the beginning of his years of teaching, Siddhartha Gautama faced a lot of criticism from those who would not agree with what he had to say. Seeing what he was going through, his disciples approached him and asked, "How can you be so calm and peaceful when people find fault in your words and ridicule you?" The Buddha answered with a question: "When someone offers you a gift and you don't accept it, to whom does the gift belong to?"

We have to decide: Shall we accept the gift, or not? The decision is ours. And the right decision will liberate us. As Eleanor Roosevelt said, "No one can make you feel inferior without your consent." I know that I will never get everyone's approval, and that there will always be people who will not agree with me. It's impossible to please everybody. Some will like me, some will not. Seeking total external approval is a sure way to unhappiness. What other people think of me should never be as important as what I think of myself, therefore I make sure to value more how I see myself than the opinions others have of me.

....

"It's none of my business what people say of me and think of me. I am who I am and I do what I do. I expect nothing and accept everything. This makes life so much easier." ~ Anthony Hopkins

....

I must thank those who criticize me. One sincere criticism is more valuable than one hundred praises. It opens up opportunities for reflection and improvement.

I can't expect that everybody will understand and agree with me. I can't expect that everybody will be gentle and kind with me. I can't expect that everybody will love me. That's unrealistic. I can't control how others will interpret what I say and do. All I can control is the purity of my intentions.

Sometimes my delivery is unskillful. Other times I am misunderstood. But negative reactions to my words and deeds do not matter if I am at peace, and able to honestly and calmly say to yourself, "My intentions are pure."

It is not realistic to believe that I have never wounded some people during my lifetime. We all did. We all had those selfish and mindless moments, those unskilled words and actions that some of us, later, came to regret. No one is totally perfect and completely innocent. I accept that I have hurt others, and that some people do not like me.

I knew I had some work to do, so I went to the center of my being, to that place of silence and stillness, and I pondered on what moved and moves me, and I forgave myself, once and for all. I left that weight of guilt and recrimination by the wayside and vowed not to get back to it ever again. I was able to say to myself, "I am here. I am safe. I know who I am. I know the ground where I stand. I have arrived. This is home." And after establishing myself in this safe place, I added, "I know that my intentions are pure. I am at peace. I am firm in my intent to be good, do good, and help other people as much as I can, for as long as I can. I am firm in my intent of not inflicting anyone any harm."

May I be able to have compassion for, and send waves of love to all of those who unjustly criticize, attack, and dislike me. May I be able to forgive all, including myself, for all unwholesome words and actions. May I be able to constantly express great gratitude for all the blessings that have been bestowed upon me.

As a teacher, I try my best to be the guide on the side, not the sage on the stage. I try to be present, sensitive, and flexible, surrendering control, and striving to get my ego out of the way. Yes, I plan my classes, but remain open to change. I am attentive to what is called for in the moment, being at peace if I have to toss away all my well-crafted plans and do something completely different. As my mentor told me, "What comes out of their mouths is gold!" Therefore I trust the intelligence that arises from the group in each moment, and do my best to offer myself as a clean conduit that allows the intelligence of the Universe to flow through making sure that my intentions are and remain pure.

……..

"Be who you are and say what you feel, because those who mind don't matter and those who matter don't mind." ~ Dr. Seuss

……..

THE GENEROSITY OF SHARING ONE'S PAIN

Thank you for sharing your pain
And for taking me to that place I have prohibited myself from visiting
That place where my sadness resides

Thank you for sharing your pain
And for allowing me to shed tears with you
Not only for your suffering, but also for mine

Thank you for letting your pain out
And for revealing a escape route for my own
And for sharing your story, 'cause it's my story too
And for reminding me that, in the end
We are all the same on this never-ending journey of change

Thank you for sharing your pain
And for reminding me that although this being human is not easy
I can find great consolation in knowing that I am not alone
That, in the most silent of all silences, we hold each other in love
And that is enough
That is enough

……..

KNOW THAT YOU ARE LOVED AND LOVE YOURSELF

"Your light is seen, your heart is known, your soul is cherished by more people than you might imagine. If you knew how many others have been touched in wonderful ways by you, you would be astonished. If you knew how many people feel so much for you, you would be shocked. You are far more wonderful than you think you are. Rest with that. Rest easy with that. Breathe again. You are doing fine. More than fine. Better than fine. You're doing' great. So relax. And love yourself today." ~ Neale Donald Walsch

……..

I love you. You have no idea of how much I love you. You have no idea of how many people love you. You have no idea of how much you are loved. You were, are, and always will be immensely loved. My love for you is not conditional. I love you regardless of anything. I love you just the way you are. I want you to be happy. Knowing that you are happy makes me happy. So, stop with all the nonsense, have some self-compassion, and accept the forgiveness and the love that were given to you. Forgive yourself as you already have been completely forgiven. Know that you are loved, and love yourself today.

……..

"And God said 'Love Your Enemy,' and I obeyed him and loved myself." ~ Kahlil Gibran

……..

TODAY

"What day is it?" asked Pooh. "It's today," squeaked Piglet. "My favorite day," said Pooh. ~ A. A. Milne

……..

Back in 1973, I went with some friends on a surfing trip to Peru. One of our stops along the Peruvian coast was Puerto Chicama, a surfing spot in the northern part of the country known for its perfect waves. When we arrived there, we asked if there was a place where we could stay. We were told to go talk to El Hombre (The Man) who rented rooms to traveling surfers. All he had to offer were bare rooms with a cemented floor: no furniture, no beds. It was good enough for us. One of the things that caught our attention was a white wall where travelers from all over the world left messages written with charcoal. It was on that wall that for the first time I got to know this quote: "Today is the first day of the rest of your life. Enjoy it!"

……..

The best days are the ones we live mindfully, paying attention and being amazed by the magic, mystery, and miracles that surround us. The best days are the ones in which, by practicing mindfulness, we see all the riches that the Universe has bestowed upon us, and realize how wealthy we already are.

Today is not just another day. Today is a special day. Today is the first day of our new lives. This is the day that we were given, the only one we have. Yes, we were given days in the past, but we don't have them anymore; they are gone now. And we cannot be sure that we will be given days in the future: it is not guaranteed. So, the only day that we really have is this one here. The only moment that we have is the one we are living right now.

Our lives are successions of present moments, and the only moment we have is this one. We must live mindfully, moment to moment, one present moment at a time, making the most of each one of them.

We have the power to make today different from all other days. Let us choose to make today a remarkable day, by being creative, being bold, taking risks, and doing something new. What are we waiting? Let's say to ourselves, "This is a new day, and I am new, too. This is a new moment, and I am new, too. I am not the same I was a day ago, or even a moment ago. Today is a special day; it is the first day of the rest of my new life."

……..

Yesterday is history. Tomorrow is a mystery. Today is a gift; that's why it's called the present.

……..

REINVENTING OURSELVES

We are presumptuous. We are confident that we know everything that there is to know about ourselves, right? And we are constantly telling everyone, including our own selves, "This is the way I am. This is the way I've always been." We go as far as saying, "It's too late for me to change now." But what about throwing all these certainties away, and assuming a posture of not knowing? What about activating the 'I-don't-know mind' and putting aside the 'I-know-it-all mind?' What about dropping those old labels and those repetitious, sometimes victimizing, self-defeating stories that we keep telling ourselves about ourselves? What about considering for a moment that we are not who we think we are? What about using a beginner's mind, not an expert's mind, letting go of all that we think we know, remaining open to explore with curiosity who we really are and also who we are not, and perhaps, with surprise, discovering ourselves anew?

In the Buddhist tradition it is said that wisdom arises through investigation, and that wisdom is the sword that cuts through delusion. We should strive to develop the ability to investigate ourselves, cut through the veil of delusion, and see ourselves honestly, as we really are. Imagine how investigation could help, for instance, a person who is always grumpy and constantly criticizing. With mindfulness practice she could catch herself in the act, and realize, "Here I am criticizing again! How do I feel right now? Well, I don't feel good. Let me accept this feeling and allow it to be. Let me investigate it deeper. Let me be a good host and treat it as a visitor: 'Hello, Criticism. How are you today? What brought you here? Please, sit down. Let's chat. I would like to get to know you better.' I must remember not to identify myself with this feeling: 'I am not a hypercritic. It's just Criticism that is visiting me.' How do I feel right now? What do I need? I need some compassion and love. I need to nurture myself. What do I get from this criticizing habit? I know that I don't benefit from this constant fault-finding in others, and that I would feel better if I could tame this pattern. Perhaps I can choose to do something different now."

Who you were does not need to define who you are, and who you are does not need to define who you will be. This is a new day. This is a new moment. You are a new you. The you that is here now is not the same who was here yesterday, or even a moment ago.

……..

"The place is here. The time is now. This is a new moment. This is a new me."

……..

You are free. You don't need to keep seeing as you have always seen. You don't have to keep believing as you have always believed. You don't need to keep reacting as you have always reacted. You don't need to keep telling yourself the same anguish-producing stories you have always told. You don't need to live with the same demeaning labels others have given you and that you have mindlessly accepted.

Enough!

If the current habits, labels, identities, self-definitions, and stories you have been retelling do not serve you anymore, abandon them. Drop the unnecessary load you have been carrying and embrace who you are today. Embrace yourself in the present moment with spaciousness, lightness, and freshness. Where you were is not as important as where you are, and where you are heading to. Look with new eyes and see the new in the old; see new possibilities for yourself. If necessary, invent new stories about yourself, stories of victory, and let go of the stories of your wounds. Get new narratives, better ones, ones that enhance your health, well-being, and the overall quality of your life. You are free to do so. You are free to reinvent yourself at any moment. Go ahead and do it. Just do it!

....

Remember:

"An unexamined life is not worth living."

"We must consciously unlearn the falsehoods we have unconsciously learned."

"When we change the way we look at things, the things we look at change."

....

LETTING GO

"I often wonder why we torture ourselves with visions of the past to perpetuate unjustified feelings of inadequacy. It makes no sense at all, as we have nothing to gain from such feelings. Let's move on, and not return to a place of pain; it has weighted us down long enough. Let us allow ourselves to be in the now because it really is the only thing we have. Time to let go of the past." ~ Florencia Clement de Grandprey

....

We should let go of the past. We should let go of all past lives that have played themselves out and do not serve us anymore. Let go of all those many characters we have played in the plays of our lives, but who no longer are who we are now. Who we were does not determine who we are, and who we are does not necessarily determine who we will be.

Our future is not inescapably shaped by our past.

We must let the old die in order to make it possible for the new to be born. We have to lose who we were to find out who we are.

……..

"One always has to know when a stage comes to an end. If we insist on staying longer than the necessary time, we lose the happiness and the meaning of the other stages we have to go through. Closing cycles, shutting doors, ending chapters – whatever name we give it, what matters is to leave in the past the moments of life that have finished… Things pass, and the best we can do is to let them really go away… Let things go. Release them. Detach yourself from them… Before a new chapter is begun, the old one has to be finished: tell yourself that what has passed will never come back... Closing cycles. Not because of pride, incapacity or arrogance, but simply because that no longer fits your life. Shut the door, change the record, clean the house, shake off the dust. Stop being who you were, and change into who you are." ~ Paulo Coelho

……..

It hurts to let go, but sometimes holding on hurts a lot more. It is better to close a chapter and start another than to stay stuck in the past, looking for old lives that do not exist anymore.

……..

WE ARE NOT WHO WE THINK WE ARE

"Let us dedicate ourselves to what the Greeks wrote so many years ago: to tame the savageness of man and make gentle the life of this world." ~ Robert F. Kennedy

……..

My definition of a selfish person is one who lives by the saying, "I do what is convenient for me without regard for the inconvenience I create for others." Do you want an example? Double-parking. Plenty of parking spaces a few feet away, and here's someone double-parked. Another example? Littering. Plenty of garbage cans within walking distance, but here's someone leaving all his trash on the beach.

Now, have you noticed how many times you did what was convenient for you without regard for the inconvenience you created for others? I have. And when I feel tempted to criticize others, and what I consider to be their selfish actions, I pause, look back at my own life, and let the urge go by, saying to myself, "I've been there and I've done that."

Sometimes we do what is convenient for us unconsciously, completely unaware of how what we do affect others, while other times we do it consciously, by choice. But since we live in community, we are called to tame our selfish instincts. We are called to share the world with others. We are called to remind that we are not the owners of this world, and the attitude contained in the saying, "This is my world, and you just happen to live in it. Therefore, I can do whatever I want," does not apply.

Yes, I am convinced that life would be much nicer if people thought more frequently about others, considered how their actions impact the community, and acted thoughtfully in order not to create nuisances.

………

Have you noticed how often we are the main characters of the stories we tell? Have you noticed how often we are the protagonists of the movies that run in the movie theaters of our heads? Well, perhaps it's time to consider that we are not the stories we tell ourselves about ourselves. Perhaps it's time to suspect that we are not those special and remarkable human beings that we believe we are, and that, as matter of fact, we are not superior to anyone else. Perhaps it's time to entertain the possibility that we got it all wrong.

Why don't we pause, put aside our preconceived ideas about ourselves, and do an honest effort to see ourselves as others see us? It's not an easy task for sure, but if we try we may be surprised with the realization that we are not those selfless, generous, and caring persons that we imagine to be. We may come to the realization that, in fact, we are very critical and judgmental, and be surprised by our inability to empathize. It may be a revelation to us how completely oblivious we are of how our egotistical behaviors affect others. The truth is that our self-centeredness makes it extremely hard for us to see how others see us, and realize how what we say and do affects others.

We all have blind spots. We all have shortcomings. We all have acted in selfish ways, unaware of how our behavior made others uncomfortable or, even, how it wounded them. Therefore, developing self-awareness is one of the most important things we can do. Learning to observe ourselves, noticing our thoughts, words, and actions, while developing the ability to put ourselves in someone else's position, is a priceless skill. This self-reflective practice allows us to get to know ourselves and others better, and grow in compassion, kindness, patience, and generosity.

Let us become kinder people and bring about a kinder world. Let us tame our own savageness and bring Heaven to Earth.

………..

We have to be cautious with our views and beliefs. Many times we believe we are better, but other times we believe we are worse than who we actually are. Someone approached the Dalai Lama and asked, "I don't feel worthwhile as a person. How can I work on this?" The Dalai Lama answered, "You should not be discouraged. Your feeling 'I am of no value' is wrong, absolutely wrong. You are deceiving yourself."

How others see you?

I hope we may be able to suspect that we are not who we think we are. I hope we may be able to get a glimpse of how others see us. I hope we may be able to get a better idea of who we really are, and perhaps come to the realization that in the grand scheme of things, we, and all the stories we tell about ourselves, are insignificant.

……..

"We need to forget who we think we are, so we can become who we are." ~ Paulo Coelho

………..

TO FIND THE ONE I LOST

Why did you come here?

I came here to see vapors rising from the lake in these cold mornings. I came here to experience a long, silent, eye-to-eye connection with the young deer before the sun came up.

Why did you come here?

I came here to remind myself of the life I want to live: a mindful life in which I am awake, attentive, alert, aware, appreciative, and joyfully alive. I came here to harness the courage to change and live this new, simpler life, free from all fears, addictions, cravings, and aversions.

Why did you come here?

I came here to immerse myself in the silence, absorb the peace of this place, and feel happy, content, and satisfied.

Tell me: why did you come here, really?

I came here to find the one I lost.

That's why.

That's what I came here for.

………

Usually, at the beginning of our silent retreats, we are asked questions such as, "Why are you here? What do you want to get from this experience?" After the first round of more obvious answers, we are asked again, and again, and again. "What do you really, really, really want?" and as we dig deeper, truer answers emerge.

………

MINDFULNESS AND A LIFE THAT IS WORTH LIVING

WISHING YOU A LIFE OF EASE

The winner is not the one who finishes first, arriving ahead of all others. The winner is the one who pauses and feels the breeze.

……..

This morning, while watching the sunrise at the beach, Reina, my good friend, reflected at the current state of humanity and said, "We are all exhausted, aren't we?" Immediately, as if stricken by a lightning of verity, I effusively agreed, "Yes! Isn't that true? Aren't we all exhausted? Yes, definitely: we are all exhausted indeed!"

When I think about our society and the way we live, I fantasize that we have been hypnotized and conditioned to believe that we are not OK, and that in order to be OK we have to do more, have more, and be more. The voices of our culture are constantly telling us, "You don't have enough. You don't do enough. You aren't good enough." It seems that we are always doing more in order to have more and be more. Our egos are constantly telling us that we are what we have, what we do, and what others think of us. So we engage in this perpetual laboring in order to accumulate possessions and achievements and build up big reputations for ourselves. Think about it: isn't that so? Let's pause for a moment and think: Isn't this mindless pursuit of Positions of Power, in order to retain Prestige that will grant Privileges and Preference, and make the accumulation of Possessions easier -- the Perilous P's, as I call them -- exhausting? And is this chase worth all the sacrifice? Will these things ever bring us enduring happiness? We know the answers, right?

So why do we continue chasing things out there when we already know that all that will bring us lasting satisfaction is already here, with us, around us, within us?

……..

How much is enough?

We have to realize that if we don't change our mindsets we will never be satisfied. If we live our lives mindlessly immersed in the material world, without engaging in a deep investigation of our desires, there will never be enough. No matter how much we may have, it will never be enough. We will constantly feel that we don't have enough money, enough toys, enough appreciation, enough love, and enough fame. So what could be the antidote to this way of life that never grants us peace? The answer: Making what we already have enough.

……..

Socrates said, "Having the fewest wants, I am nearest to the gods." If we believe that the peace we experience from being content is the highest expression of affluence, then we will conclude that the richest men are not those who have the most, but those who want and need the least.

Rest is the title I gave to the first chapter of Peaceful Ways, a book I wrote in 2014. It opens with this quote of Jesus: "Come to me all of you who are exhausted, and I will give you rest." In that chapter, I urge the readers to exercise self-compassion, be gentle and kind with themselves, and give themselves permission to do nothing, just rest. The questions that arise are:

- Is it possible, in this society of ours, to do less, or remain idle doing nothing at all, and not feel guilty for not being constantly active and productive? and,

- Is it possible that by doing less we may end up having more of the things that are truly satisfying and therefore be happier?

It is stated in the Tao-te-Ching that the Great Tao – the Universal Life Force Energy -- does nothing and yet leaves nothing undone. What about considering, and perhaps coming to the realization that actually we are not doing anything; we are just being done? What about, perhaps just for today, taking time off and giving ourselves the gift of rest? What about simply living with ease, flowing with the natural flow of life, calmly accepting whatever may come, enjoying what is pleasant without clinging, and being with the unpleasant without aversion? What about, perhaps just for today, letting the Universe fight our battles for us? What about taking time in silence, stillness, solitude, and seclusion to look at ourselves, express gratitude, and just be? Enough is the magic word. Enough. We do enough. We have enough. We are enough. We have nothing else to do and nowhere else to go. We have arrived already. We are here. And we can rest now.

…….

"I would like to pass on one little bit of advice I give to everyone. Relax. Just relax. Be nice to each other. As you go through your life, simply be kind to people. Try to help them rather than hurt them. Try to get along with them rather than fall out with them. With that, I leave you, and with all my very best wishes." ~ Nyoshul Khenpo Rinpoche

…….

THE MISLEADING DRIVE TO HAVE MORE

"I had everything a man could want. I was a millionaire. I had beautiful women in my life. I had cars, a house, an incredible, solid-gold career, and a future, and yet, on a daily basis, I wanted to commit suicide." ~ Eric Clapton

"As a Beatle, we made it. And there was nothing to do. We had money, we had fame, and there was no joy." ~ John Lennon

…….

We are told to strive, work hard, compete, struggle, sacrifice ourselves, and make every effort to produce results and be successful in the eyes of the world. We are told to achieve great goals, and to leave our mark. We are told that material success will make us happy. We are, then, seduced by the sirens of fame and fortune. We want to be remembered. We want, in some way, to be immortal. We want power and prestige, and we envy those who have them. We rationalize that the reason for our lack of happiness is because we haven't been able to become rich and famous yet.

But what about those who are rich and famous, and whose success did not make them happier as they were promised it would? How do they feel? Don't they feel disappointed and deceived? The idea that fame, fortune, and material success automatically bring about happiness, is a myth, and it is about time we unmask this deception, and stop, once and for all, propagating this illusion.

Success, fame, and wealth may be good things, but they do not automatically bring about happiness. We will never find happiness in those things alone. They are neutral to happiness, neither good, nor bad. Both rich and poor individuals may be happy, or not. Wealth and poverty are external conditions, but happiness in an internal one; it comes from the inside. It comes from being content, from living a fulfilling and contributing life, and from feeling loved.

The way to be happy is to be satisfied and grateful, but unfortunately we live in an environment that keeps telling us that we cannot settle, that we must have more, do more, and be more. The culture we are immersed in is constantly creating desires, convincing us that we need things. It creates in us a state of imbalance, of lack of satisfaction, of discontentment. It tells us that we are not enough, that we need to acquire more, do more, in order to be more.

We begin to get closer to peace when we go inside ourselves and inquire, "Who am I? What am I doing here? What was I brought here to do? What do I love? What makes me come alive? What gifts do I bring to share with others? How can I alleviate someone else's suffering? How shall I live, knowing that I will die?" We enhance our happiness when we start living more mindfully.

So sit still and listen to your inner voice. Be true to yourself, and do what makes you come alive. Renounce senseless competition and choose to work to enhance the wellbeing of all.

……...

"I don't believe we are these miserable animals wired to maximize self-interest. I think that actually goes against our nature and causes us a lot of pain."~ Josh Radnor

"It is an insane philosophy: 'gotta keep everybody separated, gotta compete against each other, whoever is the winner gets the toys and the spoils...' I believe we are in a culture that is depressing our authenticity, our creativity, it's putting us against each other, and it's up to us to give birth to a new culture." ~ Tom Shadyak

……..

We blame society, but we are society.

……...

What follows is a conversation between George Harrison and Olivia, his wife, as she remembers it:

Olivia - "They want to give you this award."
George - "I don't want it. I am not going."
Olivia - "You should go. It's a nice thing they are doing."
George - "If you want it, you go. I won't. I don't do this anymore."
Olivia (commenting on the conversation) – "He wanted to be in the garden, making it more beautiful. He wanted to use his time to meditate. He wasn't into collecting awards for his obituary."

Differently from the majority of people, George had experienced immense earthly success already at a young age with the Beatles, and he realized that fame and fortune didn't make him happy. He said, "I got fame and fortune, and I saw that it wasn't it."

……...

The monk does not need new clothes to wear, or new pots to cook. He wears his old robe and cooks in his old pot, and he is just fine.

……...

LIVING IN THE MATERIAL WORLD

"I'm living in the material world. I can't say what I'm doing here, but I hope to see much clearer, after living in the material world." ~ George Harrison

…….

What are we doing here, on this planet? Why is everybody running around so frantically? What is success, real success? It seems that we are all very busy, but not with the right things. It seems that we all are like that guy that Bob Dylan once sang about, of whom he said, "he is not busy being born, he is busy dying." It would be a wise thing to pause and meditate.

We should knock, and perhaps the door will open to reveal that the peace and happiness we so desperately seek is within us. Perhaps we will get to know the essence beyond all intellectual concepts, and find the vital sap beyond the barrage of illusions and misleading mental formations. Perhaps we will be able to free ourselves from this intellectual trap, and experience that there is no beginning and no end, that nothing is permanent, and that transformation is all that there is. Perhaps we will be able to liberate ourselves from all desires, realizing that since all is impermanent, it makes no sense to suffer by craving what is pleasant and averting what is unpleasant. Perhaps we will be able to welcome all guests, and treat them all as a good host, all of them: the good and the bad, the gain and the loss, the success and the failure, the happiness and the sadness, the birth and the death.

We give ourselves too much importance. It would be good if we constantly reminded ourselves that everything is impermanent, and that, sooner or later, we will return from wherever we came from. Every now and then, we should look at our belly buttons, see ourselves as mere fruits, and humble ourselves.

Maybe, the most important thing to learn during our lives is to learn how to die. I heard teachers saying that, "If we learn to die before we die, then, when we die, we don't die." The wisest thing we can do is to prepare ourselves for the moment of physical death, and in order for that transition to be peaceful, we have to be ready to let go of all the earthly things, all belongings, all fame, all fortune. We have to let go even of the desire to leave our mark on this physical world. And while alive, all we have to do is to live mindfully, making the best of every present moment, while constantly reminding ourselves that although in the physical dimension we are impermanent, in the mysterious one we are eternal.

....

TIME TO REST

Today is a good day to love ourselves. Today is a good day to rejoice with whom we are. There's no need to prove anything. There's no need to compete, excel, or win. There's no need to rush, finish first, or defeat anyone. Actually, the one who wins today is the one who takes more time to look around and spot miracles. Therefore, let's move slowly, savoring the beauty, and enjoying this day that was given to us. Nothing is required of us today, except for us to be content and happy with whom we are.

Let's not compare ourselves with others. Let's not put ourselves down, or feel unworthy. Again, there's no need to compete, or prove anything. Let us realize that we are wonderful just the way we are. We are children of the Universe, wonderful creations, worth of much love. Let us internalize the knowing that we are loved.

....

INNOCENCE AND REST

See yourself as a little, innocent child, and find refuge in loving arms. Rest. Rest without worries or fear.

Do not demand so much of yourself. Do not judge yourself so harshly. Let go of your ideas of good and bad.

Rediscover the beauty that surrounds you in this moment, and live in awe, grateful for everything.

Trust that everything is unfolding as it should, and that all will be fine.

Ask for the desires of the Universe to be your desires. Allow yourself to be used, and trust that you are being used for mighty purposes in mighty ways.

Be generous.

Know that you are loved.

....

FREE THE CHILD

Liberate the little kid in you, and give this child permission to play, have fun, and enjoy life. Jump up and down, ride a bike, catch a wave, play an instrument, swim, run, dance, draw, paint, do whatever makes you happy, and no matter what you do, do it with a smile on your face, always. And if you can't do those things you enjoy perfectly, do them imperfectly; just do them anyway.

Watch the sunrise, the sunset, or a blade of grass dancing with the breeze. Look up to see the clouds in the sky, and then look down to see their reflections on the pond. Let yourself be showered by the beauty of this world. Let yourself be transported by the magic, mystery, and miracles of this life. Notice the impermanence of everything, and give yourself permission to do nothing, just rest and relax. And every now and then, without caring the least about what others may think, give free rein to your basic instincts, free the child in you, and allow yourself to howl like a wolf, wildly and carefree, at the splendors of the Universe. Be content, satisfied, and grateful for this life. Be optimistic and hopeful. Be gentle with yourself. Be happy. And shower others with all this good that is in you.

....

MY LIFE IS MY MASTERPIECE

"My happiness grows in direct proportion to my acceptance, and in inverse proportion to my expectations." ~ Michael J. Fox

....

A perfect state of peace is attained when we are content and satisfied, not wanting anything. We accept with serenity everything that happens to us and that we cannot change, rejoice with the life that was given to us, and make the best out of it at every moment, being grateful for everything we have, everything we do, and everything we are.

Whenever our thoughts take us back to revisit the errors of the past, with feelings of remorse and regret, we mentally pardon ourselves and others. We say to ourselves, "Whatever happened in the past is in the past, and there is where I will leave it. Now it's time to move on, and that's exactly what I have decided to do: I am moving on to a better future."

And whenever we catch ourselves in a state of fear, afraid that something bad may happen to us, or to the ones we love, we acknowledge that object of fear, and after taking a calm and deep look at it, we, softly, let it go.

We realize the worrying is pointless. If we have a problem that can be fixed, then there is no use in worrying. And if we are dealing with a problem that cannot be fixed, then there is no use in worrying. Worrying is pointless.

With practice we curb rumination and anticipation, reaching a state where we have no regrets, no worries, no fear. We let go of the things that happened, as well as of those that perhaps will never take place, and practice to return our attention to the present moment where we find joy in the simplest things. We bring to mind the saying, "Whatever happened in the past, when it happened, actually happened in the present moment. And whatever will happen in the future, when it happens, will also happen in the present moment. The present moment is the most important moment because it is when we make the choices that affect the quality of our lives."

We avoid the struggle of trying to cling to what we want and of trying to push away what we don't want. We accept everything that comes our way with equanimity, and by doing so we become happier. When we don't struggle against what is, we experience peace.

……..

"I have learned to offer no resistance to what is; I have learned to allow the present moment to be and to accept the impermanent nature of all things and conditions. Thus have I found peace." ~ Eckhart Tolle

……..

We calmly work, doing the job that the Universe calls us to do, doing one task at a time, while having complete trust in a wonderful outcome. We say to ourselves, "Everything is OK." And if we feel it is not, we remember ourselves that "In the end, everything will be OK. And if it is not OK, it is not the end." In doing so, over and over again, our lives become our works of art, our masterpieces.

……..

"I like to think of myself as an artist, and my life is my greatest work of art. Every moment is a moment of creation, and each moment of creation contains infinite possibilities." ~ Shakti Gawain

……..

If you don't believe in miracles, perhaps it's because you've forgotten that you are one.

……..

WE ARE HERE TO LEARN

I like to think that Planet Earth is a learning campus and that we are here to learn. I keep thinking that if life is a course we are taking, it really doesn't matter what happens to us, be it good or bad. Since every occurrence is a new lesson, we should welcome all of them as opportunities to learn. What happens to us matters less than how we respond. What really matters is our ability to learn from all experiences, so we may be able to choose better responses to whatever may happen next.

....

THE WAY OUT OF SUFFERING

"To revere all of life, to live with natural sincerity, to practice gentleness, and to be in service to others is to replicate the energy field from which we originated." ~ Wayne Dyer

....

In order to alleviate suffering, the first thing we have to do is to cultivate the aspiration to know reality as it is. A lot of the suffering we experience comes from wrong perceptions, from not seeing things as they really are, and from not realizing how the constant push and pull of desires unsettle our balance. In order to see clearly, we need to develop the ability to pay focused attention and sharpen our noticing skills. We need to examine life and do our best to consciously unlearn the unwholesome notions that we may have unconsciously learned. We need to remove those distorting lenses that impair clear vision, such as wrong ideas and beliefs. We have to ponder not only on the question, "Who am I?" but also on the question "Who am I not?" We should welcome a healthy dose of doubt in our lives, and consider that perhaps we are not who we think we are, and that the many stories about ourselves we have created do not match reality. Perhaps it's time to take a good look at ourselves and realize that we are holding a series of distorted and unrealistic views about ourselves, about others, and about life.

We need to be careful with what we think, say, and do, because unwholesome thoughts, words, and actions create suffering. We must accept without hesitation that restraint, simplicity, and frugality, combined with selflessness, compassion, and a steadfast determination to do no harm, unequivocally eases suffering in the world. It is by curbing reactivity and expanding the time between receiving a stimulus and choosing a response -- which is put into practice by making unhurried and thorough assessments of the situations, applying wise discernment, and choosing the most appropriate responses -- that we trim misery down. It is by remaining awake, alert, attentive, aware, and appreciative of life in the present moment that we reduce anguish. It is through mindful living that we diminish agony and tribulation in the world. In a nutshell, conscious living is the way out of suffering.

………

NON-ATTACHMENT

No death, no change. No death, no transformation. No death, no birth. No death, no life.

………

I am known to be an upbeat and optimistic person, to such a point that some friends affectionately nicknamed me 'Mr. Happy.' But even in those moments when everything is well and I am cruising through life worry-free, I still feel the presence of melancholy in the background. I keep coming back to that underlying sensation of sadness in my life. And then I ask myself, "Why do I feel this way?" As I ponder, I come to the conclusion that I feel sad because who and what I love -- the people, the things, and the situations -- will, eventually and inevitably, be taken away from me, including my own physical existence with all its joyful moments.

It's not difficult for me to realize that my sadness derives from my cravings and attachments. I can see how my desires for people and things to be a certain way are sources of suffering. When they are not the way I want them to be, I suffer. And when they are, by getting attached to them and not wanting them to change, I set myself up to endure pain because change they will. I can see how delusional is the idea that I can create a perfect life for myself, a life situation that once attained would remain unchanged, fulfilling my needs and desires for the rest of my life. I can see the suffering I bring upon myself by my futile attempts to create permanence in a universe where everything by nature is impermanent. It's clear to me that the constant transformation of everyone and everything will never allow me to experience complete and lasting satisfaction in my lifetime. I can accept that an undercurrent of dissatisfaction will always be present, even when things are going well. I feel that all situations, no matter how good, cannot bring me complete contentment and peace. Even when things are good there is a knowing that things are not going to stay that way. I live with a sense of discomfort, an ever-present feeling that things are not quite right.

Unsatisfactoriness is ubiquitous. I understand that everything changes and nothing stays the same, and that the attempts to make permanent what is impermanent always fail and only bring about more suffering. I get that. And when I realize that this is a condition that affects everyone, I feel deep sympathy and compassion for all humanity. I guess that I am attached to life and wish not to die. Therefore, the greatest training to alleviate afflictions and agonies is the training I can undertake to reduce desires and learn to die before I die. My moment-to-moment practice must be one of letting go of attachments to everyone and everything, while, at the same time, loving everyone and everything. Oh, these paradoxes!

I know that in the physical realm everything is transient: nothing lasts forever. I can see manifestations of birth, growth, decay, and death all around me, all the time. Through observation and reflection I can easily come to an understanding that I don't own anything permanently, that in a way everything and everyone was lent to me for my temporary enjoyment, my body and my life included. In order to placate this disturbing sensation of lack and insufficiency, I cultivate a sense of enoughness, saying to myself, "I do enough. I have enough. I am enough. These accumulated lifetime experiences are enough. These relationships are enough. This knowledge is enough. This wisdom is enough. This life is enough." So, the training for not falling in states of despair and depression is one of coming back to this present moment, of appreciating this present moment, of giving thanks for this present moment, of feeling content and satisfied, over, and over, and over again, while calmly accepting the impermanence of everything in this inescapable cycle of perennial transformation. I see it. I know it. Now, what's left, is to do it. Just do it!

....

"In a truly loving relationship—which I have experienced—rather than drawing the one I love to me I give myself to him. Not merely do I prefer to do him good than to have him do good to me, I would even prefer that he did good to himself rather than to me: it is when he does good to himself that he does most good to me. If his absence is either pleasant or useful to him, then it delights me far more than his presence." ~ Montaigne

....

WISE ACCEPTANCE

Acceptance is an essential quality for living mindfully, and one that we cultivate during the practice of mindfulness. But acceptance is often misunderstood, so it's good to clarify what acceptance isn't, and what it is. Acceptance is not passive resignation. Acceptance is an active process that begins with a calm welcoming of what is followed by honest assessment and discernment, which puts in place the foundation for wise action.

Stress comes from not accepting things as they are. But not accepting and rebelling against what is insanity, because things are what they are. That's the reality that needs to be confronted and dealt with. We may not like the way things are, and wanting them to be different, and taking action to change them is perfectly understandable. But the acceptance we cultivate in mindfulness is the one that allows us to clearly see what is, guides us to not waste energy in fruitless protest, and leads us to choose the wisest courses of action.

Joseph Goldstein, the great mindfulness teacher, tells the story of dealing with a recurring fear. Being trained in mindfulness, rather than giving in to the instinct of pushing his fear away, hiding from, or running away from it, he practiced getting closer to it, looking at it, and investigating it with curiosity, which, most of the time, made its intensity subside. According to him, this went on for many years until the day when he had an epiphany and understood that he was using the technique of befriending the fear with the hope for it to go away forever. With this realization came an insight, a moment when he was able to say to himself, "Even if this fear stays with me to the end of my days, that will be OK." And that was the moment of total acceptance, when his relationship with fear changed, the load became lighter, and he felt that the fear released the powerful grip it had on him. He realized that until that moment he had been watching the fear in order for it to go away, but now he could accept that perhaps the fear would never go away, and even that would be OK. He understood that his resistance to accept, and his struggle against the unwanted were making things worse, not better. He was able to frame this event not as resignation, but as acceptance, and he continued doing what was necessary to get better, but now in a much calmer and less afflicted way.

I guess that this is what we are called to do: to practice equanimity, wise understanding, and serene acceptance of what we dislike, what is uncomfortable, what is annoying, what we would like to be different but are unable to change. We are called to accept our lives, and the uncertainty, the anxiety, the fear, and the pain that comes with being human. We are called to accept everything and everyone, even the most difficult people. We are called to ponder on the fact that everything that arises also passes away, that no one is exempt from death, and that we will die too.

Acceptance begins with wise assessment, with seeing things clearly, beyond the veil of delusion. We must start where we are. We should wisely choose what we are going to give our attention to, and where we will put effort. It is also important to constantly evaluate the quality of our effort, remembering that the right effort is gentle, calm, joyful, pleasurable, and light, while the wrong effort is hard and hurtful.

In a nutshell, acceptance is not resignation, but is a process of transformation that involves:

- accepting the situation
- not wasting energy futilely fighting what is
- remembering that everything that arises also passes away
- bringing to mind that what we resist, persists
- choosing to take time to make a wise assessment of the situation
- seeing clearly, beyond the veil of delusion
- knowing where we are, and starting the process of change from where we are
- using wise discernment, sorting what we can from what we cannot change, and what we will get involved with, and what not
- responding wisely rather than reacting impulsively
- choosing wise action, remembering the verses of the Serenity Prayer: "Give me the serenity to accept the things I cannot change, the courage to change the things I can, and the wisdom to know the difference."

....

"… the curious paradox is that when I accept myself just as I am, then I change." ~ Carl Rogers

....

ACCEPTING REALITY AND ALLEVIATING SUFFERING

Let's be clear: it is perfectly valid to desire things to be different than they are, but the first step to change anything is to accept what is. The famous quote of Carl Rogers, the humanistic psychologist, speaks volumes about this. He wrote, "The curious paradox is that when I accept myself just as I am, then I can change." All of us experience suffering, but what generates it? A big part of the suffering we experience comes from not accepting reality as it is and desiring it to be what it is not. We suffer when people, things, and events are not as we wish them to be, but we have to understand that we will also suffer when people, things, and events are exactly as we want them to be because sooner or later a change is going to come and they will no longer be as they are. Change is unavoidable, and our clinging to impermanent states and things -- our desire for conditions and circumstances not to change -- is a sure cause of suffering.

Not only we suffer, but we continue to suffer because we wrongly believe that the way to placate our suffering is to seek pleasure. So we engage again in craving and clinging, and we end up trapped in this vicious circle, spending our lives chasing people, things, events, and situations that, we imagine, will fill that void inside ourselves. But no pleasure, no accomplishment, no person, no thing, no event, nor any situation is capable of producing lasting satisfaction. If we could reduce the craving for what we want, and the aversion directed at what we don't want, we surely would suffer a lot less. We would not spend so much time judging and saying to ourselves, "I approve this. I disapprove that. I like this. I don't like that. I want this. I don't want that." We would not try to hold on so tightly to the wanted, nor engage in vain attempts of trying to push the unwanted away. We would accept reality as it presents itself, and not waste energy futilely fighting it. We would be at peace with the inexorable and perpetual change. In this aspect, mindfulness practice is extremely helpful because it is the practice that develops in us the ability to be aware and not cling.

Once and for all, we need to internalize the idea that the beginning of the process of liberation from suffering is to make a wise assessment of reality and say to ourselves, "This is what is, and from here I will use wise discernment to choose the best courses of action. I will remain aware of ceaseless change and I will not cling, remembering that nothing whatsoever should be clung to as I, me, or mine."

"Whenever you experience any pain or difficulty, always remember one of the deep meanings of the word suffering: asking the world for something it can never give you. We expect and ask impossible things from the world. We ask for the perfect home and job and that all the things we work hard to build and arrange run perfectly at the right time and place. Of course, that is asking for something that can never be given. We ask for profound meditation and enlightenment, right here and now. But that's not the way this universe works. If you ask for something that the world can't supply, you should understand that you're asking for suffering." ~ Ajahn Brahm

....

A CLOUDED MIND

Thick clouds do not allow us to see the vast sky. So it is with some mental states such as anxiety, fear, anger, jealousy, envy, desire, and depression: they act like clouds in the mind. Not only they limit -- and even at times totally obstruct our views -- but they also bring about unwholesome words and actions, which engender negative consequences in our lives and the lives of others. The three roots of all defilements, and the causes of the majority of human suffering, are attachment, aversion, and ignorance. Attachment is experienced as desire, greed, covetousness, and craving, which bring about the vain attempts to hold on, cling, and grasp a reality that is always changing. Aversion brings with it anger, hatred, ill-will, and even cruelty. Finally ignorance, or delusion, produces wrong perceptions that destabilize the peace of mind and result in hurtful actions. Mindfulness practice allows us to notice the disturbances created by our attachments, aversions, and ignorance. Diligent observation allows us to realize how much of our life energy is spent trying to reel in what we want and push away what we don't want, while ignoring that it's impossible to get all we want to the total exclusion of what we don't want. It becomes clear to us how much this pulling and pushing throw us out of balance. But once we acknowledge the presence of greed in our lives, its power over us subsides, and then renunciation, relinquishing, and generosity are revealed. And once we acknowledge our aversions, resistance subsides and a calm acceptance -- not resignation -- settles in. So, the suggestion for increasing the quality of life is to notice the pulling and pushing forces at work, while investigating and getting clear about our attachments, aversions, and ignorance.

LOOKING DEEPLY AND LETTING GO

"So, this entire week I'm practicing letting go. Letting go of many things: letting go of feelings that don't serve me, of people who want my time and attention but aren't willing to give me theirs, of judgment because it's not my job, of impatience because everything happens when it is supposed to, of the past because I'm here now, of worry because despite what I'd like to think, I don't have control on pretty much anything, and a biggie for me, letting go of outcomes. I'm really trying not to be attached to the outcome. I have to trust that the outcome will be perfect however it may look. I must focus on the now and not on what might be in the future, mainly, because I must be willing to accept failure and not only success. Maybe if I'm not attached to the outcome, I can just enjoy the process, kind of like baking a cake and having a blast while making it even if it might come out looking completely different from the pretty picture in the recipe book. So, will you join me in my practice this week? What will you be letting go of?" ~ Florencia Clement de Grandprey

…….

"My beautiful friend Florencia Clement de Grandprey reminds me, in her wisdom, that the full moon is a great time for letting go. I will practice letting go of judgment, for it is not mine to make, letting go of control, for it only ruins the fun and enjoyment of the present, letting go of attachments, for they only lead to suffering, particularly letting go of attachment to outcomes and attachment to my story, for the process is perfect and bliss is in releasing into the dance of life and flowing with whatever presents... Allowing you to be reinventing with every breath. Letting go of situations that no longer serve my joy. What would you let go of?" ~ Millie Pochet

…….

I agree with Socrates who said that "an unexamined life is not worth living." I believe that it's our duty to examine life and consciously unlearn the unwholesome notions that we have unconsciously learned. "The less you know, the more you believe," is a saying that points to the fact that many of us hold on to unwholesome beliefs that most likely we absorbed during that time in our lives when we hadn't yet developed the ability of critical analysis. It is unfortunate that many of us, even after reaching adulthood, still choose, perhaps out of fear, not only not to analyze our beliefs in order to put their veracity to test, but also not to explore points of view and beliefs from other people. It is clear that this tendency to close ourselves up to other ideas, this stubborn determination to ignore other perspectives, and this unwillingness to change, even when evidence of the inaccuracy of our positions is presented, brings about suffering not only for others, but also for our own selves. This realization alone should be enough to encourage us to look deeply and honestly within ourselves in order to let go of those beliefs that do not contribute to the betterment of life.

Enter mindfulness!

Mindfulness is a practice aimed at alleviating and eventually eliminating suffering. It takes us to a place of deep observation of the present moment and invites us to explore. It removes the fog of delusion and allows us to see clearly. It connects us with what is real and true and liberates us from our old and inaccurate beliefs. It develops in us the humility to recognize and calmly accept that we have been holding on to suffering-creating views. It shows us a universe of possibilities and empowers us to let go of what does not serve us anymore. It gives us freedom to change and in doing so, improve not only our own lives, but other people's lives as well.

. . . .

I believe that an unexamined life is not worth living, and I get great joy from the intellectual exercise of understanding ideas and making connections. It helps me to see differently, and I see value in this exercise. I see that I am changing, and I like the change. I see that the new ideas allow me to see and understand differently. They liberate me, and I like that.

I can see that we are the ones attaching meanings and labeling the occurrences as good or bad, right or wrong. We are the ones creating stories based on what happens to us. What if we stopped labeling and classifying? What if we stopped creating stories? What if we simply watched what happens and accepted what is? Wouldn't, then, everything be just what it is?

. . . .

MINDFULNESS AND SEEING CLEARLY

THE OVERCOAT

I think. I have memories. I have desires. I exist. Well, I believe I exist. But who am I? What exactly is this "I?" I think I know who I am, but the "I" that I am is certainly more than my body -- or the many bodies I've been in. It has to be so because although the "I" is the same, the body keeps changing. As I look back at my life and think about it, my "I" has inhabited many bodies: the body of a newborn, a toddler, a child, a teenager, a young adult, and of this old man now. I ask myself, "Where are the bodies that I once occupied?" They don't exist anymore. But I am still here. The feeling of "I" persists without those physical bodies.

I have recently learned that there isn't a single cell in my body right now that was there seven years ago. I am dying all the time. Looking from another angle, I realize that while some cells are dying, other cells are being born. We are not only dying; we are also being born again and again. Both processes are taking place at the same time: death and birth. I keep dying and being born again.

Thinking about my final physical death, within this framework, I realize that death is not such a big deal: it is just one more death in the stream of deaths. I believe that the "I" that has persisted without the bodies it has once occupied, will still persist even without the physical body I may be 'wearing' at the time of my final death. As my friend Bob once told me, "My body is just an overcoat. That's all it is. When I got it, it was new and beautiful. The fabric was immaculate and soft. As years went by, it started to show some wear-and-tear. It got dirty, and with time it came to a point where I wasn't able to wash the stains off anymore. The fabric lost its glow, and I couldn't get rid of the wrinkles. Some holes started to show up. The overcoat lost some buttons, and I just went on wearing it without them. It will reach a point where it will be beyond repair. And then the time will come when I will have to throw the overcoat away because I will not be able to wear it anymore."

……..

All the things I think I am, and I say I am, are so impermanent that I can't claim them as being myself.

……..

A lot of the pain and suffering we experience in life is due to our over-identification with self. But we have to come to the understanding that the "I" is just a construct of our minds, a concept that we have created, and that, as the Buddha has warned us, "nothing is to be clung to as I, me, or mine."

My friend Leslie, who had a near-death experience, tells that when she left her physical body she experienced an exuberant feeling of freedom. She tells that "the feeling of freedom was combined with a deeper feeling of peace than I have ever known before or since. I was surrounded by love in the form of light. And I was in my true home." She explains that in that moment she felt expansive, light, free, and realized how dense, heavy, and constricting the body was. Dying was, for her, a liberating and joyful experience. It was like removing a heavy overcoat. She says that although not comparable in magnitude, dying produces a feeling somewhat similar to taking off every single piece of clothing that may be bothering and constricting us after a long day of hard work, and going skinny dipping. It is a liberating and joyful feeling! She affirms that there's no need to be afraid of death.

……..

THE UNCHANGEABLE

Who am I? I am not my body. My body keeps changing, but I remain. I am not what I do. What I do keep changing, but I remain. I am not what I have. My possessions keep changing, but I remain. I am not the many characters I have played in the theater of life. My roles keep changing, but I remain. I am not the many professional positions I have occupied, the labels people have used to identify me, the tribes I belong to, or the story others choose to tell about me. My occupations, identities, tribes, and what others say about me keep changing, but I remain. I am not what I have accumulated. I am not the power I may have, the position I may occupy, the prestige I may command, or the privileged treatment I may receive. I am not whatever I am attached to or has been attached to me. Everything is impermanent and keeps changing, but I remain. Take everything away from me -- every single thing, including this physical life -- and still, I will remain.

Who am I, then, if I am not my body, if I am not what I do, and what I have? I am the one who does not change. And who, then, is this unchangeable I? I am an eternal spiritual being having a temporary human experience.

I am the one who sees the truth beyond the illusions that deceive and enslave, and the truth has set me free.

....

WHO AM I WHEN I AM NOT?

Who am I when I am not playing the character I have created?
Who am I when I am not imitating, impersonating, pretending?
Who am I when I am not trying to please or impress?
Who am I when I am not obsessing with what to say and the right words to use?
Who am I when I not striving to be perfect, wanting to be someone I am not?
Who am I when I am not thinking about what I like and dislike, what I approve and disapprove what I want and don't want?
Who am I when I am not wanting life to match my expectations, wishing the world and people in it to be as I would like them to be?
Who am I when I am not lost in pleasant fantasies, or scary dramas?
Who am I when I am not plotting how to satisfy my cravings?
Who am I when I am neither the one who is being observed, nor the one who observes?
Who am I when I am not who I think I am?
Who am I and who am I not?
What remains after all that I think I am is gone?

....

The genesis of this poem: Saki Santorelli, one of the instructors of the mindfulness retreat I am attending recited David Whyte's "Enough," a poem that I love very much, and that has been a companion in my life for many years now. He said, "David wrote this poem during a silent retreat when he was instructed, just as you were, not to write." After a pause, Saki added, "Well, I guess that, actually, he was not writing; he was listening." Well, I, too, listened to the words I've written in the middle of the silence. What emerged and became evident during these days of silence was not so much who I am, but much more who I am not. So, it made me ponder: "Who am I when I am not who I think I am?" At the end of the retreat, Saki mentioned that he was pondering on that question, and it made me think how we affect each other's lives in unexpected ways. 6/15/2016 – Omega Institute, Rhinebeck, NY.

....

UNAWARE OF THE IMPERISHABLE LIGHT

If you are familiar with The Four Agreements, a popular book by Don Miguel Ruiz, you will remember, "Don't take anything personally."

I am called to remember that even though I have been conditioned to think in terms of 'I,' the truth is that nothing is about me. As much as I am conditioned to think this way, I am not the center of the Universe, and therefore I should not give myself too much importance, or credence, or take anything personally because there is no 'I.'

The same is true for you: it's not about you. You are not the center of the Universe, so don't give yourself too much importance, and don't take anything personally because there is no 'You.'

But why do we give ourselves so much importance?

We came to explain this sense of separation that we experience through this thing that we call the 'Ego.' The ego makes us believe that we are separated from and in competition with others.

According to the Buddha, we will all experience the following eight worldly vicissitudes throughout our lives:

- Gain and Loss
- Praise and Blame
- Pleasure and Pain
- Fame and Disrepute.

Trying to cling to gain, praise, pleasure, and fame, while thinking that we can shield ourselves from experiencing loss, blame, pain, and disrepute is illogical and impossible.

The ego craves praise and recognition. It wants to win, feel superior. Well, the ego is not a good adviser. Listening to the ego and its demands is a sure source of suffering, because the ego leads us to what is unwise and unwholesome. The ego is the one who takes things personally, gets offended, and feels the need to retaliate. The ego seeks revenge and instructs us to inflict pain on someone else. The ego mistakenly believes that if we wiped out our enemies everything would be fine. The ego wrongly believes that violent means can bring about the peace we so desperately seek. The ego is the one who believes that the way to get rid of our pain is to seek pleasure, although pleasure has proven time and again to be ephemeral and never to bring about lasting happiness.

....

CLEAR COMPREHENSION

There's an urban legend of five monkeys that, as the story goes, were put inside a cage by a group of scientists. In the middle of the cage the scientists placed a ladder with bananas on its top. Naturally, when the monkeys saw the bananas they started to climb the ladder, but every time a monkey went up the ladder, the scientists soaked the other monkeys with very cold water. After a while, every time a monkey started to climb the ladder, the other monkeys pulled it down and beat it up. After some time, no monkey would attempt to climb the ladder, no matter how great the desire. The scientists then decided to take one of the monkeys out of the cage and put a new monkey inside. The first thing this new monkey did, after seeing the bananas, was to climb the ladder. Immediately, the other monkeys pulled it down and beat it up. After several beatings, the new monkey learned never to go up the ladder, even though there was no evident reason not to do so, except for the beatings. A second monkey was replaced and the same occurred. All monkeys took part in the beating of the newcomer. Soon, another of the old monkeys was replaced by a new monkey, and the same thing happened all over again. Then the fourth and the fifth old monkeys were replaced by new monkeys, leaving a group of five monkeys that without ever having received a cold shower continued to beat up any monkey who dared to climb the ladder. Now, if we could ask the monkeys why they beat up those who attempted to climb the ladder, probably their answer would be "I don't know. It's just how things are done around here."

Our beliefs really limit what we apprehend with our senses. Some scientific experiments showed that people who believe something not to be possible, will not be able to see what they consider to be impossible, even if such a thing is unfolding right before their eyes. Another factor that prevents us from seeing clearly is the pressure exerted by the many tribes we belong to and the stipulation to not question dogma and authority. To engage in an independent exploration to find the truth is often seen as dangerous, disloyal, and treasonous. Is not uncommon for the explorer to become a persona non grata and be expelled from the group. The emotional pain associated with becoming an outcast discourages many from exploring and challenging the dogmas of religious and political institutions, for instance. Rather than investigate the beliefs to see if they are really true, it is much easier, and certainly less painful, to turn a blind eye, surrender to the power structures, and bend the truth to fit the beliefs.

Perhaps the most important activity we can engage in during our lifetime is that of investigating our beliefs and behaviors, in order to get rid of all things that prevent us from seeing clearly. I love the saying "We must consciously unlearn what we have unconsciously learned." We have the tendency to look outside, and see others as the source of problems. But we have to comprehend that we cannot change others. We can only change ourselves. So, it's not about them; it is about us. It is about our dedication to unlearn the prejudices we have unconsciously learned. It is about our commitment to work on our own selves to tame our impulses of discrimination and exclusion, our violence, our biases, so we may become kinder, more inclusive, and more respectful human beings. Therefore, it is always a good idea to raise doubts, ask questions, and investigate what we know -- or think we know -- in order to consciously unlearn all the lies we were fed. This is not an easy endeavor: it demands courage, and no one can do it for us; we have to do it ourselves. With diligent effort we can get rid of all distorting lenses that prevent us from seeing clearly, and realize that when we change the way we look at things, the things we look at change.

Think about it.

....

SEEING AND NOT SEEING

"When we change the way we look at things, the things we look at change." These words, attributed to Max Planck, the father of the quantum theory in physics, and often mentioned by the late Wayne Dyer, summarize what, for me, should be our priority in life, and the highest goal we should strive for on our journey to create better lives and a better world: we must strive to see clearly because and change the way we look at things in order to see beyond what we currently see. Let's explore this "seeing" for a moment. To begin this exploration, let's entertain the fact that we don't see with our eyes, but with our brains. Some researchers went further and said that our hearts and bodies perceive and apprehend realities before our brains do. In other words, our bodies know the experience before our brain translates it in ways that we can 'understand' them. Well, we will save this for another time. For now, let's stay with the research that shows that we are very selective with our seeing, and that we favor noticing what makes sense to us, that we see what is in accordance with what we already know. Very little of what does not confirm our beliefs and our understanding of what is possible and plausible is able to go through our 'brain filters.' In other words, the majority of what we let through and let in is what matches our concepts. It seems to be very difficult for anyone to see something new if they are not open and deeply committed to do so. Therefore, the first thing to consider is that we are unable to see everything that there is to be seen, and, also, that we may be unable to see what others see. In other words, we cannot be absolutely sure that what others see is what we see, and vice versa.

Let us also contemplate that instead of seeing things freshly -- with the eyes of a child, or with the eyes of a curious tourist visiting a place for the first time -- we evoke memories of past experiences, and mentally construct images that our brains can understand. For instance, imagine yourself looking at a tree. What do you see? Do you see this particular tree, freshly, in all its uniqueness, or do you muster your past experiences with trees, mentally evoke your ideas of what trees are, construct a mental diagram of a tree, and that's what you see? Think about it. But what would happen if we didn't give it a name? What if we didn't call it a tree? What if we didn't recall what we have learned in school about trees, our accumulated notions and ideas about trees? What if we investigated this thing freshly, as something completely new and unknown, something we had never seen before? So, here are some important questions: "When we look at something, what do we actually see? Do we see reality, or do we see our idea of reality? Do we see an object, or do we build an idea of that object in our brains? Do we see all that there is to be seen, or do filter out what does not match our understanding?"

Maybe there is a lot more out there that is invisible to the eyes. Perhaps we don't even see a small portion of what there is to be seen because we are lost in our thoughts, notions, and beliefs. Many thinkers came up with the concept of multiverse, and they challenge us to imagine that we are living in a kind of virtual reality, and that there are many such parallel realities. Physicists have been trying to explain to us a new paradigm of energy that challenges our deep-seated concepts of matter, space, and time. Other thinkers talk about the existence of several dimensions. Theologians express ideas about the material and the spiritual world, of being in this world, but not of it. Buddhists teach about the relative (also referred to as provisional or conventional) truth, and the ultimate truth, and tell us that our challenge is to reconcile living in this more visible (material) world with the knowing, or without forgetting, that we are also living in a less evident world.

Well, the truth -- if there is a truth, one single truth, which is highly questionable -- is that the way we live on this planet is a reflection of the ways we see things, of our understandings of what life is, and of what we accept to be possible. This evokes a saying, "As a man thinks, so is he."

……..

"It's just a thought. Thoughts are not real. Thoughts are just thoughts. Thoughts think themselves. I am not my thoughts. This is just a thought, and I don't have to believe it."

……..

CHANGING PARADIGMS AND SEEING ANEW

"Things are seen through the lenses of our desires, prejudices, and resentments, and are transformed accordingly." ~ Rune Johannson

……..

We don't see the world as it is, but through our own personal lenses. Unfortunately, the current paradigm that the majority of us came to agree upon is that life is a violent competition for scarce resources between separated beings congregated in tribes, and that only the strongest survive. In our fear-dominated minds we feel that we must be very careful because we are surrounded by enemies that are coming to get us. We accept life as a never-ending struggle of 'us against them.' But if we change the ways we look at things, we can bring about much better arrangements of living together on this planet.

Once we reach a new, evolved consciousness, we will embrace the evident truth that this universe is immensely abundant, and that we don't need to be so afraid, and compete as much as we do. We will realize that there's more than enough for everybody here and that we don't need to be afraid of times of scarcity, and, therefore, that we don't need to accumulate as much as we do. We will come to our senses and see what is so evident: that our capacity to invent amazing things that enhance the quality of life has no end. We will reach the conclusion that no one needs to suffer, and that all individuals can be supported to have dignified, thriving, and contributing lives. Once we incorporate new understandings such as these, we will be able to be a lot kinder, cooperate much more with each other, and bring about a much better world for all.

One of the greatest changes that needs to take place in order for this to occur is our understanding of who we are. We see ourselves as separated beings, detached from one another, with our own individual lives and stories. But what if we challenged all these concepts and expanded the ideas of who we are? Some thinkers say that what we accept as reality is in fact an illusion, and that we are not these separated bodies, separated minds, or separated individuals, but that in all aspects we are one single, united, and interdependent organism. Again, the acceptance of new paradigms like this depends on the way we look at things, on our curiosity, on our openness to the strange and unknown, and on a firm commitment to work on our own selves and explore.

When we go through profound personal transformations we begin to see what we were not able to see before; we begin to have insights and epiphanies, and new paradigms, full of new possibilities, become visible to us. The truth is that when we change the way we look at things, the things we look at miraculously change!

One myth that needs to be debunked is that these deep transformational experiences are only available to a few evolved individuals. Nothing could be farther from the truth! These awakenings are accessible to all of those who commit themselves to courageous investigation, exploration, and dedicated inner work. A diligent daily discipline of mental training, such as insight meditation and mindful living, can bring about the desired change because our brains have the ability to reorganize themselves by forming new neural connections throughout life. We can move away from those automatic reactions of our primitive brains, and, with training, bring about more sophisticated and thoughtful ways of responding to stimuli.

We can train ourselves to expand the space and time between stimuli and responses. We can train ourselves to use the S.T.O.P. method which reminds us to "Stop, Take a breath, Observe, and only then Proceed." With practice we can significantly reduce the mindless "fight, flight, or freeze" reactions, and increase the instances when we pause, take time, and choose more mindful responses.

I currently accept that I am not able to see everything that there is to be seen. I accept that I unconsciously discard most of the reality that does not agree with my understanding of what life is and of what is possible. For now, based on where I am on my journey, and the experiences and insights I've had, I am calmly embracing both the reality I think I am seeing, and the one I believe exists, but I am not seeing. Therefore, I feel comfortable saying that "We are, at the same time, mortal and immortal, human and divine, body and spirit, solid matter and vibrational energy, separated and connected, independent and interdependent. We are many, and we are one."

……..

SEEING WITH THE HEART

"Here is my secret. It is very simple: It is only with the heart that one can see rightly; what is essential is invisible to the eyes." ~ Antoine de Saint Exupéry

……..

Individual inner peace is what allows us 'to see with our hearts,' and it's what will bring lasting peace to the world; in fact, it is the only thing that ever will. Once we become able to see the beauty that is invisible to the eyes of the body, once we are able to see ourselves in others, we will develop love and compassion for all, even for those whose hearts are full of hatred.

The world needs our calm, serenity, and composure, and our most crucial assignment during our lifetime is to tame our savageness and grow this individual peace. It is only by developing our reserves of inner peace that we can become bringers of peace.

The end of conflict and violence will be achieved when we all rest in a vast garden of inner peace, and see the beauty, the magic, the mystery, and the miracles through the eyes of our hearts.

. . . .

THE END OF SUFFERING

As Socrates said, "An unexamined life is not worth living." I believe that our journey during this passage here on Earth should be one of seeking greater understanding in order to experience the cessation of suffering. Liberation from suffering -- the attainment of a calm peace and lasting happiness -- comes from the practice of deep and diligent observation and examination of life. I believe that one of the most important things we can do during our lifetime is to continuously and carefully examine our beliefs in order to consciously unlearn the wrong notions we may have unconsciously learned and adopted. This practice of looking deeply into the nature of reality brings about a greater awareness which makes it easier to identify and remove wrong perceptions. This expanded view and comprehension also brings us more peace by reducing our judgment and condemnation, and by enhancing our compassion and acceptance.

Through diligent observation we become acutely aware, for instance, of the continuous transformation and impermanence of everything. This realization removes a major source of suffering in life: attachments.

If we come to recognize that everything changes, that nothing lasts forever, that nothing is created and nothing is lost, but everything is transformed; if we realize, by detailed observation, that something cannot become nothing; if we understand that there is no birth and no death, but all that there is is continuous transformation, continuation, and reintegration with the whole, we remove one of the major obstacles for lasting happiness: the fear of death.

Through conscientious scrutiny, we also come to realize that there is no isolated self, that we all are intensely interrelated, and that, therefore, as the Buddha said, "nothing, whatsoever, should be clung to as I, me, or mine," because this personalization and clinging are sources of suffering.

If we want to look deeply into the nature of reality and have a clearer understanding, mindfulness meditation is probably the best practice. In this aspect, it is very much like science, and meditators are very much like scientists who observe phenomena thoroughly, with great curiosity and ardency, while constantly checking to make sure they are not lost in a territory of wrong perceptions, fantasies, and illusions. Let's dedicate ourselves to the mission of observing and understanding ourselves and our own patterns of behavior. This shall expand our ability to make wiser choices and alleviate the suffering we may be experiencing. And if we are able to continue on this path -- practicing mindfulness diligently -- perhaps we can become examples of lives well lived. Perhaps we will inspire others to engage in this work of paying attention to life, and perhaps this is what will reveal to them a personal and collective way out of suffering. This is a noble endeavor and a greater reminder that our practice is not selfish; we don't practice for ourselves alone.

....

APPRECIATING OR WANTING?

I fluctuate between wanting the present moment to be different than it is, and appreciating it exactly as it is, with all it brings. I fluctuate between wanting to be better and appreciating myself just as I am.

My default mode seems to be the wanting one. I have this unending desire to be a better man. I want to be a kinder, gentler, a more generous and patient human being, and this desire constantly propels me to do more, read more, study more, meditate more, reflect more, and write more. And because I believe this pursuit to be a worthy one -- and one that can be reached through work -- I keep doing the things I believe will bring me closer to the desirable goal. But, unfortunately, while in the middle of doing all these things, I constantly forget to remind myself that this pursuit to be better has no end, because no matter where I may be, improvement is always possible. And since I am pursuing a target that is constantly moving -- and is always ahead of me -- this unending struggle can be exhausting! So I have to pause and ask myself, "Do I really need to do more and be more? Can't I find contentment with myself as I am? Am I not enough already? What am I chasing?" I need to remind myself that no matter how noble the goal may be, a chase is always a chase, and every pursuit is a struggle.

Those times when I am able to switch from the wanting mode to the appreciative mode, I realize that everything is fine, and that I don't need to be any different; I don't need to be more, or do more. I realize that expressing my uniqueness -- which is revealed through living with authenticity -- is the best thing I can do, the best contribution I can give to the world. But to get out of the wanting mode in order to live more in the appreciative mode, I need to practice. I need to remember to live mindfully, and as the saying goes, "It is not difficult to be mindful. What's difficult is to remember to be mindful!" Practice is needed.

Here I go again! I need to practice! Another self-imposed demand? Perhaps not a demand, but a reminder. I need to remind myself to pay attention to the here-now, and appreciate whatever the present moment brings. I have to remind myself to follow my bliss and find joy in all that I do.

I notice a lack of balance: I spend too much time striving, and not enough time appreciating. I spend too much time demanding a lot from myself, and not enough time pampering myself.

Enough with all the striving! Time to switch modes! I am enjoying the present moment, this moment, right here, right now, in all its beauty.

My body is healthy. My mind is clear. My heart is joyful. And my soul is serene.

......

ENDLESS PURSUIT

Everything that arises also passes away. Everything!
......

Life is getting better, but we are tired. Actually we are exhausted by the endless striving of trying to get somewhere else and be someone else. We are exhausted by the endless pursuit to be better, to be perfect.

We live with this sentiment that something is missing, but we are not quite sure what it is. We say to ourselves, "If only I had a better job. If only I had a better partner. I need to diet, exercise, and lose weight. I need to meditate. I need to get more education," and we put ourselves in motion to fill an ill-defined void, only to find ourselves again in a grueling pursuit that has no end.

Yes, making efforts to improve ourselves is admirable, but we should analyze how the desire to be better prevents us from accepting ourselves as we are and disturbs the enjoyment of the present moment. The work of improving ourselves, setting goals and trying to reach them is noble, but once we put ourselves in motion, we need to enjoy the ride. We should do the work at hand without obsessing with the desired outcomes, remaining open and receptive to everyone and everything the Universe sends our way, attentive to what is happening in the present moment.

It is a difficult balance. On one hand we want to improve -- and the drive and dedication we apply to improve are commendable -- but on the other hand we must let go. The never-ending pursuit brings restless and anxiety, so we must remember to be gentle with ourselves, being aware of the self-criticism that leads us to believe that we're not doing enough and therefore we are not good enough.

We should not let the pursuit of a future state of happiness be an impediment for the enjoyment of happiness right here, right now.

……..

DESIRES AS OBSTACLES

The desire to be happy is in itself an impediment to be happy. The desire to be peaceful is in itself an impediment to be peaceful. Why? Because the desire itself is an acknowledgement that we don't have what will placate the dis-ease we are experiencing, the sentiment that something is missing, something is lacking, that something is not quite right. The desire for peace and happiness is an acknowledgment that we don't have peace and happiness, which prevents us from experiencing peace and happiness here and now.

……..

TAMING THE WANTING CREATURE

Let us not waste our whole lives chasing ghosts. Let us not go through life desiring to have what we don't have, to do what we aren't doing, and to be who we are not, imagining that only then we will know fulfillment and happiness. Let's develop wise acceptance, and stop wasting energy in wanting the world to be different than what it is, and others to be different than who they are. Let us tame the wanting creature inside ourselves.

Let's find a good balance between our desires and the appreciation of who we are, what we do, and what we have, living happily in the here-now, accepting all that is, while being grateful for all the gifts that were given to us and that are at our disposal in the present moment.

Mindfulness leads to gratefulness, and gratefulness leads to happiness.

....

WHAT IF WE KNEW THAT WE CAN'T IMPROVE?

"Is there any way in which one's mind can be transformed, or is it simply a process which is nothing more than a vicious circle? What are we looking for? What are we seeking? Are we in search of some wisdom that is going to help us change ourselves, improve ourselves? Do we feel that it is our duty to do what we can to improve ourselves?

Now, can we improve ourselves? Is this possible, or is this an illusion, a vicious circle? How can we improve ourselves if the person who is going to do the improving is the one who needs to be improved?

Can we stop this pursuit and simply accept who we are? How do we know what is good for us? If we say that we want to improve ourselves, then we ought to know what is good for us. But, obviously, we don't because if we did we would be improved already.

If we are really aware of our own inner workings we will realize that there's nothing we can do to improve ourselves, and this also goes for society. Let us suppose that we can't do anything to change ourselves. What would happen if you knew beyond any shadow of doubt that there's nothing we can do to be better?

When we free ourselves from the busyness of trying to improve everything, then our own nature will begin to take care of itself, because we will not be getting in our own way all the time. We will begin to find out that the great things that we do, we are not actually doing them, but they are being done through us." ~ Alan Watts

....

It seems that we are always looking for ideas we can use to improve ourselves. We go around reading books, watching videos, listening to talks, participating in rituals, attending presentations, workshops, and retreats, and spotting new teachers, new gurus who we hope will give us the ultimate formula to make us better and happier. But who are the ones looking for improvement? We are the ones, right? We are the ones who consider ourselves to be somewhat defective and incomplete and who want to do what is necessary to achieve a state of perfection and wholeness. So, let's pause and think about this for a moment: we begin the journey with the premise that we are imperfect, and we are relying on ourselves, imperfect beings, to create what we imagine to be perfect beings. But isn't it reasonable to consider that if we knew how to create perfect beings, we would be those beings already? Do you get it? Isn't this kind of thinking and pursuit somewhat crazy? What if, instead of analyzing (and over-analyzing) ourselves (and others) -- instead of finding fault, criticizing, judging, and condemning -- we simply accepted that we are as we are, and that who we are is wonderful.

....

"We, all of us, are sacred children on a sacred journey. On this journey we are at different points physically, mentally, emotionally and spiritually. Wherever we are, that's where we are supposed to be. By recognizing these facts we can heal our wounds and become friends, no matter how different we may think we are." ~ Wally Dale

....

The mind that can improve the mind is not the same mind. The mind that can improve the mind is the mind that observes the mind and doesn't get identified with it, believing it is the real 'self.'.

The seeking for answers is innate in us. The drive to expand our consciousness is in our own nature. Or is it a thought that was implanted in us by the prevailing competitive culture and that pushes us to be better than others? Is the spiritual pursuit -- the drive to expand our consciousness -- also ego-driven?

....

Now, what if we came to accept that the premise that we are imperfect is false, and that this constant struggle to better ourselves is what is impeding us from enjoying life to the fullest? Think about it for a moment. How would this new thought affect us? What would happen if we knew, beyond any shadow of doubt, that there's nothing we can do to be better? It would, at least, be a huge relief, wouldn't it? Realizing that there's nothing we can do to improve ourselves would give us a breather in the course of which we would simply relax and allow the Forces of the Universe to work in us and through us. It would give us permission to pause and observe what is going on, and, maybe, then we would find out that this is the magic recipe for a good life, the one we have so desperately been looking for. Gloria Taraniya asks, "What if there isn't any right way to be? What if the way you are is just fine?

What if all the self-improvement just compounds the suffering? What if the only problem here is that you think there's a problem here?" ~

………..

Maybe the journey isn't so much about becoming anything. Maybe it's about un-becoming everything that isn't really who we are, so we can be who we were meant to be in the first place.

……...

JUST BEING HUMAN

The voices in our culture tell us that we only have value if we do and achieve a lot, and that one's worth is dependent on performance and success. We don't attribute value to anyone just for being human. Well, what about changing this paradigm? What about realizing that we are divine creations and that we are magnificent by nature? What about considering that we don't have to do anything to be deemed worthy? What about considering that we are human beings, and not human doings? Here's Henry David Thoreau enjoying the present moment, doing nothing, just being: "Sometimes, in a summer morning, having taken my accustomed bath, I sat in my sunny doorway from sunrise till noon, rapt in a revery, amidst the pines and hickories and sumachs, in undisturbed solitude and stillness, while the birds sing around or flitted noiseless through the house, until by the sun falling in at my west window, or the noise of some traveler's wagon on the distant highway, I was reminded of the lapse of time… I realized what the Orientals mean by contemplation and the forsaking of works. For the most part, I minded not how the hours went. The day advanced as if to light some work of mine; it was morning, and lo, now it is evening, and nothing memorable is accomplished."

……...

TO LOVE MYSELF

As part of a program aimed at enhancing health and quality of life through mindfulness and mindful eating, I participated in an exercise that brought about one of the most revealing insights I have ever had. I was invited to think about negative things I say to myself about my body. Working with a partner, I was instructed to write down a negative statement that I constantly repeat to myself in my internal dialogues (my 'old tapes,' as the course calls them), such as, "I am out of shape, my

153

body is flabby, and my belly is pathetic. I must exercise daily and make better choices regarding what I eat and drink." Then, I was instructed to read the statement out loud. Finally, it was my partner's turn to repeat to me what I had just said. When I heard her say, "You are out of shape, your body is flabby, and your belly is pathetic, and you must exercise daily and make better choices regarding what you eat and drink," I felt a rush of indignation and rage invade my body. Although absolutely conscious that I was participating in an exercise, I still felt, "How dare she say such harsh things about me? Who does she think she is to talk to me like that? This is so unkind!" And then the realization hit me... This is what I do all the time. This is the way I talk to myself all the time. This is the abusive way I treat myself all the time. I am my own worst critic. I say the most hurtful things to myself, things that I would never even consider saying to anyone else. I criticize myself harshly all the time. I use the most demanding tone. And I do all this without any compassion, kindness, or consideration for my feelings. Wow! What a revelation that was!

....

In my philosophical-spiritual musings I say to myself that I came here to Earth, and was given this life, to learn some lessons, the most important being to grow in selflessness. I wholeheartedly believe that I came here to learn to be less selfish and more unselfish. But after the awakening that took place with this exercise, I am now considering that an equally important lesson that I need to learn is to be kind and gentle with myself, and to love myself just as I am. I am now beginning to understand, in a much more profound way, something that I thought I already knew: that if I am unable to love myself fully and totally, I will never be able to love anyone else. I am beginning to realize that if I don't accept myself as I am, I will live my life criticizing not only myself, but everything and everyone else, wanting the world to be different than it is, and that, definitely, is a pitiful way to waste a lifetime. Wow! I am always in awe with the fact that learning has no end.

....

How would a friend feel if you constantly told her that you didn't like the way she looked? How would she feel if you constantly criticized her, and told her that she needed to change? How would she feel if you never showed acceptance and gratitude? Think about it. How would she feel if you treated her the same way you treat your body, because that's the way you treat your body, isn't it? Now, how do you treat your very best friend? Let me guess. You are there for her, listening attentively and doing your best to help and support her. You accept her just as she is, constantly telling tell her how grateful you are for having her in your life, letting her know how much you appreciate all the kind things she does for you, day in and day out.

It's time to treat our bodies as our best friends.

．．．．．．

HEALTHY BODY, HEALTHY MIND

My body is healthy, my mind is clear, my heart is joyful, and my soul is serene.

．．．．．．

We are called to take good care of our bodies and minds, and adopt a healthy lifestyle. Many years ago, when I was leading the Fun Fitness Youth Program and coaching cross-country runners I created an acronym to help my athletes remember that they should always strive for good nutrition, rest, stretching and exercise. I used to say, "Remember NuRSE: Nutrition, Rest, Stretching and Exercise. If you remember this NuRSE, you may never need one." Choose to eat healthy, nourishing foods. Choose to exercise and stretch your body regularly, and have plenty of rest. Take good care of your mind also. Feed it with good words, sounds, and images. Choose to read good books, listen to good music, and watch good movies. And, perhaps the most important of all, exercise your mind by meditating daily, and stretch it by exploring new points of view. And do not forget to give it some rest.

Be gentle with yourself. Do not demand too much of yourself. Have some self-compassion. Adopt a non-striving attitude, and do not put unnecessary pressure on yourself. Let go of the need to control and the strife to produce results according to your plan. Allow the changes to arise at the proper time. Do your part, relax, and the positive outcomes will come about naturally.

Finally, as much as possible, be a positive and optimistic individual. By choosing optimism, and nurturing great love for yourself, you will not only be helping your body heal itself, but you will also be helping others heal themselves. The truth is that our well-being is extremely important. Each one of us touches many lives. Let us exude optimism, and take good care of ourselves not only for our own sake, but also for the benefit of many others.

……..

MINDFULNESS AND HAPPINESS

HAPPY, CONTENT, SATISFIED

"He has achieved success who has lived well, laughed often, and loved much; Who has enjoyed the trust of pure women, the respect of intelligent men and the love of little children; Who has filled his niche and accomplished his task; Who has never lacked appreciation of Earth's beauty or failed to express it; Who has left the world better than he found it, Whether an improved poppy, a perfect poem, or a rescued soul; Who has always looked for the best in others and given them the best he had; Whose life was an inspiration; Whose memory a benediction." ~ Bessie Anderson Stanley

....

My grandmother wasn't, by any prevalent standards, the most beautiful or intelligent woman. She didn't have a huge list of extraordinary achievements to brag about. She wasn't rich either, but I remember her being happy, genuinely happy. And through this state of happiness she irradiated beauty, intelligence, and a sense of achievement.

I learned a lot about her when we went on a family vacation and we were able to spend some quality time together. By then, she had already experienced the death of her husband and of two of her four children -- my mother and one of my uncles -- perhaps the greatest of all pains for any parent.

In my mind, I can still picture her happily swinging on a hammock between two palm trees on the beach, facing the ocean, watching the sun going down, and telling me how happy she was with her life, how content she was with what she had achieved, and how satisfied she was with everything life had given her. At that stage of her life, she was constantly expressing how grateful she was for living. For her, everything was wonderful, always. She appreciated the present moments and all things they brought her, without complaining about a single thing.

When I reflected about my grandmother's life experiences, I organically expanded the popular definition of mindfulness laid out by Jon Kabat-Zinn, which states that "Mindfulness is the awareness that arises from paying attention, on purpose, to the present moment, non-judgmentally." Mindfulness is not only the awareness, but everything else that stems from it. Mindfulness is also the appreciation of life, the sense of gratitude, the contentment, and the peaceful happiness that arise from this commitment to pay attention and accept what is happening in the present moment. And this was what that time with my grandmother made evident to me.

That time together brought to light a grandma that I had not known before, an amazingly triumphant human being. She showed me a different kind of beauty and intelligence, and revealed one of the most beautiful, wise, and accomplished women I ever knew. I learned from her that true success is to be happy, content, and satisfied, and that once we reach such stage, we will have no desire to be anywhere else; we will calmly rest in the knowing that we have reached our destination.

....

DEALING WITH PAIN

My body is healthy, my mind is clear, my heart is joyful, and my soul is serene.

....

Pain is inevitable. Sooner or later, everyone will face some sort of physical, mental, and emotional pain. But although pain is inevitable, suffering, on the other hand, is optional. The Buddha told the story of the two arrows: the first arrow that hits us creates the pain, but the second arrow is one that we stick in ourselves over the original wound by reacting to the pain in unskilled ways. Resisting the pain is what creates suffering, and the more we resist, the more we suffer.

We must remember that we are in charge of the way we respond to the pain. If we fight the pain, try to push it away, get angry at it, blame ourselves for it, and make it personal by saying to ourselves, for instance, "Why me? Why do I have to go through this?" we simply add insult to injury.

The Buddha said, "Nothing, whatsoever, is to be clung to as I, me, or my," so try not to make it personal. Change the script, and say to yourself, "This is not my pain. I am not this pain. The pain is just a visitor. The pain is simply manifesting itself through me, but I am not it. I am not a victim. I am perfect and whole." Treat the pain as a visitor. If you can, don't protest, resent, or complain about it. Don't push it away. Don't suppress or repress it, but face it instead. Welcome it. Even, befriend it. What you resist not only persists, but grows in size.

On the other hand, accepting it is what will put you in the best position to deal with it, and maybe change it. Many times, those who suffer from chronic pain may benefit from being more attentive, investigating it with curiosity, and refraining from being the pain expert who says, "Here's the pain, again. I know what is going to happen. I am going to have another miserable day." Prevent the same old, repetitive tapes to run again. Explore the pain in detail and notice how it changes. Be ready to welcome it, saying, "Hi, Pain! There you are again. How are you today? O, I see, you are quite different today." And by developing a different relationship with this visitor, perhaps you may be able to enhance the quality of your life, and of the lives of those around you.

Don't make it worse by ruminating what happened in the past and anticipating what may happen in the future. Don't catastrophize. Stay in the present moment, as much as you can, as a calm observer. See worries as thoughts, just thoughts, and whenever they pop up, say to yourself, "It's just a thought, and I don't have to believe it." And what are the past and the future if not thoughts in the present moment, right? Don't allow yourself to be carried away by them. Do your best to come back to the here-now.

……..

"My body is an intelligent, self-healing organism. I know that by maintaining a positive attitude and an inner knowing that my body is constantly healing itself, I will be healed soon and enjoy a healthy life.

Knowing that my thoughts and emotions influence my physical health, I populate my mind with love and compassion for myself, and with a certainty that I am healed already. I am gentle and kind with myself. I take good care of body and mind because I know that a healthy body is the physical manifestation of a healthy mind, and a healthy mind inhabits a healthy body. *Mens sana in corpore sano. Corpore sano in mens sana.*"

....

I WANT TO NOT WANT

So many desires and so much unrest created by this constant wanting! Is it possible to be content? Is it possible to want less? Is it possible to not want? Well, I guess I am wanting something, right now. As I write these words, I want to understand, accept, and be at peace with the fact that perhaps I will always want, and that wanting is of the nature of being human. I want to understand, accept, and be at peace with the fact that in this life we will always be presented with choices, that our choices will bring about changes, and that change is the natural movement of the Universe.

What else do I want?

I want to be aware of my likes and dislikes, my wants and don't wants, my cravings and aversions, and practice to calmly tame my impulses and navigate through this ocean of desires. Actually, I want to want less. In fact, I want to not want. I want to be able to expand the amount of time between receiving a stimulus and choosing a response. I want to make thorough assessments, apply wise discernment, and improve my ability to make the best possible decisions.

I am encouraged by the unquestionable truth that all of us can make our lives better by consciously examining them. I want to remember always that "an unexamined life is not worth living," and keep examining my existence. I want to be awake, alert, attentive, aware, and appreciative of what is going on in each present moment, enjoying the beauty that surrounds me, seeing the extraordinary in the ordinary, seeing magic, mystery, and miracles everywhere. I want to immerse myself in this moment, this one -- not the previous one, nor the next one -- knowing that if I do this, the best version of myself and the best life I can live will emerge naturally.

THE INNER PEACE THAT COMES FROM WANTING LESS

At the beginning of the Mindfulness-Based Stress Reduction course, a program that I teach, we ask the participants "What do you want to get out of this program?" And soon after that, we ask, "What do you really, really, really want?" Although I ask myself this question quite often, I recently decided to do a deeper reflection. So I paused, centered myself, and asked again: "What do I really, really, really want?" And the answer that came to me this time was, "I want to want less."

What do I want?

I want the inner peace that comes from feeling that I do enough, that I have enough, and that I am enough, and that I don't need to do more, have more, or be more. I want the inner peace that comes from getting to end of my physical life feeling content with what I did, what I had, and whom I was.

....

THIS IS A GOOD MOMENT, AND I WILL REMEMBER IT

If a good life is a collection of good moments, then remember to mindfully make of every moment the best it can be! Stay alert to notice good moments whenever they arise, and do your best to capture them by bringing down your plane from the high altitude of your thoughts and landing it on this present moment, with all the feelings it brings about. Pause to mindfully notice the weather, the sights and sounds, the thoughts and emotions, the sensations in your body, and take it all in. Record the experience in your memory by saying to yourself, "This is a good moment, and I will remember it!"

Not only notice the good moments that arise spontaneously, but also create joyful moments deliberately. Do your best to populate your days with things, activities, people, and places you love by creating and spending time in environments you love, nurturing good friendships, and choosing to do the activities you like. Create the life you want to live by filling your days with moments of joy. Appreciate! Be grateful!

....

Choose Happiness. Choose Love. Ask yourself, "Does this add to my happiness and the happiness of others? Does this expand my happiness and the happiness in the world?"

....

If we claim happiness, love, and peace as our birthright, and decide to be the most peaceful, loving, and happy individuals that we can be, and do only what expands those sentiments in the world, then, no matter what may happen to us, we will always experience a deep sense of calm and an exhilarating feeling of freedom from the trappings of the world.

So, decide to be a living expression of happiness. Decide to be the happiest person you can be. Decide to live mindfully, to choose wisely, and to make of happiness a priority at every moment of your life.

. . . .

"We are individuals here on earth with our own unique purpose. Our birthright is to be happy. Your life is yours to be lived and to be cherished. Make yourself and your happiness a priority. Become a person that you're proud to be - one that lives with a wide open heart and stands for human goodness even when it's difficult or unpopular. Be honest. Be willing to change your mind as you grow, learn and love. Be humble enough to let people see your humanity, because this is when true connection is formed. Give. Give. And give more, but don't forget to be a gracious receiver too. Live each day becoming your truest, greatest self. This is your life. Live it." ~ Michelle Ploog

. . . .

DO WHAT YOU LIKE AND LIKE WHAT YOU DO

Create a list of the activities you enjoy doing, and populate your days with them. Try to do as many of them as you can every day, even if just for a short period of time. Remember that one minute counts. It may be one mindful breath, one mindful body stretch, or one mindful expression of gratitude and kindness. It may be as simple as taking a few steps outside in nature, watching the sunrise, or feeling the breeze on your skin. It may be hiking in the mountains, riding your bike, or catching a wave. It may be adding just a few sentences to the book you're writing, playing just a few chords of the song you're learning, or adding just a few touches to the watercolor you're painting. It may be simply exercising, meditating, or giving yourself permission to rest and relax. It may be taking time to listen to music you like, or calmly read that book you have always wanted to read but have repeatedly put aside, imagining that a better time to peruse it would soon come. It may be contacting your friends to tell them how much you appreciate them, or, even better, creating opportunities to hang out with them. It may be going out and serving those in need.

Whatever it may be – whatever enhances the enjoyment of your life -- go ahead and do it. And since there's not enough time to do them all, do at least a little bit of one of the things you enjoy. And if the conditions are not there to do them perfectly, do them imperfectly. Just do them anyway, today and every day!

Create the life you want to live. Don't wait any longer. Life is short.

……...

THE LIFE I HAVE DECIDED TO LIVE

I was tired of always doing what I had to do, and not having time to do the things I wanted to do. For a long time, my most ardent desire was to organize my life in such a way that I could have plenty of time, every day, to do what I love to do. So I paused to ponder on important questions, such as, "At this stage of my life, what is really important? What is my purpose in this life, and what are the best contributions I can give? What are the most important relationships in my life, and am I giving them my attention? What do I love? What am I passionate about? What do I really want to do? How does an ideal day look like for me? How shall I live, knowing that I will die?" As a result of this process, I took steps to simplify my life, and got rid of the things that prevented me from doing what I considered important and pleasant. I now live a much simpler, uncomplicated life that gives me plenty of time to do the things I want to do. And I have learned to calmly say "No" to what is unimportant, without feeling the slightest guilt about it.

Without the pressures of the have-to-dos, I now have more time to notice and appreciate all the magic, mystery, and miracles that surround me. I am in awe with the splendor of the Universe, and grateful for everyone and everything in it. I realize how blessed I am, and give thanks all the time for all the gifts that were freely given to me.

By becoming aware of this abundant wellspring of blessings, I am more optimistic and generous. And by sharing what was given to me -- by being of service to others, and helping them enhance the quality of their lives -- I experience bliss. In a nutshell, seeing people happy makes me happy. I'm fortunate. I feel I am doing what I came here to do. I do what I like, and I like what I do. Life is good!

GOOD FRIENDS

Having friends is super important. Research has shown that the best predictor of a good life, and the most important factor for mental, physical, and emotional health, is healthy social connections. Cultivating friendships is the smartest thing we can do. Loneliness is a silent killer, so let's do our best to be with those we love and make us laugh.

. . . .

COURAGE TO ACCEPT THE CALL TO ADVENTURE

I was summoned by the Forces of the Universe to do something that only I, and no one else, can do. I hesitated, postponed, and talked myself out of it as much as I could. I told myself that I couldn't afford to take the risk. But the day finally came when I could not refuse to answer the call any longer. That was the day when I stopped lying to myself, accepted who I really was, left all the voices that were holding me back with their bad advice behind, and launched myself into the world, determined to do the only thing I could do, determined to save the only life I could save. From that moment on, I was able to hear my own voice. I remembered who I really was, and what I was brought here to do. I began to see all the magic, mystery and miracles unfolding around me, and the stars burning with joy, smiling at me, and at my decision to follow my bliss. I am happy for having chosen to be authentic and honest with myself. I am proud for having had the courage to answer the call, even though, when I launched myself, I felt I wasn't prepared to face the challenges. But, later, I came to understand that we all feel that we are not ready. Given that, I realized that what it takes to follow one's bliss is the crazy courage to say, "Ready or not, here I go!"

. . . .

FACING THE DRAGON

The Hero's Journey, for me, is having the courage to look within yourself, and say, "What am I here to do? What am I most passionate about in my life? What are my greatest gifts? How do I give them to the world?" ~ Brian Johnson

. . . .

In the mythical stories, the knight has to face the dragon. It is her destiny. She has to accept the calling. There is no alternative.

The Reluctant Knight - "It's a daily struggle. I took the leap and still live in uncertainty. Every day I try to let go of what doesn't serve me. Every single day I question everything, including myself."

The Listener - "You have so much to teach. You are living the Hero's Journey. You may not be living the life many others think you should be living, the habitual, normal, pre-scripted life. The fact that you are making different choices and opening new paths in the middle of the forest just shows how brave you are: you are brave enough to be yourself. Your adventurous spirit threatens many, but for others, like me, you are a hero. Don't listen to other people's criticism and the doubts they arise. Do not judge and condemn your own self. Bask in the admiration we have for you. Be courageous and be brave. You are admirable!"

The Reluctant Knight - "I wish I believed in myself as much as you believe in me. Sometimes I wonder if I'm deceiving myself into thinking this is really the best way, the way to awareness and clarity of purpose. But then I think of the alternative and it looks even worse. So, I just keep trucking along hoping a sliver of clarity will appear along the way."

The Listener - "You are doing what is right, dealing with 'what is.' Don't think too much about the future. Deal with life as it presents itself to you, and make the best of each and every moment, right here, right now. Don't lose this moment. Stay in the Here-Now, awake, alert, attentive, aware, appreciative, and fully alive. See with the eyes of the heart, and don't let the magic, the mystery and the miracles of this moment go by unnoticed. Don't allow your mind to be caught in regrets and worries. Look around and be amazed, grateful, and happy. Yours is a victorious existence. Just consider how many are just sleepwalking through life. You are an example to all of us, so continue to be courageous and brave. Domesticate the dragon and come back to share the story with us. Just remember where the dragon is."

Two years after domesticating the dragon, the Knight returns to the village to share her story and what she had learned.

The Victorious Knight - "For those of you who have decided to stop sleepwalking through life and have taken the leap of faith of following your hero's journey, here is where I find myself now. I don't feel the existential anxiety as strongly anymore. After the struggle there is much peace. The reward for searching isn't necessarily finding all the answers but rather feeling it's OK not to have them. Surviving the journey is strengthening in itself."

My gratitude to my dear friend, Florencia Clement de Grandprey, for her example of courage and bravery.

....

Our lives can be beautiful adventures, if we accept the call. We must not ignore it. We must muster all courage and accept the mission to tame our dragons. We should not act as if we don't know where they are. We know it well. Our dragons are our own fears, and they reside inside ourselves. We should not avoid them, hide from them, or run away from them. Our challenge is to walk up straight to them, and look them in the eyes, calmly, peacefully, and fearlessly, and by doing so, they will be transformed. Let us domesticate our dragons, and return home as heroes.

....

THIS IS HOME

"Nobody has lived in the past, nobody will live in the future." ~ Arthur Schopenhauer

....

Let us remember to see thoughts just as thoughts, and choose not to allow ourselves to be carried away to the future or the past by worrisome thoughts. Let us come back to the present moment, over and over again, always remembering that both the past and the future do not exist except as thoughts in the present moment.

The present moment is the only moment when we are alive. Nobody has ever lived in the past, and nobody will ever live in the future. We lived in the present moment, and we will live in the present moment. We always live only in the present moment. The present is the only moment that there is. Nothing is more important than being present and paying attention to life in the here-now. It is in the present moment that we make choices that affect the quality of our lives. That is why this training of being present every moment, awake, alert, attentive, and aware, moment after moment, is so important. Our lives depended on it.

Let's consider that if the present moment is all that there is, then we don't have to go anywhere; we have arrived already. Planning is important and necessary, but we should not spend our time worrying excessively about the future. We should notice when we have worried enough and more worrying is not useful. Let's make it a priority to enjoy the present moment, remembering that a good life is a collection of good moments, making the best of this and every moment. Let's be here, now, in this moment, with this breath, feeling that we have arrived already. Wherever we may be is Here, and Here is our home.

"I am here. I am safe. I know who I am, and I know the ground where I stand. I have arrived. This is home."

....

THE PRIMACY OF THE PRESENT MOMENT

"I wish you all a good case of amnesia. I wish you may be able to completely forget the past and live totally in the here-now." ~ Wally Dale

....

There is great wisdom in letting go of the past, interrupting the constant playback of old stories in our heads, appreciating the present moment, and being grateful for all the magic, mystery, and miracles it contains.

To a certain extent I agree with the saying, "Where we are is less important than where we are heading to." I feel it gives me hope and motivates me to improve my life situation. But I believe in the primacy of the present moment, so I say to myself, "Where I am is more important than where I am heading to," because who and where I will be are always being determined by the decisions I make now. This moment is the most important one, and no other moment is more important than this one. Actually, no other moment even exists. And that's why living this moment mindfully is of the utmost importance.

I also believe that who I was and where I have been is less important than who and where I am now. It's only in this present moment that I can make an assessment of who and where I am, sense what I would like to see changed, and decide where I would like to be. It's only in this present moment that I can choose the right destination, set myself in motion in the right direction, and make adjustments, even changing my target altogether if that is what is called for. It's only in this moment that I can enjoy life.

This is not new. I have been doing this throughout my life, and I still do, but what changed for me is that now, in my assessments, I focus much more on what I have than on what I believe is missing. I take more time being grateful for who I am, what I do, what I have, and where I am, than focusing on what I want and believe I need. Now, I am more cautious not to ignore how fortunate I already am.

It is perfectly valid to visualize the life we want for ourselves, create plans, and put ourselves in motion to reach our objectives, but this journey has to begin with an honest assessment of who we are and what we are meant to be. Going to the internal silence and pondering on the following four fundamental questions that Wayne Muller listed on his excellent book How, Then, Shall We Live? is really beneficial: "Who am I? What do I love? How shall I live, knowing that I will die? What gifts do I bring to share with the family of the Earth?"

Let us trust the impetus inside us and heed the calling. Let's have the courage to do what we are being called to do in spite of fears of failure, criticism, and rejection. Let's go and do those things we know we cannot not do. In the end, what we will regret the most is not having answered the calls of life, not having done the things we knew we should, not having taken the risks to live the life we were called to live.

The best way to live a purposeful life is to follow our bliss and be of service to others. Let's imagine what is necessary to make the life we should live a reality, and put ourselves in motion to reach what we aspire. Then, remaining adaptable and releasing the need to control the results, let's trust that the organizing intelligence of the Universe will take us to where we are meant to be in order to learn the lessons we are meant to learn and teach the lessons we are meant to teach.

……..

Let us remember that when we return from a trip, the most exciting stories we tell are not of what unfolded according to the plan, but what happened that was extraordinary. So let's be flexible and open to the unexpected, remembering how exciting exploration feels and how rewarding discoveries are.

……..

As a reminder to come back to the present moment, I usually say the following words at the beginning of the mindfulness practices that I lead:

"We begin this mindfulness meditation acknowledging place and time. The place is here. The time is now. We are here, now, and nowhere else and no-when else. We are right here, right now. And, actually, we are always here, now. If someone asks, 'Where are you?' the answer 'Here' is always right. And is someone asks, 'What time is it?' The answer 'Now' is also always right. We are always here, now"

Let us remember that the present moment truly is the most important moment, and that the past and the future are nothing more than thoughts in the present moment because whatever happened in the past, when it happened, actually happened in the present, and whatever will happen in the future, when it will happen, will also happen in the present moment. So, this is it. This is all that there is: this moment, right now, right here. And let's realize how special this moment is. This is a completely new moment, one that has never existed before. This is the first moment of the rest of our lives: let's make it count! Let's be here, now.

Occupying ourselves fully with the task at hand, and extracting joy from doing it with great attention is what brings about a life that is worth living.

……..

"See your career as one of creating a joyful life experience. You are a creator, and the subject of your creation is your joyful life experience. That is your mission. That is your quest. That is why you are here." ~ Abraham, Esther Hicks

……..

DISCOVERING YOUR PURPOSE, FOLLOWING YOUR BLISS

"I think anyone who has seen me in these past two years can attest to my significant increase in mindfulness and overall happiness. Before then, I had many of the symptoms of depression which I tried to counteract with exercise and a brave face for years. After losing my condo, going through bankruptcy, feeling alone, and working a job where I felt grossly underpaid, overworked, and unappreciated, I reached the end of my rope. The uncertainty of not having a job was more bearable than the pain of continuing the status quo. I decided, consciously decided, that I needed a radical change; I needed to make me happy and if that meant starting from scratch and going back to basics, then that's what I needed to do. I write this because I want people to know it is possible. I want you to know that the only way to truly be happy is to dedicate yourself to what you love and are passionate about. I'm not going to say it isn't scary starting anew, but it's even more terrifying to continue living your life like a zombie. What moves and motivates you? What would you do the rest of your life if money wasn't an issue? What are you passionate about? Have you forgotten what made you smile when you were younger and carefree? Wake up and make the changes you need to bring back that joy, or maybe it's time to discover it. You don't need to know all the details of how it will work out, you just need to take the first step. The universe has a wonderful way of conspiring with you when you get to your authentic self and start living with passion and intention. Seek clarity and take the plunge however big or small it may be. You don't want to look back one day and wish you had done things differently. Don't delay. There is never a perfect time, or rather, the time is always perfect, the time is now! Exactly two years ago, when I made this announcement, someone asked, "How can you afford to quit your job?"and I answered, "I can't afford NOT to!" ~ Florencia Clement de Grandprey

....

Who am I? What did I come here to give?

Each one of us is a unique whole, a distinctive package of talents and skills. No two are the same. No one can give what I can give. No one can give what you can give. So, too, we cannot give what others can. We must figure out what gifts we are meant to give, constantly remembering that every life is valuable because everyone has inimitable gifts to give.

....

"Don't ask what the world needs. Ask what makes you come alive and go do it, because what the world needs is people who have come alive." ~ Howard Thurman

....

Let us discover and do those things we are passionate about. Let us be who we really are, and do what we really love. Let's choose to do those things that give expression to our truest selves, by seeking answers to the questions such as, "Why am I here? What is this thing we call life and what does it demand from me? Why do we live in such fear and make life so complicated? Why can't we simply get along, helping and supporting one another to be the best that each one of us can be, so we all can give our best and unique gifts to each other? Why can't we all be friends, play together, and live in harmony?"

……..

"Peace comes from being able to contribute the best that we have, and all that we are, toward creating a world that supports everyone. But it is also securing the space for others to contribute the best that they have and all that they are." ~ Hafsat Abiola

……..

WHAT IS LIFE?

"When I was 5 years old, my mother told me that happiness was the key to life. When I went to school, they asked me what I wanted to be when I grew up. I wrote down 'happy'. They told me I didn't understand the assignment, and I told them they didn't understand life." ~ John Lennon

……..

It seems that we live in a world where the majority of the people is suffering from a consumption addiction, a compulsion to acquire as many goods and have as many pleasurable experiences as possible. We are desperate to succeed, to be someone -- to be number one -- because we want power, position, possessions, prestige, and privileges. It seems that we live with the need to prove that we are good and worthy of love. Is this what life should be?

What is life? What is the purpose of living?

Is it to accumulate? Is it to compete and prove that we are, in one way or another, better than others? Many years ago I heard the saying, "He who dies with the most toys, wins." And I also heard the comment, "He who dies with the most toys, is dead, just like everyone else. He who wins the rat race is still a rat."

Why are we alive? Why are we here? What for?

Is it to learn to give love? Is it to learn to accept love and allow ourselves to be loved? Is it to have fun, laugh, and be happy? Is it to learn to pay attention and be awake, alert, attentive, and aware? Is it to learn to live consciously, appreciating the simple things? Is it to develop gratitude? Is it to learn to be less selfish and more selfless? Is it to help others? Is it to grow in compassion, and to care and share? Is it to learn to be kind, generous, patient, loving, giving, and forgiving? Is it to leave a contribution to humanity, to leave an honorable legacy? Is it to repair what is broken and make things whole? Is it to promote justice, peace, and unity? Is it to awaken ourselves and stop the sleepwalking through life? Is it to help awaken humanity? Is it to bring Heaven to Earth, or to reveal that Heaven is here already? Is it to teach? Is it to learn how to live? Or is it, simply, to learn how to prepare ourselves to die?

We need to constantly remember to ask ourselves, "Who am I? What do I love? How shall I live, knowing that I will die? What are my gifts to the family of the Earth?" as Wayne Muller so beautifully stated.

……..

"Often we want to be somewhere other than where we are, or even to be someone other than who we are. We tend to compare ourselves constantly with others and wonder why we are not as rich, as intelligent, as simple, as generous, or as saintly as they are. Such comparisons make us feel guilty, ashamed, or jealous. It is very important to realize that our vocation is hidden in where we are and who we are. We are unique human beings, each with a call to realize in life what nobody else can, and to realize it in the concrete context of the here and now. We will never find our vocations by trying to figure out whether we are better or worse than others. We are good enough to do what we are called to do. Be yourself!" ~ Henri Nouwen

……..

WE CAME HERE. WE ARE HERE. WHAT FOR?

When Mary gave me the stone, she solemnly deposited it in the palm of my hand. While holding my hand between hers, she looked me in the eyes and said, "May this remind you of who you are and what you were brought here to do." What was I brought here to do? What were we brought here to do? I believe that we came here to learn. We came here to teach. We came here to work on our own selves, undergo radical transformations, and have those experiences that make us feel that we are one. We came here to journey from the grounds of separation and exclusion to those places of unity and inclusion. We came here to realize the ever-producing and never-ending abundance of this Universe, realize that there is more than enough for everyone to live good lives. We came here to learn to let go of the need to compete, defeat, and accumulate more than we need. We came here to learn to criticize less, judge less, condemn less, and love more. We are here to walk the path from selfishness to selflessness. We came here to grow in empathy, compassion, kindness, and generosity, and learn that we have more fun when we share our toys. We came here to learn to see beyond what we see, see all the magic, mystery, and miracles that surround us, and be grateful. We came here to enjoy the splendor of this beautiful garden and have fun in this awesome playground that was given to us. We came here to give our contributions to make the garden even more beautiful and the playground even more enjoyable for all. We came here to understand -- and to help others understand -- that Heaven is here if we want it to be. We came here to observe the impermanence of all things, and learn how to live knowing that we will die. Perhaps we are here, going through all the joy and sorrow, so we can learn the most important lesson: how to die before we die. We came here to practice looking deeply, listening attentively, learning unceasingly, leading compassionately, laughing profusely, and loving wastefully in order to live fully. May we be able to leave an honorable legacy behind and let go of everything with grace and ease when the time of departure arrives.

That's what we were brought here to do.

……..

"Be ashamed to die before you have won some victory for humanity." ~ Horace Mann

……..

FEARLESS

We are children of the Universe. Be not afraid.

Inspired by the saying that "an unexamined life is not worth living," I often find myself pondering and trying to understand why we were given life. I take the engagement with this reflection as a duty. I believe we should not waste our lives in vain pursuits, but that we should constantly bring to mind the rarity of human life and the limited time we have here. We should use this time wisely, asking ourselves, "Why were we given the opportunity to live? Why are we here? What for?"

From these reflections I came to the idea that we were brought here to learn and to teach, and also to help others do likewise. Once I embraced this as the main reason for our existences, I realized, in a deep way, the immeasurable value of life. It became evident to me that we must protect all life, not kill, and oppose all killing because everyone should have chances to learn and teach, and no one has the right to deprive others of learning and teaching opportunities. The good news is that no matter how young or old we may be, there will always be plenty of opportunities to do just that: learn and teach. Each and every day is a new learning and teaching day. We came here for a limited time, but our time as spiritual beings is unlimited. So, let us take our time to ponder and ask ourselves often, "What am I supposed to learn here? What am I meant to teach here?"

Let's not regret getting old. It is a privilege denied to many. And let's not be afraid of dying. Let's connect with the feeling of eternity and don't fear death. Let's think of ourselves as manifestations of something that is much bigger. Let's imagine ourselves as entities that never cease to exist, only change form. Let's consider that we may be eternal spiritual beings having temporary human experiences.

Death can be a great counselor. It can be the best adviser on how to live a good life. If we ask and listen, Death will tell us that what really matters is the love we give. Let us accept the inevitability of aging and dying, and don't let fear of death interfere with the enjoyment of life in this present moment, or stop us from giving the contributions we can give at any stage of our lives. Since we cannot know how long we will stay here, let us give as much love as we can right here, right now.

......

GO FOR IT

Once, on a TV program, I heard Carole King saying, "If you want to do something, go for it. Try. Don't tell yourself that you can't make it. Don't let your parents tell you that you can't make it. Let the world tell you that you can't make it after having tried. Or, maybe, let the world discover you. But don't fail to try because if you don't try you can't succeed. I had hopeless times in my life about different things. You just have to persevere, because one day that door does open, but if you don't persevere, you won't be there when it does."

MINDFULNESS AND GRATITUDE

THIS MOMENT, THIS DAY, THIS LIFE

"Life is simply one damned thing after another. If it is not this one, then it is going to be the next one." Unquestionably, this is not the most upbeat definition of life, but it's a valuable one because it acknowledges life's randomness. If we look at life dispassionately, we can conclude that life is simply a succession of fortuitous phenomena. Just like the weather, so too life can be construed as sequence of situations that arise when conditions are present. When conditions come together, beings, objects, and events come into existence. While conditions are present, they continue to exist. When conditions are not there anymore, they cease to exist.

However, in the middle of all those changing and uncontrollable circumstances, we can still live a good life. If we accept that a good life is a collection of good moments, then we can do our best to notice, appreciate, savor, and absorb the good moments of life. We can learn to pause and give ourselves time to take those moments in. We can learn to register them in our long term memory by paying attention to the good in the present moment.

Although this is quite simple to do, it's not easy. As the saying goes, "It is not difficult to be mindful; what is difficult is to remember to be mindful." If our minds are always in the past or the future, then the present is rarely registered. And if that's all we do, we may get to the end of our lives and feel that we have not lived, what is very sad. So the challenge is to try to live mindfully, being totally present with whatever may be unfolding, approaching each experience, pleasant or unpleasant, with curiosity, impartiality, and equanimity, while remembering that whatever arises also passes away.

So let us make each moment count, doing our best to mindfully notice and extract the good that each one has to offer. Let's remember to treasure this moment because, in all truth, it is the only one that exists, the one in which we make the choices that ultimately affect the quality of our lives.

The quality of our lives is a result of the choices we make. That's why mindful moments, those when we observe the world around us, notice our thoughts, emotions, and body sensations, ask ourselves the important questions, and choose wisely, are so important.

So let's be here, now, present to extract the good of this moment, finding the extraordinary in the ordinary, seeing the new in the old, discovering the unusual in the usual, and noticing all the stunning magic, mystery, and miracles in which we are immersed. Let's pause and take it all in. Let's ask ourselves, "What brings me joy? How can I populate my days with the activities, things, people, and places that bring me joy?" And knowing the answers to these questions, let's create amazing moments on purpose. Let's create perfect days, deliberately. Let's create joyful lives, intentionally.

....

SEIZE THE DAY

Seize the day, put very little trust in tomorrow.

Carpe Diem, Quam Minimum Credula Postero.

This is an invitation to focus with ardency on the only available reality: this present moment, right here, right now, with all the good and bad it brings.

Seize the day, put very little trust in tomorrow.

This is an invitation to bring to mind our own mortality, and the limited duration of our physical lives so we become serious about living lives that matter.

Seize the day, put very little trust in tomorrow.

This is an invitation to deal with the challenges at hand and not worry unnecessarily about tomorrow, because tomorrow will reveal its own worries.

Seize the day, put very little trust in tomorrow.

This is an invitation to seize the present moment, and notice, appreciate, savor, and absorb all it has to offer.

……...

OUR LIVES ARE CONSTANTLY BEGINNING

Our lives are constantly beginning, again and again. Every moment is a new moment, the first moment of the rest of our lives, and the only one that really exists, the only one during which we can affect the quality of our lives by the choices we make. All that happens, when it happens, happens in the present moment. Whatever happened in the past, when it happened, happened in the present moment. And whatever will happen in the future, when it will happen, will also happen in the present moment. The past and the future are nothing more than thoughts in the present moment.

We must practice diligently and do our best to tame the tendency of our minds to roam and get lost in time and space. This wandering habit of the mind gets in the way of capturing the good of each present moment because it hinders our ability to be fully present in the here-now, noticing all the beauty that surrounds us.

Knowing that a good life is a collection of good moments, let us do our best to be present, noticing and taking in those moments, with all their magic, mystery, and miracles. Let us not only notice those good moments that come about spontaneously, but let's also create good moments on purpose. Let's ask ourselves, "What brings me joy? And how can I populate my days with more of the things, people, activities, and places that bring me joy?" Let's create those joyful moments intentionally and more often and then pause, giving ourselves all the time necessary to savor them, enjoy them, absorb them completely, and record them in our minds. Let us remember to be mindful, and to allow ourselves to be amazed, grateful, and optimistic. Let us make of this and every moment the best it can be, knowing that this is the recipe for creating fulfilling and happy lives! Let us realize and remember that today -- and every day -- is a special day. Today is the first day of the rest of our lives. Let's make it count. Let's be present and enjoy it!

UNSATISFACTORINESS AND ENOUGHNESS

We live with a perennial feeling that something is missing, in a constant state of unsatisfactoriness. We keep telling ourselves, "If only I had more money... If only I had a better job... If only I had a bigger house... If only I found the right partner... If only I were able to meditate with regularity, then I would be OK." We are constantly pursuing something, usually outside of ourselves, and this pursuit is exhausting because it has no end; once we achieve what we want, some other desire pops up. In those moments when we may be desiring to become someone better, or get somewhere better, it would be wise to counterbalance such desires with some doses of gratitude and contentment, perhaps saying to ourselves, "I am enough. I do enough. I have enough. I don't have to get anywhere. I have arrived already."

……..

The observation of life made me realize that I rarely experienced full contentment. No matter how wonderful my life was, I always felt that something was not quite right, that something was missing. I lived with the hope that something in the future would come about and fulfill the void I felt. But what would bring me contentment and peace of mind was never clear: perhaps the next academic degree, the next job, the next relationship, the next house, the next vacation, perhaps when I achieved fame and fortune. I kept pursuing those things that the culture told me would make me happy.

Not knowing what would tame my anxiety -- what would give me the feeling of fulfillment I so much longed for -- I found myself all over the place. It was as if I was shooting in the dark, hoping to hit the target. Rather than being centered and satisfied, I found myself in this state of imbalance, constantly desiring, constantly leaning forward, hoping that the next future thing would placate this sentiment that although things were good, they were not quite right, this subtle feeling in the background that something was wrong. I referred to it as 'a bug in the system, an undercurrent of uncertainty, fear, anxiety, and dissatisfaction.' I could hear Mick Jagger singing, "I can't get no satisfaction."

I came to realize that many of the things I was pursuing -- the things I was told would make me happy -- were misleading, vain promises of happiness. I realized that I was following someone else's formula for happiness, not my own. I also came to learn that a state of happiness based in conditions is only temporary because circumstances are constantly changing. Yes, everything is impermanent! And then I began to become aware of the vicious circle of desires and discontentment, desires and restlessness, desires and suffering! I became more aware of how wanting is disturbing, and how contentment is calming.

Enter enoughness!

I realize that everything, no matter how good, can be improved. I also realize that improvement has no end, and that it is necessary to practice mindfulness and know when to say, "That's enough. I am satisfied." By practicing appreciation, contentment, and gratitude for all that I do, all that I have, and who I am, I feel that I was blessed with much more than enough, and as a result of that feeling, I am more generous. And when I am all this -- appreciative, content, satisfied, grateful, and generous -- I am happier.

Give it a try.

....

"The more you pursue feeling better all the time the less satisfied you become as pursuing something only reinforces the fact that you lack it in the first place. The more desperately you want to be rich, the more poor and unworthy you feel regardless of how much money you actually make... The desire for more positive experience is itself a negative experience. And, paradoxically, the acceptance of one's negative experience is itself a positive experience... Wanting positive experience is a negative experience. Accepting negative experience is a positive experience." ~ Mark Manson

....

HOW LIFE SHOULD BE

We better pause and think... What are we doing here? What is life? Did we come here to work, make money, buy, consume, and accumulate? Is this the main purpose in life? Is this what life is supposed to be?

Apparently it is, since human beings -- the vast majority, at least -- spend more time working and acquiring stuff than in any other activity. Well, is this, then, the right way to spend our lives? What do you think?

I believe we can live better lives by engaging in the process of exploring and trying to figure out what the ultimate purpose of life is. I believe we can live better lives by organizing ourselves to live on this planet in gentler ways. I believe that, to begin with, we must learn to be mindful of the world around us, and notice the beautiful garden and wonderful playground in which we live. By doing so, we will be constantly amazed by the magic, mystery, and miracles that surround us, and this will develop in us a sense of immense appreciation and gratefulness for these gifts that were freely given to us. This awareness will open up the doors for a new realm where we will live much more joyfully.

But in order for us to manifest this new way of living, we will have to abandon some of the old ideas that we have always accepted. We will have to take a good look at those beliefs that are deeply ingrained in our minds and that we have never questioned, such as our beliefs about work and success. So, let us do that for a few moments.

We were brought up to believe that we must work hard and accumulate material wealth. Unconsciously, we feel that if we are not working hard, we are violating some sort of higher moral principle, and are, therefore, committing a transgression, a highly reprehensible offense. But is this so? Should we feel as if we have sinned because we haven't worked really hard? Should we feel that we have failed in life if we haven't amassed great wealth? We have to pause and question our obsession with hard work, consumption, and accumulation. We have to ask ourselves, "Do I really need to work as much and as hard as I do? Do I need to consume and accumulate as much as I do? Do I need to have so many possessions? Is it right to generate so much waste as I do?"

It is also important to consider some fundamental questions, such as, "Who am I? Is my individual value determined by what I do and what I have? Am I what I do? Am I what I have? Am I a human-doing and a human-having, or am I a human-being?" These are important reflections because they can lead us to rethink who we are, what we do, and the ways we have organized ourselves to live on this planet.

……..

"Our excessive possessions (and obligations) are not making us happy. Even worse, they are taking us away from the things that do.

Once we let go of the things that don't matter, we are free to pursue all the things that really do matter... Sometimes, minimizing possessions (and obligations) means a dream must die. But this is not always a bad thing. Sometimes, it takes giving up the person we wanted to be in order to fully appreciate the person we can actually become." ~ Joshua Becker

....

DON'T WORRY

You see, many of us wake up in the morning with an alarm and spend the rest of the day in a state of alarm. We don't relax a single moment. We get up, get dressed, get ready, and get going. We wake up in the morning telling ourselves, "I have to do this and I have to do that," and create those long and unrealistic to-do lists, with too many things to do and not enough time to do them.

Then we go through our days rushing and running, thinking about what we have to do next instead of concentrating on what we have in front of us, be it the work at hand, or the person we may be with, collecting all the scattered pieces and trying to put them together. Most of the time, we are not here, now; our minds are elsewhere and else when. We are not enjoying the present.

And as it invariably happens, unexpected things pop up, and there goes the plan we had for the day. When this happens, we immediately tense up. Instead of giving thanks for the unexpected, and accepting what we were given, we resist and react. We don't surrender and look for the good in the unexpected. As we don't look, we don't find. We don't go with the flow; we swim against it. As a result, irritation, impatience, frustration, anger, and anxiety become our companions for the day.

And at the end of the day, when we review our to-do list, we tell ourselves, "I have not done this. I have not done that. I should have done this. I could have done that. I haven't done enough. I am worthless." We go to bed feeling tired, guilty, and defeated.

Is this your life? What kind of life is this? Why are you going to go through life feeling this way: tired, guilty, and defeated? Can't you see that you are the one imposing too many demands on your own self? Can't you see that you are the one creating your own stress, the biggest killer of all?

Yes, we begin our days with our plans, and we may end up doing something completely different. This is OK. This is life. We have to plan. We have to put ourselves in motion to reach our goals, but we have to remain flexible, accepting, surrendering, and relaxing. In moments of mayhem, we have to breathe deeply, reconvene, recollect, and be gentle with ourselves. We have to find joy in what was brought to us. At the end of the day, instead of focusing on what we have not done and feeling guilty and defeated, we shall focus on the much that we have accomplished and feel victorious.

How can we do this?

I suggest we look at our days differently, and rather than telling negative stories, let's tell positive ones. Let's focus on all the positive aspects of the day and tell a tale of victory. "I had a fantastic day, full of unexpected occurrences and new opportunities. I took action and I am moving closer to my goals. I gave a great contribution to the world today!" No more negative stories. No more shouldas, couldas, and guilt feelings. "It was a glorious day. I am grateful. And I am moving on; the past is gone." We must learn to do our part, and let go, and let the Universe take care of the details.

....

Good morning. This is God. I will be handling all your problems and concerns today. I will not require your help. So relax and enjoy the day. Have a good day!

....

IT'S WHAT I DO

I went to my week-long silent retreat thinking what I would like to get from it. I framed it as a time of spiritual detox and rehab. I knew it was going to be demanding, so I renewed my commitment to apply myself wholeheartedly in order to get the most out of it. And then it came to me that, in the final analysis, it didn't matter so much what I thought I would do, or what I intended to do, or what I said I was going to do; what really mattered is what I actually did!

Actions really speak louder than words.

What was true for my retreat is also true for life. Good intentions that are not translated into action have no impact in enhancing the quality of life, one's own and the lives of all other sentient beings. So, let us remember that every moment of awareness and clarity, of re-commitment to noble goals, and of right action is important. May we have the strength to live mindfully. May we choose to be happy and bring happiness to others. May happiness be the chief-counselor for our decisions.

. . . .

It's not what I think I'll do.
It's not what I intend to do.
It's not what I say I'll do.
It's what I do.

. . . .

Since gratefulness is the key that opens the gates to the kingdom of happiness, it is always appropriate to express gratitude. I realize how fortunate and blessed I am. How many people in the world have a chance to attend a silent retreat? How many people in the world have a chance to take a long period of time off, go to a beautiful, secluded, and protected place where they are taken good care of, in order to work on their personal development? I am fortunate and blessed, and I am grateful.

. . . .

THE PATH TO HAPPINESS

"Happiness is available. Please help yourself to it." ~ Thich Nhat Hanh

. . . .

By being mindful we see what we weren't able to see before, both inside and outside. We begin to see all the magic, mystery and miracles that surround us. This immense beauty -- that has always been here, but that we only begin to notice now -- brings about a state of amazement. We realize how blessed we are, and we feel grateful for all that was given to us, with life itself. Feeling blessed and content with all we have, we become less afraid and more optimistic, trusting in the abundance of the Universe. We begin to move away from selfishness in the direction of selflessness. We develop compassion and become more generous. We realize that we were given the gifts that we were given not to keep them, but to give them away. We realize that it is in giving that we receive, and by doing all this, we find the happiness that we were seeking, right here, right now.

....

"People are often illogical, unreasonable, irrational, and self-centered. Forgive them and love them anyway. If you are kind and do good, people may accuse you of selfish, ulterior motives. Do good and be kind anyway. If you are successful, you will win some false friends and some true enemies. Succeed anyway. The good you do today will be forgotten tomorrow. Do good anyway. Honesty and frankness make you vulnerable. If you are honest and sincere people may deceive you. Be honest and sincere anyway. The biggest men and women with the biggest ideas can be shot down by the smallest men and women with the smallest minds. Think big anyway. People favor underdogs but follow only top dogs. Fight for a few underdogs anyway. What you spend years creating, others can destroy overnight. Create anyway. People really need help but may attack you if you do help them. Help people anyway. If you find serenity and happiness, some may be jealous. Be serene and happy anyway. The good you do today, will be forgotten tomorrow. Do good anyway. Give the best you have, knowing that it will never be enough. Give the world the best you have and you'll be attacked. Give the world the best you have anyway. In the final analysis, it is between you and God. It was never between you and them anyway." ~ Kent M. Keith and Mother Teresa

....

EXPRESSING GRATEFULNESS

I am grateful for everything. I am grateful for this body. I am grateful for my friends, and for all the people I have shared my journey with. I am grateful for my teachers, not only those who have taught me what to do, but also those who, through mistakes and suffering, have showed me what not to do. I am grateful for the good life I always had and have. I am grateful that I have always had food, water, and a roof over my head. I am grateful that I have always been healthy and surrounded by love. I am grateful that I have never been exposed to violence. My problems are nothing compared with the problems of so many other people in the world. I am blessed. I am grateful. I am happy.

Gratefulness is the key that unlocks the gates to the kingdom of happiness.

……..

"In daily life we must see that it is not happiness that makes us grateful, but gratefulness that makes us happy." ~ David Steindl-Rast

……..

FROM MINDFULNESS TO HAPPINESS

Be mindful.
Be amazed.
Be grateful.
Be content.
Be optimistic.
Be compassionate.
Be generous.
Be happy.

……..

Be mindful of all the beauty that surrounds you. Be mindful of the infinite possibilities that are always available for you. Be present in this moment, right here, right now, not lost in thoughts, ruminating the past and anticipating the future with unnecessary worries. Since in the final analysis a good life is a collection of good moments, extract all the good you can of each and every present moment. Be awake, attentive, alert, aware, and appreciative, in order to be fully and joyfully alive. Don't allow the past unhappiness, or the pursuit of an imagined future happiness, to be the sources of your present unhappiness. Again, don't ruminate and don't anticipate. Be here, now.

Be amazed with all the magic, mystery, and miracles that surround you. Cultivate a patient, childlike curiosity. Cultivate the eyes of a tourist, the mind of a beginner, the boldness of an explorer, the inquisitiveness of a scientist, the attentiveness of an investigator, the attention of a romantic lover. See beyond what you see. Look with the eyes of the body and see with the eyes of the heart. Feel the breeze, and watch the leaves and branches dancing with the wind. See the reflections on the pond, and the shining sparks on the surface of the water. See things as you've never seen them before. Be aware of the eternal and the transient. Notice the permanence and impermanence of all. Nothing lasts forever. Know that in the physical form neither you nor anyone else will last forever. Know that what is bad will not last forever, nor what is good. Everything changes. Everything passes. So do not get too attached to anything or anyone, not even your loved ones, your body, your ideas about yourself, or even the idea that a being called "I" exists. Learn to release and let go of everything.

Be grateful for all the gifts that were freely given to you. Be grateful for the life you have, for the adventure you are living.

Be content and satisfied with your share, with all that was given to you. Don't compare yourself with others. There will always be people who are, who do, and who have more than you, as well as people who are, do, and have less than you. Stop comparing. You are not less than anyone else; nor more. You are you. Be yourself. Be who you are. Be authentic and genuine. Be humble. Try not to judge and condemn.

Be optimistic, hopeful, and positive. Trust that everything in the Universe is unfolding as it should, and better things and situations are always coming your way. Remember to look at the biggest possible picture always, and see that what seems very significant, actually is not. Look at your own experience and see that many of the things you thought were good and wanted, turned out to be bad, and many of the things you didn't want turned out to be good. Cultivate a great sense of humor, and remember that many of your worries never came to be true.

Be compassionate. Develop empathy, and try to see and feel as others see and feel. Decide to do something to make someone else's life better. Be kind, patient, forgiving, and loving. Be fair, just, and honest.

Be generous. Give. Give. Give. Give love. Give of yourself -- your time and undivided attention -- to others. Give them your shoulder to cry.

Be of service to others. Be kind. Listen. Be a peacemaker, a bringer of peace, a promoter of peace. Be at peace with others and with yourself. Be gentle with others and with yourself. Do not demand too much nor be too harsh with yourself. Relax and enjoy. And, by doing all this, day in and day out, you will be happy.

……..

From Mindfulness to Amazement.
From Amazement to Gratefulness.

From Gratefulness to Contentment.
From Contentment to Optimism.
From Optimism to Compassion.
From Compassion to Generosity.
From Generosity to Happiness.

. . . .

FROM SILENCE TO HAPPINESS

Remember! Remember! Remember! It is not difficult to be mindful. What is difficult is to remember to be mindful.

. . . .

Pause for a moment, come to the here-now, and try to reflect on the following components to see if, for you, they work together to produce a state of happiness.

- Befriending the silence.
- Cultivating stillness.
- Enjoying Silence, Stillness, Solitude, Seclusion, Simplicity, and Service.
- Staying mindfully in the here-now, awake, alert, attentive, aware, appreciative, and alive.
- Paying attention.
- Coming back to this moment, over and over again, and realizing it is a new moment, and the only moment.
- Cultivating a childlike curiosity, a beginner's mind.
- Refraining from comparing, contrasting, categorizing, classifying, competing, complaining, criticizing, and condemning.
- Observing.
- Exploring.
- Noticing.
- Investigating.
- Looking with tourist's eyes, and seeing beyond what we normally see.
- Discovering magic, mystery, and miracles everywhere, and finding the sacred in the secular.
- Appreciating, enjoying, and admiring the gifts that were freely given to us, and experiencing a state of awe, amazement, wonderment, ecstasy, and reverence.

- Experiencing joy, delight, elation, bliss, euphoria, and exultation.
- Recognizing the blessings, and acknowledging the abundance of the Universe.
- Developing a sense of gratefulness, and hosting a feeling of contentment and satisfaction.
- Discovering your purpose and following your bliss.
- Accepting the call of Life, and courageously launching yourself into the adventure.
- Putting yourself in motion.
- Letting go and letting be.
- Cultivating inexhaustible hope and optimism.
- Remaining open to outcomes, no matter how unexpected they may be.
- Trusting that everything is unfolding as it should.
- Remembering that nothing lasts forever; everything changes all the time.
- Finding perfection in the present situation.
- Refraining from striving.
- Being gentle with yourself, knowing when to demand less.
- Giving yourself the gift of rest.
- Living with ease by practicing simplicity, humility, authenticity, honor, and honesty.
- Developing tenderness, solidarity, and love.
- Taking action to serve and give.
- Being generous, patient, gentle, and kind with others.
- Developing strong, meaningful, deep, high quality relationships.
- Giving people your full, undivided attention.
- Laughing and bringing laughter to others.
- Becoming a bringer of peace.
- Deciding to be happy.
- Doing what makes you happy, and, finally,
- Experiencing happiness!

....

SEPARATION, INITIATION, RETURN

"Let yourself be silently drawn by the strange pull of what you really love. It will not lead you astray." ~ Rumi

....

The Hero's Journey, the common template of tales that involve a hero who goes on an adventure, wins a victory, and then comes home transformed, can be divided in three major parts: Separation, Initiation, and Return.

So, here is our future hero, living the "normal life," living all his many predetermined roles, doing pretty much what everyone else does, doing what is expected of him, wanting the same things everyone else wants, working hard, consuming a lot, trying to fit in, be admired and loved, and hardly ever questioning anything. In his heart, every now and then, he may feel that he is not living the life he was called to live, but the pressures of the culture around him keep him doing the same things over and over again. He remains mostly unaware of his potential, of possibilities, of his options in life, living as if he is hypnotized, constantly distracted, and somewhat numb. Although internally he may feel that he is not doing what he came here to do -- or being who he came here to be -- he refuses to accept the Universe's Call to Adventure. He does not feel he is ready or capable of facing the challenges. And then, suddenly, something happens; a loss of wealth, health, or relationships. He loses his job, his money, his house, or a loved one. He faces a break-up or a divorce. He gets sick and loses vitality. These are prime moments for the hero to wake up. He can't stay put any longer. He has to go! And so, maybe reluctantly, he answers the Call to Adventure, and does what the Universe is summoning him to do. This is what Joseph Campbell called "The Separation."

....

The Call to Adventure is that persistent call from the Forces of the Universe summoning us to do what we must do if we are to fulfill our purposes and live lives that matter.

What is your mission in life? The Universe is calling. What have the Forces of the Universe summoned you to do? The Universe is calling. Answer the call! You know what you have to do. Put yourself in motion and give that contribution that only you can give.

....

Then a new phase begins. Joseph Campbell called it, "The Initiation." That is the adventure itself. It is time now for the hero to let go of lives that have played themselves out and do not serve him anymore. He needs to let go of his past, his attachments, his identities, his personae, and the stories he tells about himself. It is time for him to put himself in motion to answer the calling. It is time to question all beliefs, letting go of some, keeping others, and adding new ones. It is a time of self-discovery. It is a time for honestly answering the four fundamental questions: "Who am I? What do I love? How shall I live knowing that I will die? What gifts do I bring to share with others?" It is a moment for removing the masks and living with authenticity. It is a time to become aware of the big illusion we are immersed in. It is a time to face the challenges, despite all self-doubts and insecurities. It is time for the hero to follow his bliss, knowing that if he does so, the Universe will open doors for him where there were only walls. And it is also during this phase that teachers and helpers show up.

....

"I seek courage to live -- this day. Courage to strike out on a path I have never trod before, courage to make new friends, courage to yield myself to the full power of the dream." ~ Howard Thurman

....

And after the hero lives his adventure, he comes back, forever changed. Joseph Campbell called this phase, "The Return." He is now much more peaceful, selfless, compassionate, tolerant, content, and grateful. He becomes a blessing to all who come in contact with him.

....

"Our deepest fear is not that we are inadequate. Our deepest fear is that we are powerful beyond measure. It is our light, not our darkness that most frightens us." ~ Marianne Williamson

....

FEAR WHEN HAPPINESS ARRIVES

Have you heard of the negativity bias, the propensity of our minds to give much more attention to what is negative than what is positive? Well, many of us are always catastrophizing. No matter how good the present moment may be, we are always imagining that something bad is about to happen, that tragedy is just around the corner. We live in fear, compounding unnecessary stress and anxiety, which in turn have detrimental effects on our mental, emotional, and physical health and well-being. It's always good to pause and ask, "What do I get from this? Is this pattern of thought useful?"

It's not uncommon for fear to arise when things are just fine. Yes, everything is OK, everything is perfect, but we are not tranquil: deep inside there is this disturbing fear that something bad is about to happen. Flavio Gikovate, a Brazilian psychotherapist and scholar, lectured extensively on the irrational fear felt by many that when everything is well, or when everything is about to be well, a tragedy will strike. Many people are unaware that they may be afraid of achieving their dreams, having success, and experiencing happy moments, because they are already anticipating the pain they will experience in the event they lose all that. Have you ever noticed the sneaky fear that arises when we are about to reach our goals, or when we have reached them and are experiencing success and happiness? Dr. Gikovate alerted us that due to this fear many times we sabotage ourselves and bring our projects to failure, a dangerous tendency that becomes more present as we get closer to reaching our goals. It's not uncommon, when things are going well, for our brains to focus on the negative rather than the positive. And we have to understand that the brain's tendency to pay more attention to what is negative is natural; it's just the way our brains work and have worked throughout the ages to protect us, humans, from danger. But the good news is that our brains are trainable. Yes. Our brains are trainable!

We can, through deliberate mindfulness practice, increase our ability to be aware of those times when fear is not called for. We can also train ourselves to increase our ability to notice the good and take it in, what has the power to tame fear.

Here's an acronym that will make this practice easier to remember: NASA. Not the National Air and Space Administration of the space programs and astronauts, but the initials of four other words: Notice, Appreciate, Savor, and Absorb. NASA.

The more I pause to notice, appreciate, savor, and absorb the good things in my life, the more gratitude becomes my brain's default operating mode. I become more focused on gratitude than fear. I focus on the abundance of the Universe and marvel at it. I am more optimistic and less pessimistic. I focus on how blessed I am, how blessed we all are, and feel content, satisfied, and happy. N.A.S.A. I invite you to give it a try.

……...

REPLAY, RELIVE, REMEMBER, REFLECT

After a mindful walk in nature, I usually create an opportunity for my students to reflect in silence, voicing these instructions:

- Replay in your mind's eye what you've noticed during the walk
- Relive the sensations and emotions you've experienced
- Remember any memories those moments evoked, and
- Reflect on any epiphanies that emerged.

Finally, I ask them to sum it all up and take it all in.

……...

MINDFULNESS AND DEATH

TEARS IN RAIN

"Quite an experience to live in fear, isn't it? This is what it is to be a slave."

"I've seen things you people wouldn't believe. Attack ships on fire off the shoulder of Orion. I watched c-beams glitter in the dark near the Tannhäuser Gate. All those moments will be lost in time, like tears in rain. Time to die."

These are the final words of Roy Batty, the rebel replicant in the movie "Blade Runner," directed by Ridley Scott, based on Philip K. Dick's story "Do Androids Dream of Electric Sheep?" The screenplay was written by Hampton Fancher and David Peoples. This scene makes me think about living in fear, loving life, and the impermanence of all.

....

During a time in my life when I was dealing with a lot of uncertainty and fear, the words spoken in this scene of the movie "Blade Runner" made me reflect a lot about the disturbing effects of fear. The movie depicts a society in the future where androids are sent to other planets to do the hard work. These automatons are the slaves of the future, and the best ones are known as replicants, excellent replicas of human beings. Similar to humans, they function just for a limited amount of time until they reach that point when their systems shut down and their existences come to an end. A group of replicants come to love their lives so much that they want to prevent this from happening; they don't want to die. So they initiate a violent rebellion, and come to Earth with the intent of meeting their creator, the scientist who invented and manufactures the androids. Their hope is that, after hearing their plea, he will extend their lives from the default four-year lifespan. Special police operatives, known as Blade Runners, are assigned to hunt down and exterminate the defiant replicants. A retired police officer from the Blade Runner squadron reluctantly accepts the assignment to eliminate the rebel androids, and that's what he does, one by one. The end of the movie brings us to witness the confrontation between this detective and the last rebel left, the strongest of them all, the leader of the group. The final clash takes place on the rooftop of an abandoned building. The android clearly has the upper hand, and the detective is about to lose the fight, and his life. On the verge of dying, when the detective is showing all his fear, the slave calmly says to him, "Quite an experience to live in fear, isn't it? This is what it is to be a slave." I have reflected on these words and they have taught me a lot. The slave himself defines what slavery truly is: slavery is to live in fear. Think about it: to live in fear is to be a slave. Every time I think about this passage I reflect upon the damaging effects of fear. It is certainly not an easy endeavor, but we must find the courage to be present and curious about our fears because facing fear is what, ultimately, liberates us. "Quite an experience to live in fear, isn't it? This is what it is to be a slave." Fear holds us prisoners. If we live our lives in fear we will never be truly free. Set yourself free.

....

Knowing that all his attempts to extend his life had failed, and that the end of his existence was imminent, the replicant decides to save his enemy's life. In the final moments of his existence, he decides to give life, not to take it, maybe because of the great love for life that he had developed. I think that when you come to a deeper understanding of what life is, you come to the conclusion that because life is so precious, no one should ever kill. We understand that the preservation of life is paramount. What comes to my mind is a saying attributed to Gandhi: "For this cause I am willing to die, but there is no cause I am willing to kill for."

....

Nothing lasts forever. "All those moments will be lost in time, like tears in rain."

ACCEPTING IMPERMANENCE

"Well Marianne, it's come to this time when we are really so old and our bodies are falling apart and I think I will follow you very soon. Know that I am so close behind you that if you stretch out your hand, I think you can reach mine. And you know that I've always loved you for your beauty and your wisdom, but I don't need to say anything more about that because you know all about that. But now, I just want to wish you a very good journey. Goodbye old friend. Endless love, see you down the road." ~ Leonard Cohen

………

We are called to realize that nothing lasts forever; neither what is good, nor what is bad. Everything that is of the nature to arise, will also pass away.

Transformation is taking place all the time.

We are called to realize that since everything is impermanent, all kinds of attachments lead to suffering. So, we must be prepared to let go of everyone and everything.

We are called to accept both what we consider to be good as well as what we consider to be bad with equanimity.

While taking good care of our health, we must be ready to accept the inevitable debilitating effects of aging. We must prepare ourselves to accept that we, our loved ones, and everyone else, will eventually get ill and die, and although we are taught to love, we must learn not to cling to anyone or anything, and be prepared to let go of all that we love.

We have to come to the realization that suffering comes from the concept of 'I' and, therefore, we should let go of the stories and characters that we have created for ourselves, transcend our identification with our physical bodies, and realize that they are mere vessels of an Imperishable Light that is birthless and deathless.

We have to come to the realization that our suffering comes from forgetting that we are, at the same time, mortal and immortal, human and divine, body and spirit, solid matter and vibrational energy, separated and united, independent and interdependent.

We are many, and we are one.

………

JASMINE FLOWERS

What once was white and soft
Is now lifeless and dry
A pleasant visitor who didn't overstay
Gone now...
But the scent remains

....

INSEPARABLE SAND

I once witnessed the creation of a mandala with colored sand by the monks of the Drepung Gomang Monastery. They worked diligently for an entire week creating a beautiful piece of art destined to disappear. The tradition dictates that once the mandala is finished, the monks sweep all the sand they have used and pour it in the water. The lesson to be learned is the impermanence of all things. All things must pass, and therefore we should not get attached to anything. Sometimes we dedicate countless hours to the creation of something beautiful, but we must learn to detach ourselves from our creations. They will not last forever. In the final analysis, nothing does.

For us who are parents, it is a reminder to let our children -- our most sacred creations -- go. As hard as it may be, we have to accept that they too, just like everyone and everything else, will not last forever. And for all of us, the lesson is to realize that no matter how much effort we may have put to create our lives, and to bring about the best versions of ourselves, we still must be ready to let everything we love go, and accept that we, too, will vanish like sand in the water. Everything is transient. We should not get attached to anything, including our views of how life should be, because every attachment brings about suffering.

....

"So we fix our eyes not on what is seen, but on what is unseen, since what is seen is temporary, but what is unseen is eternal." ~ Paul, the apostle

....

Once brushed together, the once multi-colored sand with very distinct and identifiable colors became one inseparable and indivisible whole. I guess there is another lesson to be learned here: no matter how

196

different from one another we may think we are, and no matter how much effort we may put during our existences to isolate ourselves, exclude and separate ourselves from others, in the end we all become the same inseparable and indistinguishable sand.

T. S Eliot said that "what we call the beginning is often the end, and to make an end is to make a beginning." He exhorted us to explore: "We shall not cease from exploration, and the end of all our exploring will be to arrive where we started, and know the place for the first time."

....

Birth, growth, decay, death, transformation...

Everything is transitioning; death follows birth, and birth follows death.

Everything that begins will meet its end, and every end brings about a new beginning.

Every being and thing we love is impermanent, and we have to learn to peacefully accept the inevitable physical separation. We have to fix our eyes not on what is seen, but on what is unseen, since what is seen is temporary, but what is unseen is eternal. We have to prepare ourselves for our physical death, accepting that no matter how important we may think we are, in the end, we, too, will leave behind a tombstone that someday will become illegible.

It seems that we go out in life looking for something without realizing that what we have been looking for has been with us all the time. We go out looking for a treasure that we have had since the beginning. We go out to learn, forgetting that we already know and that the wisdom we seek resides in us.

There are magical moments available to all of us when we walk in the woods, when we immerse ourselves in nature, when we prepare ourselves to intentionally hear the unheard and see the unseen, when we become aware at the source of the longest river of the voice of the hidden waterfall and the children in the apple-tree.

The truth we seek is in the whispers heard in the silence. The truth that will bring us peace is not known, because not looked for, but heard, half-heard, in the stillness, between two waves of the sea. And in order for us to know this truth and experience this peace we have to be willing to let go of lives that have played themselves out and do not serve us anymore. We must be willing to live in a condition of complete simplicity, costing not less than everything.

....

PHYSICAL AND SPIRITUAL

We are physical beings. That is true, but perhaps not the entire truth. I believe we are more than these mammals. I believe we are spiritual beings too. I use the word spiritual, but perhaps I could choose to use other less-charged words, such as mysterious, or awe-struck. Now, I don't have clear evidence of that but due to all the magic, mystery, and miracles that surround me, the hypothesis that we are both physical and spiritual beings is one that I like to explore.

We inhabit this physical world, but, as many sages say, we are not from this world. And that's the human condition: having to live and operate in one realm -- the physical -- while belonging to, and not forgetting the other -- the spiritual. Our job is to constantly remember who we are, where we came from, what we were brought here to do, and where we will be going to after our passage through this physical dimension is over.

Pierre Teilhard de Chardin said that we are not human beings having spiritual experiences, but spiritual beings having human experiences. As human beings, we are faced with challenges, struggles, disappointments, tragedies, trials, tribulations and death. That's all part of being human. But, looking at these occurrences as spiritual beings we realize that they do not deserve the importance we attribute to them; what seems to be major in the physical dimension is in fact minor when seen through the eyes of the spirit.

One more time: our job is to constantly remember who we are and what we were brought here to do. We are eternal spiritual beings having temporary human experiences. We are One Consciousness revealing itself through several physical manifestations that are impermanent and separated. We are, at the same time, human and divine, mortal and immortal, separated and united, independent and interdependent, many and one. We were brought here to remember and experience our oneness. We were brought here to learn to be compassionate and learn to love others. We were brought here to learn to give love. We were brought here to learn to be unselfish, kind, patient, gentle, forgiving and generous. We were brought here to learn all these things, and also to teach them. We were brought here to promote understanding, peace and unity. That is what is asked of us.

………

WE ARE DIVINE AND WE ARE ONE

We are all human beings. Our common humanity precedes our nationality, ethnicity, ideology, or any other category. We could say that we are human before we are anything else, but this would be an incomplete statement because our divinity precedes even our humanity. We are divine before we are human. We are divine before we are anything else.

We break away from agony the moment we become conscious of our heavenly nature. This is what brings us ultimate tranquility: the conscience of our divinity. This is what brings us ultimate ecstasy: living out our divinity. This is what brings us ultimate happiness: making others happy. We must come to realize that our fate is linked with that of everyone throughout the Universe. We are all related, and the full realization of our divinity and oneness is one of the greatest insights we might come to, one that raises our consciousness to new heights and forever changes the way we see reality, and live our lives.

………

"Hope and fear are both phantoms that arise from thinking of the self. When we don't see the self as self, what do we have to fear? Empty your mind of all thoughts. Let your heart be at peace. Each separate being in the universe returns to the common source. Returning to the source is serenity. If you don't realize the source, you stumble in confusion and sorrow. When you realize where you come from, you naturally become tolerant, disinterested, amused, kindhearted as a grandmother, dignified as a king. Immersed in the wonder of the Tao, you can deal with whatever life brings you, and when death comes, you are ready." ~ Laozi

………

THE POTATO PRINCIPLE

Mycology is the branch of biology that studies fungi. I once heard Paul Stamets, a mycologist, express reassuring ideas about life. Not that what he said was new to me, but hearing from someone who, in a way, dedicates himself to observe the process of death and rebirth, was comforting. His ideas replenished my reserves of tranquility to deal with the inevitable end of life, or, to be more precise, the end of the physical life in the shape and form we currently occupy in this physical dimension.

Since my youth I have been aware of Lavoisier's principle of conservation of mass which states, in my own simplified way of putting it, that "in nature nothing goes to waste, everything is transformed."

Pause for a moment, and think about transformation. We are changing all the time, aren't we? Where are the newborns and toddlers we once were? They are not here anymore. In this physical realm, we are all part of this amazing circle of life where everything changes constantly through a process of birth, growth, decay, and death. Everyone and everything is in constant transformation. When we cease to exist as living organisms, we are transformed — we change form — and become nutrients for other organisms. For instance, the matter we are made of decomposes and becomes soil from which vegetables sprout. Those vegetables become the food that sustains life. Vegetables and animals will exist for a time and then they will die and disintegrate into soil again, only to become nutrients for other life forms. And this process keeps repeating itself, without end. My friend Audrey calls it "The Potato Principle," poetically indicating our destiny: we will all become soil, vegetables, animals, and molecules of all other creatures.

I can see that we are made of everyone and everything else. Every life form that preceded us is somehow in us now. Nothing is destroyed. Nothing is created. Everything goes through a transmutation. Everything that has ever existed, exists in me. All my ancestors are, in some way, in me. All my heroes, those people I admire and look up to, are in me. We are in everything and everyone, and everything and everyone is in us. There's no separation. We are all interconnected and interdependent: we inter-are.

………

What follows is the result of my attempt to capture Paul Stamets's ideas. This is not a word-by-word transcription of what he said, but these are his ideas, and he deserves credit for them.

"Knowing that we are connected with every organism on this planet should inspire us to pause and feel the wonder of it all. We are not a part of nature; we are of nature. I feel better about my own mortality knowing that I have sprung from nature, I am of nature, and I will return to nature. Life and death is a continuum. Molecules are assembled, disassembled, and reassembled in different forms. It gives me solace in my own mortality to realize that from this web-like ecosystem I have sprung and to this web-like ecosystem I will return. I know that when I die, my molecules will be spread throughout the Universe, free to be reassembled in different forms, free to become elements of other organisms. We all share the same molecular Universe and knowing that we are this Universe gives me great peace and gratitude."

I like to think that I am made of everyone and everything else, that I carry in me particles of everyone who has ever lived before me, and of everything that has ever existed. I like to believe that through the rearrangement of molecules, all my ancestors live in me, and that, after my physical death, my particles will also inhabit everyone and everything, and I will be omnipresent. I conclude that we are one very large organism: some parts are dying, some parts are being born, but no part ever disappears. The processes of transformation, transmutation, assembling, disassembling, and reassembling of elements never stops. We are ever-present. We are all connected, not only through total interdependent relationships, but at a deep molecular level.

....

The truth is that, in this physical dimension, nothing is permanent; everything is impermanent. Life is not about birth and death; it is about metamorphosis. Every single thing undergoes changes of form, appearance, structure, or substance. All life forms go through structural or functional modifications during their development. Mutations are happening all the time. Think about the transmutation of a tadpole into a frog, of a chrysalis into a butterfly, of a fertilized egg into a newborn animal, of a tiny newborn baby into a full developed adult human being. And even when physical death occurs, tissues degenerate and facilitate the appearance of new physical life, and metamorphosis continues. Again, the only permanent thing in life is change.

During our life journeys, we go through many of those metamorphoses; some are completely involuntary, beyond our choosing and control, but others aren't.

And here I change gears, to talk about a different kind of death and rebirth: many are the times when we can choose if we are going to heed the calls to change and leave behind lives that have played themselves out and don't serve us anymore, or if we will keep trying to hold on to what once was but isn't anymore. If we accept those calls — if we face our fears and take the leaps of faith they demand — we go through those radical transformations, those spiritual awakenings, those deaths that allow us to be born again and reappear as new beings, capable of seeing what we weren't able to see before.

I accept the existence of two universes — the physical and the non-physical — and consider that we inhabit both at the same time. I believe that we are, both, mortal and immortal, that we experience birth and death in this physical plane, but not in the spiritual one. I believe that we are, at the same time, separated and united, many and one, human and divine.

....

ARRIVALS AND DEPARTURES

Life is marked by arrivals and departures, births and deaths. It is a puzzling and yet beautiful journey. Sometimes, I imagine the entire world as a giant and extremely busy train station, with people arriving and departing all the time. For the most part, joy with the arrivals and sadness with the departures of their loved ones are the feelings of those who are not traveling. But those who are embarking on new adventures experience excitement, joy, and a renewed energy to tackle whatever the upcoming journeys may have reserved for them.

Farewells in airports. The endings of romantic relationships. I felt sad when loved ones left. I felt depressed when stages of my life came to an end, and I had to let go of lives that had played themselves out and did not serve me anymore. I felt melancholy and despair witnessing physical death of people I knew, and also of people I didn't. I empathized with other people's grief and shed tears with them. But with all that I also came to realize that endings are just new beginnings in disguise.

We are constantly losing and regaining balance: this is the natural motion of life. We are always departing and coming back. We are always returning to the Source.

We came from nowhere and we are now-here.

Many times I have entertained the idea that ultimate reason for living is to go through experiences that allow us to learn how to properly die. I have decided that I will prepare myself to embrace death, my own, as an exciting departure, one that celebrates the beginning of a new and beautiful adventure. I am happy with the life that was given to me. I feel blessed for all the love I have received and the love I was able to give. Yes, my life, like all lives, had its difficult moments and tragedies, but I guess we all want to stick around for as long as we can because we love love; we love to love and to be loved. Arrivals and departures, births and deaths, beginnings and ends are ways Wisdom uses to remind us of the inexorable transformation and the impermanence of all. It is also a way of reminding us that, in the end, it's all about love: the love we make, the love we leave, and the love we take.

……..

"This body is not me. I am not limited by this body. I am life without boundaries. I have never been born, and I have never died." ~ Thich Nhat Hanh

……..

I COULD DIE TODAY

I could die today
And that would be okay
I no longer need to see the Matterhorn on a summer day

This old wood and rusted nails
This divine sky and gentle breeze
This unhurried movement of the leaves
This sound of no sounds

Maybe I will leave without ever seeing the mountain I love in all its glory
But that's okay
That's okay
I would die peacefully today
Because today was a perfect day

DEATH IS EVOLUTION

"Death is the only wise adviser that we have. Whenever you feel, as you always do, that everything is going wrong and you're about to be annihilated, turn to your death and ask if that is so. Your death will tell you that you're wrong; that nothing really matters outside its touch. Your death will tell you, 'I haven't touched you yet.'" ~ Carlos Castaneda

....

I have been thinking of physical life as a stage in the process of our evolution, and seeing the end of our physical existence simply as a moment of transition to another educational campus. I imagine someone coming to me, when the moment approaches, and saying, "OK. Enough. You have learned the lessons you needed to learn and taught the lessons you were brought here to teach. There's no need for you to stay here anymore. It is time for you to leave this dimension and go the next one." I like to think that physical death is just another moment of transition on this evolutionary journey. It is not that we reach the end of our journey when we die; it simply continues in another dimension.

I can understand people feeling sad when a loved one dies. There is sadness in all separations. But this sadness, perhaps, is just because that person will not be around -- at least not physically -- and we won't be able to enjoy their presence any longer. I can also understand the anxiety, fear, and the sense of insecurity one feels with the loss of a family member: many new challenges may arise for which those who remained may feel unprepared or incapable of dealing with. But in the end, everything will be OK, right? As the saying goes, "In the end, everything will be OK. If it is not OK, it's not the end."

Many times people say that the person died too soon, that she had so much more to live and give still, that her life was cut short, that now, after all the hard work and sacrifice she endured, was her time to enjoy life ... But all these statements come from the assumption that the person would be happier staying here than where she is right now. What about embracing the idea that there is no better place than the one we go to after our physical deaths? What about rejoicing and celebrating the good fortune of the deceased?

What comes to my mind is the idea that babies are reluctant to leave the wombs of their mothers. They are comfortable where they are, so when the time of birth arrives, they protest and cry. They want to stay with the known because they fear the unknown. I can draw a parallel with the moment of physical death. We got accustomed with our lives in this dimension, and we don't want to die. Just like the babies, we don't want to leave the known to venture in the unknown. But who says that what we will experience is not immensely better?

We can say that we exist because certain conditions came together and brought us into existence. We continue to exist while conditions that keep us alive continue to exist. The moment that such conditions cease to exist, so do we: we die. This is a very liberating. It's an approach that invites us to consider that there is no 'self,' that there is no 'I' to be attached to, only conditions and circumstances that are constantly changing, creating and extinguishing phenomena.

Impermanence of everything is the rule, right? So, we must accept death with equanimity.

Some of my friends tell me that I shouldn't talk so much about death. They tell me that I talk about death too much. For me, that's not the problem. The problem is that we don't talk about it enough.

We're constantly asking is there life after death? We should be asking ourselves is there life before death? Am I enjoying the journey? Am I present to enjoy the journey? Am I living? Or am I going through the motions, in automatic pilot, unaware of the present, sleepwalking through life?

. . . .

"Death is a concept that refers to endings. Endings need boundaries, and your dimensionless self has no boundaries." ~ Wayne Dyer

. . . .

Henry Scott-Holland wrote a beautiful poem in which he says that death is nothing at all. Check it out.

. . . .

THE BEAUTY OF DEATH

Every end is a new beginning. Every departure is followed by an arrival.

....

I think of those people I knew and who have transitioned from this dimension to another. I also think about my own upcoming transition, and how much I want to be prepared to welcome it peacefully and joyfully when the moment comes.

The following passage is from my good friend, Paul Veliyathil, an author and hospice chaplain, who lovingly ministers to the dying and their loved ones.

"While death is a painful reality for the living I believe, it is the most joyful and beautiful experience for the dying, because it is the release of the soul from the shackles of the body which is the source of all our problems. Besides, it is a homecoming, the re-joining of the individual soul with the Universal Soul, like the waves returning to the ocean. People have always wondered what happens at the moment of death. Nobody has come back to tell us. However, Neale Donald Walsch, author of a series of books called Conversations With God, in his book, Home With God: In A Life That Never Ends, gives the following description of the death experience, which is the best I have ever seen in print. He called it the Moment Of Mergence. Here it goes..."

....

"Again, words cannot be found to adequately define or accurately describe this feeling -- partly because the feeling is huge. It might be characterized as a single, enormous conglomerate feeling that encompasses a thousand individual feelings, now slowly filling the soul. A feeble attempt would call it the feeling of being warmly embraced, deeply comforted, dearly cherished, profoundly appreciated, genuinely treasured, softly nurtured, profoundly understood, completely forgiven, wholly absolved, long awaited, happily welcome, totally honored, joyously celebrated, absolutely protected, instantly perfected, and unconditionally loved -- all at once.'" ~ Neale Donald Walsch

....

WE ARE THE WATERS OF THE GREAT SEA

We are the waters of the Great Sea
Waves brought us here, to these shores
But here we cannot stay, except for a short while
We must return to where we came from
We are the waters of the Great Sea

....

Let us begin by being aware of this moment, of what is going on right here, right now. Let us pause and listen to the sounds of the ocean and feel the morning breeze caressing our bodies. Let us, now, as we welcome the fear of death, bring to mind the fact that nothing lasts forever, that everything is impermanent, that all things in this physical dimension are being transformed all the time. Let's allow this inescapable reality of life -- the cycle of birth, growth, decay, and death -- to be understood, felt, and accepted with serenity. But let us also remember that we are, at the same time, mortal and immortal, human and divine, body and spirit, solid matter and vibrational energy, separated and connected, independent and interdependent. We are many, and we are one.

Let us live without fear, knowing that we are not alone. All of us are molecules of an immensely larger, mysterious, and glorious organism. May we be able to evoke the memory of this breeze and these sounds, and recall that we are eternal spiritual beings having temporary human experiences. This shall help us navigate through fearful times with tranquility.

....

We are the waters of the Great Sea
Waves brought us here, to these shores
But here we cannot stay, except for a short while
We must return to where we came from
We are the waters of the Great Sea

....

GEORGE

All things must pass Sunrise doesn't last all morning A cloudburst doesn't last all day ~ George Harrison

....

Our family loves The Beatles, and Pedro, my oldest son, finds a lot of similarities between George Harrison's ideas and mine. He recently sent me a video of Katie Couric interviewing Olivia Harrison after her husband's death, and titled the email, "Dad is George." We, then, engaged in a brief exchange of messages about life, death, the pursuit of an expanded consciousness during our lifetime, and about learning how to die before we die. Pedro wrote, "I would love to see George and you walking in a garden, chatting about life."

While watching the videos he sent, many things resonated with me. Here are excerpts: "He had a great sense of humor, and he was also very serious; he aspired to higher consciousness, a higher life. He reflected about life's essential questions: "Who am I? Why am I here? What am I doing here? What should I be doing here? Where am I going?" He appreciated the simple things in life. It's nature really that he loved. He felt closest to God in nature. He loved people who would appreciate a leaf on the ground, and say, "Wow! Look at that!" He said, "Sometimes I just feel I'm actually in the wrong planet. I feel great when I am in my garden, but the moment I go out the gate I think, 'What the hell am I doing here?'" He faced death with no fear, no regrets. He never really felt in control. He gave his life to God a long time ago. He wasn't trying to hang on to anything. He was fine with it. He went with what was happening. He said. "You can't just, at the end of your life, start thinking about God. It's not just something you stumble upon. Consciousness and self-realization: you have to work for it. Suffering and death are inevitable. I will not make my own suffering and my own death my enemies." George dedicated a lot of his life to attain a good ending, and I don't have any doubt that he was successful."

....

Heed the advice and don't wait until the end of your life. Work on the attainment of a higher consciousness every day. Immerse yourself in moments of silence, stillness, solitude, seclusion, simplicity, and service, however brief, and live mindfully, paying attention to the here-now. This must become your diligent daily discipline. I don't have any doubt that

that was what George did, and that he achieved success! In many of his songs, George clearly showed the spiritual path he was on, his understanding of oneness, and of the inevitable impermanence of all things, and his readiness for calmly undertaking the transition from this dimension to another.

……...

AN EPIPHANY OF ONENESS

While doing my meditation on the beach one morning -- and watching the majestic show Mother Nature was putting on -- I had an epiphany. I began my routine, as I always do, expressing gratitude. First, for the reflections of light on the surface of the water, because they take me to another dimension and make me imagine that there is more in the Universe than I can capture with my senses. Second, I was grateful for the transparency of the water and for being able to see the fish that gathered around my feet while I was standing on the ocean floor. I think they came to say "Hello," and to remind me that the Divine Miracle is everywhere; it is all around me, and in me. (On a lighter note, I also think that my legs provided some shelter and reference for them in the immensity of the ocean, and I imagined that they were grateful that I was there for them to congregate around. "No need to thank me," I thought. "I am happy that I can be of service. I am the one who should say, 'Thank you.'")

Well, let me open a parenthesis and explain that while I do Self-Reiki, I mentally say some affirmations. They are extremely useful for centering me, and helping me be a better channel for the universal life force energy. Well, the session was going as it usually goes, and I was feeling really good. As I was getting ready to recite my closing affirmations, something extraordinary happened. I suddenly felt a surge of energy running through my body - a tremor, an electric discharge -- followed by a calm realization of oneness. What I felt and understood in that moment is very difficult to describe in words. Language is too limited to explain, but for the first time, I had an understanding of "I Am" that went beyond my prior intellectual comprehension. I felt, understood, and apprehended the "I Am" concept as I never had before. With that, a new set of affirmations instantly came to me. I called it, "An Epiphany of Oneness:"

……..

I look around and see miracles. I look around and see Heaven. I look around and see the Garden and the Playground. I look around and see the Divine Presence everywhere, all around me, and in me. I am part of the whole. Actually I am not a part; I am the Whole. I am

I don't exist isolated. Separation is an illusion. I am not this little, unconnected, detached, and fearful being that I thought I was. I am the Whole. I am

Only One exists. I am the Universe. I am the Immense One. I am the Whole. I am holy. I am

……..

It was indeed a very powerful and beautiful experience of oneness. I can't deny it, and I don't want to diminish its impact on me. I believe that all of us can have the mystical experience of oneness, because it is a gift that is available to all of us.

Thomas Keating said, "The gift of God is absolutely gratuitous. It is not something you earn. It is something that is there. It is something that you just have to accept. This is a gift that has been given. There's no place to go to get it. There's no place you can go to avoid it. It just is. It is part of our very existence. And so, the purpose of all great religions is to bring us into this relationship with reality that is so intimate that no word can possibly describe it."

His words are so precise! I believe that those who live mindfully develop this intimate relationship with reality, and become able to notice the magic, mystery, and miracles that exist all around us and in us.

I have pondered why I have decided to give the title Pay Attention! Be Alert! to the book I wrote almost two decades ago, and I have to believe that I was guided to do so because to pay attention and to be alert is of the utmost importance to connect, communicate, and commune with the Unnamable. I believe that guidance and inspiration is available to all of us, especially to those who adopt the practice of living mindfully.

Thomas Keating also said, "Our project is not just to become a better human being, as desirable as that would be for our friends and relatives, but it is tò become a divine human being, or to learn how to live the human life in a divine way. The project is the transformation of individuals and, at some point, of the whole human family."

I believe, as he does, that our job on this Earth is "to learn how to live the human life in a divine way." Think about what he said: "The project is the transformation of individuals and, at some point, of the whole human family."

The more I meditate about it, the more I am convinced that what we really need is for humanity to embrace a new paradigm. We need new visions for a better future. We need more and more people to wake up and see different possibilities for living and thriving together. What we need is a widespread understanding of who we really are. Once we understand who we really are, and what life really is, we will see differently, and then a change for the better will happen. In order to bring justice and peace to our world, we need more and more individuals having profound transformational experiences which change the way they see everything: themselves, others, the environment, the planet, the cosmos, the Universe. I am convinced that the awareness of our oneness, the one that emerges from those awakenings, those deep personal transformations, is essential to bring about more unselfishness, solidarity, justice and peace to the world.

So, in my opinion, what we need for peace to prevail in our world is a bigger contingent of individuals with this evolved understanding of who we really are. Great ideas of how to organize ourselves to live in a more just society will not take us too far without a large contingent of evolved individuals. Personal transformation is essential for the success of societal transformation. Personal evolution precedes successful social progress. There have always been individuals who went through these transformative experiences and who developed this new understanding, but they have always been a small fraction of the world population.

In order for the world to radically change for the better, we need more evolved beings, and in order for their numbers to grow we need to demystify the current belief that enlightenment is hard and can only be achieved by a few gifted individuals. We need to disseminate the idea that awakening and expanded awareness is at hand.

We need to encourage everyone to engage in the practice of silent observation, meditation, mindful living, or any other similar discipline that may lead to the attainment of that new consciousness that will not only allow them to experience Heaven, but that will also enlist them in the work of revealing Heaven right here on Earth.

ONENESS AND PEACE

I work to improve the way people treat one another. Among other things, I facilitate diversity and sensitivity workshops to reduce hostility and foster more harmonious learning and working environments. During those sessions we explore the harmful consequences of prejudice, discrimination, intolerance, harassment, and bullying. We discuss how we, human beings, divide ourselves in us and them, and gather in all sorts of groups, clans, tribes, clubs, and gangs. We analyze how those alliances augment power that, ultimately, is used against others. We look into our obsession with competition, on how we derive a sense of worth from winning. We reflect on our need to put others down in order to feel superior. We talk about the pain we inflict on each other, and how hurt people hurt people. Finally, I invite the participants to consider that we, all of us, carry prejudices, that we all isolate ourselves in our little tribes, that we all discriminate, act with some degree of insensitivity, and play and fight to win the Power Game. In the end, we all come to agree that prejudice is learned and can be unlearned, and that we can do a lot better in the ways we relate to one another.

After teaching, reflecting, and writing about diversity and inclusion for many years, I am now convinced that the betterment we want in human relations cannot be achieved solely through education. Something more is needed, and that is that deep, honest, introspective investigation that leads to the inner knowing that we are all very similar, that we are all connected, that we all are parts of one same whole, and that treating others the way we want to be treated makes absolute and total sense.

……..

The transformation in human relations that we desire demands transformation at the personal level. It is through introspection that we come to realize our own discriminatory behavior. It is through inner work that we come to consciously unlearn the prejudices that we have unconsciously learned. It is through a journey within our own selves that we experience oneness, and start to see separation and exclusion -- and the violence they bring about -- as complete absurdities.

Let's take the time now -- and many more times throughout our lives -- to look deeply within your own selves for answers to the following questions: "Can I see that when I help others, I am helping myself? Can I see that other people's lives are as valuable as mine? Can I see that it is my best interest to support the growth of others, because they will bring about unique gifts that will benefit me?"

The truth is that the betterment of human relations stems from the awareness of our oneness, an epiphany that comes from the practice of diligent inner work, and from a gentle, mindful, and contemplative way of living. The realization that although education is important but not enough to bring about the change we want in the ways we treat one another is the reason why I have decided to promote the practice of moments of silence and stillness through mindfulness meditation in schools and workplaces. I invite you to meditate and improve yourself in order to become a bringer of harmony to the groups you belong. I invite you to become a bringer of peace to the world.

....

I AM AT PEACE

"This body is not me. I am not limited by this body. I am life without boundaries. I have never been born, and I have never died. Look at the ocean and the sky filled with stars, manifestations from my wondrous True Mind. Since before time, I have been free. Birth and death are only doors through which we pass, sacred thresholds on our journey. Birth and death are a game of hide-and-seek. So laugh with me, hold my hand, let us say good-bye, say good-bye, to meet again soon. We meet today. We will meet again tomorrow. We will meet at the source every moment. We meet each other in all forms of life." ~ Thich Nhat Hanh

....

I am happy, content and satisfied with my life, and thrilled with what lies ahead, both in this dimension and the next. I have had, and continue to have a rich life, full of great experiences and relationships. I am highly blessed and experience great abundance. I feel blessed because I have learned to notice beauty: the beautiful sunrise, the scents in the air, the dance of the leaves in the breeze that caresses me. I am able to see magic, mystery and miracles all around me. I am grateful for the life I have, and the people I share it with, especially my wife and sons. I am able to do what I like, and although I feel that I haven't finished giving my contribution yet, I feel that I am leaving the world a little better than I found it, not only through what I have done, but also through everything my sons have done and will do. I am proud of my accomplishments. I have no regrets. I am at peace.

……....

REINTEGRATING WITH THE WHOLE

Leslie Lott, my dear friend and the author of "Heaven's Perspective," wrote: "When we are in a body, we often feel separate from the others in the universe. We are not, of course. All things are part of the larger ONE. Still, when in a body, our skin is a physical barrier that separates us from others. But when our bodies die, the barrier of separation is gone! When we transition back to non-physical, there is a joyful and conscious reintegration with the whole. To understand this more clearly, imagine a beautiful soap bubble floating outdoors in the sunlight. The light hits it and it shines with different colors as it moves. Then, suddenly it pops. That which was within the bubble does not suddenly disappear, does it? Certainly the outer barrier of the bubble is gone, but what about what was inside that beautiful bubble? It merely merges back with the rest of the air. In a similar way, when our physical bodies die, when our body bubbles burst, that which is within us-- our divinity, our essence, the soul-- reintegrates with the larger ONE from whence it came. We maintain our awareness of self as an individual while merging back into the oneness of that which is called heaven, our true home. This realization came to me as Jack Bloomfield, Piero Falci and I sat at the beach this morning gently releasing One Planet United. It occurred to me that this is not an ending for One Planet United, but rather a merging of the ideas from OPU back into the larger universe. The paradigm shift from seeing it as an ending to seeing it as a merging into, a reintegration into the larger whole felt so incredibly good that I've decided to ask my loved ones to have a joyful Reintegration Celebration when my own bubble bursts and I return to true home. Blessed be. So be it, and so it is."

……....

For many years, with great passion and dedication, we operated a nonprofit organization, but the time came when we had to let it go. All of us who were originally involved with One Planet United were now contributing to the betterment of the world in other ways, and we didn't have the time to attend to the demands of keeping the organization operating as it should. We tried to find new leadership, we tried to pass the baton on, but we were not successful. After many attempts to keep it afloat, we decided that it was time to close and gently release it into the Universe. So we decided to do a little ceremony at the beach during sunrise, when we would reminisce about the organization, and say 'Goodbye.'

There was a little sadness, but also a calm agreement that it was the right thing to do. We understood the changing nature of everything, and were ready to let it go. OPU had served its purpose and played itself out. But something unexpected happened that morning: a calm, delicious, and nourishing experience. As we were talking about One Planet United we had this sudden realization that OPU didn't die. It became evident to us that its mission and vision remained alive and strong within us. It had always existed and always will. "Embrace diversity, promote unity, and create community," the phrase that summarizes OPU's mission, is what we and many others around the globe do, day in and day out. This realization was a great life and death insight for us. In that moment, everything became clear and made sense. As we gently released it, we felt OPU lovingly reintegrating with the whole. The nonprofit organization was no more, but what OPU stood for was, is, and will always be: birthless and deathless.

....

"There is a Light that lights every man that comes into the world. That Light is Eternal, All-Powerful and Imperishable. Only that which is subject to birth is subject to death. The Light is the extension of God into man. It is not born nor can it die." ~ Douglas K. DeVorss

....

EXPLORING AND INSPIRING

Well, more than six decades ago I transitioned from another dimension to this one. I was immersed in an aquatic environment inside my mother's womb, and came to this beautiful paradise.

Where did I come from?

This is one of those questions for which I know I will never get a conclusive answer.

Did I make a conscious choice to come here? If so, where was I, and what did I come here to do? Did I receive an assignment, a mission to complete here? Did I choose my family and the people in my life? Did they choose me? Did we agree before coming to this dimension who would be mean and who would be kind; who would wound and who would heal?

Who knows the answers to these questions, right? So many questions, so few answers. As you may have noticed, I agree with the words of Socrates, "An unexamined life is not worth living." It inspired me to call my blog "Exploring and Inspiring," and I added to it, as a subtitle, "Paying attention and living a life that is worth living!" I feel I am doing just that.

Yes! I'm sixty-four, and this reminds me of the song "When I'm Sixty-Four," written by Paul McCartney, and released in the Sgt. Pepper's Lonely Hearts Club Band album in 1967. I was fourteen years old then, and that was half a century ago. And here I am now, five decades later. The future that was so distant and I couldn't have imagined then, has arrived. Fifty years have gone by really fast. I can't phantom that I have already lived 23,376 days.

I'm sixty-four now. Wow! Life is good! Life is great! I love my life and I love my wife! It is time to celebrate!

....

MINDFULNESS AND CHRISTIANITY

CALMING THE MENTAL STORM

On that evening, Jesus said to his disciples, "Let us go across to the other side of the lake." So they left the crowd. The disciples got into the boat in which Jesus was already in, and departed. There were also other boats with them. Suddenly a strong wind blew up, and the waves began to spill over into the boat, so that it was about to fill with water. Jesus was in the back of the boat, sleeping, with his head on a pillow. The disciples, who were very agitated and afraid, woke him up and said to him, "Teacher, don't you care if we drown? Don't you care that we are about to die?" Jesus got up and commanded the wind, "Be quiet!" and he said to the waves, "Be still!" Then the wind died down, the waves disappeared, and there was a great calm. He, then, asked his disciples, "Why are you so afraid? Do you still have no faith?" They were in awe, and began to say to one another, "Who is this man? Even the wind and the waves obey him!" ~ Mark 4:35-41

....

Although I don't have a problem accepting as a miracle Jesus calming the wind and the waves in this physical realm, I have been inspired to see another meaning in this story. For me, this passage has less to do with actual weather storms, and more to do with the storms of unruly thoughts that take place inside our own heads. Although Jesus could be sleeping while waves were breaking over the boat -- what seems highly improbable -- what I envision is that Jesus was meditating while everyone else around him was running around agitated and full of fear. I

217

sense that his command, "Be quiet! Be still!" was directed not at the wind and waves, but, first, at himself and the thoughts inside his head, and, second, at his friends and the thoughts inside their heads. "Be quiet! Be still!" His was a simple command to go to a place of quiet and stillness, and experience peace. I like to think that Jesus was telling himself, his disciples, and all of us, to meditate. After being baptized by John the Baptist, Jesus spent forty days and nights in the desert. It looks like a long silent retreat for me: silence, solitude, and seclusion. Many titles have been given to Jesus. I particularly like Wonderful Counselor and Prince of Peace, but now I am giving him a new title: Jesus, the Master Meditator.

Now, going back to those tempests, here, there, and everywhere... In a boat full of fearful and agitated people, one sane, calm, and steady-minded person can find his way through the fog and storms, and take the boat safely to a harbor. Be that person. Practice mindfulness. The world desperately needs more steady-minded individuals.

………..

FROM AGITATION TO SERENITY

Be still and know that I am God. The quieter you become, the more you can hear.

………..

When I was a teacher at a Christian school, I used the gospel passage of Jesus calming the storm to introduce a short quiet time for my students at the beginning of my classes. My youngest son was one of those students at the time. My objective was to calm them down, get them out of the state of agitation, and create a more focused environment in the classroom. It was a very short practice that didn't take too long. I read that Bible passage -- or another similar in essence to that one -- and then asked my students to close their eyes, go to that quiet place inside themselves, and remain in silence for a few minutes. It took a while for the kids to learn to calm down and get into the practice, but once they did, they looked forward to it. And it worked well; it created an environment more conducive for learning and teaching. I did this for a while with great enthusiasm, certain that I was doing a good thing, and never imagining that anyone would object. But the word got out that I was doing something different, out-of-the-ordinary, strange. One of my students might have told her parents who, understandably, wanting only the best for their child, and not exactly knowing what was going on, decided to bring the matter to the attention of the school's administration.

It must be noted, again, that this was a private Christian school, and that the reading of Bible passages, followed by traditional prayer at the beginning of classes was a common practice, not only acceptable, but encouraged. But my silent prayer was something new, something that the community was not used to, something that, perhaps, wasn't very Christian.

So, to my surprise, one day I was called to the principal's office to explain myself. I told him and the assistant principal how the moments of silence at the beginning of the classes created a better learning and teaching environment. I also told them that I felt that silence led to an intimacy with God, an indisputable goal of any Christian school. I made reference to Psalm 46:10, "Be still, and know that I am God," and a passage in the Gospels -- Matthew 6:6 -- where Jesus, in teaching us how to pray, invites us to go to our "inner room" -- "But you, when you pray, go into your inner room, close your door, and pray to your Father..." -- and how I believed that this inner room Jesus referred to was not an actual room in a dwelling, but that place of peace inside ourselves that we are able to enter when we practice to be quiet and still. I also mentioned that I believed that God communicates with us in the silence, through whispers, the ones we hear when we remain silent and still, and tune in and listen to the gentle voice within us. I made reference to the passage in 1 Kings 19:11-13, which states, "Go out and stand on the mountain in the presence of the Lord, for the Lord is about to pass by." Then a great and powerful wind tore the mountains apart and shattered the rocks, but the Lord was not in the wind. After the wind there was an earthquake, but the Lord was not in the earthquake. After the earthquake came a fire, but the Lord was not in the fire. And after the fire came a gentle whisper. When Elijah heard it, he went out and stood at the mouth of the cave. Then a voice said to him, "What are you doing here, Elijah?" Since we were told that the voice of God is heard as gentle whispers, I told them that reducing the external and internal noise and familiarizing students with silence was a way of getting them closer to the Divine. Finally, I told them that my meditation was rooted in the Christian tradition of Centering Prayer, inspired by writings of major contributors to the Christian contemplative heritage including

John Cassian, the anonymous author of The Cloud of Unknowing, Francis de Sales, Teresa of Avila, John of the Cross, Thérèse of Lisieux, and Thomas Merton.

They told me although they had heard about some of those luminaries, they weren't familiar with Centering Prayer itself. Well, to make a long story short, they listened, understood, but, still, told me not to do it anymore. Considering the pressures they were exposed to, I understood.

....

Fear has led many people to believe that the deep silence we experience during meditation should be avoided because it transports us to dangerous grounds where evil forces operate, as I've heard someone say. I feel that this fear is perfectly understandable because in moments of silence and stillness a lot of buried emotions and unresolved situations come up, and this emotional unloading makes people uncomfortable and fearful.

The truth is that the practice of silent introspection is not yet widespread in Christian religious communities; few individuals have tried it, and among those who have, many have given up mainly due to fear of the unknown, or because they were told that meditation is dangerous, foreign to Christianity, and a menace to it. I, on the other hand, know that meditation creates an intimacy with God that deepens one's spiritual experience and, for that reason, is not a menace, but a blessing that can bring new vigor to stale religious communities. Those who stick with the meditative practice may harvest wonderful rewards, such as tranquility, serenity, clarity, and a much closer connection, communication and communion with the Divine.

....

BEATITUDES

We need to pause, look deeply, reflect, and understand what is being said here:

Blessed are they who are humble, modest, unselfish, and compassionate for theirs is the Kingdom of Heaven.

Blessed are they who mourn for all the injustices and suffering in the world, for they shall be comforted.

Blessed are they who have experienced the epiphany of oneness and understand the sacredness and the impermanence of all, for they shall inherit the earth.

Blessed are they who hunger for the end of all oppression and exploitation, and thirst for justice, equality, and a dignified life for everybody, for they shall be filled.

Blessed are those who see God in every person, those who renounce their own comfort in order to help others, those who look into the eyes of the abandoned and marginalized and let them know that they are loved, for they will be immediately rewarded.

Blessed are the merciful, for they shall obtain mercy.

Blessed are the pure in heart, for they shall see God.

Blessed are the peacemakers, for they shall be called the children of God.

Blessed are they who are persecuted for speaking truth to power, for being compassionate, and for doing what is just and morally right, for theirs is the Kingdom of Heaven.

Blessed are they who believe that Heaven is here, for they will be in Heaven.

Blessed are those who protect and care for our common home, for they will be overjoyed.

......

If you want to be blessed and to be a blessing, do what the Beatitudes ask us to do, and be

- gentle, kind, and generous
- loving, giving, and forgiving
- pacific, calm, and soft
- patient, humble, and quiet
- nonviolent, benevolent, and courteous
- selfless, modest, and mild

....

THE FRUITS OF THE SPIRIT

Be one of those who chooses, practices, gives, and, therefore, receives love, joy, peace, patience, kindness, goodness, optimism, gentleness, humility, and self-control.

Here's some good advice on how to live a good life (from the Christian Scriptures)

"For you have been called to live in freedom, my brothers and sisters. But don't use your freedom to satisfy your human nature. Instead, use your freedom to serve one another in love. For the whole law can be summed up in this one command: 'Love your neighbor as yourself.' But if you are always biting and devouring one another, watch out! Beware of destroying one another. So I say, let the Holy Spirit guide your lives. Then you won't be doing what your sinful nature craves. The sinful nature wants to do evil, which is just the opposite of what the Spirit wants. And the Spirit gives us desires that are the opposite of what the sinful nature desires. But the Holy Spirit produces this kind of fruit in our lives: love, joy, peace, patience, kindness, goodness, optimism, gentleness, humility, and self-control. The Spirit has given us life. Let us follow the Spirit's leading in every part of our lives." ~ Paul, the apostle, in Galatians 5: 13 - 26

……..

Choose, practice, give, and receive.

……..

MINDFULNESS AND BEGINNER'S MIND

LIVE AND LET LIVE

"We can either be passively carried along by forces and habits that remain stubbornly unexamined and which imprison us in distorting dreams and potential nightmares, or we can engage in our lives by waking up to them and participating fully in their unfolding...Only when we wake up do our lives become real and have even a chance of being liberated from our individual and collective delusions, diseases and suffering." ~ Jon Kabat- Zinn

……..

I have friends that don't think as I think, and that's OK. Many of them don't agree with my straightforward view that we are here, simply, to live, love, laugh, learn, and leave a legacy. Yes, as I see it, we are here to love one another, to help one another. This statement summarizes my understanding of life's purpose. When I love my sisters and brothers, I live more intensely, I laugh more freely, I learn more profoundly, and I leave a legacy that lasts in their hearts and minds. We are here to love one another. That's it. Period.

I am in favor of a respectful freedom, a freedom that does not restrict anybody else's freedom. People should be allowed to do what they want, and live as they decide to live, as long as this does not interfere in other people's lives. Everybody should have the right to live in freedom, and to enjoy the conditions that allow them to experience happiness. Life, liberty, and the pursuit of happiness should be unquestionable and unalienable rights.

Unfortunately, I see many of my friends still imprisoned by beliefs that they stubbornly refuse to examine. These are beliefs that lead to impose restrictions on other people's rights and liberties. These are beliefs about other people, and how others should be, live, and behave. They hold feelings that "the world and my life would be better without them." And who are those, that they refer to as them? They are people of a different color of skin, or of a different sexual orientation, or of a different religion, or of a different nationality. They are the members of other tribes, people who, as they think, "are not like us."

Well, I am not here to judge my friends, but I sincerely wish they would take on the task of examining their beliefs. I wish they could free themselves from those unexamined prejudices and collective delusions. I wish they could remove from their hearts all discrimination and exclusion. I wish they could experience the exhilarating joy that true freedom brings. But, again, I am not here to judge. I am here, simply, to love everyone, even those who judge, condemn, and do not love.

The truth is that those who do not think as I do are free to hold their beliefs; they are free, and so am I. I wish all my friends could see, as I see, that any kind of discrimination is dangerous. I wish they all could feel, as I feel, that discrimination anywhere is a threat to liberty everywhere. I wish we all could grow in compassion, and empathize with the suffering of our poor brothers and sisters. I wish we could all agree that all forms of oppression and exploitation should come to an end, and that the nefarious trend of concentration of wealth must be reverted because, in the final analysis, it will hurt us all. I wish we all could work together to create a new world where everyone can be free from the fear of not having enough to survive. I wish we could work together to create a new world where everyone can have what they need, not only to survive, but to thrive. I wish we all could work together to create a new world where every single human being can be supported to be the best they can be. I wish we could get together and make the changes so a less violent, a more gentle way of living and treating our planet and all life in it could emerge. I believe this is possible. I believe that Heaven is here, if we want it to be.

But many of my friends don't see as I see. Yes, this saddens me, but the fact that I don't see as they see, also makes them sad. So, I respect them, as I expect them to respect me. I bring to mind my own process of getting rid of my prejudices, and remember to grow in acceptance by saying to myself, "I've been there. I've done that." Some friends and I are not walking together now, but since the friendship continues, maybe in the future we will. We have chosen different paths now, but maybe our paths will touch in the future, and we will walk together again.

Well, independent of their beliefs, my commitment is to love them. I don't want to allow myself to be seduced by the illusion that I hold the only truth, that I am right and they are wrong. I don't want to hold the belief that I am better than anyone else. We are spiritual beings, all of us, having human experiences, and we all have a lot to learn. I don't want to identify myself as member of a tribe, and see them as members of another, because the moment I do this I will automatically be fueling the fires of separation that I want to extinct. I don't want to identify myself as member of a club that includes some and excludes many. At the end of the day, I'd rather be excluded for who I include, than be included for who I exclude. I want to identify myself, first and foremost, as a member of the whole humanity. Throughout this entire process, I want to remain open: open to welcome, open to embrace, open to love. Why? Because I don't want to have anything to do with hatred. I am not going to bring more judgment, condemnation, and aversion into our world. No! I will bring acceptance and love. All we need is love. Love is all we need.

I am happy because we are making progress and reducing prejudice. Prejudice -- which comes from ignorance -- is learned and can be unlearned. Our job is to consciously unlearn all the divisive stupidity that we have unconsciously learned. And I see that we, as humanity, are making progress in reducing bias and bigotry.

……..

"We hold these truths to be self-evident, that all men are created equal, that they are endowed by their Creator with certain unalienable Rights, that among these are Life, Liberty and the pursuit of Happiness." ~ The Declaration of Independence

……..

What do I want? I want to be happy, and I want everyone else to be happy. I want to be free, and I want everyone else to be free. I want to be allowed to do what I want, and I want everyone else to be allowed to do what they want. I am committed to respect everybody, and I expect everybody to respect me. I will refrain from doing whatever may deprive others from enjoying their experiences, and I expect others to refrain from doing whatever may restrict me from living out the experiences I choose to live. My desire is to live a happy life, and help others live happy lives. My philosophy is "Live, and let live. Love, and let love." Yes, we are becoming more civilized. Tolerance, acceptance, understanding, respect and love are spreading. We are moving forward, and I am happy. I am happy.

All we need is love. Love is all we need.

....

NEW POLITICAL LEADERSHIP FOR A NEW WORLD

"Are we so deaf that we do not hear a loving God warning us that humanity is in danger of committing suicide? Are we so selfish that we do not hear the just God demanding that we do all we can to stop injustice from suffocating the world and driving it to war? Are we so alienated that we fail to see, hear, and serve God where he is present and where he requires our presence, among humankind, the poor, the oppressed, the victims of injustice in which we ourselves are often involved?" ~ Dom Helder Camara

....

What we see in politics is a reflection of who we are.

We are immersed in a culture of selfishness, greed, separation, isolation, exclusion, competition, and pursuit of power, and as long as we remain in it, it will be very difficult to reach more humane political solutions for our problems.

What should we do, then?

We need to work on our own selves, transform ourselves, and experience the heavenly sense of oneness that infuses us with the knowing that our destiny is a common one, and that the ultimate goal of our existences is solidarity, cooperation, unity, and peace. We need to realize that we are here to connect, communicate, and commune with others, not to separate, compete, and isolate ourselves from others. We have to understand that we are here to bring the pieces together, and restore to wholeness what once was whole but is now broken. We have to realize that we are here to help one another, and to live by the values of civility, mutual support, and care for all beings and the entire planet.

We must understand that it is only when we grow in selflessness, kindness, and compassion -- and live our lives guided by such feelings, values, and principles -- that we will be able to manifest leaders and governments that will practice them.

The truth is that the world is an expression of who we are, and in order for us to manifest a better world, we must better ourselves first. More enlightened ways of organizing ourselves to live in society will spontaneously emerge when we change the prevailing ideas that dominate our thinking. A better world will come forth into existence when a vast number of individuals reach that deep-rooted conviction that generosity is better than greed, cooperation is better than competition, inclusion is better than exclusion, and compassion is better than mercilessness and indifference. When the number of such individuals grows, we will reach that critical mass that will tip the scale. When new, expanded visions of the ways we can better live together in harmony replace the limited views that currently prevail in our culture, we will bring about a new and better world.

Inner work will allow us to go beyond the ego-consciousness and the tribal-consciousness, and reach that level of mystical-consciousness where we don't see ourselves separated from others anymore. Then we will not give in to the demands of our own egos and of the groups we belong to. We will not feel inclined to fight, compete, and conquer. We will not feel obligated to do those things we know to be harmful to others -- and to ourselves -- and that our clans, tribes, parties, churches, and nations demand from us.

It is by going through deep mystical experiences -- the ones that make us realize our oneness, interconnection, interdependence, and inter-existence -- that all the insanity that surrounds us will become evident. It is by having those epiphanies of our oneness that we will gain the strength to calmly leave all this competitive madness behind. It is by experiencing those awakenings that we will be blessed with a clear consciousness that will guide us to think, say, and do only those things that harm no one and benefit everyone.

So, the inner work we do to better ourselves is serious political work with a vast reach, and don't let anyone convince you otherwise. This inner work is real activism, the one that changes views and beliefs, and that will bring about a new consciousness, and, with it, a new political leadership, and new political systems that will change the world and the lives of all who live in it for the better.

So, work on your own self, and move, as much as possible, maybe a little bit everyday, away from selfishness and closer to selflessness. Practice and teach kindness. Teach all children to be gentle, compassionate, and caring. Investigate your beliefs and get rid of your prejudices. Guide others on the path that leads to their personal awakening and enlightenment, therefore creating opportunities for them to experience oneness. Foster nonviolent communication and cooperation. Be peaceful and bless the world with your peace. Transform yourself, help others transform themselves, and, by doing so, transform the world.

. . . .

THE WORLD I WANT TO LIVE IN

"What we would like to do is change the world -- make it a little simpler for people to feed, clothe, and shelter themselves as God intended them to do. And, by fighting for better conditions, by crying out unceasingly for the rights of the workers, the poor, of the destitute -- the rights of the worthy and the unworthy poor, in other words -- we can, to a certain extent, change the world... We can throw our pebble in the pond and be confident that its ever widening circle will reach around the world. We repeat, there is nothing we can do but love, and, dear God, please enlarge our hearts to love each other, to love our neighbor, to love our enemy as our friend." ~ Dorothy Day

. . . .

I want to live in a world where everyone feels safe, loved, and protected. I want to live in a world without fear. I want to live in a world where all of us are free from the fear of not having enough for our survival and that of our loved ones. I want to live in a world without poverty, a world where everyone has a home that protects them from the heat and the cold. I want to live in a world where everyone lives in a clean environment, and has access to clean water, clean air, and healthy foods. I want to live in a world where everyone can get the support and attention they may need to restore their health in case they fall ill. I want to live in a world where everyone lives carefree lives, where everyone enjoys life like little children. I want to live in a world where children can be unconditionally loved, where they can enjoy the wonder of childhood to the fullest, where their joy is not interrupted by trauma, and their innocence is not abbreviated by fear. I want to live in a world where our abundant resources are well distributed in order to give a safe and dignified life to all. I want to live in a world without oppression and exploitation, without social injustices, without structural violence. I want to live in a world without direct violence, without wounding and killing, without crime, without weapons, and without war. I want to live in a world where we don't invest time, resources and energy in developing instruments of destruction, but in everything that preserves all life in the planet, and makes life better for all. I want to live in a just and peaceful world, a world without struggle for power and domination. I want to live in a nonviolent world where we all practice nonviolent communication and conflict resolution. I want to live in a world without lies. I want to live in a world where we all support each other on the journey of figuring out who we really are. I want to live in a world where we all support one another so we all can develop to the fullest in order to give our best contributions. I want to live in a world where we all acknowledge the sacredness of all. I want to live in a world where we see the water, the air, and the soil as sacred. I want to live in a world where we see the sacredness in every plant, mineral, and animal. I want to live in a world where we treat every living thing in it with reverence and respect. I want to live in a world where we do not separate ourselves from other human beings, and where we do not divide ourselves in little gangs. I want to live in a world where the us and them mindset has vanished. I want to live in a world where everyone realizes that we are all in this together. I want to live in a world where everyone collaborates with one another. I want to live in a world of maximum cooperation and minimum competition. I want to live in a world where there is liberty and justice for all. I want to live in a world where everyone sees this planet as a beautiful garden, and a joyful playground, and where people give of themselves to make the garden more beautiful and the playground more enjoyable. I want to live with people who cheerfully share their toys because they understand that the happiness of others increases their own happiness. Finally I want to live in a world where we all embrace the idea that this is Heaven. I want to empower those who will help me bring Heaven to Earth. I will empower those who will help me bring about this whole new world where I want to live. Those forward-thinkers and paradigm-changers are the ones who will get my vote.

WHAT SEPARATES US

If we are loving and helping our friends, and hating and hurting our enemies, we are not doing anything extraordinary; we are not extending ourselves beyond our primitive instincts and using the whole range of our human potential. We can certainly do better than this. We can go beyond the self-centered love for ourselves, our families, our friends, and our tribes, and lovingly embrace everyone, even those we consider to be our enemies.

....

Nothing separates us more than our different views of the world, our beliefs of how it should be, and our ideas of how to organize ourselves to live in it.

Divergent views and ideas create separation and division. Similar views and ideas create unity. But agreement and conformity are not the norm in our lives. Can we accept this? Can we accept that perhaps the world was created to have opposing views and contrasting ideas? Can we recognize that this allows us to make choices, have experiences, and learn what we need to learn?

My political views may not be same as yours. That's OK. My ideas of how we should organize ourselves to live in this planet of ours in order for everyone to have a dignified and thriving life may not be the same as yours. That's OK. My ideas of how we should conduct ourselves and protect the environment, may not be the same as yours. That's OK.

But here's the challenge: Can I listen and understand you? Can you listen and understand me?

....

THE PEOPLE I WANT TO SHARE MY LIFE WITH

As I grow in understanding, I want to share my life with everyone, even those who create aversion in me because it is from them that I learn the most: they are the toughest and most demanding teachers.

Nevertheless, I want to share my life with less selfish, less competitive, less fearful, less greedy, less aggressive human beings. I want to share my life with people who accept the responsibility to make the world a better place. I want to share my life with people who do not shy away from trying to understand complex issues, and are willing to go deep and analyze the intricate problems of life. I want to live in a world full of people who reject inaccurate simplifications and embrace the challenge of trying to understand what is difficult to grasp. I don't want to share my life with those who rush to embrace incomplete and inaccurate simplifications, only because deep reflection and thorough analysis of what is complicated demand too much effort. I want to share my life with people willing and able to use their critical thinking and do not reduce multifaceted problems to simple slogans. I want to share my life with people who do not reduce other people to stereotypes, and who understand that labeling is just another incomplete and inaccurate simplification.

I want to share my life with kind, respectful, and polite individuals; with intelligent, well-informed, and well-educated people; with generous, compassionate, and caring citizens; with courageous, hopeful, and optimistic human beings. I want to share my life with seekers of truth, curious and inquisitive people. I want to share my life with those who accept the challenge and engage in the hard work of personal development, with those who are on the path of enlightenment, and with those who have ascended and arrived at a place of higher consciousness. I want to share my life with people who ascended above all separation, all division, all classification, all competition, all criticism, all judgment, and all condemnation. I want to share my life with people who have liberated themselves from the trap of all simplistic duality, from the slavery of either-or, from seeing only yes or no, good or bad, gain or loss, birth or death, day or night, and nothing in between. I want to share my life with people who see more than only black and white; I want to share my life with those who are eager to explore all the many shades of gray.

I want to share my life with those moved by desire to bring about a peaceful world for all, those who cultivate peace, those who live peacefully, and those who spread peace. I want to share my life with people who want the best for others, and are willing to give of themselves to help others. I want to share my life with people who not only let others live, but protect their rights to live freely and pursue happiness the way they choose to. I will empower those who will help me increase the contingent of people I want to share my life with. I will empower those who will help me bring Heaven to Earth. I will empower those who will help me bring about the world I want to live in.

········

MY POLITICAL VIEWS

My position is quite simple. I'm in favor of everything that protects, celebrates, and enhances life. I'm in favor of everything that lifts people up, and creates conditions for them to give the best contribution they can give to the world. I'm in favor of everything that preserves and takes good care of the Earth, and enhances this beautiful garden and awesome playground that was given to us. I am in favor of us having a good time playing together, and sharing our toys. I am basically against anything that kills people, and destroys the planet we live on.

These are my straightforward, clear-cut, uncomplicated political views.

....

LABELING AND BLIND TRIBAL LOYALTY

"Using labels often leads to misunderstandings. Not using labels leads to long explanations that people are not patient enough to hear. It seems that you can't win." ~ Craig M. Watts

....

Life can be likened to scuba diving in a gigantic ocean full of peculiar beings. Either we enjoy with curious interest all the diverse marine life we encounter, looking forward to the many discoveries to be made along the journey with joyful expectation, or we get overwhelmed by the multitude of creatures, apprehensive for whatever threat we may come across next.

Surely it's not easy to approach every interaction with freshness, and see each individual as a singular person, with all his or her idiosyncrasies. That's why we compartmentalize the world around us and put people in different compartments; it makes it easier and faster for us to deal with a reality that is too vast, diverse, and dynamic. It also placates our fear of the unknown, by giving us the false sense of security that stems from the impression that somehow we already know whoever we may run into. We make simpler what is complex, even if our generalizations mean living with a series of inaccurate and incomplete simplifications. Rather than being mindful and trying to get acquainted with the nuances of each individual, we divide mankind in poorly defined tribes -- The Good Guys and The Bad Guys; We and They; Us and Them -- and spend an enormous amount of energy trying to figure out what teams others belong to, and if they can be trusted. We feel the need to know who is with us, and who may be against us, and after hastily labeling everybody, we incur in the mistake of believing that we know others simply based on the labels we have placed on them.

When we reduce members of the other tribes to limiting stereotypes; when we define them in detrimental ways; when judge, condemn, and confine them in demeaning compartments, the impetus to belittle and antagonize them grows, and from there on everything becomes an insane confrontation where possibilities of reasoning and civil intercourse are greatly reduced due to blind loyalty to teams and the compulsion to win at all costs.

But life should not be this never-ending competition. Life should not be reduced to blindly defending teams we once pledged allegiance to even after it has been proven that they do not serve the greater good. A good life calls for a sense of responsibility with the betterment of the world, and calls us to use our intelligence and recognize when our team is wrong. It asks us to swim in a sea of doubt and complexity, knowing that we may never get to the truth, but that, if we, fellow travelers, agree to leave our preconceived ideas behind and cooperate with one another in an honest search, we may, together, find beauty along the journey, and this may lead to one of the greatest joys in life.

. . . .

"Who understands does not preach; Who preaches does not understand. Reserve your judgments and words; Smooth differences and forgive disagreements; Dull your wit and simplify your purpose; Accept the world. Then, Friendship and enmity, Profit and loss, Honor and disgrace, will not affect you; The world will accept you." ~ Laozi

. . . .

"The test of a first-rate intelligence is the ability to hold two opposed ideas in mind at the same time and still retain the ability to function." ~ F. Scott Fitzgerald

. . . .

A Better Life in a Better World

OFFERING AND RECEIVING ADVICE

During a difficult time in my life, when I found myself unemployed, I heard many well-intentioned people saying, "You should do this. You should do that." Everyone was trying to help, but I didn't feel that many of the suggestions that I was hearing were good for me. I, also, at that time, didn't have the energy to take action and pursue many of them. I was feeling depressed and defeated, and I didn't want anyone to know that. It felt like it was rude to say, "Thank you, but no, I will not do what you are suggesting."

I would meet some of them again and they would ask me, with hope in their eyes, "Have you done what I suggested?" Sometimes I would lie because I didn't want to let them down, or make them think that I didn't pay attention, or that I didn't value their advice. Other times, when I told them that I had decided not to follow through, I could see the disappointment on their faces, and the pain I was causing them would actually hurt me back, making me feel guilty.

It came to a point when I didn't want to hear any advice anymore. I didn't want people to offer me help, simply because it became unbearable. In their desire to help, people offered a lot of ideas, opinions and suggestions. Their intentions were good, but the outcome was not good for me. I felt pressured. I felt I was letting people down for not following through. It made me feel that I was not a good person. It all compounded to make me feel worse.

I try to remember this, because given my helpful nature, giving advice comes spontaneously.

········

GENTLER ADVICE GIVING

I don't know what you are going through. I try to imagine, but I am not you. I can't possibly know what you are experiencing. I want to help, and that is why I am offering you these suggestions, but if you don't follow through, don't feel bad. I don't mind. It's no big deal. You will not be letting me down. I will not love you any less. I respect you. It is your life and you are the one who has to decide what's best for you. I hope you find the strength and courage to do what will improve the quality of your life. I don't want you to feel pressured. I want you to feel better, not worse. Take it easy. Know that you are loved.

THANKS-GIVING, THANKS-RECEIVING, THANKS-LIVING

It was a difficult season in my life. I was unemployed and facing the difficulties and emotions that come with such a situation. As a recent immigrant, not having any relatives besides my wife and little children in this country, I was afraid of what could happen to us. Would we be able to make it? I imagined the worst possible outcomes. Worries and fear were my most habitual companions. Some friends offered to help me, and I felt uncomfortable. I had always been in the giving end, and it felt strange to be receiving. I remember my friend, Guy, telling me, "You are being selfish." I was surprised. "Being selfish? What do you mean?" I asked him. "If you refuse to accept what we are offering you, you are depriving us from the joy of giving."

Wow!

What a revelation that was for me! In that moment I began to realize that there is generosity in both giving and receiving.

Today is a good day to give thanks for all that I have received and all that I have been able to give. Today is a good day to give thanks for all of those who have given something to me, and for all of those who have accepted what I had to give them. Your generosity, both in giving and receiving, has made my journey much more joyful.

....

GIVING AND GETTING

Behind everything we do there is a strong selfish motivation; this is undeniable. We always ask, even if we are not completely conscious of it, "What's in it for me?" We are always, or at least most of the time pondering, "What am I going to get from it?" Now, pause, and imagine something different. Imagine that you were invited to an event, whatever it may be, and that you have decided to go, not to get anything, but to give. Imagine that your presence and open-hearted participation is a gift to others. Imagine that your being there is an opportunity for others to learn something from you. Choose to participate with a giving, not with a getting attitude. I have learned that, as long as I keep the curiosity of a child, I always learn something. There's always a lesson to be learned. There's always something everywhere for me. I just need to pay attention and be alert.

MY CALLING AND COMMITMENT

I am here. I am safe. I know who I am. I know the ground where I stand. I have arrived. This is home.

……..

After all these years on this exciting journey of exploration, I am pausing and feeling the ground where I stand.

"Who am I? What do I love? How shall I live, knowing that I will die? What gifts do I bring to share with the family of the Earth?" (1)

I am committed to the work of improving myself, and the work of helping others with their inner explorations, discoveries, and actualizations of their full potentials and highest purposes in life. This is my calling and my commitment. I find great joy in guiding people on their journeys of finding their own answers to the four essential questions: "Who am I? What do I love? How shall I live, knowing that I will die? What gifts do I bring to share with the family of the Earth?"

I want to help as many people as possible 'remember who they are and what they came here to do.' I am committed to helping individuals let go of lives that have played themselves out and do not serve them anymore, as I, myself, continue this work. I find it very rewarding to help others let go of the load of the past -- their past identities, obsolete stories, and all the dead weight that they are unnecessarily carrying -- so they can travel light through life and achieve greater fulfillment in the here-now. I am committed to share with them some techniques that will help them live mindfully and powerfully in the present moment, understanding that they should not let the pursuit of a future happiness be the source of their present unhappiness.

I want everyone to understand that chasing dreams should not deprive anyone from the enjoyment of all the good that is always right here, right now, in every moment. I want them to be aware, also, of how the reviving of painful memories prevent them from enjoying life fully in the here-now. I am committed to teaching them how to deal with those mental images and internal conversations in a healthier way. I want to encourage people to say "Yes" to life, to trust life with all it presents, both good and bad. I want to help people recognize, accept, and give thanks for the gifts that life is constantly giving. I want them to realize that a good life is a collection of good moments, and that they should pay attention in order to make the most and the best of every moment. I am committed to encouraging people to heed their calling in life. I want them to ask, "What am I passionate about? What are the things that when I do them I don't feel the passing of time? What are the gifts that I am meant to give?" I want them to courageously live authentic lives, remembering what Joseph Campbell said: "Follow your bliss, and the Universe will open doors for you where there were only walls." I want to remind them that "If you bring forth what is within you, what you bring forth will save you. But if you do not bring forth what is within you, what you do not bring forth will destroy you." (2) I am committed to guiding people in the introspective work that begets those powerful awakenings which reveal what could not be seen before. I want to remind them that "It is only with the heart that one can see rightly; what is essential is invisible to the eye." (3) I also want them to understand that "when we change the way we look at things, the things we look at change." (4)

I believe that our thoughts create our world, and that is why I have decided to dedicate myself to practice and teach mindfulness. I believe that deep personal transformations produce wholesome thoughts, words, and actions which, then, create a wholesome world. I believe that guiding people through this process is one of the most powerful forms of political activism for bringing about a better world. Meditation yields the experience of oneness -- the sentiment that we are all in this together, and the understanding that we are one -- which is essential to develop empathy and compassion, and create the gentler world we aspire. Let us become kinder people and bring about a kinder world. Let us tame our own savageness and bring Heaven to Earth, because Heaven is right here if we want it to be.

NOTES: (1) Wayne Muller in "How Then, Shall We Live? Four Simple Questions that Reveal the Beauty and Meaning of Our Lives" (2) Jesus in "The Gospel according to Thomas" (3) Antoine de Saint-Exupéry in "The Little Prince" (4) Max Planck, German physicist, the founder of Quantum Physics

……..

THE HURRICANE AND ME

With another hurricane approaching I can feel the fear furtively creeping in. Influenced by all the upheaval and insanity around me, I notice myself momentarily lost in a world of worries and fears, imagining the worst that may happen. And, sadly, I feel myself diminishing, becoming small. But then, I pause, breathe, and ask myself, "What is the worst that can happen? Is it to lose my house, my belongings, my loved ones, or even my life?" And suddenly I remember that sooner or later, all this will be gone anyway, because nothing lasts forever. This reflection brings me peace. It wakes me up, and makes me ponder on what is really important in life. Suddenly, this clear and present danger becomes a blessing in disguise. It brings about the opportunity to put things in perspective. It helps me develop acceptance of 'what is,' whatever it may be. It gives me the impetus to expand, rather than contract. It propels me to move beyond my petty, self-centered worries, and present myself to be of service to others. It offers me the opportunity to be big rather than small. Yes, there is a storm coming in the distance, but there is also one much closer, right inside my head. The good thing is that I have developed the power to calm this one down.

....

We are bringers of peace and sanity during moments of turmoil. It is in moments like this one that our peaceful presence is needed. I thank you for your steadfast dedication to your mindfulness practice and for exuding such serenity and wisdom. Remember that in a boat full of fearful and agitated people, one sane, calm, and steady-minded person can find the way through the fog and storms, and take the boat to a safe harbor, saving not only his or her life, but the lives of everyone in that boat. Continue practicing mindfulness. The world desperately needs more steady-minded individuals. Thank you.

....

FROM SILENCE TO PEACE

Every now and then I remember that peace comes from silence. We should all cultivate healthy periods of silence, stillness, solitude, seclusion, simplicity, and service in our lives. Great discoveries and insights come from these moments. And I believe the world would be a lot better if we all learned to meditate and if we all unplugged for a while. Mother Teresa's recipe for peace is five lines long. Guess what? It starts with silence.

"The fruit of silence is prayer.
The fruit of prayer is faith.
The fruit of faith is love.
The fruit of love is service.
The fruit of service is peace."

~ Mother Teresa

The fruit of silence is prayer. What kind of prayer? A silent prayer, a prayer in which we do not speak, just listen, a prayer that puts us in touch with our inner wisdom. This silent observation -- which we call meditation -- allows us to see the intelligence of the Universe in action which, in turn, develops in us a calm acceptance that life is unfolding exactly as it should. From this acceptance, what grow in us are trust, optimism, hope, and faith that everything will be OK. This faith opens up our hearts to love: to receive and give love. We develop the ability to see all the beauty, all the magic, all the mystery, and all the miracles that surround us. We notice the abundance of the Universe, and we realize how loved and fortunate we are. We realize that there's more than enough for everybody, that we always had enough and will always have enough, and therefore we don't need to worry. We develop a grateful heart, a heart of love. This opening up to love moves us from selfishness to selflessness. We become less self-centered and more other-centered. We don't ask "What's in it for me?" as much as we did before, and begin asking "How can I help?" a lot more. We begin to serve others, soon realizing that it is in giving that we receive. We then open up our arms, look up to the skies, smile, and whisper a silent "Thank you" to the Source of All. And then we rest in great peace.

The fruit of silence is prayer. The fruit of prayer is faith. The fruit of faith is love. The fruit of love is service. The fruit of service is peace.

Think about it. Think about how your life would be with more silence, prayer, faith, love, service, and peace in it. Awesome, right? So what are you waiting for? Don't wait. Just do it!

....

Someone asked Mother Teresa, "What do you say to God when you pray?" She answered, "I don't say anything. I just listen." Then she was asked a follow-up question: "And what does God say to you?" She responded, "He doesn't say anything. He just listens." And after a while she added, "And if you don't understand that, I can't explain it to you."

. . . .

PEACEMAKERS: PARADIGM CHANGERS

"Peace through nonviolence is possible." I don't know about you, but in my attempts to promote this idea I hear a lot of, "Don't be naive. You are being unrealistic. Violence is natural, conflict is inevitable, and peace is impossible. This is the way it has always been and will always be. Attempts to curb violence without using violence will never work. We have to be strong and show strength. We have to be ruthless and eradicate everyone who threatens or is a potential threat to us otherwise they will annihilate us. We have to use violence to protect ourselves and others." In such situations, my answer usually is, "One thing we undoubtedly know is that violence will not end conflicts, reduce tensions, or bring lasting peace. We have tried it for millennia and it has already proven its ineffectiveness. Violence may curb violence temporarily, but it does not end conflicts permanently. In fact, it only creates additional ones. Violence begets violence; this we all know for sure. And I am not talking only about direct violence, the one that wounds and kills fast. I am talking also about the indirect violence, the one that through exploitation, oppression and all forms of social injustice, wounds and kills slowly. This widely accepted and often ignored violence is the root of all other expressions of violence. It is time for us to apply nonviolence and bring about equality on a large scale."

Nonviolence has already proved its effectiveness. We know nonviolence works and is an effective way of bringing about justice and peace; we have plenty of examples of that. Take a look, for instance, at the evidence presented by Erica Chenoweth and Maria J. Stephan in their book "Why Civil Resistance Works: The Strategic Logic of Nonviolent Conflict." or the compelling historical facts lined up by Mark Kurlansky in his book "Nonviolence: The History of a Dangerous Idea." Nevertheless, the majority of human beings still is not convinced of its effectiveness. Nonviolence still is not their tool of choice to dispel conflicts. And this is so because people are not aware of what nonviolence is, how it works, how to apply it, and how effective it is. It's time for us to invest massively in nonviolent education, nonviolent communication, and nonviolent conflict resolution. Although education and training in nonviolent techniques is gaining ground, we still have a long way to go. We need to expand our reach and coverage so every human being can receive training on how to communicate and solve conflicts nonviolently.

Peacemakers need to understand that changing the prevailing ideas in the world is not an easy task. And that is what we, peacemakers, are doing: we are trying to transform the culture and change the deeply rooted paradigm that violence is inescapable, conflict is inevitable, and peace is impossible. We are trying, in the middle of all skepticism, to bring people to believe that peace is possible. Even more, we are trying to bring people to accept and believe that peace through nonviolence is possible. Our final goal is to bring lasting peace to the world, but our main job right now is to take people to a place where they can see new possibilities, and by seeing new possibilities they may begin to question their current beliefs and ways, and choose to adopt new ones.

OK. This is our task, but before we move forward we must have one thing clear: even though we would like people to see as we see, and think as we think, we have to realize that all we can do is to inspire others, and hopefully instill in them the desire to look into new possibilities. That's it. From that point on it is up to them to embrace new visions and understandings, or not.

. . . .

RECOGNIZING OUR OWN VIOLENCE

We need to reflect and admit our own violence. When we talk about violence, we are, the majority of time, thinking about the violence perpetrated by others, but we ignore our own.

In what ways are we violent? In what ways do we contribute to violence in the world?

To begin with, we have to look at history and see how we may have benefited from the historical oppression and exploitation of others. We need to own the fact that some of us have been the beneficiaries of a system built on the lives of others. We have to recognize that we belong to a group that benefits from the unjust ways we have organized ourselves to live in society. We have to realize that the goods we buy may have been manufactured by workers who may be subjected to oppression and exploitation. We have to be aware that we are enjoying freedoms and privileges that others aren't, and recognize that we are the ones who have put in place organizations, structures, and repressive systems that maintain such privileges, and deprive others from enjoying them. We have to realize that we benefit from this unfair system, and that, in many ways, we contribute to this institutional violence.

We also have to recognize that we live immersed in a highly individualistic and competitive culture that promotes excessive and unnecessary consumption, praises go-getters, and separates winners from losers. We are living in a self-centered culture, where everything is about "me," and where very few think in terms of "we." We are violent, demanding a lot from ourselves and others, and we pass this on to our children. This brings about an inherently tense and violent environment of competition for the accumulation of wealth, an environment of division between those who have achieved material success and those who haven't, a culture that promotes competition over cooperation.

We must also reflect on the violence perpetrated by our groups, the ones we belong to. We must realize how we separate ourselves in all forms of clans, tribes, gangs, countries, nations, ideologies, religions, and so on, and how we use violence to impose our ideas, our ways, and all sorts of arrangements that benefit us. We like to think of ourselves as being nonviolent, but we must recognize that, in a way, we pay for the emissaries who go out and wage violence on our behalf.

There is a difference between the use of force to attack and the use of force to protect. Peacemakers must develop a good understanding of the difference between the two. Many times, the use of force to expand influence -- to conquer, dominate, subjugate, and even punish others -- is presented as force being used to protect. That's a lie, used all the time, by those who benefit from violence. I am against violence, but I am not against the protective use of force as a last resort to save lives. Lives must be protected, and we have to achieve the goal of protecting lives without ending other lives in the process, because all lives are sacred. We have to stop people from killing without killing.

We don't even notice how violent we are, and how we contribute to violence in unexpected ways, but we have to recognize that, right now, we are violent people living in a violent world.

A PLACE OF PLENTY

Ideas shape our reality. The idea that prevails is the world today is that of scarcity -- that there is not enough -- and this idea becomes an impediment for living in peace and harmony. Fear of not having enough infects our lives and all our relationships. Fear opens the floodgates for selfishness and greed. Fear leads people to hoard, to accumulate more than what they need, and to get more than give. Fear unleashes impulses to compete, fight, conquer, and subjugate. Fear propels people to move ahead at all costs, ignoring the pain and suffering they inflict on others. Fear moves people to oppress and exploit other beings without considering the effects on mankind and the environment. Fear of scarcity unleashes the worst in us, and creates a violent world. Our unconscious acceptance of this "Scarcity Paradigm" brings violence to everything we do.

But if we believed the opposite -- that this planet of ours is a place of abundance where there is more than enough for everybody, and that we will always have access to what we need -- then we wouldn't be so afraid of lack. We would be more gentle and generous with one another. We would compete less and cooperate more. We would be less violent.

So, our mission should be to inspire people to look beyond the prevailing mindset, and take humanity to consider and adopt the "Abundance Paradigm."

A day will come when it will be common knowledge that we are not independent, but interdependent, and that the well-being of others enhances our own. We will then understand the value of taking good care of our fellow human beings. In doing so, we will realize that this is a world of abundance where there is more than enough for everybody, and that we are the ones who create scarcity for others, because our fear makes us consume and accumulate more than what we need. We will realize that scarcity only exists when we let our fear dominate us.

TEACHING AND PRACTICING NONVIOLENCE

What should peacemakers do?

We must keep promoting nonviolence and its advantages. We must continue reminding people that violence is destructive, while nonviolence is constructive and creative. Those who resort to violence to solve conflicts seek to defeat, subjugate, and segregate their opponents, invariably creating new enemies in the process. Meanwhile, those who adopt nonviolent means for conflict resolution don't see opponents as enemies to be defeated, but fellow human beings who need to be heard and understood, human beings who, in essence, want the same things they want. Nonviolent practitioners seek to communicate and integrate.

Let us invest in teaching less violent ways of dealing with one another. Wouldn't it be wonderful if schools all over the planet taught that we all should work for social justice and peace? Wouldn't it be wonderful if all children learned Mindfulness, Nonviolent Communication and Nonviolent Conflict Resolution techniques early in their lives, so they could take those techniques to their homes, to their communities, and not only apply them, but also teach them to others?

So, let us continue our efforts. Let us teach the new generations that everyone's highest moral calling must be to end oppression and exploitation. Let us raise humanity's understanding that those who fought injustices and attained social justice through nonviolent means deserve more praise than violent warriors. Let us continue pushing for our history books to reduce references to armed conflicts, and give more relevance to those events when social advancement was accomplished through nonviolent civil disobedience. Let us make a concentrated effort on education, remembering that "if we want to leave a better world for our children, we must leave better children for the world."

A change in the prevailing ideas is what will change the world. Meanwhile, while we are educating the new generation, we have to find nonviolent ways of curbing the bullies of the world, and reduce the damage they do. We need to be a voice for the voiceless. We need to encourage and support the oppressed to challenge their oppressors.

……..

"Injustice anywhere is a threat to justice everywhere." ~ Martin Luther King, Jr.

……..

Peacemakers and world changers must work in two fronts: curbing existing violence and preventing new violence to erupt.

1 - Stopping both direct and indirect violence.
- Can we use nonviolence to stop direct violence? How?
- And how can we utilize nonviolence to promote social change and diminish the structural violence, the one brought about by oppression, exploitation and other forms of social injustice?

2 - Preventing the emergence of violence.
- Utilizing nonviolent methods for resolving disputes and conflicts.
- Teaching nonviolent methods of introspection and self-awareness.
- Teaching nonviolent communication, mediation, and conflict resolution to the young population.
- Promoting widespread social justice, therefore reducing tensions, and the rate of success of indoctrination and recruitment for the perpetration of acts of direct violence by radical individuals.
- Promoting a new paradigm, a new way of seeing the world and life.

......

FIXING THE INEQUALITY

Let us continue our efforts to put an end to exploitation, oppression and poverty, knowing that injustice and inequality are the breeding grounds of violence. Those who are hopeless and desperate -- those who feel that they have lost everything and have nothing to lose -- are the ones who lend their ears to radicals and their messages of hatred and violence. Let us recognize that social injustice, inequality, oppression, and exploitation are the roots of the social instability we are facing in the world, and that to tackle those problems we need a new consciousness that values life, not only our own and those of our loved ones and tribe members, but all lives, even the lives of our enemies. A consciousness that, because it values all life, and considers all life sacred, rejects all killing. A consciousness that cannot stand seeing billions of children around the world living in the dirt, scrounging for their next meals. A consciousness that knows that a child who was wounded, who lost his father in war, who saw his mother suffering and crying, who lost his home, who went to live in a tent in a refugee camp, who doesn't have a school to go to, and who was robbed of his innocence and childhood, is a child doomed to choose the ways of violent revenge. A consciousness that does not allow us to close our eyes to abject poverty any longer. A consciousness that shakes us from our indifference and moves us to change the ways we organize ourselves to live on this planet, so we can assure that every single person can have a caring family and a dignified life. A consciousness that will not only say that they value work, but that really show that work is valued by compassionately understanding the needs of their fellow human beings and paying honest wages to all workers, wages that really allow them to live with dignity. A consciousness that morally compels us to do something so everyone in the world, not just some, can have shelter, food, water, health care, and education. A consciousness that believes that where a person is born should not determine if that person is going to live or die. A consciousness that is not blind to the military industrial complex and to the interests that move those who manufacture and trade weapons, and profit from conflicts. We need a new consciousness that non-judgmentally values all life, the lives of the poor, hungry, and homeless, the lives of the less fortunate, the lives of the less able to deal with the complexity and nuances of life, the lives of those who need to label others and make sure they belong to an 'acceptable' tribe, the lives of those who find comfort in easy, rushed, primitive "us against them, good against evil, hard-workers against lazy bums, conservative against liberals, capitalists against socialists" explanations. That's what we, peacemakers, are talking about.

....

FORTUNE OR MISFORTUNE?

"Once upon a time there was a Chinese farmer whose horse ran away. That evening, all of his neighbors came around to commiserate. They said, "We are so sorry to hear your horse has run away. This is most unfortunate." The farmer said, "Maybe." The next day the horse came back bringing seven wild horses with it, and in the evening everybody came back and said, "Oh, isn't that a lot of luck. What a great turn of events. You now have eight horses! That's great, isn't it?" The farmer again said, "Maybe." The following day his son tried to break one of the horses, and while riding it, he was thrown off, and broke his leg. The neighbors then said, "Oh dear, that's too bad, isn't it?" and the farmer responded, "Maybe." The next day the conscription officers came around to recruit people into the army, and they rejected his son because he had a broken leg. Again all the neighbors came around and said, "Isn't that great?" and the farmer replied, "Maybe."

The whole process of nature is an integrated process of immense complexity, and it's really impossible to tell whether anything that happens in it is good or bad — because you never know what will be the consequences of the misfortune; or, you never know what will be the consequences of good fortune." ~ Alan Watts

. . . .

SPACECRAFT VIEW

During stressful seasons in their lives, I often instruct my students to take the "helicopter view." I invite them to imagine looking at themselves and at their situations from above, as a way of not making everything so personal. Usually they tell me that when they see the bigger picture they realize that their cases are not as dramatic, as hopeless, or as unique as they initially thought. In a way, the ampler view placates their negativity. This perspective can be a real eye-opener and have a powerful and transformational effect. It's a way of realizing how easy it is for us to play victim and say, "Poor me. Why me? Why this is happening to me?" Once we compare our entanglements with those of others, we often realize not only how self-centered we are, but also the pettiness of our dramas, and this realization often brings us some relief.

The distance also allows us to see that although we are doing many things to free ourselves from the complicated predicaments we are in, we are not doing the right things, the things we really need to do to alleviate suffering and augment peace. It becomes evident that we are not using wise assessment, wise discernment, and wise action. It becomes clear that we are not concentrating our energy on what can bring lasting change: we waste time dealing with the consequences, instead of focusing our attention to understand and correct the causes of our problems. Paraphrasing Thoreau, from above we can see that while there are thousands of us hacking at the branches of evil, there's just a few who are doing the right thing: striking at the roots. We realize, as the popular sayings go, that "we keep doing the same things, over and over again, expecting different results," and that, by doing so, we are just "spinning our wheels, but actually going nowhere, only fast." No wonder we are all exhausted.

Well, Carl Sagan invited us to take not only the helicopter view, but the spacecraft view. The farther we move away from the surface of the Earth on this imaginary flight, the more evident it becomes to us that we are not as important as we think we are. We realize that we are just these tiny animals, inhabiting a diminutive planet that spins around itself and travels around a little star of an unremarkable galaxy in the middle of a vast, huge, humongous, infinite universe. This in itself should be humbling enough to inspire us to let go of all unimportant matters and enjoy, with the other passengers and crew members of spaceship Earth, the beauty of this planet during the short lives that we were given.

....

Pale Blue Dot is a photograph of planet Earth taken on February 14, 1990, by the Voyager 1 space probe from a record distance of about 6 billion kilometers. It inspired Carl Sagan to write "Pale Blue Dot." Read it and take some time to reflect on what he had to say. Perhaps, think about all those individuals who in their frantic pursuit of power create a lot of pain and suffering for others, and never come to realize that they are just "momentary masters of a fraction of a dot."

....

"From this distant vantage point, the Earth might not seem of any particular interest. But for us, it's different. Consider again that dot. That's here. That's home. That's us. On it everyone you love, everyone you know, everyone you ever heard of, every human being who ever was, lived out their lives. The aggregate of our joy and suffering, thousands of confident religions, ideologies, and economic doctrines, every hunter and forager, every hero and coward, every creator and destroyer of civilization, every king and peasant, every young couple in love, every mother and father, hopeful child, inventor and explorer, every teacher of morals, every corrupt politician, every "superstar," every "supreme leader," every saint and sinner in the history of our species lived there—on a mote of dust suspended in a sunbeam. The Earth is a very small stage in a vast cosmic arena. Think of the rivers of blood spilled by all those generals and emperors so that, in glory and triumph, they could become the momentary masters of a fraction of a dot. Think of the endless cruelties visited by the inhabitants of one corner of this pixel on the scarcely distinguishable inhabitants of some other corner, how frequent their misunderstandings, how eager they are to kill one another, how fervent their hatreds. Our posturing, our imagined self-importance, the delusion that we have some privileged position in the Universe, are challenged by this point of pale light. Our planet is a lonely speck in the great enveloping cosmic dark. In our obscurity, in all this vastness, there is no hint that help will come from elsewhere to save us from ourselves. The Earth is the only world known so far to harbor life. There is nowhere else, at least in the near future, to which our species could migrate. Visit, yes. Settle, not yet. Like it or not, for the moment the Earth is where we make our stand. It has been said that astronomy is a humbling and character-building experience. There is perhaps no better demonstration of the folly of human conceits than this distant image of our tiny world. To me, it underscores our responsibility to deal more kindly with one another, and to preserve and cherish the pale blue dot, the only home we've ever known." ~ Carl Sagan

....

Pale Blue Dot is a photograph of planet Earth taken on February 14, 1990, by the Voyager 1 space probe from a record distance of about 6 billion kilometers (3.7 billion miles, 40.5 AU), as part of the Family Portrait series of images of the Solar System. In the photograph, Earth's apparent size is less than a pixel; the planet appears as a tiny dot against the vastness of space, among bands of sunlight scattered by the camera's optics. Voyager 1, which had completed its primary mission and was leaving the Solar System, was commanded by NASA to turn its camera around and take one last photograph of Earth across a great expanse of space, at the request of astronomer and author Carl Sagan. (Wikipedia entry)

....

SPACESHIP EARTH

The Earth is a living organism, and we, human beings, are molecules of this one organism. If Earth dies, we die. The current focus on irresponsible short-term gains and incessant accumulation, which for the most part has been endangering our planet, must be substituted by socially and environmentally responsible action inspired by a long-term commitment with preservation, sustainability, and social justice.

We need new mindsets, new prevailing ideas, new paradigms. We must evolve, embrace a new cosmic perspective, and act as one species whose members solve their problems practicing cooperation and solidarity. If not, we are not going to survive.

The good news is that a new consciousness is arising and with it a new idea of what a good life is. The current idea that a good life is one of self-indulgence, over-consumption, exclusivity, and isolation is being replaced by the idea that a good life is a nonviolent life of connecting and supporting others on their journeys to become the best that they can be. The old idea that we need to compete, defeat, and marginalize others, in order to accumulate as much wealth, have as many pleasant experiences, and as many toys as possible has already shown its absurdity, and is being put aside. The rising paradigm is that a good life is a life of cooperation, responsible consumption, and minimum waste; a life in community, where everyone feels included and happy to be contributing crew members of Spaceship Earth.

……..

"We travel together, passengers on a little spaceship, dependent on its vulnerable resources of air and soil. Our safety is conditional on peace and security on this spaceship. We succeed not to be annihilated due to the care, effort and love we give to our fragile vehicle." ~ Adlai Stevenson

……..

This is our only space vehicle. This is our home. This planet of ours is our Garden and our Playground. We are called to enjoy the beauty of the Garden and have fun in the Playground, We are called to share our toys because the enjoyment of others enhances our own, If we feel like doing it, we should give our contribution to make the Garden more beautiful and the Playground more enjoyable. We are called to understand that this is Heaven, if we want it to be!

……..

Our work, as visionaries and teachers, is to lead our fellow human beings to places where they may be able to see a much larger picture, and embrace a new paradigm that will save humanity from extinction. We, all of us, are traveling through the endless cosmos on the same vehicle -- Spaceship Earth -- and we need to take good care of it if we want to continue our journey.

Actually, we need to take much better care of our habitat if we want to survive. Planet Earth, our home, is under attack, and, regrettably, we -- short-sighted, fearful, and greedy human beings -- are the ones destroying our fragile ecosystem. Only a new vision of the future, and a new understanding of our common destiny will change this destructive behavior. We need a new common goal to strive for if the human civilization is to go on.

The old paradigm of a world divided in tribes that engage in power struggles and fight one another must be replaced by the new paradigm of the whole humanity working together as a species to protect the planet and enhance everyone's life. We need to set aside our differences and transcend our selfishness and petty tribal identities. We have to realize that, in essence, we are all very similar and that those who magnify differences among humans are the ones who, in several ways, benefit from animosity and conflict. We must go beyond the damaging loyalty to our little gangs, and understand how this misplaced loyalty is endangering our future. Instead of seeing ourselves as members of different religions, nations, ethnicities, schools of thought, or bands of brothers, we must see ourselves as fellow crew members of the same endangered spacecraft who are called to work together in order to maintain it in perfect conditions, so it may be able to continue its journey through the cosmos. We must replace the illusion that we are separate from one another with the understanding that we are all interconnected. We must remember that we are all descendants of the same ancient parents, members of the same family, brothers and sisters all.

....

"So, let us not be blind to our differences--but let us also direct attention to our common interests and to the means by which those differences can be resolved. And if we cannot end now our differences, at least we can help make the world safe for diversity. For, in the final analysis, our most basic common link is that we all inhabit this small planet. We all breathe the same air. We all cherish our children's future. And we are all mortal." ~ John F. Kennedy

....

I have dedicated myself to promote the vision that this planet of ours is our garden and our playground, and that we are called to enjoy the beauty of the garden and have fun in the playground; that we are called to share our toys because the enjoyment of others enhances our own; that if we feel like doing it, we should give our contribution to make the garden more beautiful and the playground more enjoyable; that we are called to understand that this is Heaven.

PROSPERING TOGETHER

We need to realize how inherently violent is the world we live in, and how much energy is put into domesticating, dominating, and subjugating others. But this doesn't need to be so. We can reduce the violence, and bring gentleness, compassion, and respect to all our relationships with each other and the planet, if we are able to move to a new paradigm that replaces the current one.

It is time for us to agree that the current ways we have organized ourselves to live on this planet may be working temporarily for some, but, in the long range, will certainly not work for anyone. We need to come up with better ways. The most damaging belief residing in the collective unconscious is that there isn't enough for everyone. This idea of scarcity, and the fear of impending times of lack, compels humans to engage in a process of unending competition for the accumulation of resources. As a result, to compete and to defeat others, to gain access and deprive others of access, to own and deprive others of owning resources that make life easier, is accepted, without questioning, as the rule of the game. Immersed in this competitive culture, we grow conditioned to believe that the only viable way of operating on this planet is selfishly: "Each man for himself" and "Only the strong survive" are adopted, indisputably, as guiding principles. Cooperation and solidarity are quickly disregarded as wishful thinking of the weak.

Unfortunately, we have created a global economic system based on super-sized corporations focused on short term profits. In the final analysis, what commands all major decisions is the question, "How can we maximize profit this quarter?" This short-sighted focus propels the privatization of gains and the socialization of losses. In the struggle to maximize profits and minimize costs, social responsibility gets very little attention, or is totally ignored. The care for others and the environment, the care for the health of the community, the payment of just wages, the payment of benefits for workers, the payment of taxes that, in the final analysis, benefit the entire community, are all seen as obstacles on the way of maximizing profits. This all leads to the situation we are living right now: a world of unbearable inequalities, with an absurd concentration of wealth that is bringing about a never-ending series of social and environmental problems.

Maybe the majority of our problems comes from over-consumption and waste. We don't even notice it anymore, but we have been conditioned to desire, buy, and consume much more than what we actually need. This short-sighted vision emphasizes production, consumption, and waste, as the way of living and maximizing gains. The bigger picture - the Spaceship Earth idea -- is seldom, if ever, brought into consideration by those making corporate decisions. Fueled by the drive for ceaseless accumulation, wealth and power end up concentrated in the hands of a few while the majority of individuals scramble to survive. Within this scenario, where the majority of Earth's population is focused on short-term survival , little room is left for its inhabitants to see the bigger picture. Social injustice, exploitation, oppression, inequality, poverty, destitution, and so on, make it very difficult for earthlings to join forces, work together, and tackle humanity's biggest problems.

But the truth is that it doesn't have to be this way. We have the capacity to organize ourselves differently and find better ways to live and prosper together. The truth is that we don't need much. We can live much simpler and satisfying lives. The moment we bring about a more just society, where everyone's basic needs are met, individuals will be more inclined to cooperate with one another, and our interactions with the planet and all its inhabitants will be less aggressive and damaging. A time will come when we will transcend our sense of separation, and realize our inextricable interconnection and complete oneness. We will, then, put aside whatever divides us, embrace this new cosmic perspective, and work together to repair and maintain Spaceship Earth. We will realize that we need to stop the destruction, heal the environmental wounds we have inflicted on our planet, create a sustainable future, and preserve our habitat in order to save ourselves. This is our common goal. The task is huge, and it is urgent. There's nothing more important. We are on this one planet and we, the inhabitants of this planet, are united by the same destiny. We have to understand that we are all in this together, for real.

We need new mindsets, new prevailing ideas, new paradigms.

……..

"I really believe that if the political leaders of the world could see their planet from a distance of 100,000 miles their outlook could be fundamentally changed. That all-important border would be invisible, that noisy argument silenced. The tiny globe would continue to turn, serenely ignoring its subdivisions, presenting a unified facade that would cry out for unified understanding, for homogeneous treatment. The earth must become as it appears: blue and white, not capitalist or communist; blue and white, not rich or poor; blue and white, not envious or envied." ~ Michael Collins, astronaut of the Gemini 10 and Apollo 11 missions.

……..

I have dedicated myself to promote the vision that this planet of ours is our Garden and our Playground, and that we are called to enjoy the beauty of the Garden and have fun in the Playground; that we are called to share our toys because the enjoyment of others enhances our own; that if we feel like doing it, we should give our contribution to make the Garden more beautiful and the Playground more enjoyable; that we are called to understand that this is Heaven, if we want it to be!

……..

AN APPEAL FOR SANITY

"Life's most persistent and urgent question is, 'What are you doing for others?'" ~ Martin Luther King, Jr.

……..

Every now and then I have this surge of indignation with our stupidity: mankind's stupidity, I mean. How can we, human beings, be so irrational and foolish? How can our behavior be so absurd and imprudent? Why aren't we able to come to our senses, and see the countless ways we are endangering the Earth, our home, and all life in it. What's wrong with us? And then I ask the same questions I've been asking for so long: Why do we allow the lowest parts of ourselves, such as greed, hatred, and mindlessness to command our actions? Why do we insist in this endless pursuit of power, possessions, prestige, and privileges that has proven to be incapable of producing lasting happiness, and that keeps bringing so much suffering to the world? Why do we choose to ignore how our actions hurt others and the planet? Why do we divide ourselves in all sorts of tribes and fight each other? Why don't we unite, once and for all, recognizing that we are members of just one tribe, the tribe of humanity? Why do we keep wasting resources manufacturing killing devices instead of using our talent and time to improve the quality of life for all sentient beings on this planet? Why can't we join forces to preserve, enhance, and enjoy our planet, this beautiful garden and wonderful playground that were given to us? Why can't we understand that we are all in this together? Isn't our behavior completely insane? What's wrong with us?

Every time I reflect about this absurd state of affairs, Carl Sagan's "Pale Blue Dot" exhortation comes to mind. He reflected on the minuscule size of our planet, and after bringing to our attention that the Earth is no more than a tiny dot in the immensity of the Universe, he called us to come to our senses.

We are all crew members and passengers of spaceship Earth, and we need to work together to preserve this vehicle that is taking us through the cosmos. We have to look at the big picture. We are all interconnected and interdependent. We are all in this together. We must stop all this ridiculous and pointless fighting, and cooperate unreservedly with each other, because we will either succeed and live, or fail and die, all of us together. Let's change the focus, stop worrying about ourselves, and start thinking what we can do for others. Rather than asking, 'What's in it for me?' let's ask, 'How can I serve?' We are all responsible for preserving Planet Earth and building a sustainable future for all life. Let's work together for the common good, for the greater good. And working together for common goals is completely possible. We just need to let go of fear and selfishness, and have the resolve to make it happen. So, let's stop the nonsense and the pettiness! Heaven is here, if we want it to be. It is time for us to start thinking cosmically.

So many people in the world have grown but not matured. They grow physically, but still act like spoiled, selfish, and insecure children. The world needs people who behave as true adults, adults who see with clarity, are guided by wisdom, and act with selflessness and responsibility for the well-being of all.

The practice of mindfulness brings about a new consciousness that makes us experience compassion for all sentient beings. With the realization that we are all in this together, we protect all life, without exception, being extremely careful in order not to harm any life form. We make conscious choices and abstain from instruments and activities that wound and kill, including those associated with the enslavement, exploitation, and slaughter of animals.

If we want to preserve Spaceship Earth, we must adopt much simpler and less violent lives.

CHOOSING TO BELIEVE IN LIES

"Don't worry. When you are dead, you don't know that you are dead. It is only difficult for others. The same is true if you are stupid." For sure there is a lot of judgment in these words, but there is also an eye-opening opportunity, a call to wake up, see, and come to conclusions that are fruits of thorough and intelligent investigation.

It is said that you can fool all the people some of the time, and that you can fool some of the people all the time, but that you cannot fool all the people all the time. Well, there are dishonest individuals occupying positions of power who keep their focus on those they can fool. They say, "There are people out there who can be fooled, and those are the ones who interest me." Unfortunately, this seems not only to be true, but also to pay huge dividends to the corrupt power-grabbers who practice it. They lie, lie, and lie to those who can be lied to. It's shameful. Shame on those who lie, and shame on those who believe in lies.

Perhaps the most disconcerting aspect of all this is the unwillingness of so many to do the work of tackling the complex issues, look at all their facets, think logically, develop a more complete and clearer view of reality, and realize that they are being lied to. It's exasperating to see that no matter how much we try, all our attempts to reason fall on deaf ears. Robert Heinlein once said, "Never try to teach a pig to sing. It wastes your time, and it annoys the pig." It's harsh and condescending, but unfortunately experience proves it to be true.

Our diligent mindfulness practice develops in us a greater reserve of inner peace, understanding, and compassion that allows us to handle the despair and exasperation caused by other people's dishonesty, laziness, and ignorance in healthier ways. The practice develops some sort of immunity that shields us from attacks so they don't bother us as much anymore. We become better able to ignore the pestering, and respond with humor, grace, and generosity.

……..

"I think the problem with people like this is that they are so stupid that they have no idea how stupid they are. If you're very, very stupid, how can you possibly realize that you're very, very stupid? You'd have to be relatively intelligent to realize how stupid you are." ~ John Cleese

……..

I believe that our job is, with great forgiveness and compassion in our hearts, to wake up both emitters and receivers of lies from the spell they are in, so they can open their eyes and see not only their limiting ideas, but also the infinite possibilities for bringing about a whole new and better world for all.

....

BEWARE OF DARKNESS

"Beware of greedy leaders. They take you where you should not go."
~ George Harrison

....

In times of darkness, we have to be watchful of many things, such as deceitful leaders, their lies, and their empty promises. But, more than anything else, we must watch our own thoughts and emotions, and be mindful of what we think and feel. We must not allow fear, hopelessness, and sadness to take hold of us. That is not what we are here for.

We are here to be happy. We are here to shine. We are here to thrive. We are here to express hope and optimism. We are here to have compassion for those who were hypnotized by evil sorcerers. We are here to -- with a big smile on our faces and with love for everyone in our hearts -- dispel darkness. We are here to bring a big, bright light of hope and celebration to Earth.

....

"Beware of Darkness" is a song written by English musician George Harrison and originally released on his 1970 solo album All Things Must Pass. The song warns against permitting illusion from getting in the way of one's true purpose in life.

In the verses, the listener is warned against various influences that may corrupt him or her, such as con men ("soft shoe shufflers"), politicians ("greedy leaders") and pop idols of little substance ("falling swingers"). In addition, the lyrics warn against negative thoughts ("thoughts that linger"), since these corrupting influences and negative thoughts can lead to maya, or illusion, which distracts people from the true purpose of life. The song reminds that this "can hurt you", and that "that is not what you are here for." (adapted from the Wikipedia entry)

INFINITE PARALLEL REALITIES

My recent comprehension of time and space is twofold: one is given by my sensory perception, and the other is being suggested to me by out-of-the-box thinkers.

My senses lead me to believe that we do not occupy more than one space at the same time: we move around, go from place to place, and once we leave one spot, we are not there anymore. Regarding time, it passes, and, therefore, there was a past, there is a present, and there will be a future. I see time as a linear progression of present moments, a reality that does not allow me, or anyone else, to go to the past or the future. Time travel is not possible.

The new take on time and space, if I understand it, is that we can be in many spaces at the same time. Past and future do not exist; everything is happening in this very moment. We can be the protagonists of several stories that are happening simultaneously, and that are taking place in infinite parallel realities. All this comes from supporters of a hypothesis called multiverse, which include luminaries such as Stephen Hawking and Neil deGrasse Tyson. The multiverse (or meta-universe) is the hypothetical set of possible universes, including the universe we live in, and various parallel or alternate universes.

Within this framework, we can come to imagine that we are not only living the lives that we are aware of right now, but that we are also living infinite other lives that we cannot be aware of from the place and time where we stand. In those other parallel lives, we have made other choices, therefore those lives are different than the ones we are currently conscious of.

Where could this possibility take us? If we give free rein to our imaginations, we can dream that if we are not happy with the lives we are currently living, we could choose lives that make us happier because such lives already exist in parallel realities, and are available for us in this very moment. So, a question arises: How do we transition from one dimension to another? Well, when we dream we are not restricted by space and time: we can visit other realities; we can fly; we can jump from one place to another instantly. So understanding dreaming seems to be of great importance to find clues, but the truth is that no one knows the answer. I feel that meditating, imagining, visualizing, and affirming is where the process begins.

LOOKING AT THIS WORLD FROM ANOTHER

"I have learned to offer no resistance to what is; I have learned to allow the present moment to be and to accept the impermanent nature of all things and conditions. Thus have I found peace." ~ Eckhart Tolle

……..

I am working on changing my mindset. I keep reminding myself that the way it has always been isn't the way it has to be. I am convinced that we can bring Heaven to Earth if we so want. I am learning to calmly accept what is. I came to the realization that I don't need to ferociously oppose what I dislike. I now see many possibilities, and see that I can choose to step aside, or choose another road, or even choose a new destination altogether. Why? Because this dimension in which we are operating is just one dimension among many. I have realized that I can look at this world as if I were an observer from another world.

When I do this, I am not turning away from the harsh realities of this dimension. Yes, there are people suffering and I will do what I can based on what I believe is best to alleviate their suffering. My belief is that we will be able to bring Heaven to Earth when we expand our mindsets and become able to see new possibilities in all areas. I believe our thoughts and vibrational energies are the forerunners of new realities. This is what I have been exploring and, hopefully, also inspiring others to do. Exploring and inspiring.

……..

"I am certain I create my life from a level that is even deeper than my thoughts, more than my thoughts. It is what I vibrate from the cellular level. It is what my being sends out to the universe. Even if I think "I am healthy", but vibrate with a fear of cancer, the fear of cancer overrides the thought. It is more than my thoughts. It is my Being. Everything is energy. Energy vibrates. What I vibrate is what I AM physically and creates my physical world. Vibrations become physical things if they vibrate the same way long enough." ~ Leslie Lott

……..

AN OVERWHELMING SENSE OF ONENESS

Astronaut Edgar Mitchell, who was part of the Apollo 14 space crew that flew to the moon in 1971, and one of just 12 human beings who walked on the moon, founded the Institute of Noetic Sciences, which sponsors research into the nature of consciousness, or studying the unexplained. In his 1996 memoir, The Way of the Explorer, he described the experience on his return to Earth as life-changing. "What I experienced during that three-day trip home was nothing short of an overwhelming sense of universal connectedness. I actually felt what has been described as an ecstasy of unity." I quoted Mitchell in my 2008 book Pay Attention! Be Alert! I saw him then in David Sington's documentary, In the Shadow of the Moon, and his words had a deep effect on me.

. . . .

"The biggest joy was on the way home. In my cockpit window, every two minutes, [I could see] the Earth, the Moon, the Sun, and the whole 360 degree panorama of the heavens..., and that was a powerful, overwhelming experience... and suddenly I realized that the molecules of my body, the molecules of the spacecraft and the molecules in the bodies of my partners were prototyped and manufactured in some ancient generation stars... and that was an overwhelming sense of oneness, of connectedness... it wasn't 'them and us;' it was, 'That's me! All of it! It's one thing!' It was accompanied by an ecstasy... "O, my God! Wow! Yes!"... An insight! An epiphany!" ~ Edgar Mitchell

We are all human beings. Our common humanity precedes our nationality, ethnicity, ideology, or any other category we may use to separate ourselves. We could say that we are human before we are anything else, but even this would be an incomplete statement because our divinity precedes even our humanity. We must come to realize that our fate is linked with that of everyone else. We are all related, and the full realization of our oneness is one of the greatest insights we might come to, one that raises our consciousness to new heights, and forever changes the way we see reality and live our lives.

Upon his return from space, Edgar Mitchell felt that a collective shift in consciousness was absolutely necessary. So he engaged in the work of helping others investigate their inner lives, develop their human potential, and challenge obsolete paradigms.

LOOKING FROM ABOVE

Do they see me? The ones climbing this tree; do they see me? And the ones that tickle my knee; do they see me? And the ones journeying through this old wooden table in the garden; do they see me? And these ones I carefully avoid stepping on as I mindfully walk this labyrinth; do they see me? These ants, I mean; do they see me? And if they don't, then what else is out there that I don't see? I wonder.

……..

I believe astronauts should rule the world. All of those who have been beyond Earth's atmosphere and seen it from above have been struck by our planet's beauty and fragility, and reflected on our unreasonable and preposterous behavior. Frank Borman, one of the first three human beings to orbit the moon, said, "When you're finally up at the moon looking back on earth, all those differences and nationalistic traits are pretty well going to blend, and you're going to get a concept that maybe this really is one world and why the hell can't we live together like decent people?"

When asked about what he remembered from the 1968 Apollo 8 flight, Jim Lovell had this to say: "We had pictures before of the far side of the moon, so we knew what to expect. What we didn't expect was to see the Earth as it really is. I put my thumb up to the window and could hide the Earth. Suddenly, I realized that I am 240,000 miles away, but behind my finger is a planet with about 4 billion people. That told me in a moment just exactly what we are in the universe." He also added, "There's an old saying, 'I hope to go to heaven when I die.' Suddenly, it dawned on me that we went to heaven when we were born! We arrived on a planet that had the right amount of mass to have the gravity to contain water and an atmosphere, just at the proper distance from a star. It appeared to me that God had given mankind sort of a stage to perform on. I guess how that play will turn out is up to us."

Here's my appeal for sanity: "We are all crew members and passengers of spaceship Earth, and we need to work together to preserve this vehicle that is taking us through the cosmos. We have to look at the big picture. We are all interconnected and interdependent. We are all in this together. We must stop all this ridiculous and pointless fighting, and cooperate unreservedly with each other, because we will either succeed and live, or fail and die, all of us together. Let's change the focus, stop worrying about ourselves, and start thinking what we can do for others. Rather than asking, 'What's in it for me?' let's ask, 'How can I serve?' We are all responsible for preserving Planet Earth and building a sustainable future for all life. Let's work together for the common good, for the greater good. And working together for common goals is completely possible. We just need to let go of fear and selfishness, and have the resolve to make it happen. So, let's stop the nonsense and the pettiness! Heaven is here, if we want it to be."

....

On December 24, 1968, in what was the most watched television broadcast at the time, the crew of Apollo 8 read in turn from the Book of Genesis as they orbited the Moon. Bill Anders, Jim Lovell, and Frank Borman recited Genesis chapter 1, verses 1 through 10 verbatim. Anders began by saying, "We are now approaching lunar sunrise, and for all the people back on Earth, the crew of Apollo 8 has a message that we would like to send to you." He then read verses 1–4, Lovell read verses 5–8, and Borman read verses 9–10, concluding the transmission saying, "And from the crew of Apollo 8, we close with good night, good luck, a Merry Christmas – and God bless all of you, all of you on the good Earth."

The preceding text is from a Wikipedia article under the title 'Apollo 8 Genesis reading.' I included it here because I feel that the final words pronounced by Frank Borman in that message express the feeling of inclusiveness in a very expressive way. I think his was the right message, one that includes everyone and that is worth repeating: "God bless all of you, all of you on the good Earth."

....

Here's an idea: Every elected official, or better, every person running for public office in the world, as a requirement, should spend time in outer space looking at our world from above.

....

BEING MINDFUL OF OUR CHOICES

I live in Florida, close to the ocean. Every morning I go to the beach to watch the sunrise, and every morning I pick up trash from the sand. Some days I pick up a lot, other days just a little. Some days I go well prepared, with gloves, bags, and my pickup tool. Other days I just bend down, collect items with my bare hands, and deposit them in the trash cans. But I have vowed not to leave the beach without picking up at least eleven items. And if you are asking "Why eleven?" the answer is simple: "It's just because eleven is my preferred number." Being a surfer, I have developed great love for the ocean, especially the shoreline, and beach cleanup is not new for me: it's an activity I have been performing for decades. I have made it my mission to collect the scattered rubbish people leave behind. Almost every day I hear a "Thank you for doing this" from a stranger, and it is not uncommon to engage in conversations about how much our careless littering is wounding our planet. I am not saying all this to brag, but to bring up a reflection about the way we live. Perhaps we can pause and ask ourselves, "Am I aware of how my choices affect the planet and all life on it? Am I being selfish and lazy, doing what is convenient for me without considering the inconveniences I create for others?" Perhaps this reflection can inspire us to live differently, consuming less and wasting less. Perhaps we can be more mindful of the choices we make, and limit to a minimum the amount of disposable items we use. I am trying to be more selective of what I buy, trying to reduce the consumption of products packaged in plastic and staying away from single-use plastic items, such as plastic bags, forks, knives, spoons, plates, cups, straws, and bottles.

In an article published in the May 6th, 2019 edition of the Washington Post, Darryl Fears wrote: "One million plant and animal species are on the verge of extinction, with alarming implications for human survival, according to a United Nations report released Monday. The landmark report goes further than previous studies by directly linking the loss of species to human activity. It also shows how those losses are undermining food and water security, as well as human health. Oceana senior adviser Philip Chou called the report a beacon for more action to address a crisis. 'We are seeing alarming increases in the deaths of fish, marine mammals and turtles ingesting plastics,' Chou said. 'These plastics break apart in the ocean into microscopic particles [that are] consumed by fish, fish we now eat.'"

I also have been distressed by the negative impact of livestock production on the environment. Livestock farming has a vast environmental footprint and is one of the major causes of the world's most pressing environmental problems, including deforestation, soild erosion, contamination by pesticides and herbicides, loss of biodiversity, air, land, and water pollution, greenhouse gas emissions, acid rain, ocean waters warming, coral reef degeneration, and global warming. Considering all these factors, one of the most effective ways of repairing the environment is to refrain from consuming products of animal origin.

……..

"This may surprise you because it surprised me when I found out, but the single biggest thing an individual can do to combat climate change is to stop eating animals." ~ James Cameron

……..

But this is not all. We need to be sensitive and reject the abhorrent ways we treat animals. It is wrong to enslave, torture, and slaughter animals for our benefit. Animals were not made for us. They are sentient beings and we must treat them with kindness, compassion, and respect.

……..

"It's not a requirement to eat animals, we just choose to do it, so it becomes a moral choice and one that is having a huge impact on the planet, using up resources and destroying the biosphere." ~ James Cameron.

……..

Bottom line: eating non-processed, raw plants like animals in their majority do, is good for us, good for the animals, and good for the planet.

Stephanie, a good friend, reminds me that we need the planet more than the planet needs us. This is so true, isn't it? The planet will still go on when we become extinct, just like it continued to go on when the dinosaurs died out. Unfortunately, not only we are the ones who are creating all the current ecological crises, but also the ones who are making them worse due to our neglectful and irresponsible way of living. Let's take a look at the global population. The total number of humans currently living is estimated to have reached 7.7 billion people as of April 2019. It took over 200,000 years of human history for the world's population to reach 1 billion, and only 200 years more to reach 7 billion.

I find it alarming that now that we are entertaining the possibility of someday inhabiting another planet, such as Mars for instance, we mindlessly enter in a state of delusion perhaps thinking that it is OK to trash the Earth because we will always be able to leave this planet and go live somewhere else. Really? And then what? We will trash Mars and go to Jupiter? Isn't that absurd? The bottom line is that we need to take good care of our planet, the only one we have right now, and not treat it as if it were disposable because it is not! The truth is that if we are not part of the solution -- if we aren't engaged in living more mindfully and repairing the damage that has already been done -- then we are the problem. We are the problem!

Here it is, once again, my appeal for sanity: "We are all crew members and passengers of spaceship Earth, and we need to work together to preserve this vehicle that is taking us through the cosmos. We have to look at the big picture. We are all interconnected and interdependent. We are all in this together. We must stop all this ridiculous and pointless fighting, and cooperate unreservedly with each other, because we will either succeed and live, or fail and die, all of us together. Let's change the focus, stop worrying about ourselves, and start thinking what we can do for others. Rather than asking, 'What's in it for me?' let's ask, 'How can I serve?' We are all responsible for preserving Planet Earth and building a sustainable future for all life. Let's work together for the common good, for the greater good. And working together for common goals is completely possible. We just need to let go of fear and selfishness, and have the resolve to make it happen. So, let's stop the nonsense and the pettiness! Heaven is here, if we want it to be."

....

THE WORLD WE WANT

"The question that guides my life is, 'How do you create a wisdom-based culture?' That is the question that guides my life. How do we create that? There would be social-emotional learning in every school. There would be compassion training in every school. Corporations would focus not on quarterly profits, but on the quality of connections and the impact they are having on the world. All people would be taken care of. Everyone would get a basic income so there would be a sense of likeness and {an understanding that} if others are hurting, we are also hurting. We would create a tax system that benefits not only the top but the bottom. All this has to come from an internal sense of wanting to help. So there is an inner process that each one of us has to go through to understand our own suffering, our own pain, which opens up to feel another's suffering and pain. It would not come because we are trying to convince others of our positions. So that's what inspires me and draws me... to create a wisdom-based culture where these things are not coming about because we are democrats or republicans but because we are actually seeing our humanity, and developing policies and practices based on a sense of connectedness." ~ Soren Gordhamer

Rather than asking what you want to do in the world, pause, be fully present, and ask yourself, "What is the world asking of me? What does the world wants to do through me? What wants to come out in the world through me?" Think or yourself as a conduit, and allow life to do what it wants to do through you.

....

TIME TO TEACH NONVIOLENCE

"In order for the world to become peaceful, people must become more peaceful. Among mature people war would be impossible. In their immaturity people want, at the same time, peace and the things which make war. However, people can mature just as children grow up. Yes, our institutions and our leaders reflect our immaturity, but as we mature we will elect better leaders and set up better institutions. It always comes back to the thing so many of us wish to avoid: working to improve ourselves." ~ Peace Pilgrim

....

It's time to teach nonviolence. It is time to flood the curricula of our schools with subjects that can improve human relations such as Nonviolent Communication, Nonviolent Conflict Resolution, Character Education, Mindfulness Meditation, Restorative Justice, Mediation, and Social and Emotional Learning. It is time to teach less about the violent warriors and more about the nonviolent peacemakers.

"Nonviolent Lives: People and Movements Changing the World Through the Power of Active Nonviolence," a book by Ken Butigan, inspires its readers to consider that they, too, can be agents of change through nonviolent means. This book highlights a group of individuals who dedicated themselves to bring about justice and peace through active nonviolent resistance.

Although we can more easily remember the names and great feats of those heroes who risked and lost their lives, this book also brings to light other less known peacemakers, revealing that the path to justice and peace is mostly made of small and persistent acts of defiance. Many of the individuals mentioned in Butigan's book didn't do anything tremendously daring and heroic to begin with; they simply decided that they could not remain as bystanders and allow wrongdoing to go on. They had the courage to step outside of their comfort zone, speak up, and expose the perpetrators of injustices, day in and day out. And this is something that we all can do. By carrying out small acts of civil disobedience, protest, and resistance, they initiated waves of social change that brought us closer to achieving what should be the aim of mankind: to tame the savageness of man and make gentle the life of this world. "Nonviolent Lives" is a book that proves, through many examples, the great power of active nonviolent resistance to beget social change. This book is, also, a calling to the political involvement and activism so needed nowadays in this world of ours, a world plagued by all sorts of direct and indirect violence. When will we put an end to social injustice, oppression, exploitation, bigotry, discrimination, exclusion, income inequality, and poverty? When will we say "No more!" to human rights abuses, torture, environmental aggression, war, and the continuous development of weapons of mass destruction? When will we put an end to all this insanity? When will we pause and realize that this planet of ours is a beautiful place of immense abundance with more than enough for everybody? When will we realize that we can organize ourselves to live on it in gentle and cooperative ways that will allow everyone to have dignified, thriving and contributing lives?

"Civil disobedience is not our problem. Our problem is civil obedience. Our problem is that people all over the world have obeyed the dictates of leaders...and millions have been killed because of this obedience...Our problem is that people are obedient all over the world in the face of poverty and starvation and stupidity, and war, and cruelty. Our problem is that people are obedient while the jails are full of petty thieves... (and) the grand thieves are running the country. That's our problem." ~ Howard Zinn

………

The truth is that everything we do for justice and peace, no matter how small, adds up to bring about a culture of compassion and solidarity that one day will prevail in this world. As Margaret Mead said, "Never doubt that a small group of thoughtful, committed citizens can change the world; indeed, it's the only thing that ever has." Let us to walk on the same paths of those peacemakers who came before us. If we pay attention, we can hear them calling. Let us heed their calling.

....

"Nonviolence is not a political weapon or a technique for social change so much as it is an essential art—perhaps the essential art—of civilization. Nonviolence is a way of thinking, a way of life, not a tactic, but a way of putting love to work in resolving problems, healing relationships, and generally raising the quality of our lives. Nonviolence is a skill. Love is a skill. The transformation of anger is a skill. All these can be learned. We cannot say we aren't capable of nonviolence; all we can say is we are not willing to do what is necessary to learn.' ~ Eknath Easwaran

....

A SAFE AND WELCOMING SPACE

"When you are interiorly free you call others to freedom, whether you know it or not. Freedom attracts wherever it appears. A free man or a free woman creates a space where others feel safe and want to dwell. Our world is so full of conditions, demands, requirements, and obligations that we often wonder what is expected of us. But when we meet a truly free person, there are no expectations, only an invitation to reach into ourselves and discover there our own freedom." ~ Henri Nowen

How do we create a space where others feel safe and comfortable to dwell in?

We create a safe and welcoming space by curbing our cravings and aversions, by accepting everything and demanding nothing, by diminishing our self-importance, and by just showing up as who we really are.

By doing so, we allow others to relax, feel safe, and give permission for them to be who they really are.

....

NONVIOLENT COMMUNICATION

"Out beyond ideas of wrongdoing, and right-doing, there is a field. I will meet you there." ~ Rumi

Nonviolent Communication is based on the principles of nonviolence.

Nonviolent Communication begins by assuming that we are all compassionate by nature and that violent strategies—whether verbal or physical—are learned behaviors taught and supported by the prevailing culture. Nonviolent Communication also assumes that we all share the same, basic human needs, and that all actions are a strategy to meet one or more of these needs. People who practice Nonviolent Communication have found greater authenticity in their communication, increased understanding, deepening connection, and conflict resolution. With Nonviolent Communication we learn to hear our own deeper needs and those of others. Through its emphasis on deep listening—to ourselves as well as others— Nonviolent Communication helps us discover the depth of our own compassion. This language reveals the awareness that all human beings are only trying to honor universal values and needs, every minute, every day. Nonviolent Communication can be seen as both a spiritual practice that helps us see our common humanity, using our power in a way that honors everyone's needs, and a concrete set of skills which help us create life-serving families and communities. The form is simple, yet powerfully transformative. Through the practice of Nonviolent Communication we can learn to clarify what we are observing, what emotions we are feeling, what values we want to live by, and what we want to ask of ourselves and others. We will no longer need to use the language of blame, judgment, or domination. We can experience the deep pleasure of contributing to each others' well being. Nonviolent Communication contains nothing new. It is based on historical principles of nonviolence-- the natural state of compassion when no violence is present in the heart. Nonviolent Communication reminds us what we already instinctively know about how good it feels to authentically connect to another human being. Nonviolent Communication creates a path for healing and reconciliation in its many applications, ranging from intimate relationships, work settings, health care, social services, police, prison staff and inmates, to governments, schools and social change organizations. ~ The Center For Nonviolent Communication website – cnvc.org

……..

"All that has been integrated into Nonviolent Communication has been known for centuries about consciousness, language, communication skills, and use of power that enable us to maintain a perspective of empathy for ourselves and others, even under trying conditions... When your internal dialogue is centered in a language of life, you will be able to focus your attention on the actions you could take to manifest a situation that meets your needs along with those of others."
~ Marshall B. Rosenberg

NONVIOLENT EDUCATION

Unfortunately, it seems that the majority of us are not capable of listening attentively, analyzing dispassionately, thinking rationally, and acting logically. It seems that we don't take the time to choose the best responses. What we do, most, if not all the time, is to react to the events in our lives very, very fast, often with emotionally-charged, unbalanced, and violent reactions.

It's time for us to invested massively in teaching how to expand and take control of the gap between stimuli and responses, and how to use this space-time in order to listen, connect, understand other people's feelings and needs, analyze, and choose the best responses. It's time for us to invest massively in teaching nonviolent communication and nonviolent conflict resolution.

Although education and training in nonviolent techniques is gaining ground, we still have a long way to go. We need to expand our reach and coverage so every human being can receive training on how to communicate mindfully and solve conflicts nonviolently. We must keep promoting nonviolence and its advantages, creating conditions for people to realize that violence is destructive, while nonviolence is constructive and creative.

We have to remind ourselves that those who resort to violence to solve conflicts seek to defeat, subjugate and segregate their opponents, invariably creating new enemies in the process, while those who adopt nonviolent means for conflict resolution don't see opponents as enemies to be defeated, but fellow human beings who need to be heard and understood, human beings who, in the final analysis, want the same things they want.

Nonviolent practitioners seek to listen deeply, feel compassionately, communicate respectfully, and invite others to jointly come up with creative solutions that dispel tensions, bring parties together, and make all those involved feel that a fair agreement can be reached.

Let us invest in teaching less violent ways of relating with one another. Wouldn't it be wonderful if all children were exposed to the practice of Mindfulness, Nonviolent Communication, Nonviolent Conflict Resolution, Mediation and Restorative Justice, early in their lives? Wouldn't it be wonderful is they took those techniques to their homes and communities, and not only applied them, but also taught them to others? Wouldn't it be wonderful if schools all over the planet taught programs that enhanced empathy and compassion, taught more cooperation and less competition, and taught children that we all should work to end violence through the attainment of social justice and peace?

So, let us continue our efforts. Let us teach the new generations that everyone's highest moral calling must be to put an end to the systemic, indirect violence. Let's work to put an end to oppression and exploitation. Let us continue pushing for our history books to reduce references to armed conflicts, and give more relevance to those events when social advancements were accomplished through nonviolent resistance and civil disobedience. Let us raise humanity's understanding that those who fought injustices and attained social progress through nonviolent means deserve more praise than violent warriors.

Let us teach mindfulness, introspection, meditation, and all those gentle techniques that allow people to find answers to the most essential questions within themselves. Let us develop a great love for the silence, and demonstrate the advantages of cultivating it. Let us practice and teach how to properly listen to one another, understanding each other's needs, and exploring creative ways of having those needs met. Let us make a concentrated effort on education, teaching what is really important, what really needs to be taught. Finally, let us understand once and for all that nothing in the world can make us feel better than contributing to the well-being of others. Let us remember that if we want to leave a better world for our children, we must leave better children for the world.

"He who opens a school door, closes a prison." ~ Victor Hugo

The world needs nonviolence. Humanity needs nonviolence. Every person needs to learn nonviolence.

NEITHER VICTIMS, NOR EXECUTIONERS

Who am I? Am I a murderer? Am I an accomplice of murderers?

Albert Camus was awarded the Nobel Prize for literature in 1957, the second youngest writer to receive this honor. He died three years later in an automobile accident. "Neither Victims nor Executioners," one of his writings, appeared serially in the autumn of 1946 in Combat, the daily newspaper of the Resistance, which Camus helped edit during the Nazi occupation and for a short time after the war. It was published in English in the July-August 1947 issue of Politics. What follows is an excerpt of that piece, in which Camus calls for nonviolence and preservation of life.

"All I ask is that, in the midst of a murderous world, we agree to reflect on murder and to make a choice. After that, we can distinguish those who accept the consequences of being murderers themselves or the accomplices of murderers, and those who refuse to do so with all their force and being. Since this terrible dividing line does actually exist, it will be a gain if it be clearly marked. Over the expanse of five continents throughout the coming years an endless struggle is going to be pursued between violence and friendly persuasion, a struggle in which, granted, the former has a thousand times the chances of success than that of the latter. But I have always held that, if he who bases his hopes on human nature is a fool, he who gives up in the face of circumstances is a coward. And henceforth, the only honorable course will be to stake everything on a formidable gamble: that words are more powerful than munitions." ~ Albert Camus

So, inspired by Camus, I pause and ask myself, "Who am I? Am I a murderer? Am I an accomplice of murderers? Do I send others to kill on my behalf? What part do I play in the killing? In what ways do I benefit from the killing of others?"

The truth is that even I, this flimsy and hesitant promoter of peace, am guilty. For the mere fact that I am a citizen of this country, and a taxpayer, I somewhat contribute to the killing of others. Without regard for my personal opposition to the use of violence, my government sends emissaries to kill, and that is what they do on my behalf. They may not have my explicit consent to do so, but they somehow benefit from my silent connivance, and from a system that ignores my opposition to all forms of violence and killing.

So, I hear Camus asking me, "In the midst of this murderous world, what do you choose?" And my answer is, "I choose life. I choose kindness. I choose communication. I choose active nonviolent resistance to all forms of violence, all forms of oppression and exploitation, all the inhumane forms human beings treat other human beings." May we, all of us, make a similar choice. May we all choose life. May we grow in mindfulness, experience oneness, and engage in the work of alleviating other people's suffering, and that of preserving the planet and all life in it. May we reject violence and killing. May we believe in the intrinsic goodness of man and the power of nonviolent, friendly persuasion to dispel tensions and solve conflicts. May we live with the conviction that words are more powerful than munitions. May we choose selflessness, modesty, and cooperation, not self-boasting and competition. May we choose peace, always.

……..

To all my sisters and brothers in arms, independent of what country or tribe you pledge loyalty to... To all of you engaged in fight and killing... To all of you getting physically and mentally wounded... To all of you trapped in the cross fires... To all of you, the conscientious objectors and deserters... To all of you, all over this world of ours, know that I feel your pain and that I love you all. We are all in this together. I can imagine how hard it may be to do some of the things you are ordered to do. Maybe not thinking about the insanity of all this violence and killing is the only way to cope with it, and maintain some sort of soundness of mind. I can understand that. I can feel the pain. If you are engaged in killing, and if you can find a way out, I hope you exercise this option. Please, stop! If you are, in any way, involved in hurting and killing other beings, stop, please. Stop all violence and protect all lives, especially the lives of the most innocent. Stop wounding. Stop killing. Take care of the children. Please, stop!

I want you to know that you are loved.

……..

AN APPEAL FOR SANITY

Please, stop!

Stop the violence. Put an end to the scars, wounds, mutilations, and deaths. It is our responsibility to do what we can to give all children opportunities for them to enjoy a peaceful and joyful childhood. It is our duty to do what we can so all children may enjoy their lives in safety. Save our children. Drop your weapons and put your energy, effort, and focus on saving the children. Save your children, our children.

We don't normally see the pictures of wounded children in war zones because such pictures are highly disturbing. The sad truth is that since we are shielded from seeing these images, we are not moved to do something to stop the violence; we don't connect, at a visceral level, with their pain and suffering.

Pause for a few moments and feel their pain. Listen to your inner voice. What is it calling you to do? Heed the calling and do something, anything, no matter how insignificant you may think it is, to stop the insanity. As Mother Teresa said, "It doesn't matter what you do, what matters is the love you put into the doing." Don't think that what you do has no significance. As Howard Zinn said, "If people could see that change comes about as a result of millions of tiny acts that seem totally insignificant, then they wouldn't hesitate to take those tiny acts."

Don't think that you are powerless. As Margaret Mead said, "Never doubt that a small group of thoughtful, committed citizens can change the world; indeed, is the only thing that ever has."

………

We are all connected. If one of us is not well, none of us can be totally well. Let us convince ourselves that when we care for the wellbeing of others, we are also caring for our own. Let us convince ourselves that any form of oppression and exploitation brings about pain and instability, and that we, directly or indirectly, are also benefiting from injustices that are taking place in the world. Let us convince ourselves that it is on everyone's best interest to promote social justice, because justice precedes peace. Let us convince ourselves, once and for all, as Dr. Martin Luther King Jr. once said, that "injustice anywhere is a threat to justice everywhere."

Let us put an end to violence by putting an end to poverty. Let's adopt a new paradigm for a new world. Let's convince ourselves that we live in a world of abundance where everyone can have a dignified and worry-free life, where the basic needs of every single individual in our planet can be met. Let us convince ourselves that there is more than enough for everybody to live a healthy, safe, and productive life. Let us convince ourselves that there will always be enough, that we will always be taken good care of, and that there's no need to be afraid and accumulate.

Let us convince ourselves that we don't have to deprive others of their share in order for us to have a bigger share. Let us convince ourselves that depriving others from having a happy livelihood will not make us any happier. So let us be honest and vastly generous in all our transactions with others. Let us be the agents of change, the ones who will bring Heaven to Earth.

We can do it!

. . . .

GIVING OUR CONTRIBUTION FOR A BETTER WORLD

Here, in the comfort and safety of my home located thousands of miles from the nearest war zone, I watch the news and think about the children who have been directly affected by war. My heart cries and my spirit sinks. I think how their lives have been forever tarnished.

I ponder on all the distress violence brings about.

Violence inflicts pain and suffering, and condemns little children to carry the memories of atrocities for a lifetime. Violence shatters the children's innocence and hope, and disseminates fear and mistrust. Violence brings forth the desire for revenge, and turns innocent children in slaves of hatred. Violence only produces more violence.

This insanity must stop. This is my appeal for sanity: Please, stop!

Drop your weapons and go take care of the children, all children, your own and the children of your enemies; they are your children too. We are all related. We are one family. Drop your weapons, and go take care of the children. Take care of their wounds. Feed them. Shelter them. Give them love. Give them love. Give them love. Give them hope. Give them family.

. . . .

Please, stop! If you are in any way involved with violence, especially the direct violence that wounds and kills children, I implore you to stop.

Please, stop! We are all members of the same family, the Human family. Every child is ours. Please, protect the children.

. . . .

"When you call yourself an Indian or a Muslim or a Christian or a

European, or anything else, you are being violent. Do you see why it is violent? Because you are separating yourself from the rest of mankind. When you separate yourself by belief, by nationality, by tradition, it breeds violence. So a man who is seeking to understand violence does not belong to any country, to any religion, to any political party or partial system; he is concerned with the total understanding of mankind." ~ Jiddu Krishnamurti

....

The moment you identify yourself with one tribe, and vow loyalty to that tribe, you separate yourself from the whole. The moment you create an 'Us,' you create a 'Them.' The efforts you make to separate yourselves -- the efforts you make to avoid miscegenation and keep your tribe 'pure' -- create the monsters that will eventually haunt you. Every action you take to isolate yourself breeds a potential violent reaction. What you believe is protecting you, is what, in reality, is endangering you.

....

"People, all people, belong to each other. And he who shuts himself away, diminishes himself, and he who shuts others away, destroys himself." ~ Howard Thurman

....

"Community cannot feed for long on itself; it can only flourish where always the boundaries are giving way to the coming of others from beyond them — unknown and undiscovered brothers." ~ Howard Thurman

....

So, here some guidelines to live by:

- Say "No" to tribes that exclude others.
- Refuse membership in exclusive clubs.
- Leave the gangs, all gangs, not only the most notorious ones, but also the gangs created by race, religion, ideology, sports fanaticism, and national pride.
- Don't look for refuge and safety in the ghettos populated by those who look and think like you. Go out and explore.
- Be suspicious of those who profess, "We are right, they are wrong. We are good, they are bad."

- Say "Yes" to diversity and inclusion.
- Mingle, blend, associate, join, unite with everybody.
- Embrace diversity. Promote unity. Create community.

The old paradigm of a world divided in clans and nations that engage in power struggles and fight one another must be replaced by the new paradigm of the whole humanity working together as a species to protect the planet and enhance everyone's life. We need to set aside our differences and transcend our small-minded tribal identities. We have to realize that, in fact, we are not different one from the other, and that those who invent and magnify differences among humans are the ones who, in several ways, benefit from animosity and conflict. We must go beyond the damaging loyalty to our little gangs, and understand how this misplaced loyalty is endangering our future. Instead of seeing ourselves as members of different religions, nations, ethnicities, schools of thought, political groups, or bands of brothers, we must see ourselves as fellow crew members of the same endangered spacecraft who must work together in order to maintain it in perfect conditions, so it may be able to continue its journey through the cosmos. We must replace the illusion that we are separated from one another with the understanding that we are all interconnected. We must remember that we are all descendants of the same ancient parents. We are members of the same family. We are all brothers and sisters. We are one.

"A house divided against itself cannot stand." ~ Abraham Lincoln

....

LET'S PUT AN END TO INSANITY

What are we doing? Why are we allowing the lowest parts of ourselves to act out? Why do we keep engaged in this insane pursuit of power and possessions?

Let's stop the insanity! Let's look at the big picture and see that this beautiful planet is our home, and that we have much to gain if we stop fighting one another, and begin cooperating with one another with greater fervor.

We are all in this together. We will either succeed or fail together. We will either live or die together. We are all crew members and passengers of spaceship Earth and we need to work together to build a sustainable future. So, let's stop the nonsense, the myopia, the pettiness. Heaven is here if we want it to be.

Let's change the focus. Let's stop worrying about ourselves and begin thinking what we can do for others. Let's work together for the common good, for the greater good. Rather than asking, "What's in it for me?"' let's ask, "How can I serve?" knowing that the best exercise for the heart is to bend down and lift others.

Let's do it!

……..

Please, stop! Inflicting pain on someone else will not ease anyone's suffering.

Please, stop! Renounce violence. Don't inoculate the virus of hatred in your children. Don't give them a poison that you know will stay with them until they die. Surely you don't want to do this to your children. Free them from the curse of having to carry hatred in their hearts for the duration of their lives. Liberate them from this lifetime curse. Give them a better future. Do something different. Be the one who brings about real change.

If you are one of those more closely connected with the killing, be it by manufacturing or trading weapons, or by directing others to use them, or, even, by actively using them, consider doing something else. Consider getting another job. Consider dropping your weapons. Consider speaking up against violence and becoming an agent of change. Consider dedicating yourself to end oppression and exploitation, and create conditions for everyone to have safe, hopeful, healthy, dignified existences. Consider engaging in the work of bringing Heaven to Earth. If you are fighting, if you are in the business of violence, aggression, and war, please, stop. Drop your weapons! Do not kill. Life is sacred.

In what came to be known as the First Letter to the inhabitants of Corinth , Paul, the apostle, wrote the following: "Surely you know that you are God's temple and that God's Spirit lives in you! God will destroy anyone who destroys God's temple. For God's temple is holy, and you yourselves are his temple."

For those of us who are not directly involved in wars, let us, with compassion in our hearts, direct our thoughts to the children who have lost loved ones, those who have been wounded, those who have lost hope. Let us try to empathize with them. Let us try to feel their pain, even knowing that this will never be possible. Let us pause for a moment and realize that we, indirectly, also support the violence that creates so much pain and suffering throughout the world. Let us realize that we benefit from the structural violence that oppresses and exploits so many around the world. Let us consider that we, for remaining passive and not actively opposing it, have consented in having others perpetrate violence on our behalf. Yes, it is understandable that we may choose to ignore the harsh reality, and sedate ourselves with all sorts of distractions. It is understandable our desire to protect ourselves from all this madness, and do what we can to shut our minds from being affected by this sad state of affairs. But digging holes in the ground and sticking our heads into them to avoid seeing and feeling the pain that is going on around us has never worked and never will.

The time has come to lower our shields and allow our hearts to be pierced by the arrows that carry the suffering of the children. Let us try to feel their pain, feel their despair, and may this disturb us enough to drive us to take action.

Let us promote the idea that nothing — nothing — justifies inflicting pain. Let us promote the idea that all life is sacred and that nothing — nothing — justifies killing someone else. Let us commit to always speak up against violence and promote the understanding that violence will never be an effective way of solving problems.

Let's together implore, "Please, stop!"

Let us do something — anything within our power — to bring Heaven to Earth. Let us promote the idea that this is our garden and playground and that all we need to do during our lifetime is to take good care of the garden, improve the playground, share our toys, and have a good time together. Let us promote the idea that we are all playmates who were born to be friends and play together. Let us become agents of change. Let us be promoters of peace. Believe me. We can do it! Let's do it!

………

WE ARE ONE FAMILY

"We need to decide that we will not go to war, whatever reason is conjured up by the politicians or the media, because war in our time is always indiscriminate, a war against innocents, a war against children" ~ Howard Zinn

....

Please, stop! Let us put an end to all division and fighting. Let's renounce our loyalty to our petty tribes and pledge allegiance to just one big family, the Family of Planet Earth. To say, "I am Human," should be always enough to identify our only affiliation. As Howard Zinn once said, "We need to assert our allegiance to the human race, and not to any one nation." Let us really feel that we are all in this together. Let us understand that we are all passengers and crew members of the same spaceship -- Spaceship Earth -- and that together we need to take good care of this vehicle and its crew in order to be able to continue our journey through the cosmos.

I am hopeful. I believe the day will come when we will realize that we all have been acting as immature gang members who fight other gangs for no good reason. The day will come when we will no longer pledge allegiance to nations, religions, or schools of thought that separate us from others. The day will come when the ideas that supported our separation in nations and the establishment of borders will be completely obsolete; we will not have to defend territories, and we will not be tempted to conquer territories either. There will be nothing to kill or die for.

The day will come when the words of Howard Thurman, "People, all people, belong to each other. And he who shuts himself away, diminishes himself, and he who shuts others away, destroys himself," will be effortlessly accepted as an unmistakable truth.

The day will come when we will look back in disbelief and realize how insane we were; it will be hard for us to understand what led us to divide ourselves, fight each other, and bring so much unnecessary pain and suffering upon ourselves.

....

Let us bring about a new paradigm for a new world. Let us allow our minds to be taken over by thoughts of peace, prosperity, and abundance for all. Let us work on our own selves in order to reach that evolved consciousness that allows us to see Heaven on Earth as a real possibility. Let us engage in the work of guiding others to those places where they may be able to envision all creation coexisting in peace and unity, thriving, enjoying, and having fun on Planet Earth, this beautiful garden and awesome playground that was given to us.

Believe me. We can do it! We can be powerful agents of change. Take time to envision Planet Earth as a generous gift to us, and imagine that this breathtaking garden astonishing playground simply for us to enjoy and have fun together.

Plant the good seeds. Share this vision with your friends and family. Live by it.

....

Please, stop! Stop the hatred, the fighting, the killing, the pain and the suffering. Drop your weapons, and go take care of the children.

Do you feel called to do something to change our world and make it a better place? Do you feel unsure of what to do, what you can do? Do you feel powerless? Do you feel that nothing you may do will ever be relevant? Do you feel discouraged? Do you feel that no matter what you do, whatever it may be, it will not matter? Please, stop! Don't let those negative feelings immobilize you. I invite you to go deep inside your own self and explore what you can do. Each one of us can do something. Each one of us has different talents. Each one of us has something different to give. Each one of us is called to action in different ways. I encourage you to explore and uncover your own ways of giving contributions.

You may want to join a group of people who are working to bring peace to our world. You may decide to support organizations that are bringing relief for those affected by the conflicts. You may want to join existing initiatives, or initiate something new yourself. You may be moved to express your feelings through art, hoping that you may be able to touch someone else's soul. You may be moved to write a song. You may be moved to write your own appeal for sanity. You may be moved to initiate a Silent Peace Walk. Or, you may simply make a firm commitment that you will treat everyone you meet with extra kindness, patience, and generosity. Whatever it may be, just do it!

Peace starts with you, with me, with each one of us. Let there be peace on Earth, and let it begin with me, with you, with each one of us. Let us be the peace we wish to see in the world. Let us work on our own selves to grow our inner peace and let us bestow our peace upon the world. And let us, grounded in this soil of inner peace, engage in the work of promoting justice and bringing lasting peace to the world. If not now, when? If not us, who? We can do it!

. . . .

PLEASE, STOP!

Coincidences, or, as I call them, God-incidences are those synchronicities in life; those apparently unrelated events that are related, but whose relationship is difficult to explain. Let me tell you what happened, because, at least for me, something remarkable did happen. I wrote "An Appeal for Sanity" during the evening hours of Monday, July 28, 2014. I was called to write it, if you understand what I mean. I was watching BBC World News when I got a glimpse of Lyse Doucet's report, "No place to hide for children of war in Gaza and Syria," and that was enough. I saw the children, I felt their pain, and I heard the command to do something. I had more important things to do -- or so I thought -- but The Voice Within commanded me to put all things aside and dedicate myself to "do something." I had to obey. See, I was the one who, many years ago, asked, "God, use me. Make me an instrument of your peace." And since writing is what I do, I sat down and wrote "An Appeal for Sanity" which can be summarized by the two words that plea: "Please, stop!"

Now the God-incidence... The following day -- Tuesday, July 29, 2014 -- I got to know that Pope Francis, in an impromptu plea for peace, said the following words during his Sunday address at Saint Peter's Square: "Brothers and sisters, never war, never war! I am thinking above all of the children who are deprived of the hope of a worthwhile life, of a future. Dead children, injured children, mutilated children, orphaned children, children whose toys are things left over from war, children who don't know how to smile. Please, stop! I ask you with all my heart, it's time to stop. Stop, please!"

What I find worthy of notice is that although I was completely unaware of his remarks, both of us were called to bring attention to the pain and suffering of the children, and that the same two words, "Please, stop!" powerfully emerged in different places and times.

You may be reading this and feel called to do something. If so, go ahead. Don't think too much. Just do it!

....

I WILL NOT KILL

All life is sacred. We are spiritual beings having human experiences, and I will not deprive anyone from having the experiences they are meant to have, and learning what they need to learn during their passages through the Earth, including the pain and suffering of carrying the regret and remorse of killing someone.

I may be killed, but I choose not to kill. Physical life is temporary and transient; it will eventually end. Once we understand who we really are -- that we are, at the same time, mortal and immortal, human and divine, separated and united, many and one -- then we can fully understand the greatest saints and sages, and we can let ourselves be killed, without ever killing, because we have realized that life is more.

Once we experience a spiritual awakening, we become able to see beyond what we were able to see before, and then we see that the mystery many of us call God is in everyone and everyone is in God; God is the ground in which we exist. This realization makes violence, aggression, and killing inconceivable and unacceptable.

The other realization is that since we are in God and God is in us, we are protected by God; therefore, we don't need weapons for protection. And if we are to face abuse, suffering, and even experience physical death, we understand that this is all part of the human experiences we, spiritual beings, have to live in order to learn the lessons we are meant to learn during our passage as human beings through this physical dimension.

It may sound that I am advocating the cowardly stance of remaining passive when facing injustice, threat, and aggression, and allowing the violent ones to walk all over the defenseless. This is not the case at all. I am advocating that we should be bold, stand up, resist, defend ourselves and others, speak truth to power, and engage in the work of creating a just society, and do all this, and a lot more, without ever using violence, and without ever being afraid of bringing our physical life to an end.

Whenever I witness the loss of lives through war, crime, and other senseless acts of violence -- that many times are motivated by lack of justice, by despair, and by the compulsion to take justice in one's own hands as the last resort -- what comes to my mind is this scene of the movie Gandhi. Here's a description of that scene: a meeting is taking place in a large auditorium and some participants start to advocate the use of violence as a means to stop the abuse and discrimination they are being subjected to by the authorities and the police. The idea begins to gain adepts, and people in the room begin to raise their voices and express their desire to use force and lash out against the government that passed unjust and discriminatory laws, and the law enforcement agents. This goes on for a while until Gandhi stands up and says, "In this cause, I, too, am prepared to die, but there is no cause for which I am prepared to kill."

I guess he had reached a higher understanding. I think he spoke as any enlightened being would. "For this cause I am prepared to die, but there is no cause I am prepared to kill for."

……...

"Those four words form the basis of my pacifism: 'I will not kill.' And it is amazing to me how many people respond to that with questions/arguments presenting me with hypothetical situations where I should/would/could/must kill for some 'higher' reason. I always respond, 'I will not kill,' and this makes them angry." ~ Pat Carrithers

……...

I face similar questions as the ones described by Pat Carrithers. When asked about what I would do in such hypothetical situations -- for instance, someone threatening the lives of my loved ones -- I say that I would try to stop the attacker from killing using as much nonviolence as possible, or using the minimal amount of violence possible. In an extreme situation I would sacrifice my life if this could save another life, but I would not kill. In all honesty, it is a difficult question and I hope never facing such a situation. All I know is that these words impacted me profoundly: "For this cause I am willing to die, but there is no cause I am willing to kill for." These, for me, are words coming from someone who has reached a higher ground, someone I admire.

Here's my desire and my vision:

I would prefer to live in a world without weapons, without violence, without terrorism, without aggression, without retaliation, without revenge, and without war.

I would prefer to live in a world without fear, without greed, without poverty, without oppression, without racism, without slavery, without discrimination, and without exploitation.

My world, the one I am creating, is a nonviolent world, where compassion and cooperation reign, and where everybody can live with dignity and thrive. I know this is possible. Let's create a whole new world! Heaven is here if we want it to be!

....

WHAT HAVE WE LEARNED?

April 30, 1975. At 4:03 a.m., two U.S. Marines are killed in a rocket attack at Saigon's Tan Son Nhut airport. They are the last Americans to die in the Vietnam War. At dawn, the last Marines of the force guarding the U.S. embassy lift off. Only hours later, looters ransack the embassy, and North Vietnamese tanks role into Saigon, ending the war. In 15 years, nearly a million North Vietnamese Army and Vietcong troops and a quarter of a million South Vietnamese soldiers have died. Hundreds of thousands of civilians had been killed.

What have we learned?

We have learned that war is good for nothing. We have learned that violence doesn't solve anything, it only begets more violence. We have learned that war wounds physically, mentally, emotionally, and spiritually, and leaves permanent scars that never fade away. We have learned that those who decide about waging war, and those who profit from it, don't go to the battlefield; they stay in their safe, well protected, comfortable, luxurious environments, counting their monetary and political gains without regard for the destruction, devastation, pain and suffering they bring to the world. We have learned that those who decide to send others to fight wars do so because they are greedy, not because they are compassionate. We have learned that we fight because we are fearful, not because we are brave. We have learned that we, human beings, are very much alike; we all have the same dreams, we all bleed and die. We have learned that, actually, we don't have anything against those we fight against, and that, in the end, we are all brothers and sisters.

If you believe, as I do, that we are spiritual beings having human experiences, then you have learned, as I did, that killing people deprives human beings from having the experiences they are supposed to have, and learn the lessons they are supposed to learn during their passages on this earth.

We have learned that ideas divide us, but ideas are not worth killing for.

We have learned that nations and borders, and things such as patriotic pride, are abstractions created by us, and that we can go beyond these concepts and look at Planet Earth as one indivisible whole, as one spaceship where we, all of us, are together.

We have learned that we have to strike the roots of evil, and put an end to this absurd, senseless economic system that we have created this monstrous, voracious beast that oppresses, exploits, brings about poverty and despair, concentrates wealth, enhances inequalities, creates social tensions and violence, and wounds the planet.

We have learned that we need to put an end to this system that actually doesn't benefit anyone, not even those few who believe that they are benefiting from it.

The truth is that we can organize ourselves to live on this planet in much better ways. We live in a place of abundance where there is more than enough for everyone to have safe, dignified, joyous, and blissful existences. We can put an end to poverty. We have the resources, the intelligence, and the creativity to make life immensely better. We are capable of taking care of everyone, of all creation, and preserve the environment. The time has come to redirect all the resources we currently use to attack others and defend ourselves, and use these resources to create a better world for all.

These are some of the lessons we have learned.

Yes, we are still waging war, aren't we? Can we do our part, however small, to change that? Can we stand up, be seen, and join our voices again saying, "Enough! War no more! No more war!"

It's time to put our heads together and imagine Heaven on Earth. It's time join our hands and bring about a place ruled by justice, peace, compassion, care for all sentient beings, and a thoughtful relationship with the environment. May this be the moral compass that guides us in everything we do.

....

WHAT CAN WE DO?

Continue to fill your heart with love and spread love to all around you. Practice inner peace and be peaceful. Your peaceful energy adds to the energy that eventually will bring about world peace. Be the most generous, patient, loving, giving, and forgiving person you can be to your family members, friends, the members of your many communities, as well as strangers and enemies.

Be a peaceful and comforting presence always. Be the one who provides protection. Be the one who provides a secure place to relax and rest. This, in itself, is an enormous contribution to stop violence. Then, go to the silence, listen to your inner voice. It will tell you what to do.

Find the peaceful energy in the center of your being and take action from there. In the middle of all noise and confusion, pause and listen to your inner voice. Discern what causes call you to action, and then, take action, no matter how tiny. Do something, anything. Do what you are called to do. Give your contribution using your unique set of talents and skills. Begin by taking action in the environment close to you. Act within your circle of influence. Take the first step, then the second, and continue on, one step at a time. Cultivate your inner peace. Be the peace you wish to see in the world. Since we are all interconnected, your peaceful thoughts, emotions, and actions affect the world; they add to the energy of peace that one day will prevail in the world. Get together with other people who, like you, also dream with a world of justice, peace, and unity, those who are already in action to bring this new world about, or those who don't know yet exactly what to do, but want to do something. Work together. Slowly, little by little, your circle of influence will expand, and maybe one day the circumstances will be right and you and your friends will have a huge impact in bringing about social justice, peace, unity, and the overall betterment of the world. You will be instrumental in creating a new world where violence, both direct and indirect, will no longer exist. You will manifest a world without crime and war, without oppression and exploitation. You will manifest a world of justice, peace, compassion, kindness, and generosity.

Enjoy the garden and the playground. Not only that: reveal the garden and the playground to others who haven't discovered it yet. Help others see the beauty that surrounds us. Reveal the Heaven that exists here on Earth. Continue showing that this is our Garden and our Playground, and that all we have to do is to take good care of both. All we have to do is to enjoy this amazing gift that was given to us, have fun together, and share our toys. Go forth and remind others that we are here to enjoy the beauty of the garden and have fun together, as fellow playmates, in this awesome playground. We don't need to compete. We don't need to fight. We don't need to oppress and exploit. We don't need to be afraid. We don't need to accumulate. We are here to have fun together. We are here to give our best and unique contributions, and to help others also give their best and unique contributions to the world. We are here to take good care of each other, share our toys, and have a great time together. All we have to do is to change the prevailing mindset. We don't need to be afraid, fight, or compete; we only need to cooperate. Promote these ideas. Promote this new paradigm and help people see this new possibility of enjoying life and living in peace. Keep up the good work.

Everyone is different. Everyone has different talents and skills. Everyone has different gifts to give, but realize that, just by thinking what you can do, you are already doing a lot. You are a blessing to the world, and the best thing you can do is to be the peace you wish to see in the world.

……..

It is wonderful to hear and see your awareness and how it is tuned into our modern world. Your words are here to do good, your actions reinforce the words. Keep up the good work. Your impact is greater reaching than you can even know. A movement starts with one person, then grows to two, then snowballs exponentially. If we want peace in this world, we have to live it, show it, and believe in it. I believe in you.

……..

"There are Five Fallacies about Life that create crisis, violence, killing, and war. - First, the idea that human beings are separate from each other. - Second, the idea that there is not enough of what human beings need to be happy. - Third, the idea that in order to get the stuff of which there is not enough, human beings must compete with each other. - Fourth, the idea that some human beings are better than other human beings. - Fifth, the idea that it is appropriate for human beings to resolve severe differences created by all the other fallacies by killing each other." ~ Neale Donald Walsch

....

SILENT PEACE WALK

Young Americans have not seen during their lifetime, public demonstrations as successful as the ones pro Civil Rights and against the Vietnam War that took place in the '60s. It could be said that young Americans have not yet witnessed the power of nonviolent action to better their lives. As a consequence, many individuals doubt that nonviolent actions, such as public demonstrations and civil disobedience, can be effective in bringing about change. Add to this scenario a dysfunctional political system with a representative democracy that does not equally represent all, social media that keeps us separated in our clusters, and politicians and segments of the media that shameless spread lies, and one has a recipe for the mass apathy and resignation that appears to be prevalent in our country and in many other countries of the world. It certainly would be nice to have more people actively engaged in the work of promoting social justice, peace and protection of the environment, so it's fitting to ask ourselves, "What can we do?"

Our first responsibility is to wake up and live more mindfully. We need to do the diligent work that develops wakefulness, attentiveness, alertness, awareness, and appreciation, and as much as possible we should encourage and support others to do the same. Then we should come up with creative initiatives where people can practice how to publicly express themselves. We need to find ways to attract those non-engaged individuals and get them involved and active by creating events where those more hesitant individuals can feel safe to participate and publicly advocate for worthy causes. We need to offer non-threatening venues for the shyest among us to gather and collectively express their desire for a better world.

Enter the monthly Silent Peace Walk, an easy-to-do, non-threatening, and gentle introduction to activism. The Silent Peace Walk is simple: people gather to walk in silence for good causes. Yes, it can be considered a simple walking meditation that enhances appreciation for the world and inner peace, but it is more than that; it's also is a way of bringing together a group of like-minded individuals who will meet regularly, and perhaps work together for the betterment of the world.

We have been leading monthly Silent Peace Walks in our community for many years, and this initiative has built connections that opened doors for inter-faith dialogues, cross-cultural and multicultural conversations, helping build a culture of respect and peace.

Sometimes, our nonviolent action can be as simple as sharing a hug. At the closing of every Silent Peace Walk we announce, "It's Hug Time!" and Peace Walkers know exactly what to do. Hugs bring about smiles.

"To hug is to say with the hands what the mouth is not able to, because not always there are words to say everything." ~ Mario Quintana

………

For me, the beauty of hugs is that we cannot give one without getting one. A friend brought to my attention that this wasn't true. He said, "You can give a hug without getting one back." I thought about it and concluded that he was right. And then I noticed sadness visiting me. It would heavenly to live in a nonviolent place of mutual trust, free from malice, where we all enjoyed hugging freely, and where we all could experience the joy of receiving and giving.

………

PRAYER FOR A MORE HUMANE HUMANITY

I pray for the cessation of all violence. I pray for the end of use of all deadly force. I pray for the end of all oppression and exploitation. I pray for the end of all pain and suffering. I pray for justice for all. I pray for less selfishness and more unselfishness. I pray for less competition and more cooperation. I pray that we all may experience an existence completely free from worries of not having enough for our survival. I pray we may all see Planet Earth as a place of abundance, where there is more than enough for everybody. I pray for the end of the fear that leads to accumulation. I pray that we all may see Planet Earth as our garden and playground. I pray we all may see Planet Earth as a gift that was given to us to enjoy. I pray we all may be able to share this gift, make it better, and have fun together in it as playmates who share their toys. I pray we all may use our lives to become more loving, generous, patient, tender, kind, compassionate, and forgiving human beings. I pray we may all be able to find ways of giving our best contributions to the world. I pray we all engage in the work of helping others find how they can give their best contributions to the world. Then world peace will be real. Then we will reveal Heaven on Earth. It is possible. We just need to embrace this new paradigm.

....

LETTING GO OF THE NEED TO BE RIGHT

The world does not need intelligent minds that speak, but patient hearts that listen.

....

Why do we engage in unnecessary arguments, and get so upset? Why do we let these emotions get a hold of us? Can't we see the ugly egos at play? Can't we feel our egos craving to be right? Do we want to be right, or do we want to be happy? I believe that most of the time it is better to be kind than to be right.

We have to ask ourselves if we want to win, or if we want to promote understanding and peace. We must be sensitive to the fact that reality is perceived through one's beliefs; what we see is not what they see, and what they see is not what we see. We look at the same and see different.

So let us realize that we cannot change someone else's views; only they can do that. And knowing that, let us also not hold so steadfastly to our views, opinions, and beliefs either.

In many instances – the unimportant ones -- it is better to ignore the attacks and not engage in the fight. But if we feel the need to engage, let's make sure we do so nonviolently, listening more and speaking less, being compassionate, and trying to empathize and understand, seeking first to understand, then to be understood.

Let us not oppose force with force, nor negative feelings with negative feelings. And let us not respond to negative words with negative words, nor react to insults with insults. Let us be kind, hoping that our softness will soften our opponents too. Let us realize that many times there's no need to defend, or to attack.

Remembering that hatred consumes the one who holds it and no one else, let us not hold on to grudges.

And if we cannot come to an agreement, perhaps we can make an effort to feel that the love that unites is bigger than any views that may divide.

. . . .

THE BIRTH OF THE ONE WHO EXHORTED US TO BE KIND

"This is the way of peace: overcome evil with good, falsehood with truth, and hatred with love." ~ Peace Pilgrim

. . . .

Joseph and Mary were a couple of young refugees escaping violence who depended on other people's compassion and generosity to get by. Mary was pregnant and delivered her baby boy in a mud-filled, smelly barn, surrounded by animals. Nowadays, our Nativity scenes make everything look very clean and comfortable, but pause for a moment and think about it: two scared, lonely, homeless human beings, fleeing violence and persecution, having their first baby in a barn! They named their son Jesus, and this baby, a refugee himself, grew up to become a wise teacher of nonviolent activism for justice, solidarity, and peace.

Let us think about the world we can create if we follow his teachings of selflessness, kindness, and generosity. Let us develop a compassionate and welcoming heart and bring Heaven to Earth, because Heaven is here, if we want it to be.

Many times we excuse ourselves from taking action by saying that we can't act like Jesus because he was divine, and we are not. We see injustices and do nothing, or very little, because in our minds courageous action is reserved for the super-heroes only, not for normal human beings like us. But perhaps we can take some time today day for a deep reflection on questions such as: "Am I open to welcome immigrants? Am I willing to welcome refugees? Do I have in me what it takes to welcome them?" Perhaps we can take some time to look inside ourselves and find a wellspring of courage that will make us less afraid, selfish, and judgmental. Perhaps today we may be able to expand our hearts and be more compassionate, generous, and kind. Perhaps today we can open the doors of our dwellings and welcome -- really welcome -- Mary,

Joseph, and Jesus, remembering that all of us are, in one way or another, refugees.

May we honor the memory of the one who exhorted us to be kind by mindfully practicing all the good that he has taught us.

....

THE NEW COLOSSUS

"Not like the brazen giant of Greek fame,
With conquering limbs astride from land to land;
Here at our sea-washed, sunset gates shall stand
A mighty woman with a torch, whose flame
Is the imprisoned lightning, and her name
Mother of Exiles. From her beacon-hand
Glows world-wide welcome; her mild eyes command
The air-bridged harbor that twin cities frame.
"Keep, ancient lands, your storied pomp!" cries she
With silent lips. "Give me your tired, your poor,
Your huddled masses yearning to breathe free,
The wretched refuse of your teeming shore.
Send these, the homeless, tempest-tost to me,
I lift my lamp beside the golden door!"

~ Emma Lazarus

The New Colossus is a sonnet by American poet Emma Lazarus (1849–1887), written in 1883. In 1903, the poem was engraved on a bronze plaque and mounted inside the lower level of the pedestal of the Statue of Liberty. The poem talks about the millions of immigrants who came to the United States (many of them through Ellis Island at the port of New York). The poem has entered the political realm. It was quoted in John F. Kennedy's book A Nation of Immigrants (1958) as well as a 2010 political speech by President Barack Obama advocating immigration policy reform.

....

OPENING HEARTS AND DOORS

A lot of fear erupts every time extremists perpetrate senseless acts of violence anywhere in the world. Many of those who are sensitive to the suffering of refugees hesitate about receiving more of them here. Some suggest that allowing people from many ethnicities into this country will make America unmanageable and dangerous.

Is the mix of people of many different cultures and religions a problem? I don't think so. Looking at America, and reviewing its history, we conclude that this is a land of immigrants. We are people from all over the world living together in relative peace. Some suggest that allowing immigrants into this country will only create more ghettos and make the United States less safe. They say that ghettos are the breeding grounds of terrorists. Ghetto is defined as a section of a city, especially a thickly populated slum area, inhabited predominantly by members of an ethnic or other minority group, often as a result of social or economic restrictions, pressures, or hardships. Yes, there are many ghettos in many American cities, as there are in many other cities of the world. People don't choose to create ghettos; they come about naturally. First of all, people live in those neighborhoods that they can afford. Second, people naturally choose to congregate and live together with those they can more easily communicate with. This is only natural. Finding a doctor, a dentist, or shop owner who speaks their language, will only make their lives more comfortable. They feel safer. It is a matter of mingling with people who have similar ways and views, who know, trust and understand one another, and, therefore, can make each other's lives easier. America has many Chinatowns and Little Italys. That's not the problem. Some suggest that immigrants don't make a true effort to integrate in the societies that accepted them, and that, for instance, they don't make a sincere effort to learn the ways, values, and language of the hosting countries. This is not always true. I teach English to immigrants, and I can witness the great efforts those who come to class -- many of them after a long day of hard work -- make to learn the language. I admire them.

Is there resistance to cultural integration by the immigrants? Yes, somewhat, but more than resistance, we must acknowledge that there is a natural difficulty. All adaptation demands effort. Learning a new language is not always easy, and maybe not even a priority if you are struggling to survive. The first priority is to find work, and take care of your loved ones. And if you do all this, most likely there's not too much time left for anything else. Also, the impulse to preserve one's cultures is understandable. People want to preserve their languages and customs, and want their children to marry people who share their values, and who they feel comfortable with.

But what we must acknowledge is that these are not the main causes of social unrest. The main cause is lack of opportunity and hope. This is the main cause. What is causing the violence all over the world is the marginalization of a vast number of human beings by an economic system that does not grant them opportunities to be all that they can be. They are in despair because the old promise that those who work hard will surely be blessed with upward social and economic mobility is not present in today's world as it was in years before. They see the immense divide between those who have a lot and those who have little, and they get discouraged by the extremely limited opportunities available to improve their lives, no matter how much they sacrifice, or how hard they work. This, all of it, is what generates the frustration that lashes out through irrational acts of violence. People from different ethnicities and cultures congregating geographically and living together is not the problem. Great inequality, massive concentration of wealth, and the diminishing availability of paths of upward social and economic mobility is the real problem.

Hopeful and motivated individuals -- those who see real possibilities of a better future for themselves and their loved ones, and who see that hard work really pays off -- are going to be thankful, love, and protect those who welcome and host them.

....

I HOPE COMPASSIONATE PEOPLE WILL WELCOME ME

"You and I should live as if You and I never heard of a You and an I."
~ Rumi

....

These are dangerous times of growing xenophobia. Can't we see that the people in our borders are human beings just like us, who just like our ancestors are leaving difficult life situations to try to create better lives for themselves and their loved ones?

We talk about us and them, but can we imagine, if only for a moment, that we could be them and they could be us? Can we? Perhaps, by imagining that we are them and they are us, we can reach the conclusion that there's no them, just us. Perhaps we can feel deeply that we are all in this together.

I think about my grandparents who, one century ago, courageously and desperately left Europe, and everything they knew and had, to try a new life in Brazil.

Can we find compassion and generosity, love and kindness in our hearts, and welcome frightened refugees as if we were welcoming our scared ancestors when they came to America?

I try to put myself in the shoes of my ancestors, and I pray that if someday my family and I find ourselves in a dire situation in which we shall be forced to flee this country and seek asylum in another, we may find generous, welcoming people who will take us in and treat us with kindness.

....

At the end of the day, I'd rather be excluded for who I include, than be included for who I exclude.

....

"This was the secret of America: a nation of people with the fresh memory of old traditions who dared to explore new frontiers, people eager to build lives for themselves in a spacious society that did not restrict their freedom of choice and action... Immigration policy should be generous; it should be fair; it should be flexible. With such a policy we can turn to the world, and to our own past, with clean hands and a clear conscience... Every ethnic minority, in seeking its own freedom, helped strengthen the fabric of liberty in American life. Similarly, every aspect of the American economy has profited from the contributions of immigrants... The contribution of immigrants can be seen in every aspect of our national life. We see it in religion, in politics, in business, in the arts, in education, even in athletics and in entertainment. There is no part of our nation that has not been touched by our immigrant background."
~ John F. Kennedy

....

THE NONVIOLENT JESUS

Consider learning the ways of the nonviolent Jesus. Consider responding to the challenges of life as he would. Consider imitating him.

Committed inner work leads to a deep personal transformation. Persistent and diligent inner exploration leads to a higher degree of awareness, which leads to the experience of oneness, which leads to empathy and compassion, which leads to selfless living and nonviolent activism to establish justice and peace. If you feel that you are not there yet, please consider cultivating mindfulness in silence, stillness, solitude, seclusion, simplicity, and service. This will inevitably awaken in you the desire to serve others and lead you to work nonviolently for justice and peace.

The world needs your contribution. We need each other's help to bring about a more peaceful and just world.

....

UNIVERSAL DECLARATION OF HUMAN RIGHTS

"What kind of peace do we seek? Not a Pax Americana enforced on the world by American weapons of war. Not the peace of the grave or the security of the slave. I am talking about genuine peace - - the kind of peace that makes life on earth worth living -- the kind that enables man and nations to grow and to hope and to build a better life for their children - - not merely peace for Americans but peace for all men and women - - not merely peace in our time but peace for all time. So, let us not be blind to our differences - - but let us also direct attention to our common interests and to means by which those differences can be resolved. And if we cannot end now our differences, at least we can help make the world safe for diversity. For, in the final analysis, our most basic common link is that we all inhabit this planet. We all breathe the same air. We all cherish our children's future. And we are all mortal." ~ John F. Kennedy

....

The Universal Declaration of Human Rights was adopted by the United Nations General Assembly on December 10, 1948. It arose as a response to the horrendous atrocities perpetrated during World War II. With the end of that war, and the creation of the United Nations, the international community vowed to not allow the carnage that happened in that conflict to ever happen again.

It is fitting to remember and honor John Peters Humphrey, the Canadian who wrote the draft document from which the Declaration emerged, and Eleanor Roosevelt who, at that time, was chairing the Commission on Human Rights that produced the final document. The authors of the Declaration, inspired by the desire to make peace a reality, invite all peoples of the world to recognize that all human beings are equally valuable, have the same fundamental rights, and must be treated with dignity and respect at all times. The Declaration reminds us that all human beings are born free; that everyone has the right to life and liberty; that no one shall be held in slavery or subjected to torture or to cruel, inhuman, or degrading treatment; that everyone is entitled, without any discrimination, to equal protection of the law.

The Universal Declaration of Human Rights is one of the most important documents of mankind. We should take the time to read it, get familiar with it, teach it, and demand elected officials throughout the world to abide by it, as a foundation for peace and unity in our world.

....

A TINY RIPPLE OF HOPE

"Each time a man stands up for an ideal, or acts to improve the lot of others, or strikes out against injustice, he sends forth a tiny ripple of hope, and crossing each other from a million different centers of energy and daring those ripples build a current which can sweep down the mightiest walls of oppression and resistance." ~ Robert F. Kennedy

....

It seems that our aspirations are to be rich, famous, and powerful. Compassion, kindness, generosity, civility, cooperation, and care for others and for the environment are not priorities. Neither is curiosity to explore, investigate, and expand knowledge, reflect on the meaning and purpose of life, and pursue truth and wisdom. We came to the extreme of praising ignorance and ridiculing intelligence. Unfortunately, we have dumbed ourselves down, apparently spending our time watching the empty lives of celebrities and reality TV stars. We've become selfish, careless, dishonest, indecent, cruel, and foolish people, because of our fate: we are destined to go through life brutally fighting one another for money, so we can pay for the minimum amount of resources necessary to stay alive. We fight one another so we can have food, shelter, clothing, healthcare, education. But if we are skirmishing to stay alive, we can't even think about taking care of others. So no one can even imagine contributing a bit of the little they have for the community's healthcare, for caring for children and seniors, and so on. If people are living at the edge of destitution, struggling to make ends meet, how can they take care of anyone else? It seems that this idea of "each man for himself, and each woman for herself, " has served the elites very well. We, on the other hand, have become almost too poor to contribute for creating a society where everyone is taken good care of, and where we are able to share resources, and cooperate to better one another.

In his Hierarchy of Human Needs, Abraham Maslow used the terms Physiological, Safety, Belongingness and Love, Esteem, Self-Actualization and Self-Transcendence needs to describe the pattern that human motivations generally move through. The most fundamental and basic four layers are what Maslow called deficiency needs: physical needs, security needs, friendship and love needs, and esteem needs. If these deficiency needs are not met, the individual will feel anxious and tense, and the mental and physical health will be affected. Maslow's theory suggests that the most basic level of needs must be met before the individual will be motivated to focus on the higher level needs. If you are hungry, without a safe shelter, worried about your survival, unemployed, underemployed, working in a job that you don't like, working in an unhealthy work environment, being underpaid, not having enough to cover your health care expenses may something bad happen, making just enough money to go by, most likely you will not be able to focus on what you need to be physically and mentally healthy; most likely you will not enjoy healthy relationships, you will not have time and venues to express yourself creatively, you will not have time and energy for spiritual exploration and intellectual growth, you will not have time and energy to build a good relationship and have a healthy sex life, you will not have the means to live in a healthy environment, you will not be willing to contribute to the wellbeing of others.

The world does not have to be like this. We can organize ourselves to live on this planet in much better ways. This is a place of abundance, and there is more than enough for everybody to live good lives. We can assure to everybody life, liberty, and the means to pursue happiness. We can organize ourselves so every family can have what they need to survive: food, water, clothing, shelter, sanitation, and a clean and healthy environment to live. We can guarantee health care and education for everyone. We can eradicate the basic survival worries and grant everyone the means for a dignified life.

Instead of living in fear of not having enough; oppressing and exploiting others for personal gain; accumulating more than the necessary and depriving others of the essential means to live with dignity; living in a mode of constant competition and fight, we can tame our fears, change our ways, and live much better.

We are here to express ourselves fully and give our unique gifts to the world, what Maslow referred to as Self-Actualization and Self-Transcendence. And we are here to help others develop themselves, so they too can express themselves fully and be able to give the gifts that only they, and no one else, can give to the family of the Earth.

We can do better. We can become a network of individuals who support one another on our journeys to become the best we can be. We can become a network of individuals who look after one another, and help one another reach those stages of development where each one of us will be able to give our best contributions to the world.

We need a new paradigm for a new world. We need a new set of beliefs to manifest a better world. We need to embrace solidarity, cooperation, and collaboration as the values to live by. We must help one another find ways to enjoy healthy professional lives where we may be able to do what we feel called to do, where we may be able to fully express our purpose in life, where we may give our best contribution to the world, and where we may be able to enjoy financial rewards that will allow us to live worry-free lives so we can concentrate our efforts in bringing Heaven to Earth.

....

A NEW PARADIGM FOR A NEW WORLD

We have to be careful with the ideas we accept simply because we manifest our beliefs. If we believe, for instance, that human beings will always fight, oppress, and exploit one another, then that's exactly what we will get. Within this frame of mind, mankind will never experience widespread justice and peace.

If we want to transform the world and make it better, we must first change our thoughts. We must refrain from repeating fatalistic prognostics such as, "This is the way things have always been, and will always be." We must put our pessimistic omens aside, imagine a better future, and affirm with conviction, "Things don't need to be the way they are now. We have the capacity to make them better."

It is difficult for us to understand that we are molded by the ideas we unconsciously accept. Why is it so? Because we are immersed in them. Like fish that are unable to see and understand the water in which they swim, we too, without a trained mind, are unable to see our thoughts. Fishes are surrounded by water, immersed in it, but unaware of it. We too, like fish, are surrounded and immersed in an ocean of widely accepted ideas, pervasive beliefs, far-reaching assumptions and ways of thinking that trigger automatic and unquestioned responses. And we are mostly unaware of it all. Paradigms not only condition our reflexes and bring about predictable outcomes; they also restrict how we see the world, limiting our imagination, and blocking us from considering new ideas and possibilities.

The current prevalent beliefs constrain us to accept with resignation that this undesirable reality is unchangeable, and that pessimistic outcomes are inevitable. Inequity, injustice and unfairness around us are accepted without further questioning because we believe that, "This is the way things have always been, and will always be."

Once again, our realities are shaped by the ideas we accept and the stories we tell ourselves. If we believe that unity and cooperation are impossible, we will attract experiences that will validate that belief. If we believe that humans will never transcend their selfishness, and their loyalty to tribes, ideologies, religions, and nations -- and will always be fighting one another -- we will find innumerable instances that will confirm those beliefs. If we are among those who keep saying, "We are right, and they are wrong," and if we are unable to see that every individual, independent of the group, nation, party, dogma, religion, tribe, or any other gang he or she belongs to, is saying the exact same thing -- we will continue to propagate prejudice and division. Finally, if we believe that life is a struggle without end, and that we have to compete and fight to get what we need because there isn't enough for all of us, our experiences will validate those beliefs.

But we would have a completely different experience, and manifest a much better world, if we embraced more positive, optimistic, and inclusive beliefs. We would have a completely different, and much more pleasant experience, if we were brought up hearing messages such as, "Don't be afraid. This is a place of abundance. There is plenty for everyone. We all take care of one another here on Earth. You don't have to worry. There's no need to compete and accumulate. Just give your best, collaborate and share, and you -- and everyone else -- will be fine."

The adoption of new, more optimistic ways of seeing life changes everything. We can change the world by adopting new thoughts ourselves. If we do so, eventually we will reach that tipping point when the prevailing paradigms will change. That will be the day when consciousness will shift, and we will begin to manifest a much more beautiful reality in this physical dimension.

………

I imagine that a day will come when we will be looking back, and saying, "In the past we lived in fear. We were constantly worried about not having enough for our survival. This fear created all sorts of problems. It made us extract all we could from the environment, and accumulate much more than what we needed. It made us compete, oppress, exploit and fight one another. That struggle brought about a lot of pain and suffering; while some were able to gather a whole lot, the immense majority ended up with almost nothing. Both those who had and those who didn't have lived in fear: the former were afraid of losing what they had, while the latter lived in the constant despair of not having enough to survive. But once we came to the realization that this is a place of abundance, and that we are all in this together, we changed the inefficient and unjust ways we had organized ourselves to live on this planet. We began to cooperate much more with one another, and everything changed: fear vanished, generosity flourished, solidarity blossomed, and peace became possible. We came to the realization that this is our garden and our playground, and we finally brought Heaven to Earth."

………

Once the majority of human beings come to embrace those new beliefs, a new, much better world will arise. We can change our physical world if we change the way we live in it. But in order to successfully create the conditions for everyone to thrive and enjoy life to the fullest, we must first change our thoughts and beliefs.

So here's my challenge to you: adopt these more positive, optimistic, life-enhancing beliefs. Practice them. Live them. Propagate them. Believe that Heaven is here if we want it to be. Accept that this is a place of abundance where there is more than enough for everybody. Accept that things don't need to be the way they are. Accept that we, all of us, can have our needs met and live without fear. Accept that we have the capacity to come up with better, more efficient ways of organizing ourselves to live on this planet. Believe that reason, justice, and fairness will prevail. Envision all human beings living dignified, fulfilling lives. Envision a world of solidarity, where we fully support one another, and where each one of us develops to the fullest, and gives his or her best contribution to humanity.

Look back and be optimistic! The world has changed. The world is changing. The world will continue to change for the better. Believe it! As Buckminster Fuller said, "It is now highly feasible to take care of everybody on Earth at a higher standard of living than any have ever known. It no longer has to be you or me. Selfishness is unnecessary. War is obsolete. It is a matter of converting the high technology from weaponry to livingry."

. . . .

PEACEFUL PLANET

"What do we need in order to have world peace?"

Well, naturally, we need justice. Peace is an offspring of justice. Without justice there can be no peace. We need to better organize ourselves to live in society in such ways that bring all forms of oppression and exploitation of our fellow human beings to an end. We need political, social, and economic equality: equal rights and responsibilities. Equal contributions, efforts, and rewards. We need to guarantee to all individuals access to opportunities through which they can reach positions where they can create, be productive, and fully express themselves, so they can give their best contributions to the world.

We need to reward work with real upward social mobility. Work must really pay off and bring about personal progress and advancement. The fruits of work must allow workers to provide a dignified life for themselves and their families. Workers must earn enough so they can live without fear of lack.

We need to come up with better ways of organizing ourselves to live in society, so everyone may have what they need to live with dignity, beginning with guaranteed access to healthy food, clean water, safe shelter, affordable health care, meaningful education, and safe living environments. In short, if we want peace, we must eradicate poverty.

The lack of means to support oneself brings about instability and conflict. Poverty is the breeding ground of violent fanatics. All the worries and concerns the fear of not having enough generates, brings about stress that manifests itself in more violent and less peaceful environments.

But the more I meditate about it, the more I am convinced that what we really need is for humanity to embrace a new paradigm. We need new visions for a better future. We need more and more people to wake up and see different possibilities for living and thriving together.

What we need is a widespread understanding of who we really are. Once we understand who we really are, and what life really is, we will see differently, and then a change for the better will happen. In order to bring justice and peace to our world, we need more and more individuals having profound transformational experiences which will change the way they we see everything: themselves, others, the environment, the planet, the cosmos, the Universe.

I am convinced that the awareness of our oneness, the one that emerges from those awakenings, those deep personal transformations, is essential to bring about more unselfishness, solidarity, justice, and peace to the world. So, in my opinion, what we need for peace to prevail in our world is a bigger contingent of individuals with this evolved understanding of who we really are.

Great ideas of how to organize ourselves to live in a more just society will not take us too far without a large contingent of evolved individuals. Personal transformation is essential for the success of societal transformation. Personal evolution precedes successful social progress.

There have always been individuals who went through these transformative experiences and who developed this new understanding, but they have always been a small fraction of the world population. In order for the world to radically change for the better, we need more of those evolved beings, and in order for their numbers to grow we need to demystify the current belief that enlightenment is hard and can only be achieved by a few gifted individuals. We need to disseminate the idea that awakening and expanded awareness is at hand. We need to encourage everyone to engage in mindfulness meditation and mindful living, or any other practice that may confer them that new consciousness that will not only allow them to experience Heaven, but also enlist them in the work of revealing Heaven on Earth.

Our experience is a manifestation of our inner energy. A beautiful energy manifests a beautiful world. A peaceful energy manifests a peaceful world. The more we develop our inner peace, the better will be the reality that will show up for us. The calmer we are, the calmer the world will be. Therefore, we must take on our own personal development, the one that produces more light and love, the one that dispels our own inner darkness, the one that sanctifies our souls.

Yes, it demands diligent practice, but it is within everyone's reach. Enlightenment is available to everyone, and enlightened individuals are the ones who will bring peace to the world. Period.

My recommendation? Pay attention and be alert. Be grateful. Meditate everyday, or do any other thing: pray, do yoga, sing in the shower, do Reiki, go to mass, plunge fully clothed in a cold stream, walk barefoot on the snow, eat a fruit salad with lots of mango, embark in an extended solo bike ride... do anything and all things mindfully, anything that works for you to take you beyond your self. Since we are all different, the same ritual, the same sets of beliefs, the same religion, will not work for everyone. As long as you are paying attention, anything, no matter how little, can trigger an experience that will allow you to connect, communicate, and commune with the Divine. Pay attention and make sure you are not dwelling in negative feelings such as fear, worry, anxiety, and anger. If so, pause, welcome them, and gently ask them to leave so you can entertain new guests: feelings of gratitude, fearlessness, honesty, love, kindness, generosity, compassion, and hope. This is what will initiate the process that ultimately will bring lasting justice and peace to your world, and to our world.

MINDFULNESS AND INCLUSION

DISSATISFIED AND IRRESPONSIBLE GODS

Yuval Noah Harari wrote this insightful description of the current state of affairs: "Despite the astonishing things that humans are capable of doing, we remain unsure of our goals and we seem to be as discontented as ever. We have advanced from canoes to galleys to steamships to space shuttles — but nobody knows where we're going. We are more powerful than ever before, but we have no idea what to do with all that power. Worse still, humans seem to be more irresponsible than ever. Self-made gods with only the laws of physics to keep us company, we are accountable to no one. We are consequently wreaking havoc on our fellow animals and on the surrounding ecosystem, seeking little more than our own comfort and amusement, yet never finding satisfaction. Is there anything more dangerous than dissatisfied and irresponsible gods who don't know what they want?"

....

GO TO THE SILENCE, CHANGE THE WORLD

"Our meditation practice is not selfish. We don't practice for ourselves alone. Our practice benefits the entire world. As we change, the world changes. Our practice makes us more compassionate, generous, and patient, more loving and caring human beings. Our practice is a powerful form of activism that makes the world a better place."

These are words I say to my fellow meditators at the end of the meditations I lead. And I believe in them. I really do.

I teach mindfulness, a millenary practice that helps reduce anxiety and stress. This is good, isn't it? Calmer and less reactive people are better for everyone, right? Or not?

Well, we have to consider that we live in a violent environment of oppression and exploitation. And, yes, as many critics of mindfulness point out, mindfulness can be used by those in positions of power to make citizens in general, and workers in particular, less combative, and more docile, obedient, and productive. But who can say that mindfulness is not also allowing people to see reality more clearly? Who can say that mindfulness is not making the structural violence and the hidden forms of oppression and exploitation more visible? Who can say that mindfulness is not challenging meaningless living, waking up a crowd of sleepwalkers from the vain promises of achieving happiness through consumerism? Who can say that mindfulness is not making us feel, in a very deep way, that we are all in this together, and that we are both oppressed and oppressors? Who can say that mindfulness is not augmenting the contingent of wiser activists for social justice and the preservation of our planet?

The practice of mindfulness does not make us indifferent to the suffering in the world, or oblivious to injustices. I argue that it has the opposite effect: mindfulness practice makes us more sensitive and compassionate. It makes us more aware of the suffering of others, of the damaging impact our wasteful way of living is having on the planet and its inhabitants, and of the perilous path toward extinction our civilization is on. The higher consciousness that arises through mindfulness practice activates in us the desire to engage in wise actions that can bring about a better world for everyone. Mindfulness makes us very aware of our interconnection and interrelation.

....

"We are not separate. We are inextricably interrelated. The rose is the garbage, the soldier is the civilian, the criminal is also the victim. 'This is like this, because that is like that.' No one among us has clean hands. None of us can claim that the situation is not our responsibility. The child who is forced to work as a prostitute is that way because of the way we are. The refugees who are forced to live in camps have to live like that because of the way we live. The arms dealers do their business so that our economies can continue to grow and they can benefit. Wealth and poverty, the affluent society and the poor society, inter-are. The wealth of our society is made of the poverty of the other." ~ Thich Nhat Hanh

....

I, like so many others, believe that we need to change the ways we see life, the ways we understand the world, and the ways we treat each other and all sentient beings. The way we live on this planet needs to change, and the practice of mindfulness meditation, as well as other similar practices, by changing our paradigms, is the best way I know to promote effective, healthy change. It is clear to me that it is completely possible for everyone to have a good life on this planet, but in order for this to happen, a change in the ways we currently live is necessary. The process of change starts with the realization that we, human beings, were the ones who created the ways we are currently living, and that we detain the power to organize ourselves differently and change everything if necessary. In order to do so, we should assume a 'beginner's mind' -- a mind not constrained by preconceived ideas and beliefs; a mind open to entertain infinite possibilities -- and while looking at everything anew, ask ourselves, "This is a beautiful planet. This is a place of abundance. There's more than enough here for everyone. How can we organize ourselves so everyone can have a dignified existence, while respecting all beings and preserving the health of the planet in the process?" I am convinced that it is completely possible for us to organize ourselves to live on this planet in wiser, more supportive, and less violent ways.

....

"I have the audacity to believe that peoples everywhere can have three meals a day for their bodies, education and culture of their minds, and dignity, equality, and freedom for their spirits. I believe that what self-centered men have torn down, men other-centered can build up." ~ Martin Luther King, Jr.

....

Each one of us finds his or her own way of responding to the suffering of the world. There are innumerable forms of expressing compassion and working to improve the lives of the downtrodden. We, all of us, are unique in the combination of talents and skills we came to this world with, and it is up to each one of us to discover how we will bestow the gifts that we were given in order to alleviate the suffering of others. Some will heal. Some will feed. Some will shelter. Some will teach. Some will invent. Some will make themselves available to listen and comfort those who are hurting. Some will be called to show up to protest inhumane practices, let their voices be heard, and not only precipitate change of morally wrong and unacceptable policies and practices, but also let the oppressed know that they have not been forgotten. While some will actively engage in social activism for change, I advocate that we should all meditate and live mindfully knowing that our mindfulness practice, by transforming us, will, directly and indirectly, benefit all sentient beings.

Many people challenge me, saying, "What are doing? Your mindfulness practice is not changing anything. You are not helping anyone." I am convinced that the practice of meditation, and of other similar disciplines of introspection and inner exploration in silence, stillness, solitude, seclusion, simplicity, and service have a huge positive impact in the betterment of society. By getting to know oneself more intimately, by developing a better understanding of life, by becoming more aware of the suffering of others, by becoming more compassionate and generous, meditators wisely engage in the work of restoring Heaven on Earth, and have an effective impact. Like the ripples created on the surface of the water when a stone is dropped on a pond, so too selfless acts of kindness create ripples that travel far and wide and bless others. When people accuse my meditation practice of being pointless and ineffective, I think of the impact the Buddha and Jesus had on the world; two meditators who dedicated their lives to their own awakening and the awakening of others, and whose teachings, after millennia, still influence and benefit us to this day. The exemplary lives they lived inspire us to do no harm; to do good, be good, and savor the good. They inspired and continue to inspire multitudes of social activists. To say that meditation doesn't change anything nor help anyone is, in my opinion, a misconception. Lasting change cannot really occur without individuals changing their perception of what's within them and around them.

……..

"All of humanity's problems stem from man's inability to sit quietly in a room alone." ~ Blaise Pascal

……..

Through the practice of meditation we reach the understanding that no life matters less than any other. The Dalai Lama said, "I try to treat whoever I meet as an old friend. This gives me a genuine feeling of happiness." Meditation practice makes it easier to smile and treat each person we meet as an old friend. We become sensitive to the suffering in the world and we let go of any impulses to put anyone down, replacing those impulses with the desire to bring everyone up.

....

"Here's an ancient truth about being human: we cannot give gifts to others that we are unable to give to ourselves! That's why "inner work" done well is never selfish. Ultimately, it will benefit other people." ~ Parker Palmer

....

Practicing meditation is like going home, going to a safe refuge where you center yourself, find balance, and cultivate love and peace. It is from this place of peace that you then come out into the world to distribute -- calmly, compassionately, and generously -- the love and peace you have gathered. I say to the detractors of mindfulness, "One thing does not exclude the other. Practice meditation and actively work for social justice, and see what happens. Go to the silence and be surprised by the changes in the ways you see and behave. Knowing that the most effective nonviolent civil disobedience initiatives -- the ones that brought about lasting social change -- were inspired and carried out by those who had deep disciplines of introspection and inner work, choose to be like those who have used the formula effectively. Be like the Buddha, Jesus, Thoreau, Gandhi, Dorothy Day, Howard Thurman, Martin Luther King, Jr., Peace Pilgrim, Mother Teresa, Thich Nhat Hanh, and so many others. Go to silence, know yourself, and then come out to work calmly within your circle of influence and change the world. Don't get discouraged."

I always remember that we, practitioners of mindfulness, are bringers of peace and sanity during moments of turmoil, and that's why the practice is so important. Again, our practice is not selfish; we don't practice for ourselves alone. Our formal meditation practice and our commitment to living mindfully is a powerful form of service to others. I tell my students, as an encouragement, that "In a boat full of fearful and agitated people, one sane, calm, and steady-minded person can find the way through the fog and the storm, through the winds and the waves, and sail the boat to a safe harbor, saving not only his or her life, but also everyone else's lives. Practice mindfulness. The world desperately needs more steady-minded individuals."

....

"May you have the serenity to accept what you cannot change, the courage to change what you can, and the wisdom to know the difference."

....

"You may not be able to do much about the great problems of the world or to change the situation you are in, but if you can awaken the eternal beauty and light of your soul, you will bring light wherever you go. The gift of life is given to us for ourselves and also to bring peace, courage, and compassion to others." ~ John O'Donohue

....

"Of course, I value independence, national and personal. But I also value collaboration because little that's good has ever been achieved without it. I, for one, would be utterly lost without the many people who've invested time, energy and love in me." ~ Parker Palmer

....

THE IMPORTANCE OF SILENCE

All the most influential peacemakers and social changers had a practice of silence: Thoreau, Gandhi, Howard Thurman, Martin Luther King, Jr., the Dalai Lama, Thomas Merton, Mother Teresa, Thich Nhat Hanh, Thomas Keating... They all had prayer, silence, meditation, and contemplation as part of their daily lives.

It's in the silence that we reach an elevated and expanded consciousness. It's in the silence that we get to see clearly, beyond the illusions, and get to know who we really are. It's in the silence that we touch our common essence and go beyond what separates us to realize what unites us. It's in the silence that we transcend our loyalties to our tribes and realize that we are human and divine before we are anything else. It's in the silence that we move from egoism to altruism, from individuality to community. It's in the silence that we realize that we are all in this together, that we are all connected, that we are one. It is the silence that we get that we are all in the same spaceship -- Spaceship

Earth. It's in the silence that we realize that this is a place of abundance, and that we can organize ourselves to live on this planet in new ways. Everyone can have dignified lives, free from man-inflicted lack, pain, or suffering. It's in the silence that we realize that this is our garden and playground. It's in the silence that we realize that this is Heaven, if we want it to be.

A new consciousness emerges in the silence.

The end of the impetus to compete, conquer, dominate, subjugate, and accumulate; the end of the impulse to pursue power in order to control, oppress, and exploit; the end of prejudice and tribalism; the end of aggression and violence; the end of injustices and abject poverty; the end of indifference and neglect... All these blessings come from inner work, from a practice of silence.

The understanding that we are all in this together; altruism, empathy, and compassion; forgiveness, acceptance, and tolerance; cooperation and collaboration; patience, generosity, kindness, love, nonviolence, tranquility, and peace; respect for the environment and for all sentient beings; respect and service to others... All these wonderful insights are experienced by those who practice the cultivation of wisdom through moments of introspection in silence, stillness, solitude, seclusion, simplicity, and service.

The Silence allows us to notice, appreciate, savor, and absorb the magic, the mystery, and the miracles. We look at the same things, but now we see what we were not able to see before. Now, we feel awake, alert, attentive, aware, appreciative, and alive. We feel like little children, discovering the world and living in a state of awe.

·······

BE THE PEACE YOU WANT TO SEE IN THE WORLD

Peace in my heart brought peace to my family.
Peace in my family brought peace to my community.
Peace in my community brought peace to my nation.
Peace in my nation brought peace to the world.
There is peace on Earth, and it began with me

·······

We have work to do to restore sanity in our world. We have work to do to tame our savageness and enhance our kindness. This work begins with each one of us. Mindfulness, and other similar practices of silence, stillness, simplicity, seclusion, solitude, and service develop our inner peace, our compassion, our understanding that we are all in this together, our generosity, and our reaching out to those who are lonely and hurting. We become healers. We become bringers of peace.

Let us cultivate peace. The world needs peaceful people. The world needs us. Let us do what needs to be done to protect this calm energy of peace, and let us avoid all that disturbs it. Let us be vigilant in order not to be another one of those who bring more agitation, anger, and hatred to the world. Let us be kind to one another, and be the peace we want to see in the world.

We have great responsibilities. We must expand understanding, compassion, and love, because this is the most effective way of reducing ignorance and hatred in our world. We must live lives that uphold the well-being of others, and see ourselves as bringers of peace, the ones whose mere peaceful presences bring energies of concord to places of discord.

There's a lot we can do to make this world of ours a better place for all. So, let us go ahead and ask ourselves, "What can I do to create the just world of my dreams, the world I want to live in? What, given my attributes and my personality, can I do to make this world a better place? And what, among the many things that must be done, do I feel called to do?"

The answers will vary because we are endowed with different talents and skills, but certainly one of the best things we can do, if not the best, is to take care of preserving and growing our own inner-peace while guiding and supporting others to do the same.

Knowing that hatred is not overcome by hatred, but through love alone, we should pause and ask ourselves, "How can I promote peace while preserving and expanding my inner-peace and that of others?"

Think about it.

....

WITHOUT DR. MARTIN LUTHER KING, JR

The voice of Dr. Martin Luther King, Jr. was silenced by an act of violence. I keep thinking how much he influenced me. He has been a guiding light in my life. For sure I admire his courage, his determination, his capacity to endure suffering without retaliating. I certainly admire him for always acting with the utmost civility, for exemplifying active nonviolent resistance, and for being able to bring the exchange of ideas about human rights to the highest intellectual level.

But the characteristic I admire the most in Dr. King was his ability to see. As someone who is able to foresee the beautiful butterflies that eventually will come out of the ugliest caterpillars, he was able to see fragile and gentle human beings even inside the nastiest bullies. He was able to see the best of humanity inside everyone. He was able to see himself in others. And he was able to see the Promised Land.

On April 3, 1968, one day before his death, Dr. King gave his famous I've Been to the Mountaintop speech. Referring to the death threats he was receiving, he said, "Well, I don't know what will happen now. We've got some difficult days ahead. But it really doesn't matter with me now, because I've been to the mountaintop. And I don't mind. Like anybody, I would like to live a long life. Longevity has its place. But I'm not concerned about that now. I just want to do God's will. And He's allowed me to go up to the mountain. And I've looked over, and I've seen the Promised Land. I may not get there with you, but I want you to know tonight, that we, as a people, will get to the Promised Land! And so I'm happy, tonight. I'm not worried about anything. I'm not fearing any man! My eyes have seen the glory of the coming of the Lord!"

How I wish we all could see as he saw.

I see Dr. Martin Luther King, Jr. as a hero of humanity, as an architect of peace, as an example of a dignified human being, perhaps as the greatest American who ever lived!

How I wish we all remembered the courage he had to speak the truth, and the sacrifices he made. How I wish we all imitated him, trying our best to be the best we can be.

……..

THE BELOVED COMMUNITY

Dr. Martin Luther King, Jr., called us to serve one another, especially the less fortunate among us. He said, "Life's most persistent and urgent question is, 'What are you doing for others?'" A powerful question, for sure.

I believe that we are here to be the best that we can be and to support others so they, too, can be the best that they can be. We are here to give our unique contributions to the world and to support others so they, too, can give their exceptional contributions to the world. We are here to help one another, and we do this through altruistic service. Dr. King dreamed of a just and peaceful society. He called it The Beloved Community.

The King Center website displays the following description of Dr. King's Beloved Community. "It is a global vision, in which all people can share in the wealth of the earth. In the Beloved Community, poverty, hunger and homelessness will not be tolerated because international standards of human decency will not allow it. Racism and all forms of discrimination, bigotry and prejudice will be replaced by an all-inclusive spirit of sisterhood and brotherhood. In the Beloved Community, international disputes will be resolved by peaceful conflict-resolution and reconciliation of adversaries, instead of military power. Love and trust will triumph over fear and hatred. Peace with justice will prevail over war and military conflict."

To believe that the self-serving, selfish, savage, each-man-for-himself mentality that currently prevails in world can bring about the Beloved Community that Dr. King called us to create is an unsustainable belief. In order for the Beloved Community to become a reality, we need to practice solidarity, serve one another, and be our brothers' and sisters' keepers.

Unfortunately, we have drifted away from the goal of bringing the Beloved Community into existence. We need to reflect on what governments are, and how they have to work in order to produce the kind of just society we want to live in. To begin with, we have to understand that we created governments. Governments are creations of the people who understood that we needed to cooperate and organize ourselves to make everyone's lives better. Imagine for a moment if we didn't have governments? The government is nothing more than a big public service agency and those who work there are public servants. In the final analysis, this agency that we, the people, have created exists to serve all of us, the public, and not to self-serve those who happen to be there, and those who get what they want through bribery and corruption of those who are governing. Think of the government as a service organization from which we expect the completion of certain tasks and the delivery of certain goods and services. We are the ones who contribute to this agency, so we have the right to demand it to work to create the society we want: King's Beloved Community.

Some may say that King's vision is impossible to accomplish, but the truth is that we have an abundance of resources to take good care of everyone. We have all the resources we need to eradicate homelessness and hunger. We have all that is necessary to support each other's development through education and health care. President Lincoln spoke of the kind of government we all want, a "government of the people, by the people, for the people." Let us hope that we can bring about a government that is really of all people, by all people, and for all people. This is the kind of government that "shall not perish from the earth."

……...

"If you want to be important, wonderful. If you want to be recognized, wonderful. If you want to be great, wonderful. But recognize that he who is greatest among you shall be your servant. That's the new definition of greatness. And this morning, the thing that I like about it…by giving that definition of greatness, it means that everybody can be great. Because everybody can serve. You don't have to have a college degree to serve. You don't have to make your subject and your verb agree to serve. You don't have to know about Plato and Aristotle to serve. You don't have to know Einstein's theory of relativity to serve. You don't have to know the second theory of thermodynamics in physics to serve. You only need a heart full of grace. A soul generated by love. And you can be that servant."~ Dr. Martin Luther King, Jr.

……...

CALLING US TO A HIGHER GROUND

What follows are words of a truly evolved and noble human being.

"We must work unceasingly to uplift this nation that we love to a higher destiny, to a higher plateau of compassion, to a more noble expression of humanness."

"We must develop and maintain the capacity to forgive. He who is devoid of the power to forgive is devoid of the power to love. There is some good in the worst of us and some evil in the best of us. When we discover this, we are less prone to hate our enemies."

"To our most bitter opponents we say: 'We shall match your capacity to inflict suffering by our capacity to endure suffering. We shall meet your physical force with soul force. Do to us what you will, and we shall continue to love you. We cannot in all good conscience obey your unjust laws, because noncooperation with evil is as much a moral obligation as is cooperation with good. Throw us in jail, and we shall still love you. Bomb our homes and threaten our children, and we shall still love you. Send your hooded perpetrators of violence into our community at the midnight hour and beat us and leave us half dead, and we shall still love you. But be ye assured that we will wear you down by our capacity to suffer. One day we shall win freedom, but not only for ourselves. We shall so appeal to your heart and conscience that we shall win you in the process, and our victory will be a double victory.'"

"It is time for all people of conscience to call upon America to return to her true home of brotherhood and peaceful pursuits."

"If humanity is to progress, Gandhi is inescapable. He lived, thought, and acted, inspired by the vision of humanity evolving toward a world of peace and harmony. We may ignore him at our own risk."

~ Martin Luther King, Jr.

········

WHERE WE STAND IN MOMENTS OF CONTROVERSY

On December 12, 2019, as I review my writings to put together this book, I am pleased with the announcement that Greta Thunberg, the 16 years-old girl from Sweden who decide to speak up against the apathy and inactivity of adults to tackle the environmental crisis and who brought worldwide attention to the urgency of the issue, was chosen as the TIME 2019 Person of the Year. The magazine article written by Charlotte Alter, Suyin Haynes, and Justin Worland contains this passage that made me reflect on where we stand in moments of controversy. "In May 2018, after Thunberg wrote an essay about climate change that was published in a Swedish newspaper, a handful of Scandinavian climate activists contacted her. Thunberg suggested they emulate the students from Marjory Stoneman Douglas High School in Parkland, Fla., who had recently organized school strikes to protest gun violence in the U.S. The other activists decided against the idea, but it lodged in Thunberg's mind. She announced to her parents that she would go on strike to pressure the Swedish government to meet the goals of the Paris Agreement. Her school strike, she told them, would last until the Swedish elections in September 2018. Thunberg's parents were less than thrilled at first at the idea of their daughter missing so much class, and her teachers suggested she find a different way to protest. But Thunberg was immovable. She put together a flyer with facts about extinction rates and carbon budgets, and then sprinkled it with the cheeky sense of humor that has made her stubbornness go viral. "My name is Greta, I am in ninth grade, and I am school-striking for the climate," she wrote on each flyer. "Since you adults don't give a damn about my future, I won't either." On Aug. 20, 2018, Thunberg arrived in front of the Swedish Parliament, wearing a blue hoodie and carrying her homemade school-strike sign. She had no institutional support, no formal backing and nobody to keep her company. But doing something—making a stand, even if she was by herself—felt better than doing nothing. "Learning about climate change triggered my depression in the first place," she says. "But it was also what got me out of my depression, because there were things I could do to improve the situation. I don't have time to be depressed anymore."

I originally wrote this article five years ago, on December 2014. The writing was triggered by a report on the use of torture. I reposted the writing after the February 14, 2018 mass shooting that took place at Marjory Stoneman Douglas High School, in Parkland, Florida, when 17 people lost their lives.

……...

The Senate Select Committee on Intelligence's Report on the C.I.A.'s Use of Torture was made public two days ago, and we are drowning in an ocean of opinions condemning and defending the use of torture. In the middle of all this, what came to my mind was something that my son wrote back in 2009…

……...

I'm not sure why, but what came to my mind today, after hearing the news of a mass shooting in one of my city's schools, was something that my son wrote back in 2009. Mateus, then a 17 year-old senior, penned a short essay to support his application for the Dr. Martin Luther King, Jr. Scholarship at Boston University. Let me share it with you...

Here are the instructions he received: Write a 500-word essay describing how the following quotation has affected you personally. Please use specific examples from your own life, while also connecting your answer to the quotation and the legacy of Dr. King. "The ultimate test of a man is not where he stands in moments of comfort and the moments of convenience, but where he stands in moments of challenge and moments of controversy." ~ Dr. Martin Luther King, Jr.,

And here's my son's essay...

"Despite being imprisoned and threatened, Martin Luther King, Jr. refused to use violence. Instead, he chose active nonviolence as the way to advance social change. He stood by the unpopular doctrine of nonviolence from beginning to end, and he proved to the world he was right by his unwavering determination to stay firm in moments of challenge.

My first experience against violence came in sixth grade, when "paintballing" was becoming a very popular activity. All my friends found delight in shooting each other and comparing bruises afterwards, but I felt differently. At first, I was ostracized since I was the only one not looking at guns in magazines or trying to find the best places to play paintball. I quickly discovered, though, that my choice to not participate only made me a stronger person. At the age of eleven, I was learning what it meant to have integrity against violence.

In seventh grade, I was presented with the argument over capital punishment in my Speech and Debate class. I discovered I was a forceful opponent of the death penalty. My strong arguments resounded in class, and my teacher even confessed to my parents that I persuaded her to change her position. Dr. King's words inspired my belief. He said, "We must develop and maintain the capacity to forgive. He who is devoid of the power to forgive is devoid of the power to love."

During my high school years I had to stand up and speak up for my deepest beliefs. With our country involved in war, I spoke about the ineffectiveness of violence. When our government refused to talk to our enemies, I stood up to express how much I believe in dialogue as the only way to peace. With so many defending torture as a necessity for our safety, I spoke of it as unacceptable by all means. When I heard nasty generalizations about Muslims beings terrorists, I not only spoke up but I made a point of trying to eliminate those stereotypes. In fact, as a result of my efforts, one of my closest friends today is Muslim. When I heard racist remarks in my school, or vulgar language that diminished any particular group, I spoke up to express that we are all human beings and that what unites us is immensely larger than what separates us. With so many praising a violent system, based in extreme competition and survival of the fittest, I spoke in defense of cooperation and the need for a beloved community, one where we extend a helping hand to lift up the downtrodden. My efforts culminated in the International Day of Peace Assembly, where the messages of humanitarians and peacemakers such as Dr. King were heard again by the whole school.

I have never found it easy to remain firmly planted in my beliefs when they were unpopular. I am sure it was very difficult for Dr. King as well. However, I found an inner reward in doing what I think is right. John F. Kennedy said it best when he affirmed that "true democracy... will not condemn those whose devotion to principle leads them to unpopular courses, but will reward courage, respect honor, and ultimately recognize right." ~ Mateus Cesca Falci

....

Although he was accepted at Boston University - his brother's alma mater -- after a long consideration Mateus decided to join another school. He graduated in 2014 from Harvard with the degree of Bachelor of Arts. He is currently pursuing a career as a musician in New York City, holding the belief that, through music, he will be able to influence, inspire and engage others in the joyful work of creating a better world.

....

COSMIC COMPANIONSHIP

Where is your heart? Where is your commitment? Are you in despair with the lack of justice in the world? Are you feeling that the oppression and exploitation will never end? Are you feeling that we are destined to be violent, and that nonviolence doesn't stand a chance? Are you beginning to feel that social justice will never prevail? Are you feeling that it is too late to save the planet? Are you feeling that the forces we face are too powerful, and that the possibility of a dignified and thriving life for all in a healthy, well-protected planet is impossible? Are you losing hope?

If so, let these reflections of Dr. Martin Luther King, Jr. inspire, uplift, and motivate you.

"Perhaps the suffering, frustration and agonizing moments which I have had to undergo occasionally as a result of my involvement in a difficult struggle have drawn me closer to God. Whatever the cause, God has been profoundly real to me in recent months."

"In the midst of outer dangers I have felt an inner calm and known resources of strength that only God could give. In many instances I have felt the power of God transforming the fatigue of despair into the buoyancy of hope. I am convinced that the universe is under the control of a loving purpose and that in the struggle for righteousness man has cosmic companionship."

"Behind the harsh appearances of the world there is a benign power."

~ Martin Luther King, Jr.

....

ON THE MINDLESS MENACE OF VIOLENCE

There's something very mysterious about life and its connections and coincidences. The reading of the final chapter of Bobby Kennedy: The Making of a Liberal Icon, brought me back to the speech that Bobby delivered the night Martin Luther King, Jr. was assassinated. He said then, "What we need in the United States is not division; what we need in the United States is not hatred; what we need in the United States is not violence or lawlessness, but it is love, and wisdom, and compassion toward one another, and a feeling of justice toward those who still suffer within our country."

The day after the death of Martin Luther King, Jr., Bobby Kennedy delivered another speech known as On the Mindless Menace of Violence, in which he said, "... but this much is clear; violence breeds violence, repression breeds retaliation, and only a cleansing of our whole society can remove this sickness from our souls. For there is another kind of violence, slower but just as deadly, destructive as the shot, or the bomb in the night. This is the violence of institutions, indifference, and inaction, and decay. This is the violence that afflicts the poor, that poisons relations between men because their skin has different colors. This is a slow destruction of a child by hunger, and schools without books, and homes without heat in the winter. This is the breaking of a man's spirit by denying him the chance to stand as a father and as a man amongst other men. And this too afflicts us all. For when you teach a man to hate and to fear his brother, when you teach that he is a lesser man because of his color, or his beliefs, or the policies that he pursues; when you teach that those who differ from you threaten your freedom, or your job, or your home, or your family, then you also learn to confront others not as fellow citizens but as enemies - to be met not with cooperation but with conquest, to be subjugated, and to be mastered. We learn, at the last, to look at our brothers as aliens, alien men with whom we share a city, but not a community, men bound to us in common dwelling, but not in a common effort. We learn to share only a common fear - only a common desire to retreat from each other - only a common impulse to meet disagreement with force."

Bobby's words continue to touch me deeply, especially in these times when so many individuals of questionable character are rising to power throughout the world. I truly believe that if we dedicate ourselves to work on our own selves to expand our hearts and minds, we will experience the epiphany of oneness, and realize that we can organize ourselves to live in this world in immensely gentler ways, without so many divisions and conflicts, creating a world where everyone can live thriving and dignified lives. I know that once we experience this inner transformation and grow in selflessness, sayings such as, We are all in this together, and From a distance there are no borders, gain much deeper and expanded meanings. If we forsake violence completely and practice compassion and love wholeheartedly, I am convinced that we can bring Heaven to Earth. The truth, for me, is that Heaven is here, if we want it to be.

Our political leaders are a reflection of who we are, and if we want better politicians, we, ourselves, need to be better. I also believe that one of the most productive things we can do to change our less-than-perfect political system is to engage in personal inner work. Please, don't hastily prejudge and discard this idea. May the insanity and absurdities of these political farces we see playing out before our eyes awaken in us the conscience of the need to work to change our own selves.

OUR ENDANGERED VALUES

Darkness cannot drive out darkness; only light can do that. Hate cannot drive out hate; only love can do that. ~ Martin Luther King, Jr.

....

In Chinese the word Crisis is made of two characters, one meaning Danger, and the other meaning Opportunity.

These are dangerous times for all of us. Our most cherished and admired values -- the ones that were achieved through long-fought struggles of brave women and men and that brought about a more courteous, gentle, compassionate and enlightened society -- are endangered. Division, bigotry, intolerance, hatred, lack of civility and aggressiveness have received an influx of energy, and some people, through their discriminatory and violent behavior, are bringing to light the worst in us.

At the same time, these attacks on our values and civil liberties motivate us to engage in initiatives aimed at protecting them. Crises allow us to look deeply at the systems in place, see what is not working, and come up with better ways of organizing ourselves to live together. We can see this movement unfolding right now: people are reflecting on values, cherishing them, and showing willingness to protect them with renewed commitment. Our democracy, which has been kidnapped by a few, will inevitably be reclaimed by the majority of the people of this nation through increased participation in the democratic process, increased overseeing of the politicians and bureaucrats, and increased collaboration to create a more perfect union. Meanwhile, we will be growing our ability to deal with tense situations lovingly and nonviolently. The final result of this crisis will be positive, I believe. Now, thinking more broadly about what is needed to improve the quality of life for all, I am convinced that love is and will always be the right answer. If we want to bring about a more peaceful, just, and united society, we ourselves need to cultivate and spread kindness, compassion, generosity, tolerance and solidarity. I am convinced that the personal inner work that leads to the transformation of our hearts and minds and allows us to move from selfishness to selflessness continues to be the most powerful form of political activism for our times, and for all times. Based on this belief, my experiences in life, and the type of person I am, I have decided that the best contribution I can give to make life better on this planet is to keep working on my own self, while encouraging others to engage in this personal work of transformation from the inside out. For me, that's where the creation of a just society begins; with the construction of solid moral foundations upon which it shall rest. I have decided to give my support to those who want to start or who already are on their personal journeys of transformation. Finally, I have decided to nonviolently and actively resist the forces that try to delay, or prevent the inevitable manifestation of Heaven right here on Earth. If you feel called to do something during these difficult times, I urge you to do the same.

Through those meditative and contemplative practices that utilize silence and stillness, go to the center of your being and experience the epiphany of oneness. Realizing at the deepest level that we are all in this together changes our views and all our relationships.

Practice and get good at taming your old, primitive, reactive, fearful brain, while giving more attention and power to your new, evolved brain. This will allow you to enhance the space and time between stimulus and response and give you the skills to respond mindfully rather than react mindlessly.

Practice and free yourself from the illusion of the existence of an "I," and from the belief that this "I" is under attack and needs to be protected. Realize that there is no "I," no attack, and no need of protection.

………

"I said to the wanting-creature inside me:
What is this river you want to cross?
There are no travelers on the river-road, and no road.
Do you see anyone moving about on that bank, or resting?
There is no river at all, and no boat, and no boatman.
There is no tow rope either, and no one to pull it.
There is no ground, no sky, no time, no bank, no ford!
And there is no body, and no mind!
Do you believe there is some place that will make the
soul less thirsty?
In that great absence you will find nothing.
Be strong then, and enter into your own body;
there you have a solid place for your feet.

Think about it carefully!
Don't go off somewhere else!
Kabir says this: just throw away all thoughts of
imaginary things,
and stand firm in that which you are."
~Kabir

....

Make your voice heard, and while doing it, remember these guidelines listed by my friend, Rivera Sun: "Create connections, build community, open dialogues, organize action, use our civil liberties of speech and assembly to stand up for democracy, and don't cause physical harm to anyone or anything. Keep humanity and the planet alive, stop destruction, support the life affirming, and, of course, be kind, be connected, be unafraid!" Grow in love, kindness and compassion, and help others grow too. Soften yourself, and help others become softer too. Do all this, and inspire others to do the same, because the insights produced by this diligent inner work will reveal the best ways to bring about a just, united and peaceful world . I urge you to continue to be a presence of love, peace and unity in our world.

....

STILL HIDDEN, BUT MORE VISIBLE FIGURES

It is not easy to live in America if the color of your skin is not white. It is not easy to receive the recognition, respect, and reward you deserve for the excellence of your work if you are not a man. Life is twice as difficult if you are a black woman working among white men in America.

Last night I watched "Hidden Figures," a well-crafted and sensitive movie that generated deep reflections in me about gender and racial inequality in this country of ours. Directed by Theodore Melfi and written by Melfi and Allison Schroeder, the film is based on the nonfiction book of the same name by Margot Lee Shetterly. It tells the story, among others, of Katherine Johnson, the African American mathematician who calculated flight trajectories for NASA's Mercury and Apollo programs while facing the difficulties of being a black woman in the United States, and in a workplace populated and dominated by white men. It made me realize, once again, that even though I can empathize, I really can't fathom what it is to be black, or a woman, or a black woman in America. It made me think of the tremendous advantage I have simply for the mere fact that I was born a man, and white. It made me realize, once again, that the majority of the white population of this country goes through life in a state of oblivion, completely unaware of this immense and gratuitous privilege.

But it is evident that we are making progress, in spite of all the push-backs. We are realizing that prejudice, bigotry, discrimination, and segregation are expressions of ignorance and fear. It is becoming clearer that we, all of us, are crew members of the same spaceship that is traveling through cosmos, and that we need to work together if we want Planet Earth, our space vehicle, to last. There is a scene in the movie when Al Harrison, the head of the NASA program played by actor Kevin Costner, dramatically puts an end to segregated bathrooms in that NASA facility. The scene ends with him saying, "Here at NASA, we all pee the same color." I guess that all of us -- blacks and whites, women and men -- are coming to terms with this. I highly recommend the film. May it touch you and inspire you to continue the work of growing in understanding, educating, dispelling prejudice, and bringing more justice and peace to our world. Let us remember what Dr. Martin Luther King, Jr. told us: "Injustice anywhere is a threat to justice everywhere." Let us give of ourselves to create a gentler world for all because, in the final analysis, we are all in this together.

. . . .

INSPIRING CHANGE

Yes, you can call us naive and unrealistic, but we will keep saying that we need to move to a higher ground. We need a new consciousness for a new world. Are we going to succeed? I believe that eventually we will, since a change in the prevailing paradigm is our only real hope. Let us continue moving forward. We are making progress. Soon we will reach that tipping point -- the so called critical mass -- when the majority of mankind will accept widespread social justice and nonviolence as the most effective way of solving current conflicts, preventing the emergence of new ones, and manifesting peace. This will be the new paradigm.

So, let's be patient and generous. Let us respond with love to those who scorn us and our peace-promoting efforts. Let us face the skepticism with serenity and hope. Let us compassionately realize that those who mock us are operating in a realm where they are unable to envision new possibilities, and that we are the ones who can guide them from the deepest valleys where they are now to the top of the mountains from where they will be able to see the Promised Land.

....

" ... And then I got into Memphis. And some began to say the threats, or talk about the threats that were out. What would happen to me from some of our sick white brothers... Well, I don't know what will happen now. We've got some difficult days ahead. But it really doesn't matter with me now, because I've been to the mountaintop. And I don't mind. Like anybody, I would like to live a long life. Longevity has its place. But I'm not concerned about that now. I just want to do God's will. And He's allowed me to go up to the mountain. And I've looked over. And I've seen the Promised Land. I may not get there with you. But I want you to know tonight, that we, as a people, will get to the promised land! And so I'm happy, tonight. I'm not worried about anything. I'm not fearing any man! Mine eyes have seen the glory of the coming of the Lord!!" ~ Martin Luther King, Jr. -- I've Been to the Mountaintop -- delivered 3 April 1968, Mason Temple (Church of God in Christ Headquarters), Memphis, Tennessee -- the night before he was assassinated

....

Our job is to meet our brothers and sisters where they are. We must listen. We must acknowledge their views of the world. We must allow them to feel that we have heard and understood them. No one will listen to us if we act as if we are better and know better. No one will listen to us if we talk down on them from a pedestal. We must meet them where they are, listen to them, empathize with them, and show that even if we don't agree, we sincerely understand them. This is our job. We must seek first to understand, because only after they feel that they have been deeply and completely understood is that they will be open to listen to what we have to say. We must lead by example. People will listen to us if they see something different and special in us. If we exude peace they will pay attention to what we have to say about peace. Finally, we have to understand that because each one of us has different personalities, talents and skills, each one of us will find different ways of contributing to peace. But whatever you may be called to do, I would like to encourage you to put your focus on facilitating opportunities for people to experience inner-peace. In this violent world of ours, people are always in a fast, competitive mode. We need to create opportunities for people to understand that it is perfectly OK to give themselves time to slow down, to pause, be gentle with themselves, and touch that peace that resides within.

Let us facilitate opportunities for people to see beauty and abundance. Meditate, teach meditation, and guide others to places of inner peace where they will have those awakenings that will allow them to realize our oneness, and that life is more than what we are able to see. Walk in silence in nature, touch your inner peace, and lead a Silent Peace Walk. Become a more peaceful human being yourself, and spread peace. Remember: We must be the change we want to see in the world. We must have peace in our hearts in order to give it. Peace begins with us. Be peaceful. Be patient, generous and forgiving, always. Give love. Our job is to keep the possibility of peace alive in people's hearts and minds. Acceptance of the worst scenario -- that violence will never stop and that we will never experience peace -- is very dangerous for humanity. Even though the violence and insanity of some desperate individuals push us to places of skepticism, cynicism, and pessimism, we must do what we can to highlight all the good that there is in this world, and do what we can to keep the hope that peace through nonviolent means is possible.

....

"You may say I'm a dreamer, but I'm not the only one. I hope someday you will join us, and the world will live as one." ~ John Lennon

....

CHANGE WITHOUT CONFLICT

Is it possible to bring about social justice without violent confrontation? Is it possible for social reform to take place peacefully? Is it possible not only to maintain, but actually to enhance peace during times of change?

It is my belief that the best way to promote change is to change our own selves first, and then inspire in others the desire to change. I have been asking myself how to inspire those who detain power to do what is right and just. How do we persuade leaders to become champions for justice, and defenders of the rights to life, liberty, and the pursuit of happiness for all? How to persuade them to stop the selfish accumulation, and to focus on helping others live free and dignified lives, not only with opportunities to pursue, but actually with real chances to achieve happiness?

I still don't have satisfactory answers to those questions, but I am leaning toward the idea that humanity is in need of a new way of thinking, one that values cooperation more than competition, selflessness more than egoism, and generosity more than greed and tightfistedness. It is my belief that in order for this new paradigm to grow and become prevalent, we need to guide more and more individuals to engage in practices that can allow them to have those experiences that reveal our true nature and oneness. Those are the experiences that enhance empathy, compassion, generosity, and solidarity.

While thinking about all these things, a speech delivered by my son, when he was 14 years old, came to my mind. Here's his speech:

"I'm very happy to be here and I want to thank the Martin Luther King, Jr. Committee for inviting me to speak. My name is Mateus Falci. I am a freshman at American Heritage School. We're here tonight to celebrate the life of Dr. Martin Luther King, Jr. and all the hearts he touched. I've always admired Dr. King and I know he certainly left his mark on the nation. I was traveling throughout Florida and I commented to my dad how many cities have streets named after Martin Luther King, Jr., and I truly think that is a beautiful thing. I recently saw Arun Gandhi, Mahatma Gandhi's grandson, speak in Fort Lauderdale and he spoke about nonviolence. I know that Dr. King was also a great admirer of Gandhi and emulated Gandhi in many ways. In fact, Dr. King once said, "If humanity is to progress, Gandhi is inescapable. He lived, thought, and acted, inspired by the vision of humanity evolving toward a world of peace and harmony. We may ignore him at our own risk." Seeing and speaking with Arun Gandhi was very cool. He even wished me good luck on the speech I am giving right now, and I thought to myself, "Now I can't go wrong. Gandhi's grandson himself wished me good luck!" One thing that always stood out for me and that I admired of Dr. King was his philosophy on nonviolence. I love Dr. King's message when he said, "We shall match your capacity to inflict suffering by our capacity to endure suffering." I feel it makes so much more sense than fighting back, because violence only generates more violence. He was so right when he said, "We'll wear you down by our capacity to suffer, and one day we will win our freedom. We will not only win freedom for ourselves, we will so appeal to your heart and conscience that we will win you in the process, and our victory will be a double victory."

I look back at history and I notice that many violent revolts failed, but the nonviolent ones always achieve their goal and are the ones that leave the greatest marks, such as Gandhi's for the independence of India and Dr. King's for civil rights. Nonviolence also requires the ability to forgive and Dr. King shone through in this too. I've seen the videos of defenseless African-Americans being beaten senselessly and I am always appalled. But I forget I am appalled when I become overcome with amazement over how Dr. King and the African-American community were able to forgive such acts. Once again Dr. King said, "We must develop and maintain the capacity to forgive. He who is devoid of the power to forgive is devoid of the power to love." With all the turmoil going on in the world today I believe Dr. King's message of nonviolence and forgiveness can easily apply to situations all over the world. From the war in Iraq to the genocide in Darfur his message is one that can help resolve these issues. Dr. King once said this when talking about the war in Vietnam, "It's time for all people of conscience to call upon America to return to her true home of brotherhood and peaceful pursuits." He continued by saying, "We must work unceasingly to lift this nation that we love to a higher destiny, to a new plateau of compassion, to a more noble expression of humaneness." I feel this message is just as relevant today as it was then. Dr. King's message was of peace, love, and forgiveness, and I feel all of us gathering here tonight is very important, because we can reflect on his message and continue to spread it afar. Thank you." ~ Mateus Cesca Falci, The 17th Annual MLK Jr. Celebration, Friday, January 12, 2007 - Coral Springs Center for the Arts

MINDFULNESS AND JUSTICE

CHOOSING THOUGHTS, CHOOSING FEELINGS

Human beings entertain tens of thousands of different thoughts every day. Our minds are in constant, and most of the time, frenetic and uncontrolled activity. Something happens and a thought pops up. One thought triggers the next, and all those thoughts bring about emotions. Since our minds have the tendency to retain our negative experiences, negative emotions come to the surface, and we may find ourselves feeling sad or angry for no apparent reason. Scientists have given a name to this tendency of the brain: they called it, Negativity Bias. This tendency to focus on and retain the worst experiences puts us in a place of fear. It makes us believe that there is imminent danger out there, that there are individuals out there ready to hurt us, and that, therefore, we must constantly be on the lookout, ready to flee or fight. This negativity expresses itself through a pessimistic outlook in life: "If something bad can happen, most likely it will." Unfortunately, constant fear leads to a miserable existence with a tremendous toll of one's health; this surely is a pitiful way of living.

We should, on a regular basis, investigate what is behind our feelings, especially the troubling ones, by asking ourselves, "How am I feeling right now? Why am I feeling this way? What brought this feeling up? Is this feeling justified?" Once you identify the reason why you are feeling a certain way, you can choose to understand the emotions, deal with the problem, and move on to a better place. The results of such a simple practice are amazing. It really improves the quality of one's life.

So, pause, pay attention, and investigate your feelings. It is important to acknowledge them, understand what is generating them -- the so called sponsoring thoughts -- and take the time to process them. Do not force yourself to change abruptly. Process whatever may be disturbing you, in a gentle way. Be gentle with yourself. If you are being called to grieve and cry, go ahead and do so. But remember that you always have a choice. You have the power to choose the thoughts and feelings that will make you feel better.

So, choose whatever makes you feel good. Make sure you are not dwelling in negative feelings such as fear, worry, anxiety, and anger. If so, choose good feelings. Replace them with love and hope. You always have a choice.

......

WE HAVE WORK TO DO

Holding on to the idea that we cannot bring Heaven to Earth on our own, without external help, many people simply wait, hoping for that day when a superhero will arrive and clean the mess that we have created. Think for a moment on the long list of blockbuster movies and our adored superheroes: Superman, Batman, Spiderman, Thor, Captain America, and so on. This idea -- that a superhero will come and fix our problems -- is etched in the collective unconscious of humanity. The story of the hero who sacrifices himself to save others is one that has been told and retold innumerable times in all cultures: it is the a constant tale in our universal human mythology. Joseph Campbell, the great mythologist called it The Hero's Journey. Such repetition of the story has led many of us to believe that the only possible way for justice and harmony to reign on Earth rests on the intervention of one of those prodigious beings. Many of us have convinced ourselves that this is our fate, and that we should accept it with resignation. So all we do -- all we believe we can do -- is to hope for a mighty being with super powers to come and save us. Although I don't dislike the idea of a superhero that will come to our rescue, I feel that this thought unconsciously leads us to leave the hard work in someone else's hands. It is easier to say, "We cannot do anything. Only someone with enormous power can bring the peace and unity of Heaven to Earth!"

Well, in my opinion, this is just an easy way out, an excuse we have created for doing nothing. We need to put our fear and indolence aside, roll up our sleeves, and take action. We have work to do, and I suggest we begin this work by examining the validity of the ideas we hold. Maybe those special envoys from Heaven -- the ones who we believe are the only ones capable of installing generosity, justice, and solidarity on Earth -- will actually come when they are no longer needed. Maybe we have to do the work first, fix what needs to be fixed first, and then they will come. So, let's embrace the idea that those heroes come to Earth through us. Instead of waiting, and leaving everything that needs to be done in their hands, let's put our talents and skills to work, and offer our contribution, however humble, to bring justice, peace and unity to Earth now.

We are the heroes of our own dreams. We are the ones we have been waiting for. If we imitate the Evolved Masters who came before us, and if we practice the lessons of unselfishness and loving kindness that they taught us, we will bring them back to Earth; we will bring Heaven to Earth. This is not difficult, not at all. In fact, it is quite easy.

It starts with recognizing our interconnectedness. When we recognize ourselves in others, we are compelled to treat everyone, even our enemies, with the utmost kindness. We realize that no one comes into our lives by chance, and that everyone we interact with is as important to us as we are to them. We realize that we can learn from them as they can learn from us. We come to the understanding that we can teach them as they can teach us. We develop this inner conviction that we are all in this together. Every encounter becomes a special opportunity to love, care and share, and it is through this mutual loving, caring, and sharing that we bring Heaven to Earth.

....

THE ONE LESSON WE MUST LEARN

It all boils down to two elements: healthy selfishness and open-hearted unselfishness.

When we operate in an unhealthy, selfish mode, we are, primarily, a bunch of self-centered individuals interacting with other selfish beings. We want what we want, when we want, and the way we want. In all our interactions, we all are, consciously or unconsciously, asking ourselves "What's in it for me?" Behind every action there is a self-serving motivation. Even behind the most unselfish act there is a dose of selfishness. Even when we think that we are working solely for others and selflessly giving of ourselves, we still are, to a greater or lesser degree, working for our own selves. We may be doing it because we want recognition, power, love, acceptance, or feel that we are worthy and necessary. We may be doing it just to experience the good feelings that come from doing good. And what's wrong with this? Even if people are doing it for the wrong reasons, good is still being done, isn't it? Is there a difference between a good deed fueled by selfish reasons, and good deeds motivated by unselfishness? In every unselfish deed there is a dose of selfishness. I guess we need to check what is primarily motivating us to perform the good deeds. Is it selfishness or genuine unselfishness? What is the predominant motivator? Can we distinguish between unhealthy and healthy selfishness?

....

Why am I here? Why are we here? What for?

"I am here to learn and grow." This may sound selfish, but, actually, by learning and growing we become better human beings and a blessing to others.

"I am here to be happy." This may sound selfish, but, actually, when we are happy, we bring happiness to those around us, and we make the world better for everyone. This is healthy selfishness.

....

There's good and bad selfishness. There's good and bad unselfishness. Maybe this planet is just a big practicing ground for us to learn to distinguish the good selfishness from the bad one, and the good unselfishness from the bad one, that's all.

When our life begins, we are totally, one hundred percent selfish-- that's how we are originally programmed. And then, we are given some decades of physical existence and millions of opportunities to practice in order to learn the one lesson we need to learn: to choose healthy selfishness and unselfishness.

We are here to learn, change, grow, and be happy. We are here to do what is necessary to move from the point where we care for ourselves exclusively, to this new point where we care for everyone, our own selves included. We are here to learn that the most rewarding journey is the one that takes us from sick egoism to healthy selfishness and altruism. We are here to learn how to do good, and to do good. We are here to be joyful and spread joy. We are here to be a blessing to others. We are here to make other people's lives better.

Everything that is good stems from unselfishness.

Kindness, generosity, patience, love, forgiveness, charity, all these wonderful attributes come out naturally once we tame our selfishness. It is then that we become those giving beings, ready to give of ourselves to others. But in order to give something, we must first have it. It is by giving ourselves love, that we can love others.

The purpose of life is found in service.

Selflessness allows us to 'step inside someone else's shoes,' empathize, and develop that heartfelt desire to help that comes from deeply feeling someone else's suffering. Then the questions, "How can I help you? What can I do for you? How may I serve you?" will arise spontaneously.

········

DEFEATING SELFISHNESS

Here we are, in this learning campus called Earth, enrolled in this course called Life, trying hard to get it right, so we can graduate and get the degree.

Here we are, practicing to make the right choices, the ones that will bring Heaven to Earth, both at the individual and collective levels.

What have I learned so far?

I have learned that I am here to practice in order to become less selfish and more unselfish, less self-centered and more other-centered. I have learned that it is all about making the right choices, taking the well-being of others in consideration. And in order to make the right choices I need to pay attention to my thoughts and determine where the motivation is coming from: love or fear? And remember that love is selfless while fear is selfish.

Maybe this is what life really is: a passage through a place where we are given many opportunities to practice in order to master how to defeat selfishness. I am practicing. I believe we can all get good at it!

·········

337

WE ARE IN HEAVEN

We have been exposed to the idea that the world is imperfect and unjust, and that perfection and justice can only be experienced in Heaven. But what if we were told something radically different? What if we were told that we are in Heaven already? What if, instead of hoping to get to Heaven after we die, we were brought up and lived as if we were in the most blessed place in the Universe already? How would this impact life on Earth? I now believe that in order to bring about a better world we need a sweeping new paradigm, and I feel called to offer my contribution. Heaven is here! We are in Heaven!

What if, instead of being told that we are in a 'valley of tears, trials and tribulations,' we were told something completely different, such as, that we are in a shared garden and playground? Imagine being greeted at arrival with this message, "Welcome. You made it! You are in Heaven! This is your garden. Enjoy its beauty, and take good care of it. This is your playground. Have fun, and improve it. And, by the way, share all toys." What effect would that have on us? What would happen if spiritual awakenings opened our eyes, enhanced our perception, and allowed us to feel the Divine Presence everywhere, see beauty and miracles all around, and realize that this is a world of plenty? If children were raised hearing, "You are in Heaven," what effect would that have on our relationships with one another and with all creation? What would happen if we embraced the idea that we are in Heaven already?

I envision the day when the prevailing idea on this planet will be that we are in a place engineered by the Creator to make us happy, and that those who made it here have won the biggest possible prize. Living here is a reward, not a punishment. I envision the day when this new paradigm will lead us to organize life in this planet in such a way that everyone will have their needs met, everyone will be taken care of, no one will be left behind, and everyone will be totally supported to offer their best contributions to the world.

Living in Heaven, and enjoying everything it has to offer begins with the acceptance of this new paradigm followed by the diligent practice of mindful attention, openness to be amazed by the wonders that surround us, and the practice of constant gratitude. Here it is! Enjoy Heaven, right here on Earth!

....

OUR JOB

"The day I wrote this song, I was sitting in a circle of people of all ages and we were asked, 'Why are you here?' Why am I here? This really hit me on a deep level. I realized no one had ever asked me that question before. As I prepare to give birth to a new child, I can't help and think about the world I'm bringing my baby into. No matter where we come from, when we see the state of the world today, we can all feel the growing frustration and desire to make a difference. And we all have a voice - we just need to know how to make it heard. I have a vision that I believe is more than a dream, that I know can be our reality. I believe in an empowered world community built on the true meaning of equality – where we are all considered one people, regardless of race, religion, gender, zip code, belief system, or sexual orientation. I believe all of our voices should be heard, so that our representation reflects our population. We need our leadership to reflect an equal balance of the gifts that both men and women have to offer. I believe in a world where every child born receives a quality education – where their unique gifts are nurtured so that they may be a beneficial presence in this world. I believe in mutual respect and cooperation among all peoples and all nations. It is time to end all forms of racial injustice for our black brothers and sisters and all people of color. I believe in an end to the prison industrial complex in America and a renewed justice system that is based on fairness and truth. I believe in universal global health care based on Integrative Medicine, so that our bodies are acknowledged and treated as one system, and we can help control the spread of diseases like AIDS, Malaria, TB and Ebola. I believe we have an ability to end poverty, oppression, and hopelessness that often breeds despair, terror, and violence. I believe in common sense gun laws that serve to protect children and families and society from unnecessary violence. I believe in Peace & Love & Unity. I believe that this vision can be a reality. And, it's not about me. It's about WE. Together we can give birth to a kinder and more peaceful world for ALL children. Our souls were brought together so that we can love each other sister, brother. We Are Here. We are here for all of us. That's why 'We Are Here.' Sent with Light," ~ Alicia Keys

……..

What are we supposed to do?

Our job is to live consciously in the here-now, noticing the magic, mystery, and miracles that surround us, feeling loved, grateful, and content, not allowing the regrets of the past, or the worries with the future to remove us from the enjoyment of the present moment.

Our job is to attain total liberation from the shackles of human misery caused by wanting what we don't have and not wanting what we do have.

Our job is to figure out who we really are and what we were brought here to do, and live authentic lives, striving to give our best contributions, while supporting others so they too can give their best contributions to humanity.

Our job is to let people know that they are loved by selflessly being of service to them.

Our job is to remember, and help others remember, that we don't need to be more, do more, or have more to be loved, because to be loved is everyone's birthright.

Our job is to attain liberation by not identifying ourselves with our bodies, personalities, and mental creations.

Our job is to nurture our inner-peace, so we can bless the world with our peace.

....

PROMOTING CHANGE THE GENTLE WAY

Our job here on Earth is to be love and spread love, to be happy and spread happiness, to be peaceful and spread peace, to be just and spread justice. Our job is to love unconditionally and express ourselves fully and fearlessly.

In our attempts to bring about change it would be good to ask ourselves, "How can I use happiness, laughter, love and peace to promote change, and bring about justice?"

We cannot change anyone, but we can inspire others so they develop the desire to change themselves.

Can we be a source of inspiration that will inspire them to do what is right? Can we inspire them in such a way that they will want to change? Can we promote change using love, kindness, gentleness, compassion, generosity, and peace as your tools?

Let us be happy and spread happiness. Let us smile, laugh, and make others smile and laugh. Let us have a good time and make others feel good about themselves, reminding them of their potential to do great things, to do what is right. Let's love them and let them feel that they are loved.

....

MYSTICS WITHOUT MONASTERIES

The awakening is a beautiful occurrence in one's lifetime, one that profoundly changes those who go through it. Once it takes place, we begin to see things that we weren't able to see before. We begin to have singular thoughts that are quite different from those we had before. We begin to question the predominant and widely accepted values of our modern, materialistic culture. We begin to reflect on what life really is and why we are here. The mundane themes of conversation don't seem important anymore. And because our interests change, we begin, perhaps involuntarily, to isolate ourselves.

Through practices that develop clear seeing, we have glimpses of reality beyond wrong perceptions. Then, not only we want to share these experiences, but also want to get together with those who had similar experiences to hear what they have to say. We look for companions for our journeys of exploration.

I first heard the expression 'Mystics without Monasteries' from my friend Liz. She described them as those individuals who, having had profound experiences, begin to perceive the presence of magic, mystery, and miracles everywhere. This new state of awareness radically expands their understanding of what life is, and alters their behavior in this world, leading them to respond to life's challenges in non-traditional, somewhat unexpected ways, with much more unselfishness, kindness, patience, generosity, forgiveness, and compassion. They become those individuals who emanate a calming energy and whose sole presence brings healing and peace.

I found interesting that when Liz was describing those 'Mystics without Monasteries,' I felt that she was describing herself. This is who she is: a calming presence that brings healing and peace. Liz told me that she heard the expression in 'Entering the Castle,' a live lecture on the nature of mysticism by Caroline Myss. What attracts me in this concept of 'Mystics without Monasteries' is the idea that anyone can have a transformational experience.

I am at a point in my life that I want to help demystify the current belief that the awakening experiences are reserved only to a few gifted, highly evolved individuals. I want to demystify the idea that only hard work can lead to a closer encounter with reality beyond concepts and stories. I want to popularize the idea that anyone can experience connection, communication and communion with a mystery beyond the limitations of the self.

How?

Pay attention! Be alert! Magic, mystery, and miracles are all around, all the time. Seek and you will find. Look and you will see.

Connect. Communicate. Commune. Seek connection all the time, with your inner self and with others. Communicate from heart to heart. Seek to listen to what your wisdom has to say to you, all the time. Reach a state of supreme communion with all, a state where there is no separation. Feel the connection, the unity, the communion. Feel that we, all of us, everyone and everything in the entire universe, are one.

Remember. Recognize. Reveal. Remember to be mindful. Remember to connect, communicate, and commune. Recognize the magic, the mystery, and the miracles every moment, everywhere, in every situation, in every person you meet. Reveal this wonder to everyone you meet. Become a 'Mystic without a Monastery,' one of those individuals who emanate a calming energy and whose sole presence brings healing and peace to the world, just like my friend Liz.

········

AM I DOING ENOUGH?

Knowing that peace is an offspring of justice, and that without justice there can be no peace, peacemakers ask themselves, "Am I doing enough to promote justice?" These are questions that afflict many peacemakers. It is paradoxical because in order to bring peace to the world, in an effective manner, one must be peaceful. But many bringers of peace live with some sort of peacelessness. "Blessed Unrest," the title of Paul Hawken's book, is what comes to my mind when I think about what moves peacemakers. Promoters of peace live with an inner restlessness that calls them to take action and do something to eradicate violence and bring peace to the world.

Am I doing enough? Each individual is different, and each one has different gifts to offer to the world. Some are called to get directly involved in the movements for social change. Some are called to offer support in other ways. Each one shall contribute according to their talents and skills. Some are bold, courageous and outspoken. Others are more reserved. Each one is different. Each one of those who feel called to work for peace must find the way that best suits his personality. We have to find our way of contributing to create a more just and peaceful world. Working on our own selves to enhance our peacefulness is a must. Many times, the sole presence of a peaceful being softens hearts, enhances compassion, calms down individuals, and brings about more justice and peace to places of conflict.

In an environment of unrest, where there is so much violence, how can we bring peace? What can we do? What can I do? Am I doing enough? In all honesty, I don't have conclusive answers. I guess each one has to find their own answers. Each one has to find and pursue his or her calling. Each one has to discover the way they feel they are best using their talents and skills to make the world a better place. For instance, my calling is to cultivate my inner peace and help people find and cultivate theirs. This is what I do through my inner work, my writings, and mindfulness meditation and mindful living workshops.

Am I doing enough? I am not sure if what I am doing is enough, or will ever be enough, but, at least, I am doing something. I am trying to cultivate inner and outer peace. I am trying to reflect about peace, practice peace, and teach peace. I am trying to bring peace to everything I do, every person I meet. Like all things in life, there is a circle of causation. It is true that justice is a prerequisite for peace, but I also feel that peace is a prerequisite for justice. Successful promoters of social justice begin with peace in their hearts. I believe that hateful hearts don't go far in producing lasting peace. A peaceful society is the result of social justice and hearts full of love. The desire to promote justice and the inspiration that will indicate the right, nonviolent actions to be taken are born in the hearts of those who cultivate inner peace.

Peace in our hearts brought peace to our families, our families, our communities, and the entire world. There is peace on Earth, and it began with us, in our hearts.

VISIBLE AND NOT-SO-VISIBLE VIOLENCE

Peace seekers want the end of violence, and the majority of them focus on the end of the so-called Direct Violence, the one that wounds and kills people fast. Unfortunately, not all of them make the connection between this kind of violence and the other violence, the less visible one, the so-called Indirect, Structural, Systemic Violence, the one that through oppression and exploitation erodes hope, and wounds and kills slowly. The truth is that Indirect Violence engenders Direct Violence. War, terrorism, social unrest, violent crime, and other forms of Direct Violence are rooted in the grounds of social injustice, income inequality, concentration of wealth, with its utter poverty and lack of opportunities. That is where ideas of change through violent means are born and spread. Social injustice breeds despair which breeds violence. So when violence erupts and becomes visible, we are called to remember the other violence, the one that is not so visible. Peace seekers who want the end of the visible violence are called to work to put an end to the invisible one.

....

EXACERBATED COMPETITION

We live in a non-peaceful world. Unrest seems to be the norm in our modern societies. Many forces are at play to constantly put people in some state of disquiet. Many are pushed to participate in the fight of egos early in their lives. They are taught to see themselves as separated from others, and pushed to prove their superiority in all fronts of life. They grow up being compared with others, and, sadly, they end up living pitiful and unsatisfying existences. They are the ones who are constantly comparing themselves with others. If they are not number one -- if they are not at the top -- they are not happy. They derive their sense of worth from competing, winning and defeating.

People are conditioned to believe, for instance, that to finish in second place, even among the best in the world, is reason to be ashamed. Immersed in an environment of constant comparison and competition -- feeling that they are not good enough -- people are, then, seduced by the promise that they may placate that sense of worthlessness, and the inner void they feel, through consumption, which in many cases may lead to over consumption, uncontrolled debt, and unnecessary accumulation.

Unfortunately, this is the process that down the line fuels exploitation and social injustice. In other words, there are many forces at play that move individuals away from experiencing satisfaction, recognizing who they are -- their intrinsic worth -- what they already have, and what they have achieved already. Systems currently in place do not promote self-recognition of one's innate worth independent of comparison and competition. Systems current in place do not promote gratitude and peace of mind. The prevailing paradigm is that we are separated from one another. Our interconnection, interdependence, and the importance of cooperation are not emphasized. It seems that we have created a world of perennial unrest and permanent non-satisfaction; people feel uneasy if they are not competing all the time. People feel guilty if they pause, even if just for a short moment, to appreciate life and give thanks. They feel they need to demand more and more and more of themselves all the time.

......

INTERNAL AND EXTERNAL HARMONY

It can be argued that inner peace is independent of external conditions. A destitute man can be peaceful while one who is materially rich and has his physiological and safety needs more than met may live in despair. Wealth alone does not guarantee joy and fulfillment in life. But peace, both inner and outer, is more likely to be found in just societies, those where individuals have organized themselves in such ways that all members have their basic needs met and have opportunities to develop themselves to be the best that they can be in order to give their best contributions to humanity. By doing what we were brought here to do; by doing what we do best; by doing what we love, we bring our best contributions to the world. By doing all this, we are happy, and simply by being happy we bless the world around us with happiness and peace.

A society where many of its members live without their basic needs met is not and cannot be a peaceful society. The potential for social unrest is ever-present. Repression and fear can curb discontentment only for a time. As Martin Luther King, Jr. Said, "Injustice anywhere is a threat to justice everywhere."

The paradox is that in order to promote peace one must be peaceful, while, at the same time, in order to promote justice, the prerequisite for peace, one must experience some sort of affliction. Inner unrest calls for action that many times calls for and brings up social unrest. In order to promote social justice we are called to review the ways we have organized ourselves to live on the planet, and do away with those structures that exploit the vulnerable in order to preserve the privileges of the powerful. Gandhi and Martin Luther King, Jr., known as mighty peacemakers, were leaders of social reform movements which, through the application of nonviolent active resistance, successfully brought about more just societies, while generating no shortage of social unrest in the process.

....

PEACE IS AN OFFSPRING OF JUSTICE

Imagine waking up every morning and going to bed every night worried about your survival and the survival of your loved ones. Imagine not having the means to properly provide to your family. Imagine not knowing if you will have food to eat, water to drink, or shelter to protect you and your loved ones from the rigors of the elements the next day. Imagine living day in and day out concerned with your physical safety and that of the members of your family. Imagine living in a war zone, a refugee camp, in a place ravaged by violent crime, or in the middle of the aftermath of a natural disaster such as an earthquake, a tsunami, an avalanche, a forest fire, a tornado, or hurricane. Imagine not knowing if you are going to be able to get medical assistance for you and your loved ones in the event something bad happens. Imagine being unemployed and not being able to find a job. Imagine only being able to get low paying jobs that pay by the hour and nothing more. Imagine living with the fear that you will be completely on your own if you find yourself out of work or unable to work. Imagine not being able to get a job through which you may make enough to cover the costs of your basic needs. Imagine living in debt and with the fear of losing whatever little you have. Imagine feeling like a failure for not being able to provide a worry-free existence for your family. Imagine living without seeing opportunities that will guarantee a better future for your children. Imagine having to live like this, unable to realize your dreams, unable to become the best that you can be, unable to give your best contribution to society. Imagine living day in and day out with this uncertainty, with the feeling of an impending storm approaching in the horizon. Imagine living all the time with worry, anxiety, stress caused by the fear of lack and the feeling that the situation will never get better. Imagine living without being able to see a way out. Imagine living in despair, without hope. Imagine the level of despair that moves people to leave everything behind, risk their lives in the hope of creating better lives for all, dreaming that there is a place somewhere, where everyone can be safe and have productive lives. Just imagine.

Having enough for one's survival -- having the basic physiological and safety needs met -- is the foundation to the edifice where one can experience inner peace. Peace is an offspring of some degree of equality. Without social justice there can be no peace. The world does not need to be in such a pronounced imbalance with so many people living in poverty. This is a place of abundance where there is more than enough for everybody to live dignified lives. We just need to better organize ourselves. We can do it. It is possible.

......

EXISTENTIAL DISCOMFORT

"Five enemies of peace inhabit with us - avarice, ambition, envy, anger and pride; if these were to be banished, we should infallibly enjoy perpetual peace." ~ Francesco Petrarca

......

I live in the United States of America, and I am fully aware that I am amongst the richest people on the planet. I am aware that directly or indirectly, either as a stockholder or as a consumer, I benefit from injustices that are taking place in other places in the world. I am not innocent, and I don't claim to be.

I experience an existential discomfort. I see too much pain around me. I witness too much injustice and hypocrisy. I see the rich getting richer and the poor getting poorer; rich nations getting richer and poor nations getting poorer, and as this gorge gets deeper and more difficult to cross, I see us becoming less capable of understanding one another.

I wish I could live in a world of economic and social justice, ruled by solidarity. I wish I could live in a world without violence, be it the direct violence that wounds and kills people, or the structural violence that kills people slowly by depriving them of opportunities. It is a scandal to live in a world where thousands of people die everyday of hunger and diseases that are perfectly curable, while so much is wasted in wars and frivolities. It is revolting to see exploiters making in one day what the exploited will not make in a lifetime. It is heartbreaking to live in a divided world where leaders of nations, instead of engaging in mature, respectful, and constructive interaction for the improvement of life in the planet, act like gang leaders, spying on one another, undermining each other, acting in immature ways that create unnecessary tension and conflict. It is also sickening to observe how people ignore the moral mandate to care for the downtrodden.

The truth is that we, human beings, can evolve. We must remember that what is morally right always prevails. We should always have in mind the greater good, what is best for all, and work for the advancement of all humanity.

Martin Luther King, Jr. once said, "Every man must decide whether he will walk in the light of creative altruism or the darkness of destructive selfishness. This is the judgment. Life's most persistent and urgent question is, 'What are you doing for others?'"

We should renounce our selfish impulses to solely seek personal benefit with complete disregard for the well-being of others. We should leave behind the selfish drive to advance our own personal agenda, or the narrow agendas of the groups we belong to, without concern for the distress we may bring to others, here or in other parts of the world. We must remember that the pain we inflict upon others inevitably comes back to trouble us, one way or another. What goes around, comes around. We must refrain from exploiting others because there is no victory in exploitation; only defeat.

· · · · · · · · ·

TRYING TO FIGURE IT OUT

Meditate and live mindfully. This will produce the balms that will heal your afflictions.

Welcome everything that life is bringing you, good or bad. Meet all visitors with equanimity. Be grateful for everything and give thanks for the extraordinary life you already have. Believe that great, unexpected, wonderful, joyful things are coming your way. Know that you are loved and that there's nothing to worry about. Remember: You are a child of the Universe, and nothing bad will ever happen to you. Joy is your birthright. Know that you are loved.

Connect with your inner intelligence for guidance. Know who you are and what you came here to do. Know your purpose in life. Don't wander aimlessly wasting precious time. Live your life with courage, hope, faith, and trust. Be confident that all is good, and everything that is good is coming to you. Be patient. Trust that it will all work out. Remember, "In the end, everything will be OK. If it is not OK, it's not the end."

Remember who you are, and what you came here to do. Ask yourself, "Who am I? What do I love? What am I passionate about? How shall I live, knowing that I will die? What is life calling me to do? Who do I choose to be? What are my gifts to the family of the Earth? What am I meant to do to contribute to the world in a significant way? What am I grateful for? What are the simple things in life that I find pleasure in?" Rediscover your purpose and follow your bliss!

You can only be you, so choose to be you. There isn't another you, and there will never be another you. So, be the only one that you can be. Be the one that only you can be. Say to yourself, "I'm the hero of my own life, and I will live out who I really am." By doing so, by being authentic, you will realize your purpose. You will be a blessing to the world. You will be liberating others to live out who they really are. So, shine on like a bright light, and realize that you inspire many people.

You are a fantastic manifestation of the Great Universal Force, and you are wonderful, just the way you are. Be that, now! Don't wait for anything else in the future. Just live as if you have arrived at your destination. In all truth, you already have all that fantastic you in you. So be the wonderful you that you already are. Allow the wonderful being that you are to show up in this world. Flow beautifully with the stream of life, and touch many lives in positive ways. Just claim your special place in this world now, and bless the Universe with your magnificent presence! You are special, wonderful, fantastic! Accept that! Live that!

……..

Look with the eyes of your body, and see with the eyes of your heart. Be gentle with yourself. Receive all the love and peace I am sending you. My gift is to assure you, one more time, that you are special, unique and magnificent, and that you are loved.

Godspeed!

COME WITH ME TO THE LAND OF WE

1

I feel your pain. I am in pain too. I feel your anger. I am angry too. I feel your despair 'cause I'm in despair too. You don't need to hurt me 'cause your wound is open in me. Let us leave it all behind.
 Come with me to the Land of We.

2

Remind me of all the times I've hurt you. Tell me about the times I've excluded you, and made you feel defenseless and afraid. Help me see how heartless and violent I am. Show me all the pointless and petty wars I am constantly waging. You're hurting and I'm too. Yes, hurt people hurt people, but we can forgive each other and be free. Help me! Heal me!
 Take me to the Land of We.

3

Twists of fate took us to different places; I ended up sitting on a cushion, and you, with a rifle in your hands. I could easily be you, and you could easily be me. I see myself in you. Can you see yourself in me? Yes, I am in you, and you are in me. I belong to you, and you belong to me. I need you, and you need me. Hold my hand, and let me hold yours. Fill my void, and I will fill yours. Let us melt our loneliness and despair in the warmth of this embrace. Let us cultivate kindness in a new place. Let us walk together slowly, gently to where there is no you or me.
 Let's go together to the Land of We.

....

I heard the news of the shooting and deaths in the Orlando nightclub while attending a mindfulness meditation retreat in a place of peace and beauty called Omega Institute in Rhinebeck, New York, a real example that it is possible to bring Heaven to Earth. On the early morning hours of Monday, June 13, 2016, the instructors told us about the tragedy. We meditated, walked in silence, and afterwards many of the participants shared their thoughts in what came to be a highly emotional moment. I thank all of those who expressed their feelings in such heartfelt ways, especially Andrew and Audrey.

I am convinced that we need to silently and reverently go inside ourselves to that peaceful place of wisdom, and understand the healing that needs to take place in our world. We should stop listening to and giving power to the heralds of hate, to those who divide. We need to oppose whatever promotes killing. I am committed to spreading sanity and peace through practicing and teaching the inner work that will heal this world.

Believe it. Heaven is here if we want it to be.

....

WHAT ABOUT ME?

I am a work in progress, a work that I suspect will never end.

At this stage of my life, I am doing my best to live mindfully: I try to remember to acknowledge the synchronicities, and the magic, the mystery, and the miracles in every single thing in the Universe. I am being better able to catch myself when emotions such as fear, anger, hatred, and envy begin to creep inside, and I am learning to not offer resistance, but welcome them, get to know them better, and after a while, gently invite them to leave. Learning to observe my thoughts has helped me create exceptional days. I choose to hold an optimistic outlook in life, and do simple things such practicing to be upbeat, joyful, and caring. I try to remember to smile whenever I can, and to choose prudent actions, and emanate considerate words. I continue reminding myself to choose kindness, generosity, and forgiveness as my responses to life challenges, while hoping that I may bring more peace, joy, and harmony to the lives of those I interact with.

During my moments of silence and solitude, many times I am able to visit a place of stillness beyond the relentless activity of the thinking mind. That's where I experience clarity and peace. This practice is giving me a new understanding of life. In the silence, stillness, solitude, seclusion, simplicity, and service it is becoming clearer to me that I am not the character I have created, the protagonist of the story of my life. In the silence, stillness, solitude, seclusion, simplicity, and service I go beyond the illusory boundaries created by my ego and experience the sublime feeling of oneness, reaching an understanding that we are all in this together. This practice made empathy and compassion grow in me, and from there a call to action emerged: I felt called to help other individuals get to that same place of peace. My self-assigned mission now is to bring that same peaceful awareness to as many people as possible. My desire is not only to be present to witness the mystery of life unfolding, but also to be available to give the best of me to the people I meet, helping them live richer and contributing lives.

I am practicing to live more and more in the here-now, so whenever I catch my mind entertaining regrets, remorse, and resentments with things of the past, or worries about the future, I gently remind myself to look around, see all the beauty and good that surrounds me, and rejoice with the presents in the present. By doing so I am filled with a sense of gratitude for this planet, this beautiful garden and amazing playground that was given to us. This awareness inspires me to share the good news: "Heaven is here, if we want it to be."

Some say, with resignation, that the insane, violent, selfish, and exploitative ways that we conduct ourselves in this world are the ways things have always been and will be. I refuse to accept that. The words of George Bernard Shaw come to mind: "You see things; and you say, 'Why?' But I dream things that never were; and I say, 'Why not?'"

I see as a real possibility the emergence of a whole new world, a world without conflicts where everybody can live dignified, fear-free, beautiful, exciting, joyful, thriving, and contributing lives. It is my hope that others will envision this possibility too. We all have the capacity to transform ourselves and reach a refined state of enlightenment from where we will be inspired to organize ourselves to live on this planet in such ways that will manifest Heaven on Earth. The practice of mindfulness is the way of developing the clear seeing and the saner way of living that will make this possible. This discipline made me experience inner peace, and I am convinced that widespread inner peace is absolutely necessary for lasting global peace. I am confident that we are in the process of growing a critical mass of enlightened individuals, and that one day we will reach that tipping point when humanity will experience a fundamental paradigm change that will make life on this planet immensely better for all.

Meanwhile, I continue to examine my own beliefs in order to consciously unlearn the divisive prejudices I have unconsciously learned. At this point I don't feel the need to identify myself as a member of any tribe, or to belong to any kind of exclusive club. I don't pledge allegiance and loyalty to any faction. I consider myself a citizen of the world, a child of the Universe, a member of the big family that includes everyone and excludes no one.

……..

INNER WORK AND COLLECTIVE TRANSFORMATION

Inner work is indispensable: it liberates us from old ways of thinking, allows us to consider new possibilities, brings about a new awareness, changes the way we see everything, the way we relate to others and to creation, and transforms us and the world. Committed inner work produces personal transformation: it enhances perception, brings about a new awareness, expands consciousness, and produces an experience of oneness. It makes it clear that life is much more than the mere struggle to survive, compete, and accumulate; life is an exciting journey of discovery always happening in the here-now. With the experience of oneness, empathy and compassion emerge. Empathy and compassion propel individuals to work for justice and peace in nonviolent ways. In summary, committed inner work produces positive personal transformation which leads to positive societal transformation. The personal transformation that comes from a committed inner practice is what ultimately will bring all of us together!

I am practicing and teaching mindfulness because I have been transformed by it, and am convinced that the personal transformation that comes from diligent inner work is essential to bring solutions to our collective problems and create a better world. Fundamentally, I see myself as a teacher who creates conditions for people to have insights that allow them to be better. I have come to the conclusion that everything I have done and do converges to the same point: I have been trying to bring about a better world by promoting the practice of introspective investigation and growth. Through my workshops, retreats, and counseling, I have been teaching individuals to be sensitive of other people's needs. I have been encouraging them to respect one another. I have been teaching them how to communicate compassionately, lovingly, and nonviolently, seeking to understand one another, avoiding unnecessary conflicts, and coming to agreements that are fair and good for all involved. In essence, I have been reminding people to be kind. That's all.

At this stage of my life, this is my mission: to practice and teach what brings about kindness, compassion, happiness, and peace. My work is to transform myself in a peaceful bringer of justice and peace, while sharing resources that may help others become peaceful bringers of justice and peace themselves. My mission is to educate. My hope is that each individual that learns something from me may be inspired to share what they have learned with others. My hope is for this to go on and on, increasing the number of gentle, compassionate, good-hearted people. I see it as my contribution to the good that will spread all over the world, take it over, and transform it for the better. I see myself as a humble contributor, a teacher of future peacemakers, an instructor of the upcoming generations of peaceful individuals who will achieve, cultivate, and spread a higher consciousness.

We will bring justice and peace to the world. We will eradicate poverty, hunger and homelessness from the face of the Earth. We will make indifference and neglect with the pain and suffering of others disappear. We will put an end to all forms of indirect and direct violence. We will eliminate prejudice, discrimination, oppression, exploitation, mindless consumption, senseless waste, and irresponsible destruction of the environment. We will interact with all creation on this planet in nonviolent ways. We will create a world without wounding and killing, a world without crime, war, and terrorism. We will help those unbalanced individuals, those who spread disturbance, unrest, turmoil, and conflict, so they too can find peace within themselves, change their ways, and join forces with us to reveal Heaven on Earth. We will be the bringers of Heaven to Earth.

....

INTERNATIONAL DAY OF PEACE

Today was a good day. I was joined by many peacemakers at daybreak and we walked in silence for peace. Peace-loving people all over the world did something to expand awareness about Peace Day and demand a better world for all. The People's Climate March, the Campaign Nonviolence, and the Global March for Peace and Unity are examples of actions that took place today involving millions of individuals. I sent a message to fellow peace-seekers all over the world encouraging them to meet more often: "Meeting once a year to celebrate peace is good, but meeting every month is better. Meeting once a month to walk in silence for peace creates a strong group of Peace Builders that will plan and implement many peace initiatives. Initiate a monthly Silent Peace Walk where you live. This can be the beginning of your peace movement." I wrapped up my day watching "You Can't Be Neutral on a Moving Train," a tribute to Howard Zinn, a great man who dedicated himself to promote justice and peace, and was not afraid to speak truth to power. He is an example of courage and an inspiration to me.

Like so many people in the world, I want violence, both direct and indirect, to end. I wish we stop fighting, hurting, and killing one another. I wish we use our creative energy to put an end to poverty. And I am convinced that we can do it. We have more than enough resources to achieve peace. We just need to organize ourselves in new ways and everyone will be able to have the necessary to live with dignity, and this will bring an atmosphere of tranquility to the entire world. I am happy that the Forces of the Universe brought me to this place where I feel compassion for the oppressed, the exploited, and the downtrodden, and compelled to help create a more just and peaceful world for all. I know that what I do is not much, but today I am happy for the little I have done. I am happy that I have done something.

So, here are my wishes on this Day of Peace: May we, one day soon, wake up from the sleepwalking state we find ourselves immersed in, and realize that we have all that is necessary to manifest Heaven right here on Earth. May we realize that we can create a world where everyone can be loved and nurtured to give his or her best contribution to make everyone else's lives better. May my sons, one day, live in a more just, less violent, and more peaceful world, and may they be able to say that their father did something to make the world a better place.

Today was a good day.

....

I AM NOT AN ISLAND

To all of you out there, beautiful souls, who give of yourselves to make this world a better place... To all of you out there, beautiful souls, who give of yourselves to make the lives of our fellow men better... To all of you out there, beautiful souls, who engage in the work of inner exploration and betterment of your own selves... To all of you who, despite the mundane pressures, demands and distractions of life, engage in the work of finding and cultivating justice, peace and beauty within your own selves, and who, by doing so, make the world more peaceful and beautiful for all of us... ... I say, "Thank you."

I am deeply touched by the work you do. When you feed someone, you are also feeding me. When you shelter someone, you are also sheltering me. When you clothe someone, you are also clothing me.

When you protect someone, you are also protecting me. When you give someone love, you are also giving love to me.

Every time someone's life is diminished, I am diminished, but every time a life is exalted, I am exalted. We are all connected. When you do good, good is bestowed upon all of us. When you better yourself, you aren't the only one benefiting from it; I am too. When you take good care of others, you are also caring for me. When you lift someone up, you are also lifting me up. For that, I am grateful. Receive my heartfelt, "Thank you."

………

"No man is an island, entire of itself; every man is a piece of the continent, a part of the main... any man's death diminishes me, because I am involved in mankind, and therefore never send to know for whom the bell tolls; it tolls for thee." ~ John Donne

………

TODAY AND EVERY DAY

Today, and every day, I will be grateful.
Today, and every day, I will not worry.
Today, and every day, I will not criticize, judge, or condemn.
Today, and every day, I will not get angry.
Today, and every day, I will let go of all envy, hatred, and animosity.
Today, and every day, I will be honest in all my dealings.
Today, and every day, I will be authentic, dedicating myself to be who I am meant to be and doing what I was brought here to do.
Today, and every day, I will strive to give my best contribution to the world.
Today, and every day, I will be selfless, gentle and kind with all sentient beings, including myself.
Today, and every day, I will make everyone who comes in contact with me feel happier and more peaceful.

………

MINDFULNESS AND PARENTING

MY SON, MY GUIDE, MY GREATEST TEACHER

It was late night, and the bustling daytime activity had vanished; visitors were long gone, and most of the patients and their companions were sleeping. But I couldn't. So I kissed my wife -- lovingly, gently, and carefully, trying not to disturb her sleep -- and left the room in silence. I remember how quiet and dim the corridors were; "They must turn down the lights at night," I pondered.

"That one," I said, even though I knew she could not hear me. "That one," I said again, pointing at the newborn in the little crib whose sign bore my last name. The nurse smiled, picked him up, gently nestled him in her arms, got closer to the glass, and allowed me to take a lengthy look at him. And that was it! That was the moment when my life changed forever!

Yes, I had been in middle of all the excitement in the delivery room a few hours before. Yes, I held him in my arms minutes after he was born. But that moment, in the quiet of the night, when I took that long look at him, that was the moment when the entire Universe slowed down, everything around me became a blur, and time stood still. Something mysterious and magical was happening. I didn't know then, and I only came to realize years later that who I was looking at, just then, was the greatest guide and teacher I would have in my life. And even though I was completely unaware of my role as a neophyte explorer, he immediately took me to unexplored territories. And although I was utterly oblivious of my role as his student, he, at once, exposed me to fundamental questions. I looked at him and asked myself, "Who am I? What is this thing we call life? Who creates it? How does it come about? How can I, this simple man, be a part in something so miraculous, inexplicable, and extraordinary?" And the Voice of the Universe spoke through him: "There's something bigger going on here; something that you don't quite understand. You must pay attention and be alert." And I heard a whisper, "It's time to let go of the old. It's time to embrace the new."

That was the moment when I was transformed, never to be the same again. During the years that followed, my son guided me to take a deep look at my life and change my ways. He patiently endured the pain I made him go through while I was learning. And no matter how many mistakes I made, he always reaffirmed his unconditional love for me. He taught me what real, innocent love was. He believed in me more than I did myself. He believed that the good in me would prevail. He, more than anyone else, made me a better man. I look back and I think, "How fortunate I am! How blessed I am to have him in my life! What a vast joy it is for me to have him by my side during my journey here on Earth!"

....

THE IMPORTANCE OF PRAISE

I enjoyed watching the YouTube video "Simon Sinek on Millenials in the Workplace," and I agree with the majority of what Simon Sinek says, especially the dangers associated with the instant gratification that technology brings, the addictive effects of social media, and the need to work diligently, give it time, and cultivate patience in order to make an impact and achieve dreams. But I have reservations about the way he talks about the negative effects of a gentler kind of parenting. I think that the criticism of soft parenting -- and the alleged sense of entitlement is creates -- is an idea that, by being repeated over and over again, is gaining ground, and that although it sounds right, in my opinion, is a superficial and rushed diagnostic that diminishes the importance of gentleness and praise, especially the gentleness and praise that must come from parents.

We live in an extremely competitive world where people are put down all the time. In order to counterbalance this tendency, parents should find effective ways to enhance their children's self-esteem, foster cooperation, and tame excessive competitiveness. We are a culture obsessed with winning -- at all costs if necessary. In this video, Simon Sinek points out that the corporate environment is extremely competitive and that the leadership is bad. Well, parenting that over-emphasizes competition, comparison, and criticism has a lot to do with bad leadership. When kids who experience this kind of parenting grow up they become the bosses and parents we don't want, the ones who squash self-esteem, and provide very little positive reinforcement and support. They perpetuate the existence of the violent world we abhor. Therefore, if we want less competition and more cooperation, if we want healthier working environments, then generous parenting is extremely important, otherwise we will be parenting for the perpetuation of same undesired world, and creating more of the leaders we don't want.

Many people, when they reach positions of power, instead of changing the errors of the past, simply repeat them: "I suffered and now it's your turn; I will make you suffer. I was miserable, now it's my turn of making lives miserable. I was oppressed and exploited, and now it's my turn to oppress and exploit others, and benefit from it." They don't realize that they are now in positions where they can bring about positive changes. It would be wonderful if they realized that "This is the way it was, the way it was, but it's not the way it should or has to be. Things can be changed, and I will bring about change for the better. I suffered, but I don't need to continue the same pattern and inflict suffering on others. These injustices stop here, and I will do my part in bringing about positive change." It should not be because someone was treated badly -- or because this is the common way people are treated -- that he or she, when reaching positions of power, should continue perpetuating the same erroneous trend of treating other people badly.

The reality is that parents, as a rule, criticize much more than they praise. The majority of parents are ready to point out their children's weaknesses and failures, and by doing so, they instill in them a sentiment that they are not good enough. How many times have you heard parents criticizing their children and putting them down? Spoken and unspoken messages such as "You are a loser. You are good for nothing." are not uncommon. It seems that only when their children are doing something bad, parents take notice and have something to say. When they do good things, parents usually say nothing. It is as if children are just doing what is expected of them. Good deeds go by unnoticed. Well, it shouldn't be this way.

My advice? Love your children wastefully, and say "I love you" a lot. Catch them doing good, and say something. Praises such as, "Good job! You are smart! You are unique!" go a long way in building confidence and self-esteem.

Be the best and most supporting boss you can be, and treat the people you lead as you would like to be treated if you were in their positions.

....

"Do you want to know what makes us different? It's that my parents always hugged me, and they hugged me a lot." ~ Patrick Bensadoun

....

There is always virtue in the middle. Criticism and punishment only will not do it. Praise and rewarding only will not do it either. Too much undeserved criticism and too little deserved praise are bad. On the other hand, too much undeserved praise and too little deserved criticism are also bad. Choose the middle way. Gentle criticism when warranted, and honest praise when deserved, is the way to go. Wise use of both is what is needed: calm criticism that does not put the child down, and sincere praise that does not inflate the child's ego, gives her an unrealistic perception of who she is, and instills in her a sense of entitlement. But, if we have to choose, let us be generous in our approval and applause, and parsimonious in our censure and condemnation. Let us praise!

....

PARENT'S PRAISE

How wonderful it would be if all children could say these words to their parents: "I accept myself as I am, and I am happy with whom I am. I believe that your expressions of love and your encouragement in the past were fundamental in allowing me to feel the way I feel today. What a precious gift that was! Thank you."

Many of us do not love our own selves enough. This reduced self-esteem may be the result of early experiences with unskilled parents who instead of praising their children, had unrealistic expectations, demanded too much from them, compared them with others that they deemed better, criticized them harshly when they failed, and by doing so instilled in them the feeling that they were not good enough, and , therefore, undeserving of receiving love. Those individuals, then, go through life carrying this feeling. Some become very competitive, obsessed with achieving success, trying to prove their value, but always feeling that they are not good enough, no matter how successful they may be. Others give in to the idea that they are not good enough, and give up pursuing their highest dreams. They never give full expression to their potentials.

The negative impact of this type of parenting -- where love is conditional to excellent performance -- is long-lasting and does not go away easily. Many of my friends, some of them already in advanced age, are still striving to prove their worth in order to receive approval, recognition, and praise, especially from their parents who, by the way, have passed away a long time ago.

....

Reassuring words of unconditional love and support, especially in times of defeat and failure, are of the utmost importance to build a strong self-esteem in our children. So tell your children often that you love them, and give them reasons to think highly of themselves.

"I admire you! I'm proud of you! I love you!"

Praise everywhere, but never criticize in public, and never forget that we are what we think, so make all you can for your children to think highly of themselves. As the saying goes, "If we think we can, we can. If we think we can't, we can't."

....

BE THE ADULT YOU NEEDED WHEN YOU WERE A CHILD

Be who you needed when you were younger. Be the parent you needed when you were a child. Be the teacher you needed when you were a student. Be the employer you dreamed of having when you were an employee. Treat others as they like to be treated, so they will treat you as you like to be treated. Treat them with love, patience and generosity, and then receive back all that you have given. Don't think that by limiting the love you give, by being tough, by teaching your children to be tough, you are preparing them for the world; the only thing you are doing is perpetuating a world of despicable human beings. If you are constantly criticizing your children, putting them down, squashing their self-esteem, not giving them abundant and unconditional love, you are creating parents, bosses, teachers and coaches who will be perpetuating the world you don't want to live in, the world you don't want your children to live in. Do you want a better world? Then be a better parent. Give love. If you want to leave a better world for your children, then leave better children for the world. Shower your children with love. Flood them with love. Treat your children as they should be treated, with love and respect, so when they grow up and have their own children, they will do the same. Treat your children as they should be treated, with love and respect, so when they grow up and you need them, they will return the treatment, and treat you with love and respect too. We receive what we give. It's as simple as that. So, be who you needed when you were younger.

......

HAPPY FIRST BLINK

Happy first blink, my son. You blinked and 24 years went by. Blink again, look back, and 48 years would have passed. Blink a 3rd time, and there goes 72 years. Time passes by fast, so make it a priority to follow your bliss.

I have been thinking about the fact that we are in each other's lives, and about the bond that unites us. Some say that we are spiritual beings having human existences and that before coming to this physical plane we met in the spiritual dimension and agreed what roles we would play and what we would be doing to help one another down the path of purification, enlightenment and liberation. Maybe that was the case, and when we met you said, "I am going to be your son, and I will help you," and I said, "I am going to be your father, and I will help you," and we created a sacred contract. If we believe that we come here to learn how to liberate ourselves from the cycle of human misery, and if we believe that we keep coming back until we succeed, we have to accept that some individuals are further along the path of purification and liberation than others. I remember Wally telling me that he thought you were one of those more evolved beings. And I agree with him: I recognize in you a being with special wisdom. I see you as a teacher, my teacher. I've learned and continue to learn a lot from you. Do you remember when you told me how you dealt with people who were illogical and stubborn? You showed me the wisdom contained in doing a simple shoulder shrug, saying "Whatever," and moving on. It may seen completely unremarkable to you, but believe it or not, it made a huge difference in the quality of my life. It was an eye-opener that taught me, once and for all, to let go of the compulsion to convince those who do not see as I see.

You blinked once and this globe upon which we live has traveled through the cosmos and completed 24 ellipses around the sun while rotating around its imaginary axis 8,766 times. When I first held you in my arms, I could never imagine what your life would be like. I could never imagine that one day I would have a son who would graduate from the most prestigious university in the world, who would travel to so many exotic places, and who would live in the most vibrant metropolis on the planet. I admire you very much. I think about the challenges you faced, such as moving to two countries during your childhood, and having to leave everything behind, and having to get adapted to new cultures, learn new languages, and make new friends. I know it wasn't easy, but I believe it helped to bring about the exceptional man you are. I also remember you as a stubborn and hard-headed little child, and when I see the very determined man you are now, I rest knowing that it all worked out for the good! My most precious memories are the times I used to take you to Mrs. Corrigan's first grade class. I remember our little ritual: you hung your backpack, I got down on my knees, and we hugged each other behind the classroom door. Those were long, tender, endearing hugs, not different from the ones we share now. I guess that's when our ongoing who-will-hang-in-there-longer hug challenge began. Back then, I thought you needed the hugs. Now I see that I was the one who needed them.

I think about what life has in store for you. It is my desire to be around to see you performing to thousands of people. I can see myself rejoicing while seeing the crowds having a good time, singing your songs. I know it has already happened. I can remember it. I can't resist giving some advice: Create music that makes you happy and that will make others happy. Be generous and give your audience what will make them feel good. Spread positive vibes that will make the whole world better. Dream of success, but never forget that you are greatly successful already. Do not condition your happiness to any imagined situation in the future. Don't wait. Be happy now, for no reason at all. Be happy now because you are a success already.

If someone asked me, "Do you know a good man?" I would say, "Yes," and praise your civility, generosity, honesty, good nature, and respect for others. You have a compassionate heart and a joyful, fun-loving spirit. You make people around you smile, laugh, feel better, and love life. You are such a great man! I admire you for so many things you have done, such as the work you did with One Planet United and the

OPU Club, your work for the homeless at Harvard Square, and the work you are doing now helping underprivileged children in the New York City boroughs. I admire you. You are a light that brightens the world.

"The tiny flame that lights up the human heart is like a blazing torch that comes down from heaven to light up the paths of mankind. For in one soul are contained the hopes and feelings of all Mankind."~ Kahlil Gibran

……..

Everything is impermanent, so do not get attached to anything. Pleasant things and experiences, as well as unpleasant ones, will come and pass away. As George Harrison sang, "All things must pass. All things must pass away." The most important thing is to move along the path of purification that leads to enlightenment and the liberation from the shackles of human misery and suffering. So, in your pursuit of success, stay away from obsessive craving and clinging.

……..

"They cling obstinately to lives of wealth and honor, comfort and pleasure, excitement and self-indulgence, ignorant of the fact that the desire for these very things is the source of human suffering. If one carefully considers all the facts, one must be convinced that at the basis of all suffering lies the principle of craving desire. If avarice can be removed, human suffering will come to an end." ~ The Teachings of the Buddha, Bukkyō Dendō Kyōkai

……..

You have already lived 1,252 weeks and 2 days, or 8,766 days (out of which 6,260 were weekdays and 2,506 were weekend days... Yes, I looked it up!). You have been breathing now for 210,384 hours, or 12,623,040 minutes, or 757,382,400 seconds. Be happy because you have used all this time wisely. You have built an amazing masterpiece: You.

Happy birthday, my son!

Being mindful of our impermanence is a good thing. It makes us pay more attention, and focus on what is important.

………

"I don't regret the things I did. I just regret the things I didn't do when I had a chance to do them. I regret the decisions I waited too long to make. I regret the times I hesitated and didn't approach the people I was attracted to. I regret the times I didn't say what should have been said. I don't regret the things I did; I just regret the things I didn't do and the chances I didn't take."

. . . .

Time passes by fast, so approach the prettiest girl and the people who may help you, no matter how unapproachable they may seem to be. Life is short, so choose wisely: surround yourself with uplifting, positive people, who build you up and make your days more enjoyable, and stay away from those crazy-makers, energy-draining vampires, and toxic environments. Continue to do good. Remember always that the good you make comes back to you. If you are good to others, others will be good to you. If you are generous with others, others will be generous with you. If you forgive others, others will forgive you. In the end, the love you take is equal to the love you make (you know where this line came from right?).

Remember what Daniel Barrett told you when you met: "How stoked are you willing to be? In your life, sort for pleasure." So, follow your bliss. Take risks, or as Master Yoda would say, "Do, or do not. There is not try." Do more of what makes you happy. Above all, don't die with regrets. Remember that it's all in our thoughts. Be attentive. Observe what goes on in your mind, and populate it with positive, optimistic, happy thoughts. This is the greatest truth: "We are what we think."

I love you, now and for all eternity. It's good to be your father.

. . . .

HE LIVES IN YOU

Your greatest gift to me is love, and my greatest gift to you is love, a love that is beautiful and serene. I love you immensely. I love that you are in my life, and I thank you for your generous sharing which allows me to be in your life. I love to witness your journey, and be blessed by your joy.

I think of the time when one of us will depart from this physical realm and we will not be sharing life in this dimension together anymore. Although this saddens me, I know that love is eternal and transcends this dimension. I feel that you and I have always existed, and will never cease to exist. We have always loved and will always love each other.

....

"Never was there a time when you or I did not exist, nor in the future shall any of us cease to be." ~ from the Bhagavad-Gita

....

My sons are among the best men I know. When I think about them, the quote from Mario Sergio Cortella comes to mind: "The world we will leave for our children depends on the children that we will leave for our world." I believe that raising good-hearted human beings is the most important assignment for all of us, parents. If we want to leave a better world for our children, let us make sure that we leave better children for the world. I often reflect on how Pedro and Mateus came to be the good men they are, and I am convinced that although my wife and I may have made choices during their upbringing that may have helped them, who they came to be is not due to our doing; it's all a huge mystery, with so many uncontrollable factors at play that no one can say, "Do this, and the result will be good children." So, removing myself from receiving any accolades, I remain in awe with the kind of men they are, and I do experience a sense of having accomplished the mission that was assigned to me. I feel very fortunate, blessed, and at peace, and this surely is a great feeling.

Back in 1994, when Pedro was five years old, we watched The Lion King together for the first time. In 2011, when I visited him in Los Angeles, we watched it again, this time in the famous El Capitan Theatre. The following segment of the movie is an important part of the memories we share. In it, Rafiki points out to Simba that the spirit and values of Mufasa, Simba's late father, continue to live in him, and that Simba must remember who he really is, and have the courage to accept the calling and fulfill his potential and destiny.

I like to believe that there is a sacred connection between parents and their children, and that this connection lives forever. I feel it strongly. I feel I will always be available to support and comfort my sons, even after my physical death. And I also feel that they will always be with me. I told them, copying Mufasa, "I will always be here for you, always. All you have to do is to look up. I am in the sky, in the stars. Actually, I am everywhere. I live in you and you live in me. The love that unites us lives forever."

I hope I may live an honorable life, loving and supporting my sons, and when I'm gone, I hope they may remember me with admiration and love.

....

"Look, Simba. Everything the light touches is our kingdom. A king's time as ruler rises and falls like the sun. One day, Simba, the sun will set on my time here, and will rise with you as the new king. Everything you see exists together in a delicate balance. As king, you need to understand that balance and respect all the creatures, from the crawling ant to the leaping antelope. When we die, our bodies become the grass, and the antelope eat the grass. Just as the sun rises from the night, and winter becomes the spring, so life arises from death. And so we are all connected in the great Circle of Life.

There's more to being a king than getting your way all the time. While others search for what they can take, a true king searches for what he can give.

Simba, let me tell you something my father told me. Look at the stars. The great kings of the past look down on us from those stars. So whenever you feel alone, just remember that those kings will always be there to guide you. And so will I. I will always be there to guide you. I'll live in you. You'll never be alone. I love you my son. Look inside yourself. Remember who you are. You must take your place in the Circle of Life. Believe in yourself and there will come a day when others will have no choice but to believe in you. I never left you. I never will. Remember who you are." ~ compiled from the scripts of The Lion King series of movies and cartoons.

....

Mateus once said that he sees me as a mix of Mufasa and Rafiki. For a while we joked around with some nicknames that combined both: Mufiki and Rafasa. Then, on September 22, 2019, I was given the name Kusala when I took the Eight Lifetime Precepts at the Bhavana Society Forest Monastery and Meditation Center. So Kusala it is.

....

A BETTER LIFE IN A BETTER WORLD

HEAVEN IS HERE IF WE WANT IT TO BE

Welcome! Congratulations! You've made it! You are in Heaven! This is your garden and your playground. Enjoy the beauty of the garden, have lots of fun in the playground, and remember to share your toys. That's all.

Don't worry about anything. This is a place of abundance. There is more than enough here for everybody. You will always be safe here, so don't be afraid. Share what you have and you will always be fine, I promise. Now go! Enjoy the garden and have fun in the playground. Take good care of both, and if you feel like, help make them a little bit better.

········

RETURN TO INNOCENCE

John, a good friend of mine, told me about his recent trip and the great experience he had with his little grandchildren. He told me that now that he is practicing mindfulness he was able to really be in the here-now with them, immersing himself more fully in their world, something that he hadn't experienced before. He was able to better observe them and realize the depth of their curiosity, as well as their genuine amazement with what they were seeing and discovering for the first time.

We talked about how vital it is for us, adults, to keep this curiosity and capacity for amazement alive. And we reflected on the words of Jesus, "Truly I tell you, unless you change and become like little children, you will never enter the kingdom of heaven." Yes, the kingdom is right here, right now. Heaven is here if we want it to be.

I always heard that children are innocent, but only now, decades after the birth of my first child, I can say that I understand what that truly means. The practice of mindfulness opened my eyes, allowing me to see this innocence anew and realize how incapable I was of grasping its essence, meaning, and beauty before. I feel deeply that children are the greatest teachers. They live in the here-now. We, with our fears, worries, and regrets, are the ones who remove them from the enjoyment of the present moment, telling them that they have to push themselves to do more, have more, and be more. We are the ones who instill in them all the things that spoil their innocence. I remember my kids during the first decade of their lives, when they were discovering the world. How innocent they were! How I wish I could go back with what I know now, and instead of trying to teach them, I could simply relax and learn from them.

....

I facilitated a silent retreat yesterday and spent time in nature, walking mindfully in a beautiful botanical garden.

This morning, I received an advice that I should spend more time in nature.

Unexpectedly, the music video of the song Return to Innocence by Enigma -- that I watched many times, many years ago -- came to my mind.

Watching it again made me remember the innocence of my sons. I remembered cutting my oldest son's hair and teaching him to ride a bicycle. I remembered the two of us watching the sunrise together, while he pointed at the sun, talked to the ocean in his own universal language, and smiled. I also remembered the love I received from the women who shared their lives with me. I remembered myself as the writer whose words vanished from the pages. I remembered myself as the sower of seeds of mindfulness. I remembered myself as the shepherd who followed his sheep as we, together, returned to innocence. An old man remembers. A newborn remembers. I remember.

"That's not the beginning of the end. That's the return to yourself, the return to innocence" ~ M.C. Curly

....

HEAVEN IS HERE

"We become neighbors when we are willing to cross the road for one another. There is so much separation and segregation: between black people and white people, between gay people and straight people, between young people and old people, between sick people and healthy people, between prisoners and free people, between Jews and Gentiles, Muslims and Christians, Protestants and Catholics, Greek Catholics and Latin Catholics. There is a lot of road crossing to do. We are all very busy in our own circles. We have our own people to go to and our own affairs to take care of. But if we could cross the street once in a while and pay attention to what is happening on the other side, we might become neighbors." ~ Henri J. M. Nouwen

....

Religions should be helping us -- all of us -- to develop an intimate connection, communication and communion with the Mystery. I believe that this is attained through the diligent practice of mindfulness in silence, stillness, solitude, seclusion, simplicity, and service. Attentive observation of nature brings about a greater understanding of the interplay of every single thing and being. We see the roots of the trees intermingling underground, while their branches touch each other. We sense the power of nature both in a subtle breeze and a huge storm. We develop the same great reverence for a little ant and a massive whale.

Diligent observation makes us more aware of the immense abundance of this planet, and also makes birth, growth, decay, and death -- the perennial and unstoppable transformation -- very evident, which humbles us, the observers. Once we have that deep Experience of Oneness -- a clear and deep knowing of our inter-relation, interconnection, interdependence, and inter-existence -- we are moved to proactively connect, communicate and commune with each other. Once we go through those mystical awakenings, we experience radical transformations that tame our egos and inspire us to respond to all life's challenges and difficulties selflessly, with kindness, compassion and love; and with that, the ways we treat one another, our home planet, and the entire Universe change.

We begin to see what we weren't able to see before. We begin to see how fortunate we are, and be grateful for all the gifts that we have received. We begin to see that this planet of ours is a beautiful garden and an amazing playground, and we begin to see it as a gift that was given to us.

We will, then, feel inspired to slow down to enjoy the beauty of the garden and have fun in this playground. We will soon realize that we have more fun when all others are having fun, and this realization will lead us to enthusiastically share our toys. We will feel inspired to make the garden more beautiful and the playground more enjoyable for all. We will realize the abundance that surrounds us and will organize ourselves to live on this planet in ways through which everyone will be able to have what they need to live dignified and thriving lives, realize their potentials, and give their best contributions to the world. We will be inspired to help one another, realizing that when we help others we are helping our own selves. And by doing so, we will be bringing Heaven to Earth.

If Heaven is a place where everyone is loved and taken good care of, we must wake up and realize that we have all that is necessary to manifest Heaven, right here on Earth. We just need to be kind and compassionate. All we need to do is to love and support one another.

Heaven is here if we want it to be!

....

NEW IDEAS FOR A NEW WORLD

I am very interested in bringing about an enlightened society, a community of evolved and awakened individuals. I believe that in order to get there, we all have to engage in the activity of looking deeply within ourselves, and dedicate ourselves to meditate and live mindfully every day. If everyone took time to do that, the world would be much better. I also believe that we need to take time to explore the fundamental questions. That's one of the reasons why I consider an education that gives our students an ampler view of the world, and prepares them to deal with diversity, complexity, and transformation, so important.

We have to reflect and gain a cosmic perspective of who we are, what life is, and what we are doing here. I believe that with these insights, we will live less violently and more kindly. We will be more content, happy, and peaceful.

We not only need to do the inner work ourselves, and develop our intellects though continuous education and exploration ourselves, but we should inspire others to do the same, so, with the new ideas that will emerge, we can bring to life a more just and happier society.

Again, Heaven on Earth is a choice we must make, not a place we must find. If Heaven is where everyone is loved and taken good care of, then Heaven is here if we want it to be!

....

THE IMPORTANCE OF NEW THOUGHTS

At times it is difficult to remember to think of this world as Heaven, but certainly the practice of looking for and finding beauty in it, even in the midst of the all the challenges, is a grounding and powerful one.

Every single time I write "It's a beautiful day in Paradise" on one of my blogs, images of the poor, the homeless, the children in war zones and refugee camps come to my mind, and I ask myself, "Can they find Heaven here on Earth?" And then, I pause and send them wishes of the peaceful, plentiful, and fear-free existence they all deserve -- we all deserve -- as a birthright.

I am engaged in promoting the change of the prevailing ideas in this world. I am working to spread a new paradigm for a new world, hoping that a new way of seeing life will lead to a gentler and more civilized ways of relating to one another. I believe we can bring about an enlightened society. I believe that if more and more people begin to accept these ideas, the desired change for the better will come about easier. And what ideas are those?

Here they are: Planet Earth -- and the entire Universe -- is our Garden and our Playground. These are gifts that were given to us. We are called to enjoy the beauty of the Garden and have fun in this Playground. We are called to take good care of these gifts, and make the Garden more beautiful and the Playground more enjoyable. We are called to be kind and share our toys with our playmates because this enhances their joy, and their augmented joy enhances ours. We are called to realize that if Heaven is a place where everyone is loved, then Heaven is here if we want it to be; all we have to do is to selflessly -- and, in a way, selfishly, because of all we get from it -- love one another.

If you are one of those who are working to make the world a better place for all sentient beings, here are my request and wishes to you:

"Embrace these ideas! Talk about them! Write about them! Spread them! Let's continue planting the seeds that will open up minds, bring about new paradigms, and ultimately change the ways we have organized ourselves to live on this planet. Let us continue spreading new ideas and implementing the changes that will make life better for all on this beautiful home of ours.

Be optimistic and spread optimism. Bring hope and energize the people you meet. Be a shiner of the light that can drive out darkness.

Sending you my optimistic energies, my fellow lightshiners! It is a great joy for me to be on this journey with you."

....

A NEW SOCIETY

Consider the following: we don't even think about it, but today we are conditioned to work, make money, and exchange that money for goods and services. But what will happen when the demand for labor dwindles? As we all know, technology and machinery are replacing human labor, and if the need for human work shrinks down considerably, or even eventually disappears, the possibility of exchanging work for money may also shrink and disappear. What will happen then? Will the reduced need for human labor create a situation where a vast contingent of human beings will find themselves unable to find work, and, therefore, unable to earn money, unable to provide for themselves and their loved ones, unable to survive?

Since we are moving to a new reality where the demand for human work will diminish, we better start thinking of new ways we can collaborate to create a new world society where everyone will have all their basic needs met, independent of work. Let us envision a new global social arrangement where everyone will work less and enjoy life a lot more. Let us bring about a new society where everyone will have more time to pursue their dreams, do what they love, and develop themselves to give their best and unique contributions for everyone's welfare.

I believe this is possible. I believe that there is great abundance in this world, and that there is more than enough for everybody to live good lives. I believe that if we develop new social arrangements based on a deep sense of solidarity, we will bring about a new reality where everyone will be able to live with dignity and without the fear of not having enough. In fact, I believe we can, for good and forever, completely eradicate this damaging fear. I believe that if we reach a deep understanding of the real purpose of life, we will develop the ability to control our selfishness and greed. This will allow us to create a whole new world where all sentient beings will be properly taken care of.

I believe we have all the means and resources necessary to take care of all people in the world, and for everyone to have dignified and thriving existences. I believe we have all the means necessary to support every child and young adult during their formative years, and that we can mentor them to follow their dreams, engage in careers that match their talents, and do what they love. I believe we can support them to be the best that they can be, so they may be able to give their best contributions to the world. I believe that if we remain open to consider new possibilities, we can create a better world for all. I believe that we will find out that Heaven is here, if we want it to be!

....

CAN MINDFULNESS SAVE US FROM OURSELVES?

"In general, mindfulness begins with one-pointed focus on where we are and what's going on inside and out. Over time, though, this will bleed into a wider awareness that sees connections and explores what drives us and what effects we're having on the world around us and the people, plants, and animals in it. It brings us into direct contact with our values, and the fundamental aspiration all of us have to make a better world, the part of us that cares." ~ Barry Boyce

....

To say that people suffer solely due to their individual choices evidently is not true. Personal stress has many causes, including structural violence. A lot of the suffering comes from the competitive environments and structures we have created and inhabit. We live with the stress caused by the fear of not having enough, by long days of work, by the family problems that emerge from absent and exhausted parents. To say to someone that he is solely responsible for his happiness just adds more stress to an already stressful life. I wonder how much the incidence of personal stress would decrease if we organized ourselves to live together in gentler and more cooperative ways.

Although it is true that a lot of the stress stems from the societal, cultural, political, and economic frameworks in which we live, it is also true that personal choices can be made in order to reduce stress. We do have some control to take action, live differently, and be happier.

Enter mindfulness!

The practice of mindfulness opens up our minds and shows us new possibilities of how we can organize ourselves to live in immensely better ways on this planet of ours. Mindfulness allows us to see that this is a place of great abundance, where there is more than enough for everyone to live dignified and thriving lives.

It is in the silent that we can tame our fear and the compulsion to accumulate. It is in the silent stillness that we can feel that we are all in this together, and that when we help others, we are helping our own selves.

Is there a recipe of how the practice of mindfulness can change society? The answer, for me, lies in the practice itself.

1 - Practice mindfulness and encourage others to practice it. Teach mindfulness and help others become teachers. Spread the seeds of mindfulness far and wide.

2 – Understand and promote the understanding of the root causes of societal and environmental problems, such as, among others, the massive concentration of wealth, and how wild, unrestrained capitalism is devastating the planet and endangering survival.

3 - Develop and promote a vision for a better world. Let people see that Heaven is here if we want it to be. Help people see that we can organize ourselves to live on this planet differently than the way we have been living, and that we can live much better. Encourage people to join forces and work together to make this vision a reality.

4 - Based on your talents and skills, practice activism for social change. Encourage others, based on their talents and skills, to become activists for social change. Teach others how to become nonviolent disruptors of the social order that oppresses and exploits. Teach others so they may become teachers of nonviolent active resistance.

5 – Practice, teach, and encourage others to practice and teach nonviolence in its many forms, such as nonviolent communication, nonviolent active resistance, nonviolent civil disobedience, nonviolent social disruption for social change, nonviolent conflict resolution.

6 - Cultivate peace. Become a bringer of peace. Be that peaceful presence that brings sanity to the places in our world where insanity is present.

Just do it!

. . . .

I'M NOT THE ONLY ONE

Well, here I am, savoring the beauty of this garden and having fun in this playground. I am blessed and so are you. Imagine if everyone received this message upon arrival on this planet, how much better things would be.

Congratulations! You've made it! You're in the best place in the Universe. This is your Garden and your Playground, created for your enjoyment. Now, go have fun, make friends, share your toys, and, if you can, make the garden and the playground more beautiful and enjoyable for everyone. And, by the way, don't worry about anything. Be not afraid. This is a place of abundance. There's more than enough here for everybody to have a good life. Just share. You will be OK.

. . . .

I admire John Lennon's vision, and I would be thrilled if we all accepted his invitation to pause, imagine, and create a whole new world. Yes, I do believe that we can organize ourselves to live in new and improved ways, manifesting, right here, whatever we imagine Heaven to be. We have all the resources and the knowledge we need to create a brotherhood of man. We just need to imagine, believe, and take action, each one of us doing our part, however small, day in and day out. Live for today. Live in peace. Share the entire world. We can do it. Let's do it!

IMAGINE

John Lennon invited us to imagine a new world, inviting us to let go of ideas that do not serve us anymore, so we can embrace new ones. He encouraged us to develop a new paradigm, a new way of seeing the world: a world without countries, without reasons to kill or die for, and where all the people would be living their lives in peace. He also invited us to reduce the fear about the future and live for today, sharing and caring for one another.

"You may say I'm a dreamer But I'm not the only one. I hope someday you'll join us, and the world will live as one" ~ John Lennon

....

PARADISE

Many of us have been exposed to the idea that the world is imperfect and unjust, and that perfection and justice can only be experienced in Heaven. But what if we were told something radically different? What if we were told that we are in Heaven already? What if, instead of hoping to get to Heaven after we die, we were brought up and lived as if we were in Heaven? How would this impact life on Earth?

I have known prosperity and adversity in life. After living comfortably for a large part of my existence, I experienced the limitations imposed by extended periods of unemployment and the absence of a regular income. That new reality forced me to better empathize with the poor and become more sensitive to their needs. I came to better understand social injustice and the widening gap between those who don't have enough and those who have too much. I also realized that an unconscious fear of not having enough is what ultimately propels people to unnecessary accumulation which brings about the inequality and many of the problems we face in our world. It was during that period that I experienced an awakening that allowed me to see what I was not able to see before. I began to notice beauty and miracles surrounding me. A world of abundance revealed itself to me.

I now believe that in order to create a better world we need a new paradigm. What would happen if we embraced the idea that we are in Heaven? If children were raised hearing, "You are in Heaven, and there's nothing to fear," what effect would that have on our relationships with one another and with all creation? I envision the day when the prevailing idea on this planet will be that we live in a place of plenty, with more than enough for everyone. Sharing and serving will, then, be commonplace and widespread practices.

Heaven is here, if we want it to be.

. . . .

Imagine a complete change in mankind's mindset. Imagine every baby coming into this planet being greeted in the delivery room with these words: "Welcome! You made it! You are in Heaven! This is your garden and your playground. Take good care of both: make the garden more beautiful and the playground more enjoyable, and go have lots of fun with everything and everyone in this planet!" Imagine we also receive this message at birth: "Welcome! You made it! You are in Heaven! Don't worry. This is a place of abundance. There is more than enough for everyone. You don't have to be afraid. You don't have to accumulate. Just take good care of the garden and the playground, help one another, share your toys, and go have lots of fun with your friends." Imagine these messages becoming the truth we all live by. Imagine how the idea that this is Heaven — that we are in Heaven already — could change everything. Imagine how a slight change in mankind's mindset could create a whole new world. Imagine a whole new world. Imagine.

. . . .

I believe that we can organize ourselves to live on this planet in such ways that everyone can have a good, thriving life. Our planet is a place of abundance, and everybody can have all they need to live a dignified life, without the fear of not having enough. We only need to change the prevailing ideas and ways we have been operating on Earth. We need to find a cure to the disease of obsessive hoarding that plagues our minds. There's no need for some of us to accumulate as much as we do. And why we do it? Mainly because we are afraid of not having enough in times of need. And why? Because we live in a very selfish and individualistic culture, a dog-eat-dog environment where, as we were told since we were young, only the strong survive. We are brought up being told that it's each man for himself and each woman for herself. Naturally, we grow afraid that if something bad happens to us, no one will come to our rescue. What we witness in the world today is a lot of competition and greed.

Well, I believe we can use a lot more of compassion, cooperation and solidarity. I believe we can organize ourselves in ways that everyone can be supported to be the best that they can be, what, in turn, will allow each one of us to give our unique contributions for the betterment of the world. Unfortunately, we are immersed in a very greedy and selfish reality. But this is just a thought, a paradigm, a way of seeing that can change.

....

WORLD OF SOLIDARITY

"If you could stand on someone else's shoes, hear what they hear, see what they see, feel what they feel, would you treat them differently?" ~ in the Cleveland Clinic video "Empathy: The Human Connection to Patient Care"

....

OK. Good news, finally! Charity is no longer needed. Government sponsored programs, fundraisers, donations, and all other forms of charitable initiatives used to raise money to help the poor are no longer necessary. Poverty, homelessness, and hunger have been eradicated from the face of the Earth. We finally came to our senses, and came up with better ways of organizing ourselves to live on this planet.

Oppression and exploitation of workers in general, and of women, minors, immigrants, minorities, and of people living in underdeveloped areas of the world in particular, is over. All forms of slavery are ancient history. Sweat shops are completely gone. Work is valued and well rewarded. One member of the family working no more than 40 hours a week is now not only able to provide for all the needs of his or her family, but also able to save money for a comfortable retirement. Both parents do not have to leave their homes and work extended hours in multiple on-call, part-time, low-paying jobs as they did in the past to make ends meet. As a result, we now have less stressed-out parents, healthier families, better children, better citizens, and less social problems. Better salaries led to an increase in demand of goods and services and a reduction in joblessness.

The young population is now finding other forms, besides work as we knew it, of contributing to society with their talents and skills. This gives them renewed hope to invest and build a future for themselves. Upward social mobility, that had almost completely disappeared, is back now, and investing time and money in higher education makes sense again.

Corporations, those irrational and insensitive man-made monsters whose only goal was to amass the highest quarterly profit without regard for the pain inflicted on others and for the damage to the environment, are things of the past. With their disappearance, old forms of government susceptible to corruption also came down. The nefarious influence of money on politics that made elected representatives turn away from representing the interests of their electorate to advance the interests of those who paid them the most, is also a thing of the past. Those imperfect forms of government have been replaced by a modern social democracy where people, using electronic communication, vote on issues directly, or constitute educated individuals who have a better understanding of the specific issues to vote on their behalf. Voting became an easier, safer, and wiser process.

Advancements in the understanding of how the brain works, and breakthroughs in science in general, and quantum physics in particular, came up with explanations that could only be formulated through spirituality before. A great awakening took place when science and spirituality found common ground. People engaged in a series of development practices that led them to the understanding that we are all in this together. Since this shift took place, we overcame our tribal mentality, and violence is now at an all time low. The concept of nations, territories, and borders is vanishing. Expansionism and conquest are irrelevant since we came to the understanding that we all share the same planet. The state-sponsored violence is gone, and the military industrial complex has been dismantled. The amount of money and resources used to build weapons and maintain military supremacy has been redirected to take care of human needs, such as good housing, healthy food, clean water, sanitation, transportation, health care, and education for all. The capacity of radical ideologies to influence people and recruit extremists to perpetrate acts of violence has diminished considerably since people now live better lives, have hope, and can see the possibility of a better future for themselves and their families.

At the same time, we have adopted new technologies that preserve the natural resources and don't wound the planet as we did in the past. Sustainable communities are the new norm. Consumption is not what it used to be. People are much more educated and scrupulous, and mindless consumption and waste are things of the past. We have become more conscientious members of the global society, caring much more for the health and preservation of the planet. "Small is beautiful" is the new economic trend.

Through the growth of mindfulness practice, we finally came to our senses, grew in compassion and solidarity, and created a wonderful new world. We have decided to better distribute the fruits of the increased productivity and pay workers more than mere living wages. Now everyone has enough to live without the fear of not having enough. People now live with a real sense of belonging to a community where each member helps and is helped by all others. With that, the ever-present fear of not having enough is gone; it is a thing of the past. People are not as afraid and anxious as they once were of not having the necessary to provide for themselves and their loved ones. The stubborn tensions of the past subsided, people became more relaxed, less anxious, healthier, and social interactions improved immensely.

We finally realized that this planet of ours is a place of abundance where there is more than enough for everybody. It was amazing to realize that the only thing that we had to do was to change our thoughts and organize ourselves differently in order for everyone to have what they needed to thrive. Since everyone is now taken good care of if something bad happens, the fear of not having enough is gone, and the desperate compulsion to accumulate as a protective mechanism against potential times of lack has vanished. Since we are less fearful of not having enough for our own survival, we are now better able to love, care, and share. We finally have organized ourselves to live on this planet in new ways, and as a result of this new order we, all of us, are now able to live dignified lives, take care of ourselves and our loved ones, share from the much we have, and give our best contribution to society.

"The day everyone opened their hearts and became charitable, charity became unnecessary."

Charity is no longer needed. Government sponsored programs, and charity organizations to help the poor are no longer necessary. Poverty has been eradicated from the face of the Earth. No more poverty. No more hunger. No more homelessness. No more fear. No more greed. No more oppression. No more exploitation. No more indifference. No more neglect. No more violence. No more fanaticism. No more terrorism. No more crime. No more wars.

While all this is taking place, we are also transitioning to a time when work as we know it is becoming obsolete. Work is not what it used to be. The idea that one has to necessarily work to be deemed worthy to live in society is long gone. New technologies create what is needed in abundance. Advancements in science and technology are making work unnecessary. We are coming to a new time in humanity's history when people will not have to work, or exchange labor for money any longer. Machines and automation are replacing human labor, and something new is happening: people are now earning the means they need to live dignified lives without having to work as it was done in the past. And with the creative ways we have organized ourselves to embrace this new reality, and with the active sharing of all Earth's immense abundance, everybody has more than enough to pursue their vocations and live beautiful, creative, contributing lives. Everybody is supported to be the best that they can be. Everybody is developing their innate talents and giving their unique contributions to the betterment of the world community. People, now, occupy themselves satiating their curiosity, doing what they love, following their passions, exploring their innate talents and skills, and making great contributions to society, while living happy and thriving lives.

....

"We must do away with the absolutely specious notion that everybody has to earn a living. It is a fact today that one in ten thousand of us can make a technological breakthrough capable of supporting all the rest. The youth of today are absolutely right in recognizing this nonsense of earning a living. We keep inventing jobs because of this false idea that everybody has to be employed at some kind of drudgery because, according to Malthusian-Darwinian theory, he must justify his right to exist. So we have inspectors of inspectors and people making instruments for inspectors to inspect inspectors. The true business of people should be to go back to school and think about whatever it was they were thinking about before somebody came along and told them they had to earn a living."~ Richard Buckminster Fuller

....

We have attained a higher consciousness. We became able to see beyond what we once saw. We went beyond the illusion of separation and became aware of our oneness. We made it!

The day everyone opened their hearts and became charitable, charity became unnecessary; that was the day when charity was replaced by justice, and we brought Heaven to Earth! We can now celebrate life as brothers and sisters, as members of the same one human family, who live in peace, and rejoice with each other's accomplishments and successes. We made it! We live in a new world of solidarity! Let's celebrate!

....

"Could a greater miracle take place than for us to look through each other's eyes for an instant?" ~ Henry David Thoreau

....

THE LIGHT OF UNITY AND PEACE

Maybe, one day, we will go beyond the need to display flags and national colors. Maybe, one day, we will go beyond the need to identify ourselves as members of this or that clan. Maybe, one day, we will evolve beyond the need to pledge allegiance and loyalty to this or that nation, and we will present ourselves simply as human beings, all brothers and sisters who inhabit the same planet. Unity and peace are already here, and will always be, as long as we want them to be.

....

THE PEACE POEM

We are peaceful! All beings are peaceful!
We are happy! All beings are happy!

Peace in our hearts brought peace to our families.
Peace in our families brought peace to our communities.
Peace in our communities brought peace to our nations.
Peace in our nations brought peace to the world.
There is peace on Earth and it began with me.

One world. . One community. One family.
One heart. One love. One planet united.

CONCLUSION

Remember that whatever happened in the past, when it happened, actually happened in the present moment. And whatever will happen in the future, when it will happen, will also happen in the present moment. This is it! The present moment is all that there is! It is when life happens. And that's why this moment is the most important moment because it is when we make the choices that affect the quality of our lives. So, repeat often, "The place is here. The time is now." And whenever you find yourself lost in thoughts, bring the mind to where the body is: right Here, right Now. Notice when you are Comparing and Contrasting, Categorizing and Classifying, Competing and Complaining, Criticizing and Condemning, and as much as possible refrain from these habits in order to experience Freedom. Remember that it is not difficult to be mindful; difficult is to remember to be mindful. So whenever you catch yourself acting mindlessly, don't worry too much: simply Start Over, Begin Again, mindfully reconnecting with the present moment, the only one that really matters.

Befriend the Silence, the Stillness, the Solitude, the Seclusion, and the Simplicity. Find your purpose and be of Service to others, in order experience Peace. Planet Earth is a place of great abundance, so be not afraid. Protect the Earth because it is the spaceship that is taking us through the cosmos. The Earth is also our garden and playground. So, if you feel called to do it, make the garden more beautiful and the playground more enjoyable. Share your toys. Believe that Heaven is here, if we want it to be.

Beware of the mindless pursuit of Position, Power, Prestige, Privilege, Preference, and Possessions, and recognize the impossibility of this chase bringing about lasting happiness. Remain Awake, Alert, Attentive, Aware, and Appreciative, in order to be fully Alive. Be Mindful, Amazed, Grateful, Content, Optimistic, Compassionate, and Generous, in order to be Happy.

Finally, remember to Look deeply, Listen attentively, Learn unceasingly, Lead compassionately, Laugh profusely, and Love wastefully. By doing so, you will Live fully and also Leave an honorable legacy. And prepare yourself to Let go of everything.

Wishing you mindful moments, however brief, many times.

A Better Life in a Better World

ABOUT THE AUTHOR

Piero Falci teaches Mindfulness Meditation and Mindful Living, and the acclaimed Mindfulness-Based Stress Reduction (MBSR) program. He leads mindfulness silent retreats and organizes silent peace walks. He believes that the inner work that leads to personal awakening is indispensable to create a wholesome world. He is a promoter of social justice and peace who believes in advancing the idea that Heaven is here if we want it to be. He lives in Florida, USA.

www.PieroFalci.com   pierofalci@gmail.com

Made in the USA
Columbia, SC
27 January 2020